THE ART OF ITALIAN COOKING

THE ART OF ITALIAN COOKING

Exeter Books

NEW YORK

Front cover photograph by James Murphy
Compiled by Myra Street
Edited by Myra Street and Sonia Mills
Translated from Italian by Stefano and Natalie Ruggero
Designed by Groom and Pickerill

First published in USA 1987
by Exeter Books
Distributed by Bookthrift
Exeter is a trademark of Bookthrift Marketing, Inc.
Bookthrift is a registered trademark of
Bookthrift Marketing, Inc. New York, New York

ISBN 0-671-09307-X

Set in Plantin by
Servis Filmsetting Limited, Manchester, England
Printed in Hong Kong

Note: *when making any of the recipes in this
book, follow one set of measures only as Metric, Imperial
and American measures are not interchangeable.
Time given at the end of each recipe
includes preparation and cooking.*

CONTENTS

INTRODUCTION

Everyone eats to live, but the Italians' enthusiasm for good food is so great that they must be counted among those who live to eat.

The origins of Italian cooking are Greek, Roman and Byzantine, with a dash of the Oriental. The obsession with food has a long historical background going right back to the gastronomical excesses of Roman times. When the Holy Roman Empire was swept away and hordes of barbarians descended on Europe, the art of civilized cooking almost disappeared outside the archives of the monasteries. It was not until the Renaissance of the arts which took place in the 15th century that the art of cooking was revived along with others such as painting and literature.

The Venetians and the Florentines became the gourmets of the West during Renaissance times. The Italians claim that much of the refinement of French cooking was introduced by Catherina de Medici and the many Italian cooks she took to the court of France when she married the Dauphin, later Henry II.

Italy did not become unified into one nation until 1861. Because of this there are still vast regional differences in both cultural and culinary traditions. These regional differences are jealously guarded and give Italian food its rich variety. If you travel round the country these differences become very apparent: for example the way that rice is popular in the north, whereas pasta is the staple food in the south.

Unlike the French the Italians have never lost sight of their basic principles: simple methods of cooking, top-quality fresh ingredients and simple sauces to complement the food rather than mask its taste. The basic ingredients of Italian meals – relatively small portions of meat or fish, plenty of fresh vegetables and fruit, boiled rice or pasta rather than fried potatoes – and the use of olive oil rather than animal fat for cooking – mean that Italian cooking is very much in line with today's ideas on healthy eating. Many Italian recipes are outlines rather than blueprints, and can be adapted to suit the needs of those on special diets.

A glance through this book will convince you that producing a superb meal is not difficult, and with the endless variety of recipes there is a dish for every day of the year and for every occasion.

Herbs and Spices

Basil

(BASILICO)

Perhaps the most important of all the herbs used in Italian cooking, contributing a unique flavour and wonderful spicy aroma, particularly when combined with tomatoes. The large leaves should be finely chopped or pounded to bring out both these qualities. Dried basil is a poor substitute, and unfortunately fresh basil is scarce to find outside of Italy and the Mediterranean region, where it grows in abundance. But it is perfectly possible to grow basil, given a sheltered sunny spot. It is sometimes available in the larger supermarkets and Italian delicatessen shops during the summer.

Bay leaves

(LAURO)

These are used in very much the same way as in American or British cookery: to flavour stews, soups and marinades. Dried bay leaves are perfectly good, particularly if the dish has a long cooking time which brings out the flavour. If the cooking is short, leaves can be very finely chopped or pounded to intensify the flavour.

Parsley

Bouquet garni

Italian cooks also use the classic French bunch or faggot of mixed herbs, basically consisting of parsley stalks, thyme and bay leaf, although others may be added for particular dishes. When fresh herbs are in short supply commercially prepared sachets of bouquet garni can be used.

Fennel

(FINOCCHIO)

In Italy this usually means the vegetable Florence fennel, the bulbous swollen stems of which are served both raw and cooked. But the feathery leaves of the fennel herb are also used occasionally, typically chopped with garlic as part of a stuffing. Fennel seeds are used in some regions to flavour salami and other sausages; and in Bari to flavour dried figs. All three have an aniseed taste.

Anise

Marjoram

(SWEET MARJORAM; OREGANUM MAJORANA; ORIGANO)

Being in the same family as oregano, this herb can be used if the latter is not available. It is blander and sweeter when fresh, but when dried the difference may be hardly detectable. In Italy marjoram is used as a variation on oregano, or combined with it.

Mint

(MENTUCCIA, MENTA ROMANA)

This herb does not feature greatly in most of Italy, but is quite popular in Roman cooking, and is used to garnish salads. The powerful flavour survives drying fairly well.

Oregano

(ORIGANO)

Although this herb is *Origanum vulgare*, wild marjoram, the strain grown in Italy, and the sunny climate, combine to produce an intense scent and flavour quite unlike that of the English wild marjoram. It is gathered from the rocky hillsides where it grows wild, and hung up to dry in the kitchen; or bought already dried, when provided it is not old and stale the flavour is still good, although the scent will have faded. Oregano is used extensively in Italian cooking, typically in *pizza Napoletana*.

Parsley

(PREZZEMOLO)

This is very widely used, both as an ingredient and a garnish, for its unique combination of bright green colour, fresh scent and pleasant taste. In Italy parsley usually means the flat-leaved variety, which has a stronger flavor. Dried parsley is virtually useless, but fortunately fresh is fairly widely obtainable, and also easy to grow (unlike most herbs it likes shade).

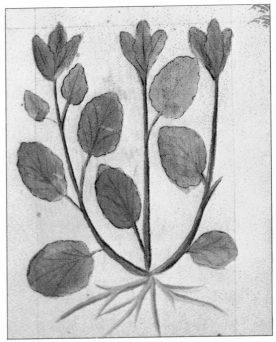

Left Juniper

Right Marjoram

Sage

Note: When using shop-bought dried herbs, try to buy freeze-dried herbs as they have more flavour than commercially dried herbs. Buy in small quantities and use within a few weeks.

Rosemary

(ROSEMARINO)

Italians adore rosemary, and make great use of it, especially to flavour meat. When fresh it is extremely strong, and sprigs should be used sparingly; when dried it is less powerful but, being more concentrated, must be used in very small quantities or it will overpower all other flavours in the dish. Rosemary is a decorative evergreen shrub, but needs a sheltered sunny spot and even so may die during a hard winter.

Sage

(SALVIA)

The large oval leaves of the sage plant, *Salvia officinalis*, are frequently used, especially with the veal and calf's liver dishes which feature so prominently in Italian cooking. Its rather sharp taste is a good foil for any rich or fatty meat. Both fresh and dried sage is strongly flavoured and should be used sparingly.

9

To prepare fresh herbs for the freezer
1 Wash the herbs and dry on absorbent kitchen towels. Wrap in clingfilm or small squares of foil; freeze and use during the winter months.
2 Parsley can be frozen by removing the sprigs from the stalks and packing.

Tarragon

(DRAGONCELLO)

Although not particularly as-sociated with Italian food, tar-ragon is used in some regions, particularly Siena, and in asso-ciation with artichokes. The narrow shiny green leaves have a spicy flavour, particularly if it is the true French variety.

Thyme

(TIMO)

This is not often used in Italian cooking, oregano or marjoram being preferred. But if these are unavailable it can be substitut-ed, although it is used in smaller quantities.

Garlic

(AGLIO)

The distinctive smell and taste of garlic makes it one of the best known flavourings. It is a pe-rennial bulb of the onion family and the plant grows about 60 cm/2 feet high. The bulb is used for flavouring and when fully grown it is made up of a number of little bulbs known as cloves.

It is a common misconcep-tion that nearly all Italian food is cooked with lots of garlic. By and large most Italian dishes, with the exception of a few special sauces such as Genoese Pesto and some soups, contain much less garlic than the food cooked in Provence and the south west of France. You may notice that many of the recipes in this book suggest cooking the garlic in the pan to be used for the dish and then removing be-fore the end of the cooking time. This gives a hint of garlic fla-vouring to the dish without overpowering the food. One or two cloves of garlic will add extra flavour to most fish soups, stews, stuffings for vegetables and for sauces used with pasta.

A garlic crusher is a most useful tool to have in the kitchen as it crushes the cloves releasing the flavour. Otherwise garlic may be finely chopped or crushed on the edge of a board with a little salt and the flat blade of a palette knife. Rinse the board, hands and knife well to avoid flavouring other foods.

Garlic bulbs and cloves

Capers

(CAPPERI)

The capers used so frequently in Italian cooking, to enliven an otherwise bland dish with their sharp flavour, are the berries of a low prickly shrub which grows round the Mediterranean region. They are preserved in salt and desalted before use. Outside Italy these are hard to find and those preserved in vinegar or brine have to serve; drain well before use.

Chillies

(PEPERONCINI)

Although these small green or red relations of the sweet pepper are more associated with Mexican or Indian cooking, Italians use them too when an extra hot taste is called for. They prefer fresh chillies and only use them sparingly, always removing the seeds inside to tone down their fiery taste. Always wash after handling fresh chillies – the raw juice burns if it gets into the mouth or on the skin.

Cinnamon

(CANNELLA)

Both cinnamon sticks and ground cinnamon are used in sweet dishes, and occasionally with meat or game.

Juniper

(GINEPRO)

As in other countries, the sharply flavoured and scented berries of the juniper bush are used to flavour meat and game; also stuffings and marinades.

Salt and black pepper

Cloves

(CHIODI DI GAROFANO)

Like cooks from other countries Italians use cloves to stud an onion before putting it in a marinade or stock. Cloves are also used in sweet dishes and cakes, the most famous being the Sienese *panforte*.

Nutmeg

(NOCE MOSCATA)

Grated nutmeg is a frequently occurring ingredient in both sweet and savoury dishes, especially ones containing spinach or Ricotta cheese. For the best flavour keep whole nuts and grate them immediately before use on a fine grater or special nutmeg grater.

Pepper

(PEPE)

Black and white peppercorns are a universal seasoning in all countries. Black ones, which are ground skin and all, have the best flavour and are preferable except for light-coloured dishes or white sauce where black specks would be inappropriate. Always buy whole peppercorns and grind them in a peppermill when required; the aroma is lost if the pepper is ready ground.

Salt

(SALE)

Italian cooks rely on top-quality fresh ingredients to produce full-flavoured food, and so do not use large quantities of salt. But it is essential to bring out the flavour of both pasta and rice during boiling. They prefer sea-salt, much of which comes from huge salt lagoons in Sardinia. If in doubt as to how much to use to season an unfamiliar dish use sparingly and have a salt mill on the table to use if more is needed.

Saffron

(ZAFFERANO)

One of the most expensive of all spices, consisting of the thread-like pistils of the autumn crocus. Saffron is an essential ingredient of the best Italian risottos contributing both subtle golden colour and pungent, rather bitter flavour. Buy saffron strands, not powder; although cheaper, the latter is likely to have been undetectably adulterated.

Fortunately a very little saffron goes a long way. Always soak in a little boiling water for 30 minutes before using to extract the full flavour; add both liquid and strands to the dish.

Other popular flavourings

Anchovies

(ALICI)

These little fish, which are preserved in brine or oil, are used a great deal to flavour many Italian dishes. They are easily obtainable preserved in jars or cans but some are highly salted and it is better to wash in warm water or soak in a little milk before using.

Mushrooms

(FUNGHI)

Dried mushrooms are usually of the type called *boletus* in Italy and *cèpes* in France. Make sure that they are a good cream and brown colour, not shrivelled and black, which is caused by long storage. They need to be soaked for about 30 minutes at the most and will cook in 20 minutes when added to the dish.

The cultivated mushrooms should be wiped thoroughly with a clean damp cloth and used as required in the recipe.

Wild mushrooms should be carefully checked to make sure they are of an edible variety. Peel the skins off, wash and use as directed in the recipe.

Vanilla

(VANIGLIA)

Italian cake and desserts often call for vanilla sugar. In Italy this can readily be bought in little sachets; but it is easy to produce it by storing a vanilla pod or bean in a jar of sugar; the flavour is so strong it soon permeates the contents. Whole pods are boiled in milk to flavour it for custards or sweet sauces; they can be rinsed and re-used many times. Sometimes it is more convenient to use vanilla extract; this is extremely concentrated and a few drops are all that is needed.

Basket of wild, cultivated and dried mushrooms

The Cheeses of Italy

Cheese plays an important part in Italian cuisine. It has been a staple food since Roman times, and as well as being used to round off a meal (before rather than after the dessert) it features in many recipes. Dishes which combine cheese with meat, poultry or anchovies are an Italian speciality. Soft cheeses like Ricotta are not only used extensively in savoury dishes but are also sweetened and eaten as a dessert. The very hard grating cheeses, especially Parmesan, form the universal garnish for soup and pasta.

Many Italian cheeses were originally produced in very localized areas, and owed their highly individual characters to the animals' milk (cows, sheep, goats and buffalo), the local climate and the type of grazing. Nowadays many are factory-made throughout Italy, and imitated in other parts of the world, from Denmark to the USA. But names such as Gorgonzola and Parmigiano Reggiano are protected under Italian law and can only be used for cheeses produced in specified areas under strict quality control.

Asiago

VICENZA

A firm, straw-coloured cheese with a scattering of holes, made from cows' milk. It is mild flavoured and eaten as a table cheese when under 1 year old, or grated when older and harder.

Bel Paese

LOMBARDY

One of the most popular cheeses in the world, only invented in the 20th century. The name means beautiful country, and it is sold in foil-wrapped discs featuring a map of Italy (or, if made in the USA, a map of the American continent). Made from cows' milk, it is semi-soft and bland, with shiny yellow rind.

Asiago, Grana Padano, Parmesan and Gorgonzola cheese

Caciocavallo

CAMPANIA

A distinctive-looking cheese shaped rather like a pear with a ball shape on top. Produced by cooking the curds until they become elastic, then stretching and shaping them. The name is thought to refer to the way the cheeses were dried: tied up in pairs and slung over poles as if on horseback (*a cavallo*). Made from cows' milk, it is firm and close textured with a golden yellow rind, and eaten at the table when young and mild, or grated and cooked when older and sharper.

Dolcelatte

The brand name of a mild creamy type of factory-made **Gorgonzola**.

Italian peasant making cream cheeses

Fontina

PIEDMONT

Genuine Fontina is made only in the Val d'Aosta region of northern Italy, from the milk of alpine cattle. Reminiscent of Swiss Gruyère, but softer and sweeter, with only tiny holes, it is a superb table cheese. Similar cheeses made elsewhere in Italy are called Fontal.

Formaggio

Italian for cheese.

Grana Padano

LOMBARDY, PIEDMONT

Hard-pressed cheese made from cows' milk, similar to **Parmigiano Reggiano**. Both belong to the *Grana* family of cheeses with brittle, grainy interior structures.

Gorgonzola

LOMBARDY

One of the great cheeses of the world: similar to Roquefort or Stilton, but creamier in texture, with veins more green than blue. It is made from cows' milk, in big foil-wrapped wheels. Although it has a strong smell the flavour should be rich but not sharp. Primarily a table cheese but also used in Italian regional dishes like *Milanese the pere ripiene*, stuffed pears.

Making Mozzarella cheese
Below Different shapes of Fior di Latte

Mascarpone

LOMBARDY

Very rich fresh cows' milk cheese rather like clotted cream, usually eaten as a dessert with fruit or liqueur.

Torta san Gaudenzio, or **Torta Gorgonzola**, is the name given to a luxury dessert consisting of layers of Mascarpone and Gorgonzola.

Mozzarella

THROUGHOUT ITALY

Fresh mild white cheese moulded into balls and wrapped in small bags with a little whey to keep it moist. Outside Italy it is best known as pizza cheese, but there it is often eaten sliced and sprinkled with olive oil. Originally it was made from buffalo milk, but nowadays most is made from cows' milk; in Italy this type is officially called *Fior di Latte*, cream of the milk.

Pasta Filata

Italian words meaning spun paste, which describe cheeses where the curd is stretched and kneaded until it becomes elastic. Mozzarella, Caciocavallo and Provolone are examples.

Pecorino

CENTRAL AND SOUTHERN ITALY

This word covers a wide variety of cheeses, as it includes all made from sheeps' milk. But usually it means a hard grating cheese, used in the same way as Parmesan, but with an extra tang due to the flavour of the sheep's milk. Such cheeses are widely made, but the best known are Pecorino Romano, Pecorino Siciliano and Sardo, from Sicily and Sardinia.

Two stages in the making of Parmesan cheese

Parmigiano Reggiano (Parmesan)

EMILIA-ROMAGNA

Genuine Parmesan cheese is made under strictly controlled conditions in restricted areas of Italy; imitations can be a shadow of the real thing. Its exquisite flavour and granular structure have made it world-famous as a grating cheese, but in Italy it is also enjoyed as a table cheese when young. A genuine cheese is a large golden drum with the words Parmigiano Reggiano pricked all over the bulging sides. It must be matured for at least 1 year; more expensive grades are matured for up to 4 years and develop an even finer flavour.

Provolone

CAMPANIA, SOUTHERN ITALY

A *pasta filata* (spun paste) cows' milk cheese moulded into various shapes (pear, cone, melon, ball etc) and tied with cords to be hung up while drying or awaiting sale. They have a smooth pale golden rind and soft but springy interior; flavour ranges from mild (*dolce*) to sharp (*piccante*), according to age. A good cooking cheese.

Ricotta

CENTRAL AND SOUTHERN ITALY

This pure white soft fresh cheese was traditionally made from the whey left over after making other cheese, but nowadays some whole or skimmed milk is added. It can be made from cows' or sheeps' milk, or a mixture of both. Traditionally it was drained in basin-shaped baskets which left their imprint on the cheese, and this is still sometimes imitated. Fresh Ricotta is the most familiar outside Italy, but there it is also salted and matured, or ripened even longer so it is hard enough to grate. The fresh variety is widely used in Italian cooking for both savoury and sweet dishes, as the bland but delicately sour flavour combines well with other ingredients.

Stracchino

LOMBARDY

Highly distinctive rindless cheese, very soft and creamy and almost white in colour. It is made from cows' milk in rather unglamorous-looking slabs, but the flavour is mild and delicious – rather like American cream cheese. Stracchino-Crescenza is a particularly rich version.

Taleggio

LOMBARDY

Cows' milk cheese made in square blocks, with soft and supple interior and thin pinkish-grey rind (factory-made ones may be foil-wrapped). Flavour can be bland, but when properly aged it has an acidic tang and makes a perfect after-dinner cheese.

The Wines of Italy

A selection of the better-known wines of each region

WHITE WINES | RED WINES

PIEDMONT — *Piemonte*

WHITE WINES	RED WINES
Asti Spumante	Barbaresco
Moscato D'Asti	Barbera
Vermouth	Barola
	Dolcetto (*red grape of the region*)
	Dolcetta d'Acqui
	Dolcetto d'Asti
	Grignolino d'Asti

LOMBARDY — *Lombardia*

WHITE WINES	RED WINES
Pinot Bianco grape (*makes sparkling wines in this region*)	Valtellina (*made from Chiavennasca [Nebbiolo] grape*)
Frecciarossa	Oltrepo Pavese
Franciacorta Pinot	Franciacorta Rosso

SOUTH TYROL — *Trentino-Alto-Adige*

WHITE WINES	RED WINES
Chardonnay	Santa Maddalena
Gewürztraminer	Lagrein del Trentino
Sylvaner	(*Lagrein is a Tyrolean grape*)
Rhine Riesling	Teroldego Rotaliano

FRIULI-VENEZIA-GIULIA — *Friuli-Venezia-Giulia*

WHITE WINES	RED WINES
Picolit	Merlot di Friuli
Pinot Grigio	Merlot di Pramaggiore
Tocai di Lison	(*made from the Cabernet grape*)
Tocai del Piave	
Grave Del Friuli	

VENETO — *Veneto*

WHITE WINES	RED WINES
Chardonnay grape	Bardolino
Bianco di Custoza	Raboso
Soave	Recioto di Valpolicella

EMILIA ROMAGNA — *Emilia-Romagna*

WHITE WINES	RED WINES
Albana di Romagna	Lambrusco
	Sangiovese di Romagna

TUSCANY — *Toscana*

WHITE WINES	RED WINES
Trebbiano (*the white grape of Tuscany*)	Chianti
Galestro	Vino Nobile di Montepulciano
Vinsanto (*strong sweet wines*)	Rosso di Montalcino
Vernaccia di San Gimignano	Brunello di Montalcino
Carmignano	

UMBRIA — *Umbria*

WHITE WINES	RED WINES
Orvieto	Colli del Trasimeno
	Tortiano

MARCHES — *Marche*

WHITE WINES	RED WINES
Verdicchio dei Castelli di Jesi	Rosso Conero

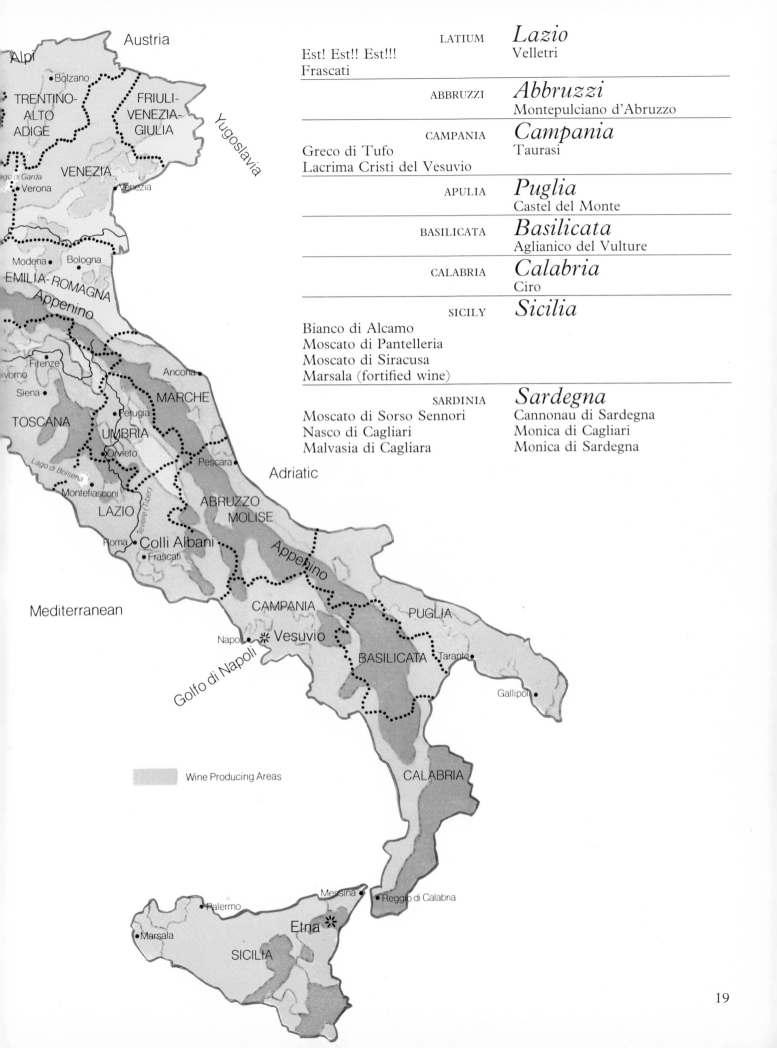

	LATIUM	*Lazio*
Est! Est!! Est!!!		Velletri
Frascati		

	ABBRUZZI	*Abbruzzi*
		Montepulciano d'Abruzzo

	CAMPANIA	*Campania*
Greco di Tufo		Taurasi
Lacrima Cristi del Vesuvio		

	APULIA	*Puglia*
		Castel del Monte

	BASILICATA	*Basilicata*
		Aglianico del Vulture

	CALABRIA	*Calabria*
		Ciro

	SICILY	*Sicilia*
Bianco di Alcamo		
Moscato di Pantelleria		
Moscato di Siracusa		
Marsala (fortified wine)		

	SARDINIA	*Sardegna*
Moscato di Sorso Sennori		Cannonau di Sardegna
Nasco di Cagliari		Monica di Cagliari
Malvasia di Cagliara		Monica di Sardegna

Wine Producing Areas

19

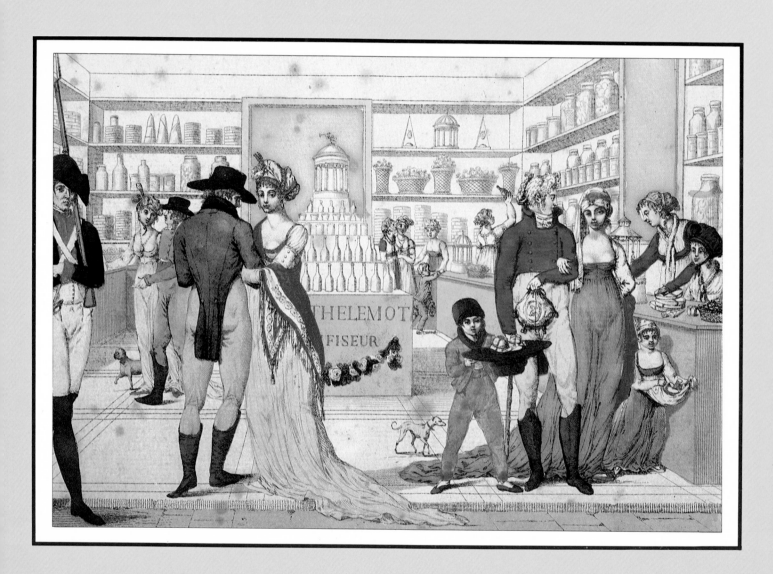

SAUCES
AND
SAVOURY BUTTERS

*The sauces of Italy are quite unlike those of
France. Made from fresh vegetables they are
simple to prepare and have few pitfalls for even
the most inexperienced cook.
Apart from Béchamel sauce, which was evolved in
Italy, and the ever popular mayonnaise;
Italian sauces are mainly made from olive oil,
tomatoes, wines, other vegetables and herbs.
They are sometimes thickened with breadcrumbs
and cheese. There are probably as many variations
on a sauce as there are cooks in Italy.
Savoury butters are useful to serve with grilled
fish, meat and poultry as well as
for sandwiches and cãnapés.*

Brown Sauce

SALSA BRUNA O SPAGNOLA

Ingredients	Metric/Imperial	American
bacon or ham fat	50 g/2 oz	2 ounces
carrot	75 g/3 oz	3 ounces
onion	60 g/2½ oz	2½ ounces
mushroom	1	1
plain (all-purpose) flour	50 g/2 oz	½ cup
brown stock (page 23)	2 litres/3½ pints	2 quarts
celery	25 g/1 oz	1 ounce
sprigs of parsley	4	4
bay leaf	½	½
chopped thyme	¼ teaspoon	¼ teaspoon
clove	½	½
garlic clove	1	1

Heat the bacon fat in a deep pan; chop the carrot and onion coarsely and slice the mushroom into 3. Add the vegetables to the pan and cook over a medium heat for a few minutes until softened. Stir in the flour and cook until it turns golden. Pour in a scant 750 ml/1¼ pints/3 cups of the stock, add the chopped celery, herbs, clove and crushed garlic. Cover and leave to cook until the mixture thickens, stirring from time to time.

Add another 750 ml/1¼ pints/3 cups of stock and continue to simmer very gently for about 1½ hours until the mixture has reduced to 750 ml/1¼ pints/3 cups, skimming if necessary.

Pass through a fine sieve, add the remaining stock and continue cooking for another hour until the sauce has reduced to 1 litre/1¾ pints/1 quart.

Time: 2½ hours　　　　*Makes 1 litre/1¾ pints/1 quart*

White, Golden and Brown Roux

ROUX BIANCO, BIONDO E BRUNO

Ingredients	Metric/Imperial	American
butter	150 g/5 oz	10 tablespoons
plain (all-purpose) flour	150 g/5 oz	1¼ cups

White roux Melt the butter in a small pan over a low heat so that it does not colour, add the flour and stir with a wooden spoon for a few minutes.
Golden roux Leave the butter and flour mixture just a little longer so that it turns golden.
Brown roux Cook the mixture until it is quite a dark brown.

Use as appropriate to thicken sauces of different colours.

1 Cook the carrot, onion and mushrooms with the bacon over a medium heat. Stir in the flour and cook until golden.
2 Pour in some of the stock and mix.
3 Add the celery, clove, garlic and herbs. Cook until the mixture thickens. Add more stock and skim.
4 Pass the sauce through a fine sieve.
5 Add the remaining stock and continue cooking.

1 Melt the butter, add the meat. Brown over a medium heat. Add water.
2 Add the bouquet garni and prepared vegetables.
3 Bring to the boil, add the clove, salt and peppercorns; skim.
4 Strain and remove pieces of bone, mash the meat and vegetables through a sieve to extract all the liquid.

Simple Brown Veal Stock

FONDO BRUNO DI VITELLO SEMPLIFICATO

Ingredients	Metric/Imperial	American
boned shoulder of veal	350 g/12 oz	¾ pound
veal hock	350 g/12 oz	¾ pound
meaty veal bone	450 g/1 lb	1 pound
small carrot	1	1
small onion	1	1
celery stalk	1	1
garlic clove	1	1
butter	50 g/2 oz	¼ cup
bouquet garni	1	1
clove	1	1
salt		
peppercorns	6	6

Cut the pieces of meat into walnut-sized chunks. Break the bone into small pieces (or get the butcher to do it). Prepare and chop all the vegetables; crush the garlic.

Melt the butter in a deep pan; add the meat and brown over a medium heat for a few minutes. Pour in 1.5 litres/2½ pints/1½ quarts of water, add the bouquet garni and the prepared vegetables. Bring rapidly to the boil. Add the clove, a little salt and the peppercorns; cover with a lid and simmer over a low heat for 2 hours, skimming the surface every so often.

Strain and remove the pieces of bone. Mash the meat and vegetables with a wooden spoon to extract every drop of liquid.

Time: 3 hours   *Makes 1 litre/1¾ pints/1 quart*

This stock is ideal for making Brown Sauce (see page 22). It is a simplified version of an elaborate and laborious classic recipe. It will keep for 3–4 days in the refrigerator or, if poured into small containers and sealed, for up to 4 months in a freezer.

Simple White Chicken Stock

FONDO BIANCO DI POLLO SEMPLIFICATO

Ingredients	Metric/Imperial	American
veal hock	350 g/12 oz	¾ pound
chicken portion	350 g/12 oz	¾ pound
chicken carcass plus neck and giblets	1 kg/2 lb	2 pounds
salt and pepper		
carrot	50 g/2 oz	2 ounces
onion	50 g/2 oz	2 ounces
celery stalk	25 g/1 oz	1 ounce
bouquet garni	1	1

Put all the meat in a large deep pan, cover with 1.5 litres/ 2½ pints/1½ quarts of water and bring slowly to the boil. Skim the surface, season with salt and pepper and add the chopped vegetables along with the bouquet garni. Cover and simmer on a low heat for about 1½ hours, skimming the surface from time to time.

Pass the stock through a sieve; remove the bones and mash the meat and vegetables with a wooden spoon to extract the last drop of liquid.

Time: 2½ hours   *Makes 1 litre/1¾ pints/1 quart*

This stock will keep for 3–4 days in the refrigerator. Alternatively pour into small containers, seal and freeze for up to about 4 months.

Velouté Sauce

SALSA VELLUTATA

Ingredients	Metric/Imperial	American
butter	25 g/1 oz	2 tablespoons
plain (all-purpose) flour	25 g/1 oz	¼ cup
veal stock (page 23)	600 ml/1 pint	2½ cups
small sprigs of parsley	3–4	3–4
salt and pepper		
grated nutmeg	¼ teaspoon	¼ teaspoon

Melt the butter in a deep pan over a low heat. Add the flour and cook, stirring constantly, until golden.

Gradually add the stock and bring to the boil, stirring constantly. Add the parsley sprigs, season with salt, pepper and nutmeg and simmer very gently for 20 minutes, stirring from time to time.

Remove the parsley and pass the sauce through a fine sieve into a bowl. If it is to stand for any length of time pour 1 tablespoon of melted butter over the top to prevent a skin from forming.

Time: 30 minutes Makes a scant 600 ml/1 pint/2½ cups

Use chicken or fish stock instead of veal where appropriate.

Vegetable Sauce

SUGO DI VERDURE

Ingredients	Metric/Imperial	American
courgettes (zucchini)	2	2
aubergine (eggplant)	1	1
large onion	1	1
pepper (sweet)	1	1
butter	75 g/3 oz	6 tablespoons
plum tomatoes	350 g/12 oz	¾ pound
vegetable stock	225 ml/8 fl oz	1 cup
salt and pepper		
chopped parsley	1 tablespoon	1 tablespoon

Wash and cube the courgettes, aubergine, onion and deseeded pepper. Melt the butter in a large pan, add the vegetables and cook for 10 minutes over a low heat.

Peel the tomatoes if using fresh, chop roughly and add to the pan along with the stock and seasoning. Simmer for another 30 minutes and flavour with parsley just before switching off the heat.

This quantity is enough to dress 350 g/12 oz/¾ pound of pasta.

Time: 45 minutes   *Serves 4*

Onion Sauce

SUGO DI CIPOLLE

Ingredients	Metric/Imperial	American
onions	4	4
bacon	75 g/3 oz	3 ounces
butter	50 g/2 oz	¼ cup
stock	125 ml/4 fl oz	½ cup
salt and pepper		
eggs	2	2

Slice the onions very thinly. Derind and dice the bacon. Melt the butter in a deep pan, add the onions and bacon and cook for 3 minutes on a medium heat. Cover with a lid and leave over a low heat for 20 minutes, if necessary adding a little stock to prevent the sauce from becoming too dry.

Season with salt and pepper when cooked. Leave until tepid and stir in the lightly beaten eggs.

This quantity is enough to dress 350 g/12 oz/¾ pound of pasta.

Time: 45 minutes   *Serves 4*

Sausage and Mascarpone Cheese Sauce

SUGO DI SALSICCIA E MASCARPONE

Ingredients	Metric/Imperial	American
fresh Italian sausages	25 g/8 oz	½ pound
butter	25 g/1 oz	2 tablespoons
Mascarpone cheese	100 g/4 oz	¼ pound
eggs, separated	2	2
Parmesan cheese, grated	25 g/1 oz	¼ cup
grated nutmeg	¼ teaspoon	¼ teaspoon
salt		

Skin the sausages and crumble into little pieces. Melt the butter in a pan, add the sausage and cook over a low heat for 5 minutes until lightly browned.

Mix the Mascarpone cheese with 2 egg yolks and 1 white, beating hard with a wooden spoon. When soft add the Parmesan cheese, nutmeg and a pinch of salt.

Mix the sausage and cooking juices with the cheese mixture.

This quantity is enough to dress 350 g/12 oz/¾ pound of pasta.

Time: 25 minutes   *Serves 4*

Tuna and Mushroom Sauce

SUGO DI TONNO E FUNGHI

Ingredients	Metric/Imperial	American
mushrooms	50 g/2 oz	2 ounces
oil	4 tablespoons	⅓ cup
garlic clove	1	1
anchovy fillets	4	4
plum tomatoes	225 g/8 oz	½ pound
vegetable stock	125 ml/4 fl oz	½ cup
tuna in oil	100 g/4 oz	¼ pound
salt and pepper		
chopped parsley	1 tablespoon	1 tablespoon

Wipe the mushrooms and dice. Heat the oil in a medium-sized pan, add the crushed garlic and cook over a medium heat until golden.

Add the drained and chopped anchovy fillets and cook for a few minutes, mashing with a wooden spoon, then add the diced mushrooms.

Peel the tomatoes if using fresh, drain if canned, chop and add to the pan along with the stock. Cook over a low heat for 30 minutes, then drain the tuna and flake it into the sauce.

Taste and adjust the seasoning, sprinkle with parsley and remove from the heat.

This quantity is enough to dress 350 g/12 oz/¾ pound of pasta.

Time: 45 minutes   *Serves 4*

Béchamel Sauce

SALSA BESCIAMELLA

Ingredients	Metric/Imperial	American
milk	600 ml/1 pint	2½ cups
small onion	1	1
carrot	½	½
bouquet garni	1	1
bay leaf	1	1
peppercorns	4	4
butter	50 g/2 oz	¼ cup
plain (all-purpose) flour	50 g/2 oz	½ cup
salt and pepper		
grated nutmeg	¼ teaspoon	¼ teaspoon

Put the milk in a pan with the quartered onion, the carrot cut into slices, the bouquet garni, bay leaf and peppercorns. Bring to the boil slowly. When the milk boils turn off the heat, cover and allow to infuse for 10 minutes, then strain into a jug.

Melt the butter in a deep pan over a low heat. Add the flour and cook, stirring constantly, for a few minutes. Gradually stir in the milk and continue cooking until the mixture thickens slightly. Turn the heat right down (put a heat diffuser under the pan if available), cover with a lid and leave to cook for 15 minutes, stirring from time to time.

Season with salt, pepper and nutmeg and remove from the heat.

Time: 15 minutes + 10 minutes: infusing
Makes 600 ml/1 pint/2½ cups

This is a thick or coating sauce referred to as white sauce in the recipes. For a thin or pouring sauce use 40 g/1½ oz/1½ tablespoons butter and 40 g/1½ oz/scant ½ cup flour.

Tomato Sauce

SALSA DI POMODORI

Ingredients	Metric/Imperial	American
fresh plum tomatoes	1 kg/2 lb	2 pounds
or canned tomatoes	450 g/1 lb	1 pound
Parma ham or bacon	50 g/2 oz	2 ounces
celery stalk	1	1
carrot	1	1
onion	$\frac{1}{2}$	$\frac{1}{2}$
butter	50 g/2 oz	$\frac{1}{4}$ cup
basil leaves	3	3
salt and pepper		

If using fresh tomatoes drop them into boiling water briefly, remove all at once, peel and deseed. Drain and deseed canned tomatoes. (A mixture can be used.)

Chop the ham, celery, carrot and onion. Melt the butter in a heavy pan, add the chopped ingredients and cook over a medium heat until the onion is golden. Mash the tomatoes and add to the pan along with the basil leaves. Season with salt and pepper, cover and simmer over a medium heat for 20–25 minutes (less if using canned tomatoes), stirring from time to time.

Use the sauce as it is or pass it through a sieve, blender or food processor to make it completely smooth.

This quantity is enough to dress 350 g/12 oz/$\frac{3}{4}$ pound of pasta.

Time: 40 minutes   *Serves 4–5*

Tomato and Herb Sauce

SUGO DI POMODORO AROMATIZZATO

Ingredients	Metric/Imperial	American
onion	1	1
garlic cloves	2	2
butter	50 g/2 oz	$\frac{1}{4}$ cup
dry white wine	225 ml/8 fl oz	1 cup
plum tomatoes	450 g/1 lb	1 pound
salt and pepper		
chopped parsley	1 tablespoon	1 tablespoon
chopped basil	1 tablespoon	1 tablespoon

Finely chop the onion and crush the garlic. Melt the butter in a heavy shallow pan, add the onion and garlic and cook over a low heat for 5 minutes until softened but not coloured.

Add the wine and leave for 5 minutes to evaporate. Peel the tomatoes if using fresh, chop roughly and add to the pan. Season and simmer gently for 20 minutes, stirring from time to time to prevent the sauce from sticking to the pan.

Add the parsley and basil just before turning off the heat.

This quantity is enough to dress 350 g/12 oz/$\frac{3}{4}$ pound of pasta.

Time: 40 minutes   *Serves 4*

Red Sauce with Peas

SUGO ROSSO CON PISELLI

Ingredients	Metric/Imperial	American
smoked bacon	100 g/4 oz	$\frac{1}{4}$ pound
butter	50 g/2 oz	$\frac{1}{4}$ cup
frozen peas	100 g/4 oz	$\frac{1}{4}$ pound
plum tomatoes	450 g/1 lb	1 pound
vegetable stock	225 ml/8 fl oz	1 cup

Derind and dice the bacon. Melt the butter in a small pan and cook the bacon over a medium heat. Before it becomes crisp add the peas and leave to flavour for 2 minutes.

Peel the tomatoes if using fresh and chop roughly. Add to the pan, adjust the seasoning, pour in the stock and cook over a low heat for 30 minutes, stirring from time to time to prevent the sauce from sticking to the pan.

This quantity is enough to dress 350 g/12 oz/$\frac{3}{4}$ pound of pasta.

Time: 45 minutes   *Serves 4*

Tomato Purée

PASSATO DI POMODORI

Make tomato purée when tomatoes are cheap to buy or if you have a home-grown surplus.

Flavour a 4.5 kg/10 pound quantity of tomatoes with 2 onions, 2 bay leaves, 2 bouquet garnis, the rinds of 2 lemons, salt and pepper to taste and 1 tablespoon of sugar.

Wash the tomatoes and cut into quarters; quarter the onions. Put in a large deep pan along with the remaining ingredients and cook for 30 minutes, stirring from time to time.

Allow to cool slightly, then pass through a vegetable mill or coarse sieve. Store in sterilized preserving bottles or jars; or pack into plastic boxes or bags and freeze.

Time: 1 hour   *Makes about $1\frac{3}{4}$ kg/4 pounds*

Tomato Juice **1** Quarter the ripe plum tomatoes.
2 Tip the tomato pieces into a vegetable mill or sieve.
3 Press the tomato pieces through in batches, discarding the skins and pips before adding the next.
4 Pour the juice into a jug and flavour with a few drops of lemon juice, salt, pepper, Tabasco or Worcester sauce to taste. Serve chilled as a drink or use in cooking.
Tomato Purée **1** Put the ingredients for the purée in a deep pan, bring to the boil and simmer for 30 minutes.
2 Press through a vegetable mill or sieve.

Anchovy Fondue

Anchovy Fondue

BAGNA CAUDA

Ingredients	Metric/Imperial	American
mixed raw vegetables: celery stalks, sweet peppers, cauliflower florets, carrots, mushrooms, fennel, cardoon	1 kg/2 lb	2 pounds
lemon	1	1
garlic cloves	6	6
butter	75 g/3 oz	6 tablespoons
anchovy fillets	225 g/8 oz	½ pound
olive oil	225 ml/8 fl oz	1 cup

Prepare all the vegetables and chop into bite-sized pieces. Put in separate bowls and sprinkle with lemon juice to prevent discoloration.

Peel the garlic cloves and slice very thinly. If liked soak in milk for 1–2 hours to remove their strong smell, then drain and dry.

Melt the butter in a fondue pan with the flame set low. Add the garlic and cook for a few minutes until softened. As soon as it starts to turn golden add the anchovy fillets with their oil. Gradually add the olive oil, stirring with a wooden spoon in the same direction. Simmer for 10 minutes until the anchovies have completely dissolved.

Take the fondue to the table and keep the sauce warm over a low flame. Present the vegetables in separate bowls or arranged on a platter for guests to help themselves and dip in the sauce.

Time: 30 minutes + soaking: 1–2 hours   Serves 4–6

This is a regional speciality from Asti.

Clam Sauce

SALSA ALLE VONGOLE

Ingredients	Metric/Imperial	American
medium-sized onions	2	2
garlic cloves	2	2
olive oil	4 tablespoons	6 tablespoons
canned plum tomatoes	2 (400 g/14 oz)	2 (14 ounce)
or fresh tomatoes	1 kg/2 lb	2 pounds
dry white wine	4 tablespoons	6 tablespoons
chopped oregano	½ teaspoon	½ teaspoon
salt and pepper		
canned clams	200 g/7 oz	7 ounce
chopped parsley	2 tablespoons	3 tablespoons

Finely chop the onion and crush the garlic. Heat the oil in a deep pan, add the onion and garlic and cook over a low heat until transparent.

Add the tomatoes (peeled if using fresh), wine, oregano and seasoning. Simmer for 20 minutes.

Drain the clams, add to the sauce and heat gently for 8 minutes. Stir in the parsley, taste and adjust the seasoning.

This quantity is enough to dress 350 g/12 oz/¾ pound of pasta.

Time: 35 minutes   *Serves 4*

Putanesca Sauce

SALSA PUTANESCA

Ingredients	Metric/Imperial	American
onion	1	1
garlic clove	1	1
carrot	1	1
olive oil	2 tablespoons	3 tablespoons
fresh tomatoes	2	2
canned tomatoes	400 g/14 oz	14 ounces
dry white wine	4 tablespoons	6 tablespoons
bay leaf	1	1
basil leaves	3–4	3–4
salt and pepper		
anchovy fillet	50 g/2 oz	2 ounces
capers	1 tablespoon	1 tablespoon
black olives	50 g/2 oz	2 ounces
Tabasco sauce		
chopped parsley	1 tablespoon	1 tablespoon

Finely chop the onion and crush the garlic. Scrape and chop the carrot.

Heat the oil in a shallow pan, add the onion and garlic and cook over a low heat until transparent. Add the carrots and cook for another minute, stirring, then add all the tomatoes, peeled and chopped, along with the wine, bay leaf, basil, seasoning and 4 of the anchovy fillets. Bring to the boil, then reduce the heat and simmer for 30 minutes.

Purée the sauce in a blender or food processor. Return to the rinsed-out pan and add the drained and chopped capers and anchovies, stoned and chopped olives and a few drops of Tabasco sauce. Add the parsley and reheat gently. (The flavour of this sauce improves if it is cooled, stored in the refrigerator overnight and reheated next day.)

This quantity is enough to dress 350 g/12 oz/¾ pound of pasta.

Time: 45 minutes   *Serves 4*

Quick Meat Sauce

SUGO DI CARNE RAPIDO

Ingredients	Metric/Imperial	American
small onion	1	1
carrot	1	1
celery stalk	1	1
butter	50 g/2 oz	¼ cup
minced (ground) beef	225 g/8 oz	½ pound
red wine	125 ml/4 fl oz	½ cup
plum tomatoes	225 g/8 oz	½ pound
salt and pepper		
chopped parsley	1 tablespoon	1 tablespoon

Finely chop the onion, carrot and celery. Melt the butter in a large pan, add the chopped vegetables and cook for 5 minutes on a low heat. Add the meat and cook over a medium heat, stirring all the time. Pour in the wine and leave for 4–5 minutes.

Peel the tomatoes if using fresh, chop roughly and add to the pan. Season with salt and pepper, reduce the heat and cook gently for a further 30 minutes. Sprinkle with parsley just before serving.

This quantity is enough to dress 350 g/12 oz/¾ pound of pasta.

Time: 45 minutes   *Serves 4*

Beef Ragu

SALSA BOLOGNESE

Ingredients	Metric/Imperial	American
onion	1	1
celery stalks	2	2
carrot	1	1
garlic cloves	2	2
butter	25 g/1 oz	2 tablespoons
oil	2 tablespoons	3 tablespoons
slices of bacon	2	2
chicken livers	100 g/4 oz	¼ pound
minced (ground) beef	350 g/12 oz	¾ pound
chopped oregano	1 teaspoon	1 teaspoon
bay leaf	1	1
sprig of parsley	1	1
red wine	125 ml/4 fl oz	½ cup
plum tomatoes	450 g/1 lb	1 pound
beef stock	225 ml/8 fl oz	1 cup
salt and pepper		

Prepare the vegetables: finely chop the onion and celery, coarsely grate the carrot and crush the garlic. Heat the butter and half the oil in a deep pan, add the onion, celery and garlic and cook over a low heat for 5 minutes. Add the carrot and cook for a few more minutes.

Derind and dice the bacon. Wash and chop the chicken livers. Heat the remaining oil in a separate pan, add the bacon and cook on a medium heat for 2 minutes. Add the beef, raise the heat to high and cook for a few minutes, stirring constantly, until lightly browned. Then add the washed and chopped chicken livers; mix until lightly browned all over.

Tip the meat into the pan with the vegetables. Add the oregano, bay leaf and parsley. Pour in the wine and allow it to evaporate slightly.

Peel the tomatoes if using fresh, chop or mash and add to the meat and vegetable mixture along with the stock. Season well and simmer gently for 45 minutes.

This quantity is enough to dress 450 g/1 lb/1 pound of pasta.

Time: 1 hour *Serves 6*

Sweet Pepper Sauce

SALSA DI PEPERONI SOTT'OLIO

Ingredients	Metric/Imperial	American
green (sweet) peppers in oil	3	3
anchovy fillets	2	2
chopped parsley	1 tablespoon	1 tablespoon
Parmesan cheese, grated	50 g/2 oz	½ cup
olive oil	125 ml/4 fl oz	½ cup

Drain the peppers, cut in half if whole and deseed. Chop finely along with the drained anchovies. Put in a bowl with the parsley and Parmesan cheese. Add enough oil to make a thick soft sauce.

If possible keep the sauce in the bottom of the refrigerator for a few days before using to allow the flavour to mature.

Serve with boiled meats, grills and hard- or soft-boiled (cooked) eggs.

Time: 15 minutes *Serves 4*

Green Sauce

SALSA VERDE

Ingredients	Metric/Imperial	American
slice of bread	1	1
wine vinegar	2 tablespoons	3 tablespoons
garlic clove	1	1
anchovy fillets	3	3
chopped parsley	2 tablespoons	3 tablespoons
olive oil	125 ml/4 fl oz	½ cup
salt and pepper		

Remove the crust from the bread and soak the crumb in the vinegar. Crush the garlic, chop the anchovies and mix with the parsley. Put the chopped mixture in a bowl, add the squeezed breadcrumbs and stir briskly. Finally add the oil and season lightly with salt and pepper.

Alternatively mix all the ingredients together in a blender or food processor.

This sauce should be fairly liquid and is used as an accompaniment to boiled beef.

Time: 15 minutes *Serves 4*

Chantilly Sauce

SALSA CHANTILLY

Ingredients	Metric/Imperial	American
whipped cream	125 ml/4 fl oz	¼ cup
mayonnaise (page 34)	225 ml/8 fl oz	1 cup
egg white (optional)	1	1

Fold the whipped cream into the mayonnaise just before serving. For a lighter sauce also fold in a stiffly beaten egg white.

This sauce makes a good accompaniment for asparagus and other boiled vegetables when served cold.

Time: 10 minutes   *Serves 4–6*

Horseradish Sauce

SALSA AL RAFANO

Ingredients	Metric/Imperial	American
mayonnaise (page 34)	225 ml/8 fl oz	1 cup
grated horseradish	2 tablespoons	3 tablespoons
white wine vinegar	1 tablespoon	1 tablespoon
whipped cream (optional)	2 tablespoons	3 tablespoons

Mix the mayonnaise with the horseradish and vinegar; stir well. If liked fold in whipped cream just before serving.

Use to accompany beef.

Time: 15 minutes   *Serves 8*

Celery Sauce

SALSA AL SEDANO

Ingredients	Metric/Imperial	American
green (sweet) pepper	½	½
small cucumber	1	1
head (bunch) of celery	1	1
small onion	½	½
lemon juice	2 tablespoons	3 tablespoons
paprika	¼ teaspoon	¼ teaspoon
mayonnaise	225 ml/8 fl oz	1 cup

Prepare all the vegetables and chop very finely. Sprinkle with the lemon juice and paprika and leave to stand for 10 minutes.

Mix the vegetables into the mayonnaise. Stir carefully until all the ingredients are well blended.

Serve with cold meats or fish salads.

Time: 15 minutes + 10 minutes: standing   *Serves 8*

Andalusian Sauce

SALSA ANDALUSA

Ingredients	Metric/Imperial	American
yellow (sweet) pepper	1	1
mayonnaise (page 34)	225 ml/8 fl oz	1 cup
Tomato Sauce (page 26)	125 ml/4 fl oz	½ cup

Char the skin of the pepper on all sides in a flame or under a hot grill (broiler). Peel and dice. Add the pepper to the mayonnaise and fold in the tomato sauce.

Serve as an accompaniment to meat, chicken or eggs.

Time: 15 minutes   *Serves 4–6*

Walnut Sauce

SUGO DI NOCI

Ingredients	Metric/Imperial	American
walnuts	225 g/8 oz	$\frac{1}{2}$ pound
pine nuts	1 teaspoon	1 teaspoon
garlic cloves	2	2
butter	50 g/2 oz	$\frac{1}{4}$ cup
salt and pepper		
Parmesan cheese, grated	25 g/1 oz	$\frac{1}{4}$ cup
single (thin) cream	225 ml/8 fl oz	1 cup

Shell the walnuts. Toast the kernels lightly in the oven, then remove the skins. Chop finely along with the pine nuts and garlic (or put in a blender or food processor).

Melt the butter in a pan, add the chopped nut mixture and cook on a medium heat until golden. Season with salt and pepper, remove from the heat and stir in the Parmesan cheese. Pour over the cream and mix well.

This quantity is enough to dress 350 g/12 oz/$\frac{3}{4}$ pound of pasta.

Time: 5 minutes　　　　　　　　　　　　　*Serves 4*

Black Olive Sauce

SUGO ALLE OLIVE

Ingredients	Metric/Imperial	American
garlic cloves	2	2
fresh chilli	$\frac{1}{2}$	$\frac{1}{2}$
oil	125 ml/2 fl oz	$\frac{1}{4}$ cup
plum tomatoes	225 g/8 oz	$\frac{1}{2}$ pound
salt and pepper		
capers	1 tablespoon	1 tablespoon
black olives	100 g/4 oz	$\frac{1}{4}$ pound
chopped parsley	1 tablespoon	1 tablespoon

Crush the garlic; deseed and chop the chilli. Heat the oil in a deep pan, add the garlic and chilli and cook over a medium heat until golden.

Peel the tomatoes if using fresh and chop roughly. Add to the pan, season with salt and pepper and cook over a low heat for about 20 minutes or until the sauce has thickened.

Just before serving add the drained and chopped capers, halved stoned olives and chopped parsley. Leave on the heat for 2–3 minutes before using.

This quantity is enough to dress 350 g/12 oz/$\frac{3}{4}$ pound of pasta.

Time: 40 minutes　　　　　　　　　　　　*Serves 4*

Genoese Pesto Sauce

PESTO ALLA GENOVESE

Ingredients	Metric/Imperial	American
basil leaves	25 g/1 oz	1 ounce
garlic cloves	2	2
pine nuts	1 tablespoon	1 tablespoon
Parmesan cheese, grated	25 g/1 oz	$\frac{1}{4}$ cup
Pecorino cheese, grated	25 g/1 oz	$\frac{1}{4}$ cup
olive oil	125 ml/4 fl oz	$\frac{1}{2}$ cup
salt and pepper		

Wash and dry the basil, put in a mortar with the garlic and pine nuts and crush with a pestle. Add the Parmesan and Pecorino cheeses and continue to crush until all the ingredients are well blended.

Add the oil a little at a time. Just before using season and moisten with 2–3 tablespoons of the pasta cooking water.

This is the traditional way of making pesto: nowadays it can be done much more quickly in a blender or food processor.

The quantity given is enough to dress 350 g/12 oz/$\frac{3}{4}$ pound of pasta.

Time: 25 minutes if making by hand　　　*Serves 4*

Sauces and Stocks
From the top, clockwise:
1 Tomato Sauce, page 26.
2 Simple Brown Veal Stock, page 23.
3 Beef Stock (as simple Brown Veal Stock, page 23, using 225 g/8 oz/$\frac{1}{2}$ pound of stewing beef and beef marrow bones).
4 Brown Sauce, page 22.
5 White Roux, page 22.
6 Béchamel Sauce with onions, page 25.
Centre:
7 Simple White Chicken Stock, page 24.

Blender Mayonnaise

SALSA MAIONESE PREPARATE NEL FRULLATORE

Ingredients	Metric/Imperial	American
egg	1	1
salt and freshly ground white pepper		
mustard (optional)	½ teaspoon	½ teaspoon
lemon juice	1 tablespoon	1 tablespoon
olive oil	225 ml/8 fl oz	1 cup

Make sure that all the ingredients are at room temperature. Put the egg, seasoning, mustard and lemon juice into a blender or food processor and blend at high speed for about 1 minute. Remove the top cap from the centre of the lid and put in a funnel. With the machine switched on, trickle the oil into the egg mixture until it thickens.

Use as for ordinary mayonnaise.

Time: 7 minutes   *Serves 4*

Coating Mayonnaise

SALSA MAIONESE COLLATA

Ingredients	Metric/Imperial	American
gelatine	3 teaspoons	3 teaspoons
stock	125 ml/4 fl oz	½ cup
mayonnaise	225 ml/8 fl oz	1 cup

Sprinkle the gelatine powder on to 150 ml/¼ pint/⅔ cup of boiling water and stir until dissolved. Mix with the hot stock, then leave until cool.

Gradually add the mayonnaise to the gelatine mixture.

Use coating mayonnaise to dress eggs, fish, boiled chicken and salads.

If required the sauce can be made firmer by increasing the amount of gelatine.

Time: 10 minutes + 30 minutes: cooling   *Serves 4*

Mayonnaise

SALSA MAIONESE

Ingredients	Metric/Imperial	American
large egg yolk	1	1
salt and freshly ground white pepper		
olive oil	125 ml/4 fl oz	½ cup
lemon juice	2 teaspoons	2 teaspoons

Make sure all the ingredients are at room temperature. Put the egg yolk into a bowl with a little salt and pepper. Stir rapidly with a wooden spoon, then begin to add the oil in a thin slow trickle, beating constantly. If the mayonnaise thickens too quickly add 1–2 drops of the lemon juice. Finish by checking the seasoning and beating in the remaining lemon juice.

If the mayonnaise curdles (due to oil being added too fast) start the operation afresh in another bowl, trickling in the separated mayonnaise instead of oil, and continuing with any remaining oil.

Use to dress salads of all kinds.

Time: 15 minutes   *Serves 4*

Vinaigrette Dressing

OLIO ACETO

Ingredients	Metric/Imperial	American
olive oil	125 ml/4 fl oz	½ cup
wine vinegar	50 ml/2 fl oz	¼ cup
wild mustard	1 teaspoon	1 teaspoon
salt and pepper		

Put all the ingredients in a screw-top jar and shake thoroughly to mix.

Chopped parsley, tarragon, chervil, chives or crushed garlic can be added to suit different salads.

Time: 5 minutes   *Makes 175 ml/6 fl oz/¾ cup*

Tartare Sauce

SALSA TARTARA

Ingredients	Metric/Imperial	American
hard-boiled (cooked) eggs	4	4
small onion	1	1
mild mustard	2 teaspoons	2 teaspoons
salt and pepper		
chopped parsley	1 tablespoon	1 tablespoon
olive oil	175 ml/6 fl oz	¾ cup
wine vinegar	3 tablespoons	4 tablespoons

Shell the eggs and separate the whites from the yolks. Mash the eggs in a bowl with a fork.

Add onion, mustard, seasoning and parsley. Trickle in the oil and mix until the sauce is frothy. Finally add the vinegar and chopped egg whites. Taste and adjust the seasoning.

Serve with fish.

Time: 20 minutes   *Serves 4–6*

Mayonnaise
To make 300 ml/½ pint/1¼ cups
1 Separate the eggs and put the yolks in a bowl.
2 Add seasoning and beat in the oil in a slow trickle. Use a wooden spoon, whisk or electric mixer.
3 If the sauce becomes too thick add a few drops of lemon juice. Taste and adjust seasoning; flavour with remaining lemon juice.

Hollandaise Sauce

SALSA HOLLANDAISE

Ingredients	Metric/Imperial	American
white wine vinegar	3 tablespoons	4 tablespoons
peppercorns	6	6
bay leaf	1	1
blade of mace	1	1
egg yolks	2	2
salt		
softened butter	100 g/4 oz	½ cup
lemon juice	1 tablespoon	1 tablespoon

Put the vinegar, peppercorns, bay leaf and mace in a small pan and reduce by boiling until there is 1 tablespoon left.

Mix the egg yolks in a heatproof bowl with a pinch of salt and 25 g/1 oz/2 tablespoons of the measured butter. Place the bowl on top of a pan of hot water, without the water touching the bottom of the bowl. Put on a low heat. Beat the mixture until it is slightly thickened with a wooden spoon.

Strain in the reduced liquid and beat well. Gradually add the softened butter in very small pieces beating between each piece.

Remove the sauce from the heat when it has become light and thick and season to taste with a little lemon juice. Keep the sauce warm by standing in a bowl of warm not hot water.

Poached Fish with Hollandaise Sauce

This sauce will curdle if overheated therefore it is essential to make sure the water does not boil while the sauce is being cooked.

Serve as an accompaniment to fish and vegetables.

Time: 20 minutes   *Serves 4*

Garlic Sauce

SALSA ALL'AGLIO

Ingredients	Metric/Imperial	American
garlic cloves	5	5
egg yolk	1	1
salt and pepper		
olive oil	225 ml/8 fl oz	1 cup
lemon juice	1 tablespoon	1 tablespoon

Crush the garlic to a pulp in a garlic crusher or with a pestle and mortar; alternatively chop very finely. Mix with the egg yolk and a little salt in a bowl.

Add the oil drop by drop as if making mayonnaise, beating constantly.

When the sauce is thick season with salt and pepper and stir in the lemon juice.

Serve with boiled or raw vegetables and with toast.

This sauce can also be made in a blender or food processor.

Time: 20 minutes   *Serves 4*

Maître d'Hôtel Butter

BURRO ALLA MAITRE D'HOTEL

Ingredients	Metric/Imperial	American
butter, at room temperature	100 g/4 oz	$\frac{1}{2}$ cup
chopped parsley	1 tablespoon	1 tablespoon
lemon juice	$\frac{1}{2}$ teaspoon	$\frac{1}{2}$ teaspoon
salt and white pepper		

Cream the butter and mix it with the parsley, lemon juice, salt and pepper.

Roll the butter into a cylinder, wrap in foil and chill in the refrigerator for at least 1 hour.

Cut into thick slices and use to garnish meat, poultry and fish. Use for savoury sandwiches and canapés.

Time: 10 minutes + 1 hour: chilling   Makes about 8 slices

Anchovy Butter (Burro all'acciuga)
Flavour the butter with 40 g/1$\frac{1}{2}$ oz/1$\frac{1}{2}$ ounces of anchovy fillets, drained and finely chopped, and a seasoning of pepper only.

Garlic Butter (Burro all'aglio)
Flavour the butter with 3 crushed garlic cloves, 1 tablespoon of lemon juice, salt and pepper.

Gorgonzola Butter (Burro al Gorgonzola)
Mix the butter with 60 g/2$\frac{1}{2}$ oz/2$\frac{1}{2}$ ounces of Gorgonzola cheese.

Mustard Butter (Burro alla Senepe)
Mix the butter with 1 tablespoon of mustard, medium or hot to taste.

To Make Open Sandwiches and Canapés
Remove the crusts from the bread (brown or white). Spread with the savoury butter and cut into shapes with cutters. Diamond and oblong shapes can be cut with a knife.

Prawn Butter (Burro ai Gamberetti)
Mince (grind) 40 g/1$\frac{1}{2}$ oz/1$\frac{1}{2}$ ounces of cooked peeled prawns. Mix with the butter along with 1 teaspoon of lemon juice and a little salt.

Smoked Salmon Butter (Burro al Salmone Affumicato)
Mince (grind) 25 g/1 oz/1 ounce of smoked salmon. Mix with the butter along with a seasoning of pepper only.

Tuna butter (Burro al Tonno)
Mince (grind) 50 g/2 oz/2 ounces of drained, canned tuna in brine or oil and mix with the butter.

Savoury Butters
Cream the ingredients together. Shape into a long roll. Wrap in cling film or foil and roll to perfect the shape. Chill before using.

It is convenient to freeze rolls of savoury butter ready for use. After freezing for 1 hour portions can be cut off the roll and frozen individually to use on steaks, chops, fish and vegetables.

ANTIPASTI

*Antipasti (hors d'oeuvre or starters) are found
on most lunch time menus in Italy
particularly when pasta is not being served.
The antipasti can be a collection of small
dishes which usually contains some type
of salame sausage.
Olives and raw vegetables, dressed with olive oil,
can be served with the sausage, or alternatively
smoked ham (*prosciutto*), or smoked pork.
Fish such as prawns, squid, mussels, tuna fish or
anchovies are all popular additions to the
antipasti, served either hot or cold. Arrange the
dishes attractively and good antipasti will make
an excellent light lunch or supper dish as well as
a starter to a main meal.*

Mussel Kebabs

Mussel Kebabs

SPIEDINI DI COZZE

Ingredients	Metric/Imperial	American
mussels	1 kg/2 lb	2 pounds
dried breadcrumbs	50 g/2 oz	½ cup
chopped parsley	1 tablespoon	1 tablespoon
chopped oregano	½ teaspoon	½ teaspoon
chopped thyme	½ teaspoon	½ teaspoon
salt		
butter	65 g/2½ oz	5 tablespoons
smoked bacon	75 g/3 oz	3 ounces
lemon wedges		

Scrub the mussels well, put in a saucepan, cover and heat for a few minutes, shaking the pan, to make them open. Discard any which stay shut. Remove the remainder from their shells and set aside.

Mix together the breadcrumbs, chopped herbs and a pinch of salt. Melt the butter in a small pan, dip in the mussels and then coat them in herbed breadcrumbs.

Remove the rind from the bacon and cut the bacon crossways into strips. Thread on to skewers, with the mussels, working the bacon over and under the mussels. Cook under a hot grill (broiler), turning for about 8 minutes until cooked. Serve with lemon wedges.

Time: 30 minutes   *Serves 4*

Mussels with Orange

COZZE ALL'ARANCIA

Ingredients	Metric/Imperial	American
mussels	1 kg/2 lb	2 pounds
dry white wine	125 ml/4 fl oz	½ cup
oranges	2	2
salt and pepper		
chopped parsley	1½ tablespoons	2 tablespoons

Scrub the mussels, removing the beards and any encrustations. Put in a large pan with the wine, juice of the oranges (reserve the rinds) and a little salt and pepper. Cover, put on a medium heat and cook for about 10 minutes until the shells have opened.

Meanwhile cut the zest of the oranges into very fine slivers.

Remove the mussels from the pan, discard any which failed to open and remove one of each pair of shells from the rest. Arrange on a heated serving plate.

Boil the cooking juices hard to reduce to a sauce. Stir in the orange slivers and chopped parsley; pour over the mussels. Serve at once.

Time: 30 minutes   *Serves 4*

Mussels with Orange

Deep-fried Mussels

COZZE FRITTE ALLA VIAREGGINA

Ingredients	Metric/Imperial	American
mussels	1.4 kg/3 lb	3 pounds
salt and pepper		
plain (all-purpose) flour	50 g/2 oz	$\frac{1}{2}$ cup
eggs	2	2
oil for deep frying		
lemon	1	1

Scrub the mussel shells thoroughly, put in a large pan with a pinch of salt and heat in the water remaining on the shells for about 10 minutes until they have opened. Discard any which do not open.

Remove the mussels from the shells and dip in flour. Beat the eggs with a pinch of salt and pepper in a bowl; dip the mussels into the egg. Allow excess egg to drain and dip into the flour again.

Heat the oil to 190 c/375 f. Drop in the mussels, keeping them apart with a fork, and fry for about 3 minutes until golden. Drain on absorbent paper towels and serve hot accompanied by a wedge of lemon.

Time: 40 minutes   *Serves 4*

Deep-fried Mussels

Lobster Salad Starter

ANTIPASTO DI ARAGOSTA IN BELLA VISTA

Ingredients	Metric/Imperial	American
For the court bouillon:		
butter	25 g/1 oz	2 tablespoons
carrot	1	1
onion	1	1
dry white wine	125 ml/4 fl oz	½ cup
sprig of parsley	1	1
sprigs of thyme	2	2
bay leaves	2	2
salt		
peppercorns	6	6
lobster	1 (1 kg/2 lb)	1 (2 pounds)
small artichokes	4	4
hard-boiled (cooked) eggs	2	2
mayonnaise	125 ml/4 fl oz	½ cup
capers	1 teaspoon	1 teaspoon
rice	225 g/8 oz	1¼ cups
lettuce heart	1	1

To prepare the court bouillon finely chop the carrot and onion. Melt the butter in a large pan, add the carrot and onion and cook over a low heat for a few minutes until the onion is transparent. Pour in the wine, and 1 litre/1¾ pints/1 quart of water; add the herbs, salt and peppercorns. Bring to the boil. Carefully immerse the lobster, reduce the heat and simmer for 20 minutes. Leave to cool in the cooking liquid.

Meanwhile prepare and cook the artichokes: cut off the stalks, pull off tough outer leaves and cut the points off the remainder. Cook in lightly salted boiling water for about 20 minutes until just tender; drain and cool. Spread the leaves apart, pull out the soft inner leaves and scrape out the bristly choke with a spoon.

Cut the eggs in half, mash the yolks with a fork and mix with the mayonnaise and capers. Stuff the egg whites with the mixture.

Cook the rice in lightly salted boiling water until just tender and cool under running water. Drain well and pile on to one end of an oval serving plate. Cover the rest of the plate with lettuce leaves, washed, drained and dried.

Remove the lobster from the court bouillon, put on a chopping board and cut in half from head to tail with a sharp knife and scissors. Carefully remove the meat and slice it evenly. Put the shell on the serving plate with the head resting on the rice; cover the body with slices of lobster meat, slightly inclined. Arrange the stuffed artichokes and eggs alternately round the edge of the plate.

Time: 45 minutes   *Serves 4*

Polenta with Seafood

MEDAGLIONI DI POLENTA AI FRUITTI DI MARE

Ingredients	Metric/Imperial	American
Polenta slices cooked as instructed (page 148)	8	8
mussels	350 g/12 oz	¾ pound
whole cooked prawns	350 g/12 oz	¾ pound
onion	½	½
garlic clove	1	1
stock	225 ml/8 fl oz	1 cup
baby octopus or squid	350 g/12 oz	¾ pound
dry white wine	3 tablespoons	scant ¼ cup
plum tomatoes	3	3
salt and pepper		
fresh chilli	1	1
chopped parsley	1 tablespoon	1 tablespoon
basil leaves	4	4

Grill (broil) the slices of polenta until golden. Arrange on a serving dish and keep warm.

Scrub the mussels thoroughly and remove the beards; discard any that are open. Put the mussels in a saucepan with 2.5 cm/1 in of water, cover and cook until they have opened. Shell, discarding any that remained shut. Shell the prawns.

Chop the onion finely and crush the garlic. Heat the stock in a flameproof casserole, add the onion and garlic and cook until transparent.

Meanwhile prepare the octopus: Cut the tentacles off the head, then slit open the body envelope and remove the stomach, head and transparent spine. Wash tentacles and body under running water and chop them.

Add the octopus to the casserole, sprinkle with the wine and leave until it has evaporated. Peel the tomatoes, if they are fresh ones, chop them roughly and add to the pan. Season with salt and pepper. Deseed the chilli pepper; chop the flesh finely and add it to the pan. Continue cooking over a low heat for 40 minutes.

Add the mussels and prawns to the pan and sprinkle with the parsley and chopped basil. Remove from the heat and divide amongst the polenta slices.

Time: 1 hour   *Serves 4*

Polenta with Seafood
1 Grill (broil) the polenta until golden.
2 Prepare the mussels and cook in the pan with a little water until they open.
3 Add the prawns to the pan for a few minutes if liked. Remove shells from the prawns and mussels from the open shells.
4 Heat the onion, garlic and stock together. Add the octopus and wine.
5 Mix in the tomatoes and chilli.
6 Stir in the mussels and prawns. Garnish with sprigs of parsley.

Frogs Lombardy Style

Frogs Lombardy Style

RANE ALLA MODA DI VERCELLI

Ingredients	Metric/Imperial	American
frogs, prepared	36	36
plain (all-purpose) flour	50 g/2 oz	$\frac{1}{2}$ cup
butter	100 g/4 oz	$\frac{1}{2}$ cup
garlic clove	1	1
mushrooms	150 g/5 oz	1 cup
anchovies	3	3
dry white wine	175 ml/6 fl oz	$\frac{3}{4}$ cup
salt and pepper		
chopped parsley	1 tablespoon	1 tablespoon

Wash the frogs well, pat dry on paper towels and dip lightly in flour.

Melt the butter in a deep pan, add the crushed garlic and cook for a few minutes over medium heat until golden. Add the frogs and cook, turning, until golden on all sides. Clean and finely slice the mushrooms and add to the pan. Chop the anchovies, stir into the pan and leave over a low heat for the flavours to blend.

Pour in the wine and season with a pinch of salt and plenty of pepper. Cover and continue to cook over a low heat for about 30 minutes. Taste and adjust the seasoning, stir in the parsley and serve very hot.

Time: 50 minutes　　　　　　　　　　*Serves 6*

Stuffed Zucchini (Courgettes)

ZUCCHINE RIPIENE DI CARNE

Ingredients	Metric/Imperial	American
courgettes (zucchini)	800 g/1$\frac{3}{4}$ lb	1$\frac{3}{4}$ pounds
bread roll	1	1
milk	1 tablespoon	1 tablespoon
minced (ground) beef	350 g/12 oz	$\frac{3}{4}$ pound
egg	1	1
Parmesan cheese, grated	25 g/1 oz	$\frac{1}{4}$ cup
onion	$\frac{1}{2}$	$\frac{1}{2}$
chopped parsley	1 tablespoon	1 tablespoon
salt and pepper		
plum tomatoes	450 g/1 lb	1 pound
garlic clove	1	1

Put the courgettes in a large pan of boiling salted water and simmer for about 5 minutes. Drain, cut in half lengthwise and hollow out the centres with a teaspoon, reserving the pulp.

Pull out the centre of the bread roll and soak it in a little milk. Put the scooped-out pulp from the courgettes into a bowl with the soaked bread, beef, egg, grated Parmesan cheese, finely chopped onion and parsley. Season with a pinch of salt and pepper, mix well with a fork and use to stuff the courgettes. Arrange them in large shallow ovenproof dish.

Peel the tomatoes if they are fresh; chop them into a pulp and season with a pinch of salt and crushed garlic. Pour the mixture into the spaces between the courgettes. Put in a moderately hot oven (200 c, 400 f, gas 6) for 30 minutes or until cooked.

Time: 1½ hours   *Serves 4*

Stuffed Celery Stalks
1 Remove the rind from the cheeses and cream in a bowl together.
2 Shell the walnuts and chop roughly. Add to the creamed cheeses and mix well.
3 Prepare the celery stalks, removing the strings. Cut into suitable lengths and stuff the stalks with the cheese and walnut mixture.

Stuffed Celery Stalks
SEDANO RIPIENO

Ingredients	Metric/Imperial	American
whole walnuts	100 g/4 oz	¼ pound
Gorgonzola cheese	150 g/5 oz	5 ounces
Robiola or cream cheese	225 g/8 oz	½ pound
celery head	1	1

Shell and chop the walnuts. Remove the rind from both cheeses, cut and mix together in a bowl with the walnuts.

Trim the celery and wash the stalks thoroughly, removing any stringy bits. Cut into 10 cm/4 in lengths.

Stuff the celery stalks with the cheese mixture and arrange on a plate. Keep in a cool place until ready to serve. Garnish with celery leaves and walnuts.

Time: 20 minutes   *Serves 4*

1

2

3

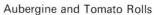

Aubergine and Tomato Rolls
1 Slice the aubergines lengthwise and sprinkle with salt.
2 Drain and pat dry. Fry the aubergines in hot oil until softened.
3 Mix the cheese with the herbs, tomatoes and breadcrumbs.
4 Place a little mixture in the centre of each slice of aubergine. Roll up and secure with a skewer or cocktail stick.

Aubergine (Eggplant) and Tomato Rolls

INVOLTINI DI MELANZANE CON POMODORI

Ingredients	Metric/Imperial	American
medium-sized aubergines (eggplants)	4	4
salt		
oil for frying		
canned plum tomatoes	400 g/14 oz	14 ounce
garlic clove	1	1
chopped basil	1 tablespoon	1 tablespoon
fresh breadcrumbs	4 tablespoons	6 tablespoons
Mozzarella cheese	1	1
Parmesan cheese, grated	2 tablespoons	3 tablespoons

Cut the aubergines lengthways into slices about 1 cm/½ in thick. Sprinkle with salt and leave to rest on an inclined board for 30 minutes to drain off excess water. Rinse, drain and dry on paper towels.

Heat the oil in a heavy pan over a medium heat. Fry the aubergine slices a few at a time until softened but not browned. Season with a pinch of salt and stack on a plate.

Drain the tomatoes, mash with a fork and mix with the finely chopped garlic, basil, breadcrumbs and cubed Mozzarella cheese. Put a little of the mixture on the centre of each aubergine slice, roll up and secure with a wooden cocktail stick (toothpick).

Brush a rectangular ovenproof dish with oil. Add the rolls, sprinkle with Parmesan cheese, cover with foil and put in a moderate oven (180 c, 350 f, gas 4) for 20 minutes. Remove the foil and serve at once.

Time: 1 hour + 30 minutes: resting *Serves 4*

Stuffed Sweet Pepper Boats

Stuffed Sweet Pepper Boats

NAVICELLE DI PEPERONI FARCITE

Ingredients	Metric/Imperial	American
large yellow (sweet) peppers	2	2
minced (ground) veal	100 g/4 oz	½ cup
sausage with fennel seeds	50 g/2 oz	2 ounces
cooked ham	50 g/2 oz	2 ounces
Parmesan cheese, grated	25 g/1 oz	¼ cup
sprig of basil	1	1
garlic clove	½	½
egg yolk	1	1
whole egg	1	1
salt and pepper		
oil	4 tablespoons	6 tablespoons
Mozzarella cheese	1	1

Wash the sweet peppers, cut in half vertically, remove the stalks, seeds and pith and cut again to make 8 'boats'.

Put the veal in a bowl, crumble in the sausage, add the chopped ham, grated Parmesan cheese, finely chopped basil and garlic, egg yolk and whole egg. Season with salt and pepper and mix well.

Brush an ovenproof dish with oil, pack the sweet pepper boats with the prepared stuffing and arrange in the dish. Sprinkle with oil and put in a moderate oven (180c, 350f, gas 4) for about 25 minutes or until the peppers are cooked.

Cut the Mozzarella cheese into slivers, put on top of the stuffed peppers, leave to melt, serve at once.

Time: 50 minutes   *Serves 4*

Artichoke Hearts with Tuna

Artichoke Hearts with Tuna

CUORI DI CARCIOFO AL TONNO

Ingredients	Metric/Imperial	American
artichokes	8	8
lemon	1	1
tuna in oil	350 g/12 oz	¾ pound
Ricotta cheese	225 g/8 oz	½ pound
Parmesan cheese, grated	25 g/1 oz	¼ cup
egg	1	1
salt and pepper		
garlic clove	1	1
chopped parsley	1 tablespoon	1 tablespoon
stock	225 ml/8 fl oz	1 cup

Prepare the artichokes by removing the hard outer leaves and stems and trimming off the sharp points. Put them in a saucepan; cover with water and add a dash of lemon juice. Bring to the boil, then cook for a further 15 minutes. Drain upside down and remove the chokes.

Meanwhile drain the tuna and put it in a bowl with the Ricotta, Parmesan, egg and a pinch of salt and pepper. Finely chop the garlic, mix it with the parsley and add to the bowl. Mix well and use to stuff the artichokes.

Pack the artichokes tightly into a straight-sided pan. Pour in the stock and remaining lemon juice, cover and cook over a medium heat for 15 minutes.

Time: 45 minutes   *Serves 4*

Crispy Rolls

INVOLTINI CROCCANTI

Ingredients	Metric/Imperial	American
plain (all-purpose) flour	225 g/8 oz	2 cups
salt		
eggs	3	3
oil	1 tablespoon	1 tablespoon
thick white sauce (page 25)	225 ml/8 fl oz	1 cup
Gruyère cheese	100 g/4 oz	¼ pound
milk	2 tablespoons	3 tablespoons
dried breadcrumbs	100 g/4 oz	1 cup
oil for deep frying		

First prepare the pastry; sift the flour into a bowl, stir in a pinch of salt, 2 of the eggs and the oil. Work together to form a soft dough and leave in a cool place to rest.

Prepare a thick white sauce and allow to cool. Mix in the very finely diced Gruyère cheese.

Roll out the pastry and cut into 9 × 15 cm/3½ × 6 in rectangles. Spoon a strip of sauce down the centre of each one and roll up. Beat the remaining egg lightly with the milk and a pinch of salt. Dip the pastry rolls into this mixture, then into the breadcrumbs. Leave to rest in the refrigerator for 30 minutes.

Heat the oil to 190 C/375 F and fry the rolls in batches until golden. Drain on absorbent paper towels and keep hot until ready to serve.

Time: 1 hour + 30 minutes: resting *Serves 4*

Fried Cheese

Fried Cheese

SCIATT

Ingredients	Metric/Imperial	American
plain (all-purpose) flour	350 g/12 oz	3 cups
buckwheat flour	350 g/12 oz	3 cups
salt		
Grappa liqueur	1½ tablespoons	2 tablespoons
Fontina cheese	225 g/8 oz	½ pound
oil for frying		

Sift the plain and buckwheat flour into a bowl with a pinch of salt. Stir in enough water to make a soft elastic dough. Add the Grappa and wait for it to be absorbed. Form the dough into a ball and leave covered in a cool place to rest for 1 hour.

Cut the cheese into small dice. Heat the oil in a heavy-based deep pan until hot but not smoking. Take out pieces of dough with a teaspoon and insert a piece of cheese in the centre. Fry in the hot oil, a few at a time, until golden. Remove with a slotted spoon, drain on paper towels and keep hot until ready to serve.

Note: This is a regional dish from the Sondriain mountains of northern Italy, where it is served not as a starter but as a dessert.

Time: 1 hour + 1 hour: resting *Serves 6–8*

Crispy Rolls

Bread and Cheese Kebabs

SPIEDINI DI SCAMORZE

Ingredients	Metric/Imperial	American
anchovy fillets	4	4
milk	125 ml/4 fl oz	½ cup
Scamorza or Mozzarella cheese	450 g/1 lb	1 pound
salt and pepper		
olive oil	5 tablespoons	½ cup
slices of crusty bread		

Soak the anchovy fillets in a little milk.

Cut the cheese into slices, season with salt and pepper and put in a bowl with one-third of the oil to marinate for 10 minutes, turning now and then.

Bread and Cheese Kebabs

Cut the slices of bread to the same size as the cheese and toast lightly. Thread alternate pieces of toast and cheese on to 4 metal or wooden skewers, ending with toast.

Brush an ovenproof dish with oil and put in the kebabs, resting the ends of the skewers on its edges. Put in a moderately hot oven (200 c, 400 f, gas 6) for 20 minutes, brushing every so often with the cooking juices.

Just before the kebabs are ready heat the remaining oil in a very small pan and fry the drained anchovy fillets until melted.

Arrange the kebabs on a heated serving dish, pour the anchovy sauce over and serve hot.

Time: 45 minutes   *Serves 4*

Aubergine (Eggplant) and Tomato Casserole

MELANZANE CON POMODORI IN FORNO

Ingredients	Metric/Imperial	American
anchovy fillets	4	4
milk	1 tablespoon	1 tablespoon
aubergines (eggplants)	3	3
salt and pepper		
fresh plum tomatoes	6	6
garlic clove	1	1
bunch of basil	1	1
oregano	¼ teaspoon	¼ teaspoon
Mozzarella cheese	150 g/5 oz	5 ounces
oil	50 ml/2 fl oz	¼ cup

Put the anchovy fillets to soak in a little milk.

Prepare the aubergines: remove the stems, wash and dry and cut into 2.5 cm/1 in thick rounds. Sprinkle with salt and allow to stand for 30 minutes on a tray, then drain with paper towels.

Brush a large ovenproof casserole with oil and arrange the rounds in it in a single layer. Season with salt and pepper. Slice the tomatoes thickly and put them on top.

Crush the garlic and chop the basil leaves; drain and chop the anchovies. Scatter them over the tomatoes and sprinkle with oregano. Chop the Mozzarella cheese finely, spread it over the top and sprinkle with the oil.

Bake, uncovered, in a moderate oven (180 c, 350 f, gas 4) for 20 minutes and serve hot.

Time: 30 minutes   *Serves 4*

Saxon Frankfurters
1 Slice the aubergines and prepare in the usual way. Pat dry with a towel and fry in hot oil until golden. Season well.
2 Slit the frankfurters lengthwise and stuff with the grated cheese.
3 Wrap the frankfurters in the slices of fried aubergine and place in an oiled dish.
4 Sprinkle with cheese and breadcrumbs and pour over some of the wine and stock before cooking.

Saxon Frankfurters

WURSTEL ALLA SASSONE

Ingredients	Metric/Imperial	American
medium-sized aubergine (eggplant)	1	1
oil	150 ml/5 fl oz	$\frac{2}{3}$ cup
salt and pepper		
large frankfurters	5	5
Gruyère cheese, grated	100 g/4 oz	1 cup
dry breadcrumbs	2 tablespoons	3 tablespoons
dry white wine	50 ml/2 fl oz	$\frac{1}{4}$ cup
stock	50 ml/2 fl oz	$\frac{1}{4}$ cup
pinch of oregano		

Wash the aubergine, slice it lengthwise and pat dry on paper towels. Heat the oil in a heavy pan, add the slices and fry them until golden. Season with salt and pepper and drain on absorbent paper towels.

Meanwhile slit the frankfurters lengthwise without going right through and stuff them with the grated cheese. Brush a rectangular ovenproof dish with oil.

Wrap each frankfurter in a slice of aubergine, secure it with a wooden cocktail stick (toothpick) and put it in the prepared dish. Sprinkle the top with the breadcrumbs and 1 tablespoon each of the wine and stock. Put in a moderate oven (180 c, 350 f, gas 4) for 25 minutes, sprinkling twice with the wine and stock.

Sprinkle the top with a pinch of oregano and serve hot straight from the dish.

If using small frankfurters allow 2 per person and use 2 aubergines.

Time: 1 hour   *Serves 4–5*

Sweet and Sour Onions

CIPOLLINE IN AGRODOLCE

Ingredients	Metric/Imperial	American
silverskin onions	24	24
butter	25 g/1 oz	2 tablespoons
clove	1	1
salt		
sugar	1 tablespoon	1 tablespoon
stock cube	½	½
wine vinegar	3 tablespoons	scant ¼ cup

Wash the small onions under running water for a few minutes, then drain and dry well.

Melt the butter in a heavy pan, add the onions and turn them gently. Add the clove, a pinch of salt and the sugar and crumble the stock cube over the top. Pour in the vinegar, cover and cook over a very low heat for about 40 minutes. Serve either hot or cold.

Time: 50 minutes　　　　　　　　　　*Serves 4*

Brussels Sprout Puffs

BIGNE DI CAVOLINI DI BRUXELLES

Ingredients	Metric/Imperial	American
Brussels sprouts	450 g/1 lb	1 pound
lemon juice	2 tablespoons	3 tablespoons
oil for frying		
For the batter: plain (all-purpose) flour	100 g/4 oz	1 cup
salt		
oil	2 tablespoons	3 tablespoons
eggs	2	2
lager or light beer	2 tablespoons	3 tablespoons

Brussels Sprout Puffs

Trim and wash the Brussels sprouts and drop into 300 ml/½ pint/1¼ cups cold water acidulated with the lemon juice. Cook in lightly salted boiling water for 15 minutes; drain and cool under running water.

To make the batter sift the flour and a pinch of salt into a mixing bowl, add the oil and lightly beaten eggs. Mix together with a wooden spoon, then gradually add the lager and enough cold water to make a thick creamy batter. Cover and leave to rest for 30 minutes.

Put a generous amount of oil in a heavy deep pan over a high heat until hot. Dip the sprouts into the batter one at a time and place in the pan. Fry in small batches until golden and drain on absorbent paper towels.

Sprinkle with salt, pile on to a heated serving plate and serve at once.

Time: 1 hour + 30 minutes: resting　　　*Serves 4*

Tuscan-style Spinach Balls

RAVIOLI ALLA TOSCANA

Ingredients	Metric/Imperial	American
spinach	1.4 kg/3 lb	3 pounds
salt and pepper		
Ricotta cheese	450 g/1 lb	1 pound
eggs	3	3
Parmesan cheese, grated	100 g/4 oz	1 cup
grated nutmeg	¼ teaspoon	¼ teaspoon
plain (all-purpose) flour	50 g/2 oz	½ cup
butter	25 g/1 oz	2 tablespoons

Wash the spinach thoroughly in cold water, remove coarse stems and drain. Cook over a low heat in the water still clinging to the leaves until tender; about 5 minutes. Drain, leave to cool and then chop.

Put first the Ricotta cheese, then the spinach through a sieve, or purée in a blender or food processor. Put in bowl with the lightly beaten eggs, three-quarters of the Parmesan cheese, the nutmeg and a little salt. Mix well. Form the mixture into little balls, roll in flour and spread out on a clean dry tea towel.

Bring a large pan of salted water to the boil. When boiling rapidly drop in 3–4 balls at a time. When cooked they will turn yellow; remove with a slotted spoon, drain and put in a heated serving dish. Continue until all are cooked.

Serve the spinach balls tossed in the butter and sprinkled with the remaining cheese. Tomato sauce (see page 26) may be served with this dish.

Time: 1 hour 10 minutes　　　　　　*Serves 6*

Marinated Olives

OLIVE CONDITE DI MONTEFIASCONE

Ingredients	Metric/Imperial	American
large black olives	600 g/1¼ lb	1¼ pounds
orange	½	½
lemon	1	1
fennel seeds	1 teaspoon	1 teaspoon
garlic cloves	2	2
olive oil	125 ml/4 fl oz	½ cup

Wash the olives in warm water, drain, remove the stones and place the olives in a small shallow dish.

Cut the orange and lemon zest into fine shreds; add to the olives with the fennel seeds and halved garlic cloves.

Pour over the juice of the lemon and the olive oil. Mix well and leave in a cool place to marinate for 1 hour.

Remove the 4 pieces of garlic before serving.

Time: 15 minutes + 1 hour: marinating   *Serves 6*

This is a dish from Montefiascone near Viterbo in the region of Lazio.

Broad Bean and Pecorino Starter

ANTIPASTO DI FAVE E PECORINO

Ingredients	Metric/Imperial	American
fresh broad beans	2 kg/4½ lb	4½ pounds
Pecorino cheese	350 g/12 oz	¾ pound
salt		

Shell the beans, rinse under running cold water, drain and dry. Put into a large serving bowl.

Cut the Pecorino cheese into small pieces and put on to a serving plate or 6 side plates. Give each person a small pot of salt so that they can help themselves to beans, skin them, dip into salt and eat accompanied by the Pecorino cheese.

Time: 10 minutes   *Serves 6*

Double-quick Patés
1 Cook the onion in a heavy pan over a medium heat until golden.
2 Add the diced chicken breasts with the brandy and simmer for 10 minutes. Add the chopped liver and seasoning. Cook and allow to cool. Purée the meat mixture and mix with half the Mascarpone cheese. Place in an oiled mould and leave to chill in the refrigerator.
3 Remove the fat from the ham and chop very finely. Stone and chop the olives.
4 Stir both into the remaining Mascarpone cheese. Place in a second oiled mould and chill in the refrigerator. Turn out both moulds when chilled and serve garnished with salad and triangles of toast.

Double-quick Pâtés

PATE RAPIDI CON CROSTINI

Ingredients	Metric/Imperial	American
onion	½	½
butter	65 g/2½ oz	5 tablespoons
boneless chicken breast	225 g/8 oz	½ pound
brandy	4 tablespoons	6 tablespoons
calf's liver	225 g/8 oz	½ pound
salt and pepper		
Mascarpone cheese	350 g/12 oz	¾ pound
cooked ham	350 g/12 oz	¾ pound
green olives	10	10
slices of bread	16	16
lettuce or radicchio leaves to garnish		

Chop the onion finely. Melt the butter in a heavy pan, add the onion and fry over medium heat for a few minutes until golden.

Dice the chicken breast and add to the pan with the brandy. Simmer for about 10 minutes, then add the finely chopped liver. Season with salt and pepper and leave for a few minutes, stirring occasionally, to allow the liver to cook. Remove from the heat and cool.

Purée the meat mixture in a blender or food processor, then stir in half the Mascarpone cheese. Brush a plain mould with oil, fill with the mixture and chill.

Remove any fat from the ham and chop the lean finely; stone and chop the olives. Add both to the remaining Mascarpone cheese, put into a second oiled mould and refrigerate.

When ready to serve toast the bread and turn the pâtés out by dipping the moulds briefly into boiling water and inverting on to plates. Garnish with red or green salad leaves and accompany with the toast cut into triangles.

Time: 30 minutes + 1–2 hours: chilling   *Serves 8*

Egg and Pâté Ramekins

TEGAMINI DI UOVA AL PATE

Ingredients	Metric/Imperial	American
shallot	1	1
butter	40 g/1½ oz	3 tablespoons
cornflour (cornstarch)	1 teaspoon	1 teaspoon
Marsala wine	50 ml/2 fl oz	¼ cup
stock	125 ml/4 fl oz	½ cup
milk	150 ml/¼ pint	⅔ cup
thin slices of duck liver pâté	4	4
eggs	8	8
salt		
cayenne pepper	¼ teaspoon	¼ teaspoon

Finely chop the shallot. Melt the butter in a small pan over a low heat, add the shallot and cook until transparent. Stir in the cornflour, then the Marsala. When almost evaporated stir in the stock, quickly followed by the milk. Mix well and cook until thickened.

Place a slice of pâté in the bottom of 4 large ramekins and break 2 eggs over each one. Season with a pinch of salt and cayenne. Pour a quarter of the prepared sauce over each one.

Put in a moderate oven (160C, 325F, gas 3) for 8 minutes and serve at once.

Time: 25 minutes   *Serves 4*

Ham Puffs

BIGNE DI PROSCIUTTO

Ingredients	Metric/Imperial	American
butter	50 g/2 oz	¼ cup
salt		
plain (all-purpose) flour	150 g/5 oz	1¼ cups
eggs	4	4
lean cooked ham	100 g/4 oz	¼ pound
Parmesan cheese, grated	2 tablespoons	3 tablespoons
oil for deep frying		

Put the butter and salt in a pan with 225 ml/8 fl oz/1 cup of water and bring to the boil. Add the sifted flour all at once, remove from the heat immediately and beat hard with a wooden spoon until the ingredients are well mixed. Return to a low heat for a few minutes and continue beating until the mixture comes away from the sides of the pan. Turn into a bowl and allow to cool.

Add the eggs to the mixture one at a time, beating constantly and waiting for each one to be absorbed before adding the next. Dice the ham and stir into the mixture along with the Parmesan cheese.

1 Prepare the celery, remove the strings and cut into strips.
2 Place the walnuts whole into a bowl with the diced cheese.
3 Crumble the Dolcelatta cheese into a bowl and mash with the milk and seasoning. Pour into the centre of the salad. Sprinkle over the olive oil. Stir well when serving.

Celery, Walnut and Cheese Starter

ANTIPASTO DI SEDANO, NOCI E FORMAGGIO

Ingredients	Metric/Imperial	American
young celery heads	2	2
whole walnuts	225 g/8 oz	½ pound
Fontina cheese	350 g/12 oz	¾ pound
Dolcelatte cheese	100 g/4 oz	¼ pound
milk	175 ml/6 fl oz	¾ cup
salt and pepper		
olive oil	125 ml/4 fl oz	½ cup
small slices of bread	24	24

Trim the celery and scrub the stalks, removing the strings. Cut into small strips.

Crack the walnuts without breaking the kernels and put in a salad bowl with the celery. Dice the Fontina cheese and stir into the bowl.

Crumble the Dolcelatte cheese into a small bowl, add the milk and mash with a fork to make a thick sauce. Pour over the salad and season with a little salt and plenty of pepper. Sprinkle on the olive oil and stir well.

Toast the bread lightly, cut into triangles and cover with a tea towel to keep warm. Serve the salad with the toast handed separately.

Heat the oil to 190 C/375 F. Add teaspoonfuls of the mixture, a few at a time, and fry until puffed up and golden. Drain on absorbent paper towels and keep hot until cooking is completed.

Time: 40 minutes   *Serves 4*

Time: 30 minutes   *Serves 8*

Cold Beef Appetizer

Cold Beef Appetizer
RIFREDDO STUZZICANTE DI BOLLITO

Ingredients	Metric/Imperial	American
anchovy fillets	4	4
gelatine	5 teaspoons	5 teaspoons
Mortadella sausage	100 g/4 oz	$\frac{1}{4}$ pound
cold cooked beef	350 g/12 oz	$\frac{3}{4}$ pound
chopped parsley	1 tablespoon	1 tablespoon
hard-boiled (cooked) eggs	2	2
cold boiled potatoes	3	3
salt and pepper		
Marsala wine	1$\frac{1}{2}$ tablespoons	2 tablespoons
mayonnaise	5 tablespoons	$\frac{1}{3}$ cup
single (thin) cream	3 tablespoons	scant $\frac{1}{4}$ cup
lemon	$\frac{1}{2}$	$\frac{1}{2}$
For the garnish:		
mayonnaise	225 ml/8 fl oz	1 cup
black stoned olives	16	16
strips of red (sweet pepper)		
pickled gherkins		
artichokes in oil		

Soak the anchovy fillets in a little milk to remove excess salt. Sprinkle the gelatine on to 125 ml/4 fl oz/$\frac{1}{2}$ cup of boiling water and stir until dissolved.

Chop the Mortadella and beef and put through a mincer (grinder) twice. Add the parsley, eggs mashed with a fork, chopped potatoes and drained anchovy fillets. Mince (grind) once more.

Put the mixture in a bowl and season with salt and pepper. Add the Marsala, prepared gelatine, mayonnaise, cream and lemon juice; mix well.

Brush a sheet of foil with oil, put the mixture on it and roll up in the shape of a long sausage. Put in the refrigerator for 3 hours. Blanch the pepper strips.

Remove foil, cut the meat roll into slices and put on a serving plate. Garnish the meat with mayonnaise and olives. Surround with peppers, gherkins and artichokes.

Time: 25 minutes + 3 hours: chilling   *Serves 6*

Ham and Salad Rounds

TARTINE DI PANE NERO

Ingredients	Metric/Imperial	American
large slices of brown bread	16	16
butter for spreading		
lettuces	2	2
olive oil	4 tablespoons	6 tablespoons
salt and pepper		
slices of Parma ham	16	16

Cut the crusts off the bread and spread the slices with butter. Cut each slice into a round using a large pastry cutter.

Wash and dry the lettuce leaves. Season the oil with salt and pepper to taste, sprinkle on the lettuce and mix well.

Divide the lettuce into 16 bunches, roll each one inside a slice of ham and place on the bread rounds. Serve at once so that the lettuce remains crisp.

Time: 15 minutes   *Serves 8*

Ham and Salad Rounds
1 Remove the crusts from the bread, spread with softened butter. Cut out rounds using a large fluted pastry cutter.
2 Wash and dry the lettuce leaves, tear any large leaves into strips. Season the oil with salt and pepper and dress the lettuce.
3 Arrange the slices of ham flat on a board. Divide the lettuce leaves into 16 bunches. Roll each slice of ham around a bunch of lettuce.
4 Place the lettuce and ham rolls on a round of buttered bread and serve immediately. The lettuce will wilt if prepared too far in advance. This recipe can also be made with slices of cooked, boiled ham. Garnish with wedges of tomato.

SOUPS

*Many Italian soups are a meal in themselves.
They fall roughly into three types; broths and
consommés, thick vegetable soups containing both
fresh and dried vegetables usually thickened with
pasta or rice, and broths with pasta.
As most Italian soups are served with grated
cheese or* crostini *(toasted or fried bread,
plain or spread with cheese) the result is a
dish to be savoured either at the beginning
of a meal or as a snack.
Any left-over vegetable soups can be puréed in a
blender or food processor for variety.*

Pancakes

CRESPELLE

Ingredients	Metric/Imperial	American
eggs	2	2
plain (all-purpose) flour	100 g/4 oz	1 cup
salt	½ teaspoon	½ teaspoon
milk	175 ml/6 fl oz	¾ cup
butter	1 tablespoon	1 tablespoon

Beat the eggs in a bowl with the sifted flour and the salt until the mixture is well blended, with a little milk. Add the remaining milk gradually beating the batter until smooth.

Heat a non-stick pan lightly rubbed over with a knob of butter and pour in 1 tablespoon of batter at a time, shaking the pan to spread evenly to form a very thin pancake, turn when golden. Repeat until all the mixture is used.

Allow the pancakes to cool, roll up and cut into very thin strips. Place the strips at the bottom of the soup bowls ready to pour over soup or consommé.

Time: 30 minutes   *Serves 8*

Crespelle are often found on the menu of famous restaurants.

Croûtons

CROSTINI E CROSTONI

Ingredients	Metric/Imperial	American
loaf of bread, sliced	1	1
oil or	225 ml/8 fl oz	1 cup
butter	175 g/6 oz	¾ cup

Croûtons can be any size for Italian recipes. *Crostini* are small cubes of bread. *Crostoni* are slices.

Use slightly stale bread to prevent excessive fat being absorbed during the cooking. Remove the crusts from medium-thick slices of bread and cut into cubes. Heat the oil or butter in a shallow pan on a medium heat and fry the bread on each side until golden brown. Alternatively use a deep fat fryer.

Drain on absorbent paper towels. Serve at once with soup.

To save time cut a whole loaf into *croûtons* and fry in batches. Spread out on baking trays and dry in a moderate oven (180 c, 350 f, gas 4) for 5 minutes. Cool and store in an airtight box or bag. If they are to be kept for more than 2 weeks put in the freezer.

Profiteroles for Consommé

PROFITEROLES PER CONSOMME

Ingredients	Metric/Imperial	American
butter	15 g/½ oz	1 tablespoon
plain (all-purpose) flour	35 g/1¼ oz	5 tablespoons
egg	1	1
salt		

Preheat the oven to 200 c, 400 f, gas 6.

Bring to the boil 5 tablespoons/⅓ cup of water in a pan with salt and butter on a medium heat until the fat has melted and allow to bubble vigorously before removing the pan from the heat. Quickly beat in the sifted flour all at once.

Continue beating until the mixture comes away from the sides of the pan and forms a ball: do not overheat or the mixture will become fatty. Allow to cool slightly.

Beat in the egg gradually until the pastry is smooth and glossy. Put the mixture into a forcing bag fitted with a small plain nozzle. Pipe small balls the size of cherry stones on to a lightly wetted baking tray, leaving plenty of space between.

Leave to cook in a moderately hot oven for 15 minutes until doubled in size and golden in colour.

Make a slit in each bun with a sharp knife and return to the oven for 5 minutes.

Serve the profiteroles as a side dish with consommé.

Time: 30 minutes   *Serves 6*

Delicate Fresh Pea Soup (page 64) garnished with *crostoni*

Little Crespelle in Soup

CRESPELLINE IN BRODO

Ingredients	Metric/Imperial	American
egg	1	1
plain (all-purpose) flour	75 g/3 oz	¾ cup
salt and pepper		
finely chopped parsley	1 teaspoon	1 teaspoon
Parmesan cheese, grated	1 tablespoon	1 tablespoon
single (thin) cream	1 tablespoon	1 tablespoon
milk	300 ml/½ pint	1¼ cups
frozen peas	100 g/4 oz	¼ pound
butter	65 g/2½ oz	5 tablespoons
stock	1 litre/1¾ pints	1 quart
extra Parmesan cheese to serve		

Break the egg in a bowl, add the sifted flour, a pinch of salt and pepper, parsley, Parmesan cheese and cream. Beat with a fork, adding milk a little at a time, the mixture should be creamy like a batter. Cover and place in the refrigerator to rest for 1 hour.

Butter a small shallow pan, place on a medium heat and when very hot pour in a small ladleful of batter, tip the pan quickly so that the batter runs over the bottom of the pan. Leave to set, then with a spatula turn over to cook on the other side. Tip on to a plate and continue to cook the pancakes until all the batter is used.

Roll up the pancakes and with a sharp knife cut into thin strips.

Melt 25 g/1 oz/2 tablespoons butter in a large pan, add the peas and leave to simmer for 4 minutes, season with salt and pepper, then add the boiling stock and simmer for 10 minutes.

Drop in the strips of pancake. Turn off the heat, pour the soup into a tureen and serve immediately accompanied with Parmesan cheese.

Time: 30 minutes + 1 hour: resting   *Serves 4*

 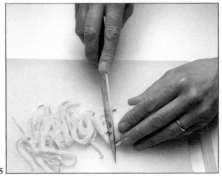

1 Break the eggs into a bowl. Sift the flour on to a piece of paper, then return to the measuring cup. Add a little flour and a pinch of salt to the eggs.
2 Beat the mixture and gradually add the milk until a smooth batter forms. Leave to rest for 15 minutes in a cool place if the time is available.
3 Rub a non-stick pan with butter. Put on a medium heat for a few seconds, then pour in 1–2 tablespoons of batter (depending on the size of the pan). Shake the pan to spread the mixture evenly and form a thin pancake; turn with a spatula when golden. Continue until all the batter is used up.
4 Allow the pancakes to cool, then roll up 2 or 3 at a time.
5 Cut into very thin strips with a sharp knife. Put in the bottom of soup bowls ready for soups or consommés to be poured on top.

Rice and Lettuce Soup

MINESTRA DI RISO E LATTUGA

Ingredients	Metric/Imperial	American
salt		
lettuce	400 g/14 oz	14 ounces
olive oil	1½ tablespoons	2 tablespoons
garlic cloves	2	2
risotto rice	250 g/9 oz	1⅓ cup
stock cube	1	1
Parmesan cheese, grated	1 tablespoon	1 tablespoon

Bring a large pan with 2 litres/3½ pints/2 quarts of cold salted water to the boil. Add the washed lettuce, cut into slices. Bring back to the boil and cook for about 20 minutes on a medium heat.

Drain the lettuce and save the cooking water in a bowl. Pour the olive oil into a deep pan and fry the peeled, sliced garlic. When golden remove it, add the rice and the lettuce to the pan. Mix for a few minutes and then cover the lettuce with the cooking water and crumble in the stock cube; stir in well.

Cook without the lid until rice is tender. Sprinkle the Parmesan cheese into the pan and serve hot in bowls.

Time: 1 hour   *Serves 4*

Rice Picker's Soup

MINESTRA ALLA MODA DELLE MONDINE

Ingredients	Metric/Imperial	American
frogs, cleaned and ready to cook	600 g/1¼ lb	1¼ pounds
large onion	1	1
butter	50 g/2 oz	¼ cup
small asparagus	350 g/12 oz	¾ pound
stock cube	¼	¼
fresh peas	350 g/12 oz	¾ pound
rice	150 g/5 oz	⅔ cup
salt and pepper		
chopped parsley	1 tablespoon	1 tablespoon
Parmesan cheese, grated	40 g/1½ oz	3 tablespoons

Blanch the frogs in lightly salted boiling water for 10 minutes. Drain and bone, retaining the cooking water.

Chop the onion finely, place in a pan with melted butter. Cook over a low heat for 5 minutes, add the frogs

and simmer on the same heat, stirring with a wooden spoon.

Wipe the asparagus stalks clean and remove and reserve the woody part at the base. Chop the remaining pieces into 3–4 sections depending on the length.

Crumble the stock cube into the cooking water in the pan, add the woody asparagus stalks, bring to the boil and cook for 15 minutes. Remove the stalks with a slotted spoon and discard.

Add the shelled peas to the liquor in the pan, lower the heat and cook gently for 10 minutes.

Tip the asparagus pieces into the pan together with the onion and frogs, stir well. Sprinkle the rice into the soup, stir well and allow to cook on a medium heat for 15 minutes.

Adjust the seasoning, sprinkle with the parsley and cheese. Mix well, pour into a heated soup tureen and serve hot.

Time: 1 hour   *Serves 4*

Semolina and French Bean Soup

ZUPPA DI SEMOLA DORATA AI 'CORIANDOLI VERDI'

Ingredients	Metric/Imperial	American
frozen french beans	150 g/5 oz	5 ounces
butter	50 g/2 oz	¼ cup
semolina	4 tablespoons	6 tablespoons
salt		
beef stock	600 ml/1 pint	2½ cups
Parmesan cheese, grated	25 g/1 oz	¼ cup
chopped fresh coriander	1 tablespoon	1 tablespoon

Blanch the french beans in 5 cm/2 in of salted boiling water, drain and dry with a tea towel. Chop the beans into ½ cm/¼ in pieces. Melt half the butter in a heatproof casserole dish, toss in the beans over a low heat, cook for 4 minutes.

Turn the heat to medium, sprinkle in the semolina and mix with a wooden spoon until toasted. Add a pinch of salt, then pour in the hot stock a little at a time, stirring constantly. Reduce the heat under the pan and continue to cook slowly for 20 minutes.

Pour the soup into a tureen with the remaining butter, softened, and the Parmesan cheese. Quickly mix together the cheese with the soup and serve sprinkled with coriander.

Time: 30 minutes   *Serves 4*

Rice Soup with Lettuce and Peas

MINESTRA DI RISO CON LATTUGA E PISELLI

Ingredients	Metric/Imperial	American
fresh peas	225 g/8 oz	½ pound
large lettuce	1	1
butter	75 g/3 oz	6 tablespoons
spring onions	3	3
beef stock	1.5 litres/2½ pints	1½ quarts
salt and pepper		
rice	100 g/4 oz	⅔ cup
chopped basil leaves	6	6
chopped parsley	1 tablespoon	1 tablespoon
single (thin) cream	50 ml/2 fl oz	¼ cup
Parmesan cheese, grated	25 g/1 oz	¼ cup

Semolina and French Bean Soup

Shell the peas, wash, drain and place in a bowl. Clean the lettuce, remove any coarse or damaged leaves, wash, drain and chop into thin strips.

Melt the butter in a large heavy pan, add the finely chopped spring onion and leave to cook for 4 minutes over a low heat.

Add the lettuce and peas to the onion, mix with a spoon. Simmer for 5 minutes on a medium heat covered with a lid.

Add the stock to the lettuce mixture with seasoning, cover and bring to the boil. Sprinkle the rice into the soup, stir and leave to cook for about 15 minutes, stirring from time to time over a medium heat. Taste for seasoning.

Chop the basil and parsley finely together, mix with the cream and the Parmesan cheese. Prepare this mixture at least 10 minutes before serving the soup to allow the flavours to mingle.

Remove the soup from the heat. Stir the cheese mixture into the soup and serve in a warm soup tureen.

Time: 1 hour — *Serves 4*

Delicate Fresh Pea Soup

MINESTRA DELICATA DI PISELLI FRESCHI

Ingredients	Metric/Imperial	American
fresh peas	1.2 kg/2¾ lb	2¾ pounds
butter	25 g/1 oz	2 tablespoons
olive oil	2 tablespoons	3 tablespoons
small onions	3	3
salt and pepper		
beef stock	1 litre/1¾ pints	1 quart
eggs	2	2
single (thin) cream	2 tablespoons	3 tablespoons
Parmesan cheese, grated	40 g/1½ oz	3 tablespoons
cooked ham, diced	75 g/3 oz	8 tablespoons
slices of bread	4	4

Remove the peas from the pods, rinse in a colander. Melt the butter with the olive oil in a heavy pan and gently cook the finely chopped onions until soft on a low heat.

Add the peas and cook for a few minutes, season well then add the hot stock, bring slowly to the boil and simmer for 35 minutes.

Beat the eggs in a serving bowl with the cream, the Parmesan cheese and the ham. Trickle 225 ml/8 fl oz/1 cup hot stock into the bowl, stir quickly with a spoon. Stir in the remaining soup.

Serve the soup accompanied by squares of toasted bread.

Time: 1 hour　　　　　　　　　　　　　　*Serves 4*

Potato Soup with Parsley

MINESTRA DI PATATE GRATTUGIATE E PRESSEMOLO

Ingredients	Metric/Imperial	American
medium-sized potatoes	4	4
salt and pepper		
beef stock	1.5 litres/2½ pints	1½ quarts
egg yolk	1	1
hard-boiled (cooked) egg yolk	1	1
single (thin) cream	50 ml/2 fl oz	¼ cup
Parmesan cheese, grated	50 g/2 oz	½ cup
chopped parsley	1 tablespoon	1 tablespoon
croûtons	100 g/4 oz	¼ pound

Peel and coarsely grate the potatoes, sprinkle with salt and pepper and drop into boiling stock. Cook for about 15 minutes, stirring from time to time.

Beat the egg yolk in a soup tureen and add the mashed hard-boiled egg yolk. Blend the cream, Parmesan and finely chopped parsley into the egg mixture and whisk together.

Pour 225ml/8 fl oz/1 cup of the stock into the egg mixture. Reheat the remainder of the stock and potatoes and add gradually to the soup tureen.

Serve the croûtons separately.

Time: 30 minutes　　　　　　　　　　　　*Serves 4*

Delicate Fresh Pea Soup
1 Fry chopped onions in oil and butter until soft.
2 Add peas, stir over heat for a few minutes and season.
3 Add stock and bring to the boil.
4 Mix eggs with cream, grated Parmesan cheese and diced ham.
5 Add a little soup to the egg mixture, mix and return to the pan.

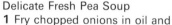

Country Rice Soup

MINESTRA DI RISO ALLA RUSTICA

Ingredients	Metric/Imperial	American
leeks	3	3
onion	1	1
oil	2 tablespoons	3 tablespoons
Italian sausages	100 g/4 oz	¼ pound
potatoes	2	2
stock cubes	2	2
fresh spinach	350 g/12 oz	¾ pound
salt and freshly ground black pepper		
rice	150 g/5 oz	⅔ cup
Pecorino cheese, grated	2 tablespoons	3 tablespoons
olive oil	1 tablespoon	1 tablespoon

Clean and slice the onion and leeks very finely. Heat the oil in a large pan over a low heat, add the onions and leeks together with the skinned and crumbled sausages. Peel the potatoes and cut into cubes, add to the pan, stir from time to time for 10 minutes.

Mix the stock cubes with 1.5 litres/2¾ pints/1½ quarts of water and pour over the vegetables; cook for 30 minutes.

Wash the spinach in several changes of cold water, remove the stalks and damaged leaves, cook in a pan with only the water which is already on the leaves from the final rinse and a pinch of salt for 4–5 minutes. Drain and squeeze out excess moisture. Chop finely and add to the soup.

Bring the soup to the boil, sprinkle in the rice, mix well and simmer until cooked. Add the Pecorino cheese, a sprinkling of pepper, the olive oil and mix well before serving.

Time: 50 minutes   *Serves 4*

Grandmother's Soup

Grandmother's Soup

MINESTRA DELLA NONNA

Ingredients	Metric/Imperial	American
onion	1	1
leeks	2	2
oil	2 tablespoons	3 tablespoons
butter	25 g/1 oz	2 tablespoons
pumpkin flesh, cubed	350 g/12 oz	¾ pound
canned plum tomatoes	200 g/7 oz	7 ounces
salt and pepper		
stock	1.5 litres/2½ pints	1½ quarts
rice	150 g/5 oz	⅔ cup
chopped parsley	1 tablespoon	1 tablespoon
Parmesan cheese, grated	75 g/3 oz	¾ cup

Chop the onion coarsely with the white parts of the leeks. Heat the oil and butter in a large deep pan and cook the onion and leeks over a low heat for 6 minutes. Add the cubed pumpkin, mix with a wooden spoon and leave to cook on the low heat for a further 10 minutes.

Add the tomatoes mashed with a fork, stir well and cook for 10 minutes, then add salt and pepper. Pour in the hot stock and allow to cook for 30 minutes.

Sprinkle the rice into the boiling soup, simmer until just cooked, then add the chopped parsley and half the Parmesan cheese.

Mix the soup well and pour into a heated soup tureen. Serve with a bowl of Parmesan cheese.

Time: 45 minutes   *Serves 4*

Broad Bean and Artichoke Soup

MINESTRA DI FAVE, CICORINO E CARCIOFI

Ingredients	Metric/Imperial	American
fresh podded broad (fava) beans	225 g/8 oz	⅔ cup
chicory (endive)	1	1
artichokes	3	3
onion	½	½
oil	3 tablespoons	scant ¼ cup
large potatoes	2	2
stock	1.5 litres/2½ pints	1½ quarts
egg yolks	2	2
single (thin) cream	2 tablespoons	3 tablespoons
salt and pepper		
Parmesan cheese, grated	2 tablespoons	3 tablespoons
chopped parsley		
croûtons	100 g/4 oz	¼ pound

Remove the skin from the podded beans. Wash and dry the chicory and slice very thinly. Clean the artichokes, wash and remove coarse outer leaves. Finely chop the onion.

Heat the oil over a low heat in a deep pan and cook the onion for 4 minutes, add 125 ml/4 fl oz/½ cup stock and leave to cook gently for 4 minutes.

Add the beans and artichokes, mix well and cook for 5 minutes, add the peeled and thickly sliced potatoes and the slices of chicory. Cover with the remaining stock and bring gently to the boil. Simmer for about 45 minutes. Remove the potato slices with a slotted spoon, mash and return to the soup.

Beat the egg yolks in a soup tureen with the cream, a pinch of salt and pepper, Parmesan cheese and the parsley. Trickle into the soup, mix quickly. Adjust the seasoning and serve hot with croûtons.

Time: 1 hour   *Serves 4*

Three-coloured Soup

MINESTRA TRICOLORE

Ingredients	Metric/Imperial	American
large ripe tomatoes	2	2
medium-sized potatoes	2	2
courgette (zucchini)	1	1
garlic clove	½	½
chopped parsley	2 tablespoons	3 tablespoons
beef stock	1.25 litres/2¼ pints	1¼ quarts
salt and pepper		
ditalini pasta (tiny tubes)	100 g/4 oz	¼ pound

Peel the tomatoes and potatoes and cut both into tiny cubes. Wash the courgette and slice into thin rounds; crush the garlic. Place all the vegetables and half the parsley in a large pan with the stock and bring to the boil; turn down the heat and simmer for 10 minutes.

Taste and adjust the seasoning. Add the ditalini and continue cooking for 10 minutes.

Serve sprinkled with the remaining chopped parsley. Grated cheese may be served separately.

Time: 30 minutes   *Serves 4*

Barley Soup

MINESTRA D'ORZO

Ingredients	Metric/Imperial	American
celery stalks	2	2
carrot	1	1
small leek	1	1
potato	1	1
medium-sized onion	1	1
chopped parsley	1 tablespoon	1 tablespoon
garlic clove	1	1
pearl barley	200 g/7 oz	1 cup
salt and pepper		
stock cube	1	1

Wash, peel and cube the vegetables, chop the onion. Chop the parsley and garlic together finely, keep in a small dish.

Wash and drain the barley, place in a large pan with 2 litres/3½ pints/2 quarts of water, the cubed vegetables and the chopped onion. Add a pinch of salt, cook on a low heat for 45 minutes, stirring from time to time.

Add the crumbled stock cube, cook for 15 minutes and at the end of the cooking time, add the garlic, parsley and pepper and stir well. Serve piping hot.

Time: 1¼ hours   *Serves 6*

Rich Soup with Ham

MINESTRA RICCA

Ingredients	Metric/Imperial	American
butter	65 g/2½ oz	5 tablespoons
semolina	4 tablespoons	6 tablespoons
Parmesan cheese, grated	50 g/2 oz	½ cup
eggs, beaten	4	4
grated lemon rind	½ teaspoon	½ teaspoon
salt and pepper		
celery stalk	2	2
beef stock	1.25 litres/2¼ pints	1¼ quarts
sherry	2 tablespoons	3 tablespoons
cooked ham, cubed	100 g/4 oz	¼ pound

Melt the butter in a heavy shallow pan over a low heat, remove from the heat. Reserve 1 tablespoon of the melted butter in the pan and pour the remainder into a bowl with the semolina, half the Parmesan cheese, eggs, lemon rind, salt and pepper. Mix well with a wooden spoon.

Heat the pan with the butter on a medium heat and pour in the prepared mixture. Spread the semolina with a wooden spatula to form a flat cake, when one side is golden, turn with the help of a lid.

Cook the mixture until golden on both sides, then turn out on to a wooden board. Allow to cool and cut into cubes with a sharp knife.

Scrub the celery, dry and cut into equal-sized pieces. Put in a pan on a medium heat with the stock, bring to the boil and simmer for 15 minutes. Add the prepared cubes and cook for 10 minutes. Flavour the soup with the sherry.

Divide the cubes of ham between individual soup bowls, pour the soup over and serve with a bowl of Parmesan cheese.

Time: 45 minutes   *Serves 4*

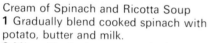

Cream of Spinach and Ricotta Soup
1 Gradually blend cooked spinach with potato, butter and milk.
2 Mix with stock, return to the heat and bring slowly to the boil.
3 Beat an egg with sieved Ricotta and grated Parmesan cheese. Add grated lemon rind and season with pepper.
4 Whisk the cheese mixture into the soup a little at a time.

Cream of Spinach and Ricotta Soup

CREMA DI SPINACI E DI RICOTTA

Ingredients	Metric/Imperial	American
spinach	450 g/1 lb	1 pound
salt		
boiled potato	1	1
butter	50 g/2 oz	¼ cup
milk	600 ml/1 pint	2½ cups
stock	750 ml/1¼ pints	3 cups
beaten egg	1	1
Ricotta cheese	200 g/7 oz	7 ounces
Parmesan cheese, grated	25 g/1 oz	¼ cup
grated lemon rind	1	1
white pepper		
croûtons	100 g/4 oz	¼ pound

Clean the spinach by washing several times under cold water and remove any coarse stalks. Cook in a covered pan with a pinch of salt with 1 tablespoon water. When cooked remove from the heat, allow to cool slightly and drain well.

Purée the spinach in a blender or food processor gradually adding the potato, butter and milk. Return the purée to the pan with the stock. Gradually bring to the boil and simmer for 15 minutes.

Beat the egg in a bowl with the sieved ricotta and Parmesan cheese. Add the lemon rind and a little white pepper, then trickle this mixture into the soup.

Whisk the soup and leave on a low heat for 5 minutes. Pour into individual soup bowls; serve with the croûtons.

Time: 30 minutes   *Serves 4*

Beat together the cream, egg yolks and Parmesan cheese with a wooden spoon in the soup tureen, add the tarragon and mix well. Pour in the soup a little at a time, mixing with the wooden spoon.

Taste, adjust the seasoning and serve hot.

Time: 1 hour   *Serves 4*

Cream of Cucumber, Courgette and Tomato Soup

CREMA DI CETRIOLI, ZUCCHINE E POMODORI

Ingredients	Metric/Imperial	American
tomatoes	400 g/14 oz	14 ounces
olive oil	5 tablespoons	$\frac{1}{3}$ cup
medium-sized onion	1	1
garlic clove	1	1
chopped basil	1 teaspoon	1 teaspoon
chopped parsley	1 tablespoon	1 tablespoon
sugar	$\frac{1}{2}$ teaspoon	$\frac{1}{2}$ teaspoon
salt and pepper		
chicken stock	1 litre/1$\frac{3}{4}$ pints	1 quart
courgettes (zucchini)	600 g/1$\frac{1}{4}$ lb	1$\frac{1}{4}$ pounds
slices of bread	2	2
cucumber	1	1

Dip the tomatoes into a bowl of boiling water to remove the skins, remove the seeds, cut into strips. Heat half the oil in a large pan, add the finely sliced onion, crushed garlic and cook for 4 minutes. Add the tomatoes, basil leaves, parsley, sugar and a little salt and pepper. Cover with a lid and cook for 15 minutes. Add half the stock and cook for 10 minutes.

Wash and dry the courgettes, slice into rings. Heat the remaining oil in a pan and cook the courgettes over a medium heat, add 2–3 tablespoons stock and when the courgettes turn golden, put them into the large pan and cook without the lid for 5 minutes.

Purée the mixture in a blender or food processor gradually adding pieces of crustless bread, and the remaining stock until creamy.

Peel and cube the cucumber, sprinkle with salt and leave to stand in a sieve over a bowl, cover with a lid.

Pour the soup into a tureen and leave to cool in the refrigerator for at least 2 hours.

Dry the diced cucumber with absorbent paper towels and serve in a separate dish with the chilled soup.

Time: 50 minutes + 2 hours: chilling   *Serves 6*

Cream of Tarragon Soup

Cream of Tarragon Soup

CREMA DELICATA AL DRAGONCELLO

Ingredients	Metric/Imperial	American
medium-sized potatoes	4	4
onions	2	2
courgettes (zucchini)	6	6
milk	1 litre/1$\frac{3}{4}$ pints	1 quart
stock cubes	2	2
single (thin) cream	6 tablespoons	8 tablespoons
egg yolks	2	2
Parmesan cheese, grated	2 tablespoons	3 tablespoons
chopped fresh tarragon	1 tablespoon	1 tablespoon
salt and pepper		

Peel and finely slice the potatoes, onions and courgettes.

Place the vegetables in a large pan with the milk, 600 ml/1 pint/2$\frac{1}{2}$ cups of water and the crumbled stock cubes. Gently bring to the boil, then allow to cook for 40 minutes on a low heat.

Turn off the heat and cool. Purée in a blender or food processor, reducing to a cream. Return to the pan and reheat on a medium heat.

Cream of Green Vegetable Soup

CREMA ALLE ERBE AROMATICHE

Ingredients	Metric/Imperial	American
spinach	225 g/8 oz	½ pound
lettuce heart	1	1
watercress	200 g/7 oz	7 ounces
bunch of parsley	1	1
courgettes (zucchini)	200 g/7 oz	7 ounces
onion	½	½
garlic clove	1	1
butter	75 g/3 oz	6 tablespoons
medium-sized potatoes	3	3
stock	1.5 litres/2½ pints	1½ quarts
salt and pepper		
chopped basil	½ teaspoon	½ teaspoon
chopped thyme	½ teaspoon	½ teaspoon
chopped marjoram	½ teaspoon	½ teaspoon
Parmesan cheese, grated	2 tablespoons	3 tablespoons
single (thin) cream	125 ml/4 fl oz	½ cup
small croûtons	100 g/4 oz	¼ pound

Clean, wash and dry the spinach, lettuce, watercress and parsley. Wash the courgettes, peel the onion and garlic and cut them into thin rings.

Melt the butter in a large pan over a low heat, add the onion, garlic and courgettes, stir for 2 minutes.

Tear the spinach, lettuce, watercress and parsley into small pieces and toss into the pan. Stir from time to time, add a few tablespoons of water after 5 minutes and cook for a further 10 minutes.

Add the peeled, diced potatoes, stock and seasoning, cook for 30 minutes. Add the basil, thyme and marjoram towards the end of this cooking period.

Stir well, allow to cool slightly. Purée in a blender or food processor until thick and creamy, return to the pan.

On a low heat stir in the grated Parmesan cheese, the cream and a little pepper, simmer for 5 minutes and serve in soup bowls with croûtons.

Time: 1¼ hours   *Serves 6*

Cream of Shrimp Soup

VELLUTATA DI GAMBERETTI

Ingredients	Metric/Imperial	American
whole shrimps	1.2 kg/2¾ lb	2¾ pounds
fish stock (page 152)	1 litre/1¾ pints	1 quart
onion	½	½
garlic clove	1	1
butter	40 g/1½ oz	3 tablespoons
plain (all-purpose flour)	2 tablespoons	3 tablespoons
dry white wine	50 ml/2 fl oz	¼ cup
ripe plum tomatoes	2	2
salt and pepper		
egg yolks	3	3
single (thin) cream	225 ml/8 fl oz	1 cup
chopped parsley	1 tablespoon	1 tablespoon

Remove and reserve the heads and shells from the shrimps. Crush the shrimps, keeping a few whole ones to garnish the soup. Put the heads and shells in a pan, cover with fish stock and simmer for 1 hour, skimming any scum from the surface.

Meanwhile chop the onion finely and crush the garlic. Melt the butter in a large pan, add the onion and garlic and cook over medium heat until golden. Add the crushed shrimps, sprinkle with the flour and simmer for 2 minutes, stirring continuously. Peel and dice the tomatoes and add to the pan; season to taste.

Strain the shrimp stock into the pan, bring to the boil and then simmer for 15 minutes. Sieve or blend the soup, then return to the rinsed-out pan and simmer for a few minutes longer.

Meanwhile beat the egg yolks into the cream, season with pepper and add the chopped parsley. When ready to serve pour the egg and cream mixture into the soup, remove from the heat and stir for a few minutes. Serve hot garnished with the reserved shrimps.

Time: 1 hour 10 minutes   *Serves 6*

Cream of Shrimp Soup

1 Reserve the heads and shells from the shrimps. Crush the shrimps, retaining a few for garnish. Put the heads and shells in a pan with the fish stock. Simmer for 1 hour. Skim the soup, cook the onion and garlic separately, add the crushed shrimps. Sprinkle with flour, simmer, then add the tomatoes.

2 Strain the stock into the pan, bring to the boil and simmer for 15 minutes. Sieve or blend the soup.
3 Beat the eggs yolks into the cream, add seasoning and chopped parsley. Trickle the mixture into the soup and stir well.

Courgette (Zucchini) Soup with Basil

ZUPPA DI ZUCCHINE AL BASILICO

Ingredients	Metric/Imperial	American
olive oil	4 tablespoons	⅓ cup
butter	25 g/1 oz	2 tablespoons
large onion	1	1
fresh courgettes (zucchini)	700 g/1½ lb	1½ pounds
potatoes	2	2
chicken stock	1.25 litres/2¼ pints	1¼ quarts
fresh basil leaves	12	12
garlic clove	1	1
eggs	2	2
Parmesan cheese, grated	25 g/1 oz	¼ cup
salt and pepper		
slices of crusty bread	6	6

1 Prepare the soup, cool slightly.
2 Purée the soup in a blender or food processor.
3 Add chopped basil and garlic to the egg, butter and Parmesan cheese mixture. Beat well.
4 Trickle the soup into the egg mixture, whisk and season.

Heat the oil and 15 g/½ oz/1 tablespoons of butter in a heavy deep pan. Chop the onion finely and cook in the oil and butter over a low heat until transparent.

Wash and dry the courgettes, slice into rings, add to the onion, mix well and cook for about 10 minutes.

Peel and dice the potatoes, add to the pan and stir on a medium heat for 3–4 minutes before adding the chicken stock. Bring to the boil slowly, cover the pan with a lid and simmer on a medium heat for 40 minutes until cooked. Purée the soup in a blender or food processor to obtain a creamy mixture.

Chop the basil finely together with the garlic. Place in a bowl with the eggs, remaining softened butter and the Parmesan cheese, beat with a wooden spoon or whisk. Trickle the creamed soup into the beaten egg mixture season with salt and pepper. Reheat on a low heat.

Place a slice of crusty bread on the bottom of each soup bowl, pour over the hot soup and serve immediately.

Time: 1¼ hours　　　　　　　　　　　　　　　　*Serves 6*

and the stock cube dissolved in 225 ml/8 fl oz/1 cup boiling water. Mix and bring slowly to the boil. Mix the flour with a little of the milk and add to the pan; stir constantly to avoid lumps.

Cook for 25 minutes on a medium heat, then whisk in the grated Parmesan cheese and the remaining butter cut into pieces.

Butter the stale bread and toast in a moderately hot oven (200 c, 400 f, gas 6) for 10 minutes. Place the toast in the bowls and pour the soup over. Serve piping hot.

Time: 1 hour *Serves 4*

Endive Soup

Endive Soup

ZUPPA DELICATA DI INSALATA RICCIA

Ingredients	Metric/Imperial	American
onion	1	1
butter	75 g/3 oz	6 tablespoons
endive	2	2
salt and pepper		
dry white wine	50 ml/2 fl oz	$\frac{1}{4}$ cup
milk	1 litre/1$\frac{3}{4}$ pints	1 quart
chicken stock cube	1	1
cornflour (cornstarch)	2 tablespoons	3 tablespoons
Parmesan cheese, grated	2 tablespoons	3 tablespoons
slices of stale bread	8	8

Chop the onion into dice. Heat 50 g/2 oz/$\frac{1}{4}$ cup of the butter in a pan on a low heat, taking care not to brown. Add the washed endive, dried and finely chopped.

Mixed with a wooden spoon, leave to cook slowly in the butter and after 10 minutes season with a pinch of salt and little pepper. Pour in the dry white wine and when this has slowly evaporated, add most of the milk

Tasty Bean Soup

CREMA DI FAGIOLI SAPORITA

Ingredients	Metric/Imperial	American
dried haricot beans	350 g/12 oz	$\frac{3}{4}$ pound
salt		
carrot	1	1
onion	1	1
bouquet garni	1	1
cooked smoked ham	100 g/4 oz	$\frac{1}{4}$ pound
butter	40 g/1$\frac{1}{2}$ oz	3 tablespoons
oil	3 tablespoons	scant $\frac{1}{4}$ cup
shallots	2	2
garlic clove	1	1
chopped parsley	1	1
freshly ground black pepper		
croûtons	100 g/4 oz	$\frac{1}{4}$ pound

Soak the beans overnight in cold water, drain.

Bring the beans to the boil over a medium heat in a large pan with 2 litres/3$\frac{1}{2}$ pints/2 quarts lightly salted water. Add the chopped carrot, the onion cut into quarters, bouquet garni and the cubed ham. When the beans are tender put the soup in a blender or food processor, first removing the bouquet garni. Return the purée to the pan and reheat over a medium heat.

Finely chop the shallots and crush the garlic, cook in the butter in a heavy pan, when golden add the chopped parsley and mix quickly. Turn off the heat and add this mixture to the bean purée.

Mix well with a wooden spoon, add a good sprinkling of pepper, then pour into individual bowls. Serve the croûtons separately.

Time: 2 hours 30 minutes (or 45 minutes in a pressure cooker) + 12 hours: soaking *Serves 4*

Baden Onion Soup

ZUPPA DI CIPPOLLE ALLA BADESE

Ingredients	Metric/Imperial	American
onions	450 g/1 lb	1 pound
butter	75 g/3 oz	6 tablespoons
plain (all-purpose) flour	25 g/1 oz	$\frac{1}{4}$ cup
stock	1.1 litres/2 pints	5 cups
dry white wine	125 ml/4 fl oz	$\frac{1}{2}$ cup
egg yolks	2	2
single (thin) cream	125 ml/4 fl oz	$\frac{1}{2}$ cup
salt and pepper		
chopped sorrel	1 teaspoon	1 teaspoon
chopped fennel	1 teaspoon	1 teaspoon
chopped chives	1 teaspoon	1 teaspoon
slices of bread	8–12	8–12

Finely slice the onions, heat half the butter in a large pan, add the onions and allow to cook until they turn pale golden. Sprinkle with flour and mix well. Wet with hot stock a little at a time until about 1 litre/1$\frac{3}{4}$ pints/1 quart has been used. Pour in the wine and cook on a low heat for about 30 minutes.

Place the egg yolks in a bowl, mix with the cream, stir in remaining stock and a little salt and pepper.

Remove the saucepan containing the onions from the heat and stir in the egg yolk mixture.

Cream the remaining butter and flavour with the sorrel, fennel and chives. Spread on the bread.

Time: 1 hour *Serves 4–6*

Oat Soup with Onions and Bacon

ZUPPA DI AVENA, CIPOLLE E BACON

Ingredients	Metric/Imperial	American
oatmeal	90 g/3$\frac{1}{2}$ oz	1 cup
onions	5	5
bacon	100 g/4 oz	$\frac{1}{4}$ pound
butter	15 g/$\frac{1}{2}$ oz	1 tablespoon
salt and pepper		
Gruyère cheese, grated	100 g/4 oz	1 cup

Place the oatmeal to soak overnight. Drain and retain the water. Make up the oatmeal water to 1 litre/1$\frac{3}{4}$ pints/ 1 quart with cold water. Put in a large pan, add the oatmeal, bring to the boil, stirring, and simmer for 1 hour.

Place the onions in the pan with the oats and cooking liquid, add the derinded and chopped bacon, butter and seasoning. Bring to the boil and cook for 20 minutes, taste and adjust the seasoning and stir in the grated Gruyère cheese.

Time: 1$\frac{1}{2}$ hours + 12 hours: soaking *Serves 4*

Onion Soup with Cheese Balls

BRODO DI CIPOLLE CON PALLINE AL FORMAGGIO

Ingredients	Metric/Imperial	American
onions	450 g/1 lb	1 pound
butter	65 g/2$\frac{1}{2}$ oz	5 tablespoons
stock	750 ml/1$\frac{1}{4}$ pints	3 cups
milk	750 ml/1$\frac{1}{4}$ pints	3 cups
plain (all-purpose) flour	65 g/2$\frac{1}{2}$ oz	scant $\frac{2}{3}$ cup
salt and pepper		
grated nutmeg	$\frac{1}{4}$ teaspoon	$\frac{1}{4}$ teaspoon
egg yolk	1	1
Gruyère cheese, grated	100 g/4 oz	1 cup
flour	25 g/1 oz	$\frac{1}{4}$ cup

Peel and finely slice the onions. Heat 25 g/1 oz/2 tablespoons of the butter on a low heat, add the onions and cook for 5 minutes, then add a few tablespoons of stock. Cook for 10 minutes then add half the stock and cook for 10 minutes; add one third of the milk. Allow to cool slightly and purée in a blender or food processor. Return to the pan with the remaining stock.

Prepare the cheese balls. Melt the remaining butter in a pan, stir in the flour, mix well with a wooden spoon, then add 225 ml/8 fl oz/1 cup of hot milk, stir until the mixture is thick and smooth. Season with salt, pepper and nutmeg. Remove from the heat, beat in the egg yolk and Gruyère cheese. Mix well and turn the mixture on to a damp plate, cool completely. Divide into small portions and form lots of tiny balls 2 cm/$\frac{3}{4}$ in across. Roll the balls in sifted flour.

Add the remaining milk to the onion soup and bring to the boil; drop in the cheese balls.

Cook for 5 minutes then remove carefully with a slotted spoon, divide evenly amongst the soup bowls and cover with boiling soup.

Time: 1 hour *Serves 4*

Onion Soup with Cheese Balls
1 Cook the onion in butter until soft, add a little stock, then one-third of the milk.
2 Allow to cool, then blend or purée.
3 Return to the pan with the remaining stock.
4 Prepare the cheese balls: melt the butter in a pan, add the
flour and stir in hot milk. Remove from heat; add the egg yolk.
5 Beat well, then add seasonings and cheese.
6 Cool, form into small balls, roll in flour.
7 Mix the remaining milk into the soup, bring to the boil, add the cheese balls and cook.

Savoy Cabbage Soup

ZUPPA DI VACOLO VERZA

Ingredients	Metric/Imperial	American
Cotechino (Italian spiced sausage)	1	1
beef stock	1.5 litres/2½ pints	1½ quarts
savoy cabbage	450 g/1 lb	1 pound
brown bread, stale	350 g/12 oz	¾ pound
grated nutmeg	¼ teaspoon	¼ teaspoon
Fontina cheese	50 g/2 oz	2 ounces

Wash the sausage, prick with a needle, wrap in a piece of muslin and place in a pan filled with cold water, bring to the boil and simmer for 1¾ hours. Allow to cool, then slice thinly.

Bring the stock to the boil, add the chopped cabbage and cook for 10–20 minutes.

Slice the stale bread 1 cm/½ in thick and toast. When all the ingredients are prepared, place a layer of toast at the bottom of an ovenproof dish, followed by the finely sliced Fontina cheese, and then a layer of cabbage with some slices of sausage. Repeat until all the ingredients are used, pour over the boiling stock and season with a pinch of nutmeg. Place in a very hot oven (240 C, 475 F, gas 9) for 10 minutes.

Time: 2½ hours   *Serves 4*

Naples Fish Soup

ZUPPA DI PESCE ALLA NAPOLETANA

Ingredients	Metric/Imperial	American
celery stalk	1	1
carrot	1	1
onion	1	1
ripe tomatoes	4	4
cod	350 g/12 oz	¾ pound
grey or red mullet	350 g/12 oz	¾ pound
oil	3 tablespoons	scant ¼ cup
sprig of fennel	1	1
sprig of thyme	1	1
salt and pepper		
grated nutmeg	¼ teaspoon	¼ teaspoon
slices of crusty bread	4	4

Wash and prepare the vegetables; peel the tomatoes if using fresh, chop roughly. Wash, skin and bone the fish and cut into large pieces.

Heat the oil in a deep pan over a low heat, add the vegetables and cook for 6 minutes, then add the thyme, fennel leaves and the fish.

Season with salt, pepper and nutmeg, pour in 1 litre/ 1¾ pints/1 quart of water bring to the boil and simmer for 40 minutes. Strain the stock, removing bones left in the fish, taking care not to break up the flesh.

Bake the bread brushed with oil in a moderately hot oven (200 C, 400 F, gas 6). Place bread in soup bowls, pour in the fish soup and serve piping hot.

Time: 1 hour   *Serves 4*

Venetian Fish Soup

BRODETTO DI PESCE ALLA VENETA

Ingredients	Metric/Imperial	American
mixed fish	800 g/1¾ lb	1¾ pounds
(2 grey mullet, 2 small crayfish, 2 inkfish, 1 piece of monkfish)		
medium onion	½	½
oil	4 tablespoon	6 tablespoons
plain (all-purpose) flour	1 tablespoon	1 tablespoon
canned plum tomatoes	400 g/14 oz	14 ounces
chopped parsley	1 tablespoon	1 tablespoon
garlic clove	1	1
wine vinegar	1 tablespoon	1 tablespoon
salt and pepper		

Clean the fish, wash thoroughly and dry. Divide into even-sized pieces, removing the inedible parts.

Cut the onion into thin slices. Heat the oil in a large pan, cook the onion until golden, sprinkle on the flour and stir well to prevent lumps.

Add the chopped tomatoes, the parsley and the crushed clove of garlic with a little water. Cook, stirring from time to time, for about 30 minutes.

Spoon in the fish, vinegar and a little salt and pepper. Simmer until the fish is tender without stirring, to avoid breaking the pieces. Hold the handles of the pan and gently move the liquid to mix.

This soup is better cooked at least 1 hour in advance and reheated gently before serving.

Time: 1½ hours   *Serves 4*

Soup with Mussels and White Wine

ZUPPA DI COZZE AL VINO BIANCO

Ingredients	Metric/Imperial	American
mussels	1 kg/2 lb	2 pounds
shallots	2	2
onions	2	2
chopped parsley	2 tablespoons	3 tablespoons
thyme	½ teaspoon	½ teaspoon
bay leaf	1	1
cayenne	½ teaspoon	½ teaspoon
dry white wine	225 ml/8 fl oz	1 cup
butter	40 g/1½ oz	3 tablespoons
single (thin) cream	225 ml/8 fl oz	1 cup
salt and pepper		
egg yolk	1	1

Scrape and clean the mussels well, remove the beards, place in a large pan. Chop the shallots and the onions into thin rings, add to the mussels with the parsley, thyme, bay leaf, cayenne, wine and butter.

Shake the pan, cover and bring to the boil for about 10 minutes until the mussels are open. Discard any which are still closed.

Strain the cooking juice into a heatproof casserole and remove the mussels from their shells.

Add the cream to the juice and bring to the boil, adjusting the seasoning.

Beat the egg yolk in a small bowl with a whisk, pour in some of the broth, mix well. Return to the casserole with the remaining broth and the mussels and reheat for a few minutes. Remove the bay leaf and serve.

Time: 35 minutes   *Serves 4*

Mussel Soup
1 Shake the cleaned mussels over a medium heat until they open.
2 Add water and tomatoes and cook for 15 minutes.
3 Heat butter in a small pan and cook the garlic and herbs.
4 Pour the herb butter over the mussels. Rinse the small pan with water and add to the pan with the mussels.
5 Toast the slices of bread and rub over with cut cloves of garlic.

Mussel Soup

ZUPPA DI COZZE

Ingredients	Metric/Imperial	American
mussels	1.6 kg/3¼ lb	3¼ pounds
tomatoes	2	2
butter	50 g/2 oz	¼ cup
garlic cloves	2	2
chopped parsley	1 tablespoon	1 tablespoon
basil leaves	3	3
slices of crusty bread	4	4
salt and pepper		

Clean the mussels carefully, scrub the shells and remove the beards, wash well under plenty of cold running water. Place in a large heavy pan without water and shake over a medium heat until the shells open in their own juices; discard any which do not open.

Add 225 ml/8 fl oz/1 cup of boiling water with the peeled cubed tomatoes and cook for about 15 minutes.

Heat the butter in a small pan and brown the crushed garlic. Remove garlic, add the parsley and basil. Pour the buttered herbs over the mussels, rinsing the pan with a little hot water. Bring to the boil and simmer gently for 5 minutes.

Toast the slices of bread, rub over with the remaining garlic. Arrange the toast in 4 large bowls and sprinkle with pepper. Adjust the seasoning and divide the mussels and liquid evenly amongst the bowls.

Time: 30 minutes   *Serves 4*

Garlic Soup
1 Peel the garlic cloves and slice the bread.
2 Heat the oil in a pan, add the garlic and cook until golden.
3 Fry the bread until golden. Drain.
4 Add the stock to the garlic. Cook for 30 minutes. Strain the stock and return to the pan with the bread.

Hunters' Soup

MINESTRA DEL CACCIATORE

Ingredients	Metric/Imperial	American
minced (ground) veal	150 g/5 oz	$\frac{2}{3}$ cup
egg	1	1
cheese, grated	50 g/2 oz	$\frac{1}{2}$ cup
butter	25 g/1 oz	2 tablespoons
grated nutmeg	$\frac{1}{4}$ teaspoon	$\frac{1}{4}$ teaspoon
salt		
beef stock	1 litre/1$\frac{3}{4}$ pints	1 quart
Parmesan cheese, grated		

Mix the veal with the egg in a bowl (if the egg is large just use the yolk). Add the grated cheese, melted butter, a pinch of salt and the nutmeg.

Work the mixture together until well mixed and form into firm balls, about the size of walnuts, in the palms of your hands.

Heat the stock until boiling, then add the veal balls and cook for 15 minutes.

Serve the soup hot, with grated Parmesan cheese in a bowl on the table.

Time: 20 minutes   *Serves 4*

Garlic Soup

ZUPPA D'AGLIO

Ingredients	Metric/Imperial	American
garlic cloves	20	20
stale bread	450 g/1 lb	1 pound
olive oil	8 tablespoons	$\frac{2}{3}$ cup
salt and pepper		
stock cube	1	1
chopped thyme	$\frac{1}{4}$ teaspoon	$\frac{1}{4}$ teaspoon

Peel the garlic cloves. Slice the bread and remove the crusts. Heat 6 tablespoons/4 fl oz/$\frac{1}{2}$ cup of olive oil in a large pan. Add the garlic and cook over a moderate heat for about 5 minutes until golden.

Pour in 1 litre/1¾ pints/1 quart of boiling water, season with salt and pepper, crumble in the stock cube, add thyme and boil for 30 minutes. Strain the stock into a bowl, return to the pan. Add the bread and stir together for a few minutes.

Serve the soup in individual bowls with a little olive oil trickled over the top.

Time: 1¼ hours *Serves 4*

Variation: The bread may be sprinkled with grated cheese and toasted under a hot grill (broiler) just to melt the cheese before the garlic soup is poured over.

Chicken and Beetroot Leaf Soup

MINESTRA DI DADINI DI POLLO CON BIETOLINE

Ingredients	Metric/Imperial	American
beetroot leaves	225 g/8 oz	½ pound
large potato	1	1
onion	½	½
celery stalk	1	1
oil	2 tablespoons	3 tablespoons
chicken stock	1.5 litres/2½ pints	1½ quarts
chicken breast	175 g/6 oz	6 ounces
salt		
pastina (tiny pasta shapes)	150 g/5 oz	5 ounces
butter	1 tablespoon	1 tablespoon
Parmesan cheese, grated	1 tablespoon	1 tablespoon
chopped parsley	1 tablespoon	1 tablespoon

Wash the beetroot leaves and chop coarsely. Chop the potato, onion and celery finely. Heat the oil in a high-sided pan, add the onion and celery and cook over a low heat until the onion is transparent. Pour on the stock and cook over a low heat.

Cut the chicken into thin strips, add to the onion mixture and cook until tender. Add the beetroot leaves and potato, mix well and cook for a few minutes longer, season with a pinch of salt and pour in the boiling stock. Mix well and cook over a medium heat for 20 minutes.

Add the pasta and continue cooking (about 5 minutes) until the pasta is *al dente*.

Garnish the soup with butter, Parmesan cheese and parsley before serving.

Time: 45 minutes *Serves 4*

Farmhouse Soup

MINESTRA PAESANA

Ingredients	Metric/Imperial	American
spinach	1 kg/2 lb	2 pounds
large onion	1	1
garlic clove	1	1
bacon	25 g/1 oz	1 ounce
butter	25 g/1 oz	2 tablespoons
salt and pepper		
stock	1 litre/1¾ pints	1 quart
egg yolks	2	2
single (thin) cream	4 tablespoons	⅓ cup
Parmesan cheese, grated	25 g/1 oz	¼ cup
To serve:		
croûtons	100 g/4 oz	¼ pound
cooked ham, cubed	100 g/4 oz	¼ pound

Wash the spinach thoroughly and put in a colander to drain.

Finely chop the onion and crush the garlic clove. Remove the rind and chop the bacon. Melt the butter in a large deep pan, add the onion, garlic and bacon and cook over a low heat for a few minutes until the onion is transparent.

Chop the spinach, add to the pan and leave for a few minutes on a fairly high heat. Lower the heat and season to taste. Pour in the stock, bring to the boil and simmer for 20 minutes.

Purée the spinach with the stock in a blender or food processor and return to the rinsed-out pan. Beat the egg yolks lightly with the cream, Parmesan cheese and a pinch of salt; add to the pan and mix well.

Serve the soup accompanied by a dish of croûtons and a dish of ham.

Time: 50 minutes *Serves 4*

Farmhouse Soup

Pasta Soup with Courgettes (Zucchini)

MINESTRA DI PASTA E ZUCCHINE

Ingredients	Metric/Imperial	American
small courgettes (zucchini)	450 g/1 lb	1 pound
pork fat	50 g/2 oz	2 ounces
garlic clove	1	1
marjoram	$\frac{1}{4}$ teaspoon	$\frac{1}{4}$ teaspoon
thyme	$\frac{1}{4}$ teaspoon	$\frac{1}{4}$ teaspoon
oil	2 tablespoons	3 tablespoons
butter	25 g/1 oz	2 tablespoons
plum tomatoes	3	3
salt and pepper		
ditalini	200 g/7 oz	7 ounces
Parmesan cheese, grated	2 tablespoons	3 tablespoons

Wash and dry the courgettes: top and tail and cut into dice. Finely chop the pork fat with the garlic, marjoram and thyme.

Heat the oil and butter in a deep pan, add the pork mixture and cook over a medium heat for a few minutes. Add the courgettes, stir well and leave for a few minutes for the flavours to blend. Peel the tomatoes if using fresh, chop and add to the pan. Pour in 1 litre/1$\frac{3}{4}$ pints/1 quart of water, season with salt and pepper and bring to the boil. Add the pasta and cook for about 7 minutes until *al dente*.

Pour the soup into a tureen, sprinkle with Parmesan cheese and serve.

Time: 45 minutes   *Serves 4*

Cabbage and Egg Soup

ZUPPA DI VERDURE E UOVA

Ingredients	Metric/Imperial	American
cabbage or spring greens	800 g/1$\frac{3}{4}$ lb	1$\frac{3}{4}$ pounds
salt and pepper		
Italian sausages	100 g/4 oz	$\frac{1}{4}$ pound
oil	2 tablespoons	3 tablespoons
beef stock	1.5 litres/2$\frac{1}{2}$ pints	1$\frac{1}{2}$ quarts
large slices of bread	4	4
garlic cloves	2	2
eggs	2	2
Parmesan cheese, grated	25 g/1 oz	$\frac{1}{4}$ cup

Trim and wash the cabbage, then put in boiling salted water for 5 minutes to blanch.

Slice the sausages. Heat the oil in a large deep pan, add the sausages and fry for a few minutes over a medium heat. Drain and chop the cabbage leaves and add to the pan. Pour in the stock, bring to the boil, then cover and simmer for 30 minutes.

Prepare the crostini (see page 60). Put the toasted bread into a soup tureen.

Beat the eggs lightly with a pinch of salt and pepper and the Parmesan cheese. Add to the pan and cook, stirring constantly, just long enough to set the egg. Pour into the tureen and serve at once.

Time: 50 minutes   *Serves 4*

Celery Soup with Ham

CREMA DI SEDANO AL PROSCIUTTO

Ingredients	Metric/Imperial	American
medium-sized onion	1	1
large potatoes	2	2
celery stalks	6	6
butter	50 g/2 oz	$\frac{1}{4}$ cup
plain (all-purpose) flour	2 tablespoons	3 tablespoons
milk	750 ml/1$\frac{1}{4}$ pints	3 cups
stock cube	1	1
dry white wine	125 ml/4 fl oz	$\frac{1}{2}$ cup
salt and pepper		
Parmesan cheese, grated	25 g/1 oz	$\frac{1}{4}$ cup
single (thin) cream	125 ml/4 fl oz	$\frac{1}{2}$ cup
lean cooked ham to garnish	100 g/4 oz	$\frac{1}{4}$ pound

Finely chop the onion and potatoes; trim and scrub the celery stalks and cut into short thin strips.

Melt the butter in a large pan, add the onion and cook for a few minutes over a low heat until transparent. Stir in the potatoes, cook for 2 minutes and then add the celery. Leave for a few minutes to absorb the flavours. Meanwhile heat the milk.

Stir in the flour, then gradually add the hot milk. Follow with 150 ml/$\frac{1}{4}$ pint/$\frac{2}{3}$ cup of water, the crumbled stock cube, wine and a pinch of salt. Cook over a very low heat, stirring frequently, for about 30 minutes.

Taste and adjust the seasoning, then purée the soup in a blender or vegetable mill. Return to the rinsed-out pan, put on a medium heat and add the Parmesan cheese and cream. Pour into soup bowls and garnish with the ham cut into very thin strips.

Time: 30 minutes   *Serves 4*

Cream Soups garnished with Cooked Ham, Chives and Leeks

Cauliflower Soup

MINESTRA DI CIMETTE DI CAVOLFIORI

Ingredients	Metric/Imperial	American
cauliflower	1	1
potatoes	3	3
onions	2	2
oil	125 ml/4 fl oz	½ cup
milk	450 ml/¾ pint	2 cups
stock cubes	2	2
butter	25 g/1 oz	2 tablespoons
garlic clove	1	1
chopped parsley	1 tablespoon	1 tablespoon
salt and pepper		
Parmesan cheese, grated		

Remove the outside leaves and stem and cut the cauliflower into florets; wash and chop. Dice the potatoes and chop the onion.

Heat 4–5 tablespoons of the oil in a deep pan, add the onion and cook for a few minutes over medium heat until golden. Add the potatoes and cook for a few minutes, then add 1 litre/1¾ pints/1 quart of water and the milk. Crumble in the stock cubes and simmer until potatoes are cooked.

Meanwhile melt the butter and remaining oil in a large deep pan; add the crushed garlic, parsley and cauliflower florets. Cook for a few minutes over medium heat, then season with salt and pepper, moisten with 2–3 tablespoons of the hot stock and reduce the heat.

Pass the potatoes and stock through a blender, food processor or vegetable mill and return to the rinsed-out pan. Add the cauliflower mixture and leave for a few more minutes for the flavours to blend. Serve hot, accompanied with grated Parmesan cheese.

Time: 60 minutes   *Serves 4*

RICE

*The famous Italian dish of risotto
is cooked by a completely different method from
other rice dishes.
The small round-grained risotto rice is
cooked carefully on top of the stove and the liquid
is added in small amounts. The risotto is stirred
over a low heat until the mixture is creamy and
the grains remain almost firm, with a slight bite,
to the taste. Any additions such as meat,
fish or other vegetables are incorporated into
the dish during cooking.
Rice is as popular with the inhabitants of
northern Italy as pasta is with those
who live in the south.*

Rice

The regional cookery of Italy provides a wide variety of rice dishes. These delicious savoury recipes need some care during cooking to ensure that the rice grains remain separate.

Risottos Short-grain Italian rice is best for making a risotto. This must not be confused with the Carolina rice which is used for puddings. Risotto is cooked on top of the stove and the liquid is added gradually. It is best to have a pan of simmering stock next to the risotto pan. Use a large heavy round-bottomed pan to prevent sticking and coat the rice in the oil or butter first. Add the hot liquid gradually and stir with a wooden spoon until each addition of liquid is absorbed. Cook the rice until *al dente*, this will take about 25 minutes on a constant medium heat. The result should be creamy but firm to the bite.

Boiled Rice Many varieties of long-grain rice are available which are suitable for boiling. Find out if you are buying plain rice or a pre-cooked variety. Use the manufacturer's instructions when using easy-cook rice. Only wash non-processed rice and do not add too much salt to the water, as it is absorbed. Only stir when the rice is first added to the pan. Boil plain rice in a large covered pan with plenty of boiling water for 12 minutes. Drain and keep warm in a serving dish. Do not leave in the pan or the rice will cake.

Yellow Risotto

RISOTTO GIALLO

Ingredients	Metric/Imperial	American
saffron strands	½ teaspoon	½ teaspoon
butter	100 g/4 oz	½ cup
onion	1	1
raw beef bone marrow	25 g/1 oz	1 ounce
dry white wine	50 ml/2 fl oz	¼ cup
risotto rice	350 g/12 oz	1⅔ cups
beef stock	1.5 litres/2½ pints	1½ quarts
salt		
Parmesan cheese, grated	25 g/1 oz	¼ cup

Soak the saffron strands in a small bowl in 1 cm/½ in of hot water.

Melt half the butter in a heavy pan over low heat. Chop the onion very finely and add it to the pan together with the bone marrow and wine.

Toast the rice under a hot grill (broiler) for 2–3 minutes until golden. Heat the stock gently.

When the liquid in the pan has reduced by half stir in the rice and saffron liquid. Raise the heat to medium and add the hot stock a little at a time, stirring frequently. Cook and stir until all the stock has been absorbed and the rice is cooked but still *al dente*. Season with salt if necessary.

Stir in the remaining butter and the grated Parmesan cheese. Switch off the heat and leave to rest for 2–3 minutes before serving.

Time: 25 minutes   *Serves 4*

Labourer's Risotto

RISOTTO ALLA PILOTA

Ingredients	Metric/Imperial	American
salt and pepper		
risotto rice	350 g/12 oz	1⅔ cups
butter	65 g/2½ oz	5 tablespoons
fresh spicy sausages	150 g/5 oz	5 ounces
Parmesan cheese, grated, or any favourite cheese	65 g/2½ oz	5 tablespoons

Place 750 ml/1¼ pints/3 cups of salted water in a large pan and bring to the boil. Pour the rice in through a funnel to ensure that it all falls into the middle of the pan in the shape of a pyramid with the last 1 cm/½ in of the point out of the water. If the point is under the water remove some water with a ladle.

When the water has returned to the boil, shake the pan by the handles to enlarge the base of the pyramid slightly; cook over a high heat for about 10 minutes until the rice is softened. Remove the pan from the heat, cover with a cloth and then fit the saucepan lid on tightly and weight it down. Leave in a warm place such as on the top of the cooker but away from direct heat for 15 minutes.

Heat the butter in a pan, add the sausages and turn with a fork while cooking to brown evenly. Add 2–3 tablespoons of Parmesan cheese, salt and pepper.

Remove the risotto from the saucepan and drain. Pour into a serving dish, add the sausages with the cooking juices, mix, then sprinkle with plenty of cheese and serve immediately.

Time: 1½ hours   *Serves 4*

Melt half the butter in a deep pan, add the chopped vegetables and cook over a low heat for a few minutes until the onion is transparent. Add the bone marrow, then the sausage meat; after a few minutes add the chicken. Mix together and cook for 10 minutes.

Put the stock in a pan over a low heat.

Drain and chop the mushrooms; add to the onion mixture together with the chicken livers. Mix well, season to taste and pour in the Marsala wine. Leave until this has evaporated, then add to the tomato paste diluted with a little warm stock. Cover the pan and simmer for 20 minutes.

Add the grated ginger, then the rice. Stir for a few minutes until well mixed, then add a ladleful of hot stock. Cook and stir until this has been absorbed, and repeat the operation until the rice is cooked but still moist.

Take the pan off the heat and stir in the remaining butter and the Parmesan cheese. Mix well and pile on to a heated serving dish.

Time: 45 minutes   *Serves 6*

Gypsy Risotto

Gypsy Risotto

RISOTTO ALLA MODA ZIGANA

Ingredients	Metric/Imperial	American
dried mushrooms	40 g/1½ oz	1½ ounces
boneless chicken	350 g/12 oz	¾ pound
chicken livers	100 g/4 oz	¼ pound
sausage meat	100 g/4 oz	¼ pound
onion	1	1
garlic clove	1	1
carrot	1	1
celery stalk	1	1
butter	65 g/2½ oz	5 tablespoons
beef bone marrow	25 g/1 oz	1 ounce
stock	1.5 litres /2½ pints	1½ quarts
salt and pepper		
Marsala wine	50 ml/2 fl oz	¼ cup
tomato paste	1 tablespoon	1 tablespoon
fresh root ginger, grated	1 teaspoon	1 teaspoon
risotto rice	400 g/14 oz	2 cups
Parmesan cheese, grated	2 tablespoons	3 tablespoons

Soak the mushrooms in warm water for 30 minutes.

Chop the chicken, wash and chop the chicken livers; chop the sausage meat. Prepare the vegetables by finely chopping the onion, garlic, carrot and celery.

Sage Risotto

RISOTTO ALLA SALVIA

Ingredients	Metric/Imperial	American
stock	1 litre/1¾ pints	1 quart
oil	2 tablespoons	3 tablespoons
butter	25 g/1 oz	2 tablespoons
shallot	1	1
risotto rice	350 g/12 oz	1⅔ cups
dry white wine	50 ml/2 fl oz	¼ cup
salt and pepper		
fresh sage leaves	20	20
single (thin) cream	2 tablespoons	3 tablespoons
Gruyère cheese, grated	25 g/1 oz	¼ cup

Put the stock in a pan on a very low heat.

Heat the oil and butter in a large pan. Add the finely chopped shallot and cook over a medium heat until golden. Trickle in the rice, stir well and cook for a few minutes.

Add the wine and simmer until it has completely evaporated, then add the hot stock a little at a time and cook, stirring, until it has all been absorbed and the rice is tender but still firm. Taste and season if necessary.

At the end of the cooking time add the finely chopped sage leaves, cream and Gruyère cheese. Turn off the heat, cover and leave to rest for a few minutes before serving.

Time: 30 minutes   *Serves 4*

Just before the rice is cooked, add the Parmesan cheese, pepper, nutmeg, the remaining butter and oil. Serve the risotto steaming hot.

Time: 1 hour   *Serves 4*

Risotto with Sweet Pepper and Aubergine (Eggplant)

RISOTTO CON PEPERONI E MELANZANE

Ingredients	Metric/Imperial	American
red (sweet) pepper	1	1
aubergine (eggplant)	1	1
salt and pepper		
shallot	1	1
butter	40 g/1½ oz	3 tablespoons
oil	2 tablespoons	3 tablespoons
stock	1 litre/1¾ pints	1 quart
risotto rice	350 g/12 oz	1⅔ cups
dry white wine	50 ml/2 fl oz	¼ cup
chopped parsley	1 tablespoon	1 tablespoon
chopped basil leaves	4	4
Parmesan cheese, grated	25 g/1 oz	¼ cup
single (thin) cream	2 tablespoons	3 tablespoons

Cut the sweet pepper in half, remove the seeds, wash and cut into tiny squares. Wash and dry the aubergine (eggplant), chop finely, put in a colander, sprinkle with a little salt and leave for 30 minutes to drain off excess bitter juices.

Finely chop the shallot. Heat the butter and oil in a deep pan (reserve 1 tablespoon of butter to use later). Add the shallot and cook over medium heat for a few minutes until golden. Rinse and dry the aubergine and add to the pan with the diced pepper. Cook for about 5 minutes on a fairly high heat. Meanwhile put the stock in another pan over a medium heat.

Add the rice to the vegetable mixture, stir for a few minutes, then add the wine. When this has evaporated pour in a little boiling stock. Continue adding stock, stirring frequently, until the rice is tender but firm.

Taste and adjust the seasoning, add the reserved butter, chopped herbs, Parmesan cheese and cream. Mix well and serve at once.

Time: 40 minutes + 30 minutes: resting   Serves 4

Apple Risotto

Apple Risotto

RISOTTO ALLE MELE

Ingredients	Metric/Imperial	American
apples	4	4
lemon	½	½
butter	65 g/2½ oz	5 tablespoons
olive oil	4 tablespoons	⅓ cup
risotto rice	350 g/12 oz	1⅔ cups
dry white wine	50 ml/2 fl oz	¼ cup
beef or chicken stock	1 litre/1¾ pints	1 quart
salt and pepper		
Parmesan cheese, grated	50 g/2 oz	½ cup
grated nutmeg	¼ teaspoon	¼ teaspoon

Peel the apples, remove the core and cut into cubes. Bring a pan of acidulated water (water with lemon juice) to the boil. Immerse the apples, bring back to the boil and cook for 3 minutes. Drain and place in a small pan with one-third of the melted butter, fry for a few minutes until golden but not dark, remove and keep warm.

Place 25 g/1 oz/2 tablespoons of butter in a pan with some of the oil to heat, sprinkle in the rice and allow to turn golden. Mix well, moisten with the wine and leave to evaporate. Start adding a little hot stock, add the remainder gradually, stirring from time to time to mix well.

Add the apples after 10 minutes and continue to stir, season to taste.

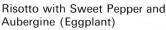

Risotto with Sweet Pepper and Aubergine (Eggplant)

1 Cut the red pepper into small dice. Dice the aubergine.

2 Heat the butter and oil in a deep pan and cook the shallot over a medium heat until golden. Add the pepper and aubergine, cook for 5 minutes, then stir in the rice.

3 Moisten with the wine and allow to evaporate.

4 Add the stock gradually, stirring with a wooden spoon until the rice is almost cooked.

Mushroom Risotto

RISOTTO CON FUNGHI ALLA MIA MANIERA

Ingredients	Metric/Imperial	American
large flat mushrooms	225 g/8 oz	½ pound
butter	60 g/2½ oz	5 tablespoons
oil	1 tablespoon	1 tablespoon
salt and pepper		
sprig of parsley	1	1
garlic clove	1	1
onion	1	1
risotto rice	350 g/12 oz	1⅔ cups
dry white wine	50 ml/2 fl oz	¼ cup
stock	1 litre/1¾ pints	1 quart
Parmesan cheese, grated	50 g/2 oz	½ cup

Wipe the mushrooms and chop finely. Heat one-third of the butter with the oil in a small pan, add the mushrooms and fry over medium heat for a few minutes. Season with salt and pepper.

Chop the parsley with the garlic clove and set aside.

Finely chop the onion. Melt half the remaining butter in a deep pan, add the onion and cook over medium heat until golden. Stir in the rice and leave for a few minutes for the flavours to blend. Add the wine; when it has evaporated start adding hot stock, a little at a time. Continue, stirring constantly, until the stock has all been absorbed and the rice is almost cooked.

Add the mushrooms and their juices and lastly the parsley and garlic mixture and Parmesan cheese. Turn off the heat, stir in the remaining butter, cover and leave to rest for 2 minutes.

Turn the risotto into a heated serving dish and serve at once.

Time: 1¾ hours   *Serves 4*

Sailor's Risotto

Sailor's Risotto

RISOTTO DEL MARINAIO

Ingredients	Metric/Imperial	American
uncooked scampi	550 g/1¼ lb	1¼ pounds
salt and freshly ground black pepper		
shallots	2	2
bay leaves	2	2
garlic cloves	2	2
mussels	700 g/1½ lb	1½ pounds
onion	1	1
olive oil	4 tablespoons	⅓ cup
butter	75 g/3 oz	6 tablespoons
risotto rice	600 g/1¼ lb	scant 3 cups
dry white wine	225 ml/8 fl oz	1 cup
tomato paste	1 heaped tablespoon	1 heaped tablespoon
chopped parsley	4 tablepoons	⅓ cup
Parmesan cheese, grated	2 tablespoons	3 tablespoons

Wash the scampi and boil for 5 minutes in 1 litre/1¾ pints/1 quart of salted water, with 1 shallot, crumbled bay leaves and 1 crushed clove of garlic added. Drain, remove the shells and put the flesh to one side. Return the shells to the water and boil for a further 20 minutes.

Scrub the mussels and remove the beards, place in a large pan with a piece of onion and 125 ml/8 fl oz/1 cup of water. Shake over a medium heat until the shells have opened, remove the mussels from their shells and place the cooking juices to one side.

Heat the oil and half the butter in a large pan, add the crushed garlic, 1 diced shallot and the remaining chopped onion and cook until golden. Sprinkle in the rice and, mixing with care, allow it to colour.

Add half the mussels, chopped; mix well, then pour in the wine and allow to evaporate. Continue to cook adding the strained stock from the scampi, alternating with the strained mussel juices. Season halfway through and then add the remaining mussels and the scampi. Add a little more boiling water, if necessary, to cook the rice.

When the rice is cooked, stir in the tomato paste diluted with a little warm water, the remaining chopped butter, chopped parsley and grated Parmesan cheese. Mix well, cover and leave to rest for 2 minutes before serving.

Time: 1¼ hours   *Serves 6–8*

Risotto with Saffron

RISOTTO ALLO ZAFFERANO

Ingredients	Metric/Imperial	American
saffron strands	½ teaspoon	½ teaspoon
beef stock	1 litre/1¾ pints	1 quart
butter	75 g/3 oz	6 tablespoons
spring onions	2	2
risotto rice	400 g/14 oz	2 cups
dry white wine	125 ml/4 fl oz	½ cup
salt and pepper		
Parmesan cheese, grated		

Soak the saffron in 50 ml/2 fl oz/¼ cup of hot stock.

Heat two-thirds of the butter in a large pan, add the finely chopped onion and cook over a medium heat until it just begins to change colour.

Sprinkle in the rice and stir for a few minutes, pour over the wine and allow to evaporate.

Add the saffron and all the stock gradually, stirring as it is added. Cover with a lid, lower the heat and leave to cook for 8 minutes.

Remove from the heat, taste and adjust seasoning, stir in the remaining butter and mix well. Serve with a bowl of grated Parmesan cheese.

Time: 25 minutes   *Serves 4*

Aubergine (Eggplant) Risotto

RISOTTO CON MELANZANE E PREZZEMOLO

Ingredients	Metric/Imperial	American
aubergines (eggplants)	2	2
salt and freshly ground black pepper		
butter	25 g/1 oz	2 tablespoons
oil	2 tablespoons	3 tablespoons
small onion	1	1
garlic clove	1	1
anchovy fillets	2	2
risotto rice	350 g/12 oz	1⅔ cups
dry white wine	50 ml/2 fl oz	¼ cup
stock	1 litre/1¾ pints	1 quart
chopped parsley	1 tablespoon	1 tablespoon
oregano	¼ teaspoon	¼ teaspoon
Parmesan cheese, grated	25 g/1 oz	¼ cup

Wash, dry and cube the aubergines, sprinkle with salt and allow to stand for 20 minutes on a tray.

Melt the butter with the oil in a large pan, add the chopped onion, crushed garlic, drained, chopped, anchovy fillets and cook on a low heat. Drain the aubergines on absorbent paper towels, add to the pan and leave to soften.

Sprinkle in the rice, allow to blend with the other ingredients, then pour over the wine. Allow wine to evaporate and cook the risotto by adding the boiling stock gradually.

When the rice is *al dente*, mix in the chopped parsley, oregano and Parmesan cheese. Serve piping hot sprinkled with pepper.

Time: 40 minutes   *Serves 4*

Sicilian Risotto

MONTICELLO GIALLO DI RISOTTO

Ingredients	Metric/Imperial	American
vegetable stock cubes	2	2
long-grain rice	350 g/12 oz	1⅔ cups
egg yolks	3	3
single (thin) cream	225 ml/8 fl oz	1 cup
grated nutmeg	¼ teaspoon	¼ teaspoon
Marsala wine	1 tablespoon	1 tablespoon
butter	40 g/1½ oz	3 tablespoons
Parmesan cheese, grated	50 g/2 oz	½ cup
hard-boiled (cooked) eggs	3	3

Bring 1 litre/1¾ pints/1 quart of water to the boil, add the crumbled stock cubes. Sprinkle in the rice, stir with a wooden spoon until the rice has absorbed all the stock.

In a bowl beat the egg yolks with the cream, nutmeg, Marsala wine and chopped butter. Mix into the hot rice, stir in the Parmesan cheese and leave the risotto to rest for 2 minutes.

Turn into a heated deep serving dish and serve sprinkled with sieved hard-boiled (cooked) eggs.

Time: 30 minutes   *Serves 4*

Aubergine (Eggplant) Risotto

Rice Mould with Creamy Mushroom Sauce

RISO IN FORMA CON SALSA SPECIALE

Ingredients	Metric/Imperial	American
mushrooms	225 g/8 oz	½ pound
onion	1	1
leek	1	1
celery stalk	1	1
butter	100 g/4 oz	½ cup
stock cube	1	1
salt and pepper		
Marsala wine	50 ml/2 fl oz	¼ cup
milk	4 tablespoons	⅓ cup
single (thin) cream	100 ml/3½ fl oz	scant ½ cup
long-grain rice	350 g/12 oz	1⅔ cups
Parmesan cheese, grated	65 g/2½ oz	5 tablespoons
shallot	1	1
parsley sprigs to garnish		

Wipe the mushrooms, trim the stalks and cut into slices. Clean and chop the onion, leek and celery.

Place half the butter in a pan over a low heat, add the chopped vegetables, cook for 5 minutes, stirring from time to time, then add the mushrooms and cook for a further 5 minutes.

Preheat the oven to 180 C, 350 F, gas 4.

Mix the crumbled stock cube, salt, pepper, Marsala and hot milk together, pour over the vegetables and leave to cook for a further 30 minutes on a low heat adding the cream slowly towards the end of the cooking time.

Cook the rice in boiling salted water, drain when *al dente* and place in a bowl. Mix with the remaining butter, Parmesan cheese and finely chopped shallot.

Turn the rice into a buttered ring mould and place in a moderately hot oven for 15 minutes.

Purée the vegetables in a blender or food processor to finish the sauce, add a little more milk if it is too thick. Taste and adjust the seasoning.

Turn the rice out on to a heated round serving plate, pour the sauce over the ring and garnish with sprigs of parsley before serving.

Time: 1 hour   *Serves 4*

Boatman's Rice

RISO DEL BARCAIOLO

Ingredients	Metric/Imperial	American
small white onions	350 g/12 oz	¾ pound
butter	25 g/1 oz	2 tablespoons
oil	2 tablespoons	3 tablespoons
stock	225 ml/8 fl oz	1 cup
freshly ground black pepper		
dry white wine	50 ml/2 fl oz	¼ cup
long-grain rice	350 g/12 oz	1⅔ cups
tuna in oil	200 g/7 oz	7 ounces
chopped parsley	1 tablespoon	1 tablespoon
sprig of basil	1	1

Cut the onions into quarters. Heat the butter and oil in a large pan, add the onions and leave over a low heat until softened. Add the stock and season with pepper. Pour in the wine, reduce the heat and leave until the onions are cooked through.

Meanwhile cook the rice in boiling salted water.

Drain the tuna and mash it with a fork. Add it to the onions at the end of the cooking time, together with the chopped herbs. Mix with the rice and serve hot.

Time: 30 minutes   *Serves 4*

Rice with Tuna and Caper Sauce

RISO CON SALSA DI TONNO E CAPPERI

Ingredients	Metric/Imperial	American
long-grain rice	400 g/14 oz	2 cups
salt and pepper		
bunch of parsley	1	1
spring onions	2	2
olive oil	3 tablespoons	scant ¼ cup
lemon juice	1 tablespoon	1 tablespoon
tuna in oil	200 g/7 oz	7 ounces
natural yogurt	150 ml/¼ pint	⅔ cup
hard-boiled (cooked) eggs	2	2
mayonnaise	4 tablespoons	6 tablespoons
capers	2 tablespoons	3 tablespoons
double (thick) cream	100 ml/3½ fl oz	scant ½ cup

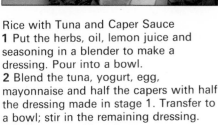

Rice with Tuna and Caper Sauce
1 Put the herbs, oil, lemon juice and seasoning in a blender to make a dressing. Pour into a bowl.
2 Blend the tuna, yogurt, egg, mayonnaise and half the capers with half the dressing made in stage 1. Transfer to a bowl; stir in the remaining dressing.
3 Fold in the whipped cream.
4 Mix most of the sauce with the rice. Mix in the remaining capers and put on a dish. Top with sauce and garnish with parsley and egg.

Boil the rice in salted water. Wash and dry the parsley, wash and roughly chop the spring onion, put in a blender with the olive oil, lemon juice, a pinch of salt and pepper. Pour the mixture into a bowl.

Now blend the tuna, yogurt, 1 egg, mayonnaise and a tablespoon of capers with half the previous mixture. When ready pour into a bowl and add the remaining parsley mixture. Finally gently fold in the whipped cream.

When the rice is *al dente*, drain and rinse under cold running water. Pour the sauce over and mix. Add the remaining capers and remix. Place on a serving plate, garnish with slices of egg and serve cold. This makes an excellent dish for the summer.

Time: 30 minutes *Serves 4*

Rice Mould with Tomato and Mozzarella
1 Put onion and garlic in a large pan and pour on wine. Cook for 4 minutes.
2 Sprinkle the rice on to the onion, stir, then gradually add the stock, stirring until the rice is almost cooked.
3 Add the herbs. Mix well, adding the Parmesan cheese during the mixing.
4 Place half this mixture in the dish; cover with tomatoes and cheese.
5 Cover with the remaining rice mixture and cook in the oven. Turn out and garnish as liked. Parsley, basil leaves or sliced tomatoes may be used.

Rice Mould with Tomato and Mozzarella

SFORMATO DI RISO AGLI AROMI

Ingredients	Metric/Imperial	American
chopped parsley	1 tablespoon	1 tablespoon
chopped basil	1 teaspoon	1 teaspoon
garlic clove	1	1
onion	1	1
white wine	125 ml/4 fl oz	$\frac{1}{2}$ cup
risotto rice	350 g/12 oz	$1\frac{2}{3}$ cups
stock	1 litre/1$\frac{3}{4}$ pints	1 quart
Parmesan cheese, grated	25 g/1 oz	$\frac{1}{4}$ cup
salt and pepper		
ripe tomatoes	2	2
Mozzarella cheese	1	1
Tomato Sauce (page 26)		

Chop the herbs and garlic together finely, slice the onion. Place the onion in a large pan with the wine, cook for 4 minutes, sprinkle in the rice, stir and allow wine to evaporate. Add the hot stock gradually and stir until the rice is *al dente*. Add the herbs and garlic.

Add the Parmesan cheese. Pour half the risotto into a non-stick cake pan or ring mould, season well. Cover with slices of peeled tomato and Mozzarella cheese, sprinkle with salt and cover with the remaining risotto.

Place in a moderately hot oven (200 c, 400 f, gas 6) for about 20 minutes. Turn out on to a warm serving dish and serve at once.

Tomato Sauce (see page 26) may be served separately.

Time: 40 minutes   *Serves 4*

Rice with Gorgonzola and Fontina Cheese

RISO CON FONTINA E GORGONZOLA

Ingredients	Metric/Imperial	American
long-grain rice	350 g/12 oz	1⅔ cups
salt and pepper		
Fontina cheese	150 g/5 oz	5 ounces
Gorgonzola cheese	150 g/5 oz	5 ounces
milk	450 ml/¾ pint	2 cups
butter	75 g/3 oz	6 tablespoons
plain (all-purpose) flour	40 g/1½ oz	6 tablespoons
single (thin) cream	175 ml/6 fl oz	¾ cup

Boil the rice in salted water, drain when *al dente*.

Remove the rind from the Fontina cheese, cut into cubes and place in a bowl. Cut the Gorgonzola cheese into very small pieces. Put the milk in a small pan over a low heat.

Soften two-thirds of butter in a pan, add the flour, stirring well, then gradually add the hot milk, stirring continuously to make a sauce. Gradually add the small pieces of Gorgonzola, season with a pinch of salt and pepper. Remove from the heat and stir in the cream.

Add the drained rice to the bowl with the cubed Fontina cheese and mix with the remaining butter.

Make a layer of rice in a buttered ovenproof dish, cover with one-third of the Gorgonzola sauce, add another layer of rice followed by half the remaining Gorgonzola sauce, repeat for the third time.

Place the dish in a moderate oven (180 C, 350 F, gas 4) for 10 minutes, then serve immediately. For best results the rice needs to be very hot but the sauce on the top should not brown.

Time: 40 minutes　　　　　*Serves 4*

Rice and Leeks

RISO E PORRI

Ingredients	Metric/Imperial	American
leeks	450 g/1 lb	1 pound
cooked ham	75 g/3 oz	3 ounces
salt and pepper		
milk	125 ml/4 fl oz	½ cup
risotto rice	350 g/12 oz	1⅔ cups
stock	1.25 litres/2¼ pints	1¼ quarts
Parmesan cheese, grated	25 g/1 oz	¼ cup

Trim the leeks, remove the coarse external leaves and cut into rings. Wash under running water. Chop the ham and put in a pan with the leeks. Season with salt and pepper, pour in the milk and simmer gently until the leeks are tender and the milk has dried up.

Add the rice and a ladleful of the hot stock. Cook and stir, adding more stock as it becomes absorbed, until the rice is tender but still moist. Sprinkle with Parmesan cheese and serve hot.

Variations: Add lots of chopped parsley, or 2 chopped cooked potatoes.

Time: 35 minutes　　　　　*Serves 4*

Chicken Liver and Rice Soup

MINESTRA DI RISO E FEGATINI CON PREZZEMOLO E UOVA

Ingredients	Metric/Imperial	American
chicken stock	1.25 litres/2¼ pints	1¼ quarts
onion	½	½
butter	25 g/1 oz	2 tablespoons
chicken livers	150 g/5 oz	5 ounces
sage leaves	3	3
salt and pepper		
brandy	1 tablespoon	1 tablespoon
large potato	1	1
long-grain rice	150 g/5 oz	⅔ cup
chopped parsley	1 tablespoon	1 tablespoon
eggs	2	2
Parmesan cheese, grated	2 tablespoons	3 tablespoons

Put the stock in a pan over a very low heat.

Chop the onion finely. Melt the butter in a large pan, add the onion and cook over a low heat until transparent. Add the chicken livers and sage leaves. Allow to absorb flavour, then turn up the heat, season with salt and pepper and sprinkle in the brandy. Remove the chicken livers and chop coarsely.

Dice the potato and add it to the pan. Stir for a few minutes, then pour in the hot stock. Bring to the boil and drop in the chicken livers. When the stock returns to a full boil trickle in the rice and simmer gently for 15 minutes. Taste and adjust seasoning if necessary.

Put the parsley in a bowl with the eggs and Parmesan cheese and beat together. Trickle into the soup, whisking vigorously, until the egg floats in strands. Remove the sage leaves and serve.

Time: 45 minutes　　　　　*Serves 4*

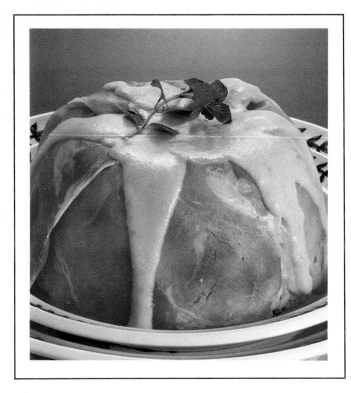

Rice Mould with Cheese Sauce and Ham

Rice Mould with Cheese Sauce and Ham

SFORMATO DI RISO CON PROSCIUTTO E
FONDUTA

Ingredients	Metric/Imperial	American
For the cheese sauce:		
Fontina cheese	350 g/12 oz	$\frac{3}{4}$ pound
milk	200 ml/7 fl oz	scant 1 cup
butter	1 tablespoon	1 tablespoon
egg yolks	4	4
salt and white pepper		
For the mould:		
long-grain rice	350 g/12 oz	$1\frac{2}{3}$ cups
salt and white pepper		
butter, melted	75 g/3 oz	6 tablespoons
grated nutmeg	$\frac{1}{4}$ teaspoon	$\frac{1}{4}$ teaspoon
Parmesan cheese, grated	2 tablespoons	3 tablespoons
oil	1 teaspoon	1 teaspoon
thin slices of smoked ham	100 g/4 oz	$\frac{1}{4}$ pound

Slice the Fontina cheese thinly, put in a bowl and cover with the milk. Cover and leave for 2 hours.

To cook the sauce first melt the butter in the top of a double pan set over a low heat. Strain the slices of Fontina cheese, reserving the milk, add to the pan and whisk until stringy. Increase the heat a little and beat hard, adding the milk. Beat the egg yolks lightly with a pinch of salt and pour into the pan. Mix rapidly and cook, stirring, until the mixture is thick and smooth. Season with white pepper and remove from the heat, but keep warm.

Cook the rice in lightly salted boiling water. Drain and return to the pan, stir in the melted butter, nutmeg and Parmesan cheese. Brush a ring mould with oil and press the rice tightly into it. Cook in a moderately hot oven (200 C, 400 F, gas 6) for 10 minutes.

Turn the mould out on a heated serving dish and cover with the slices of ham. Pour the cheese sauce in the centre and over the top. Serve at once.

Time: 1 hour + 2 hours: soaking   *Serves 4*

Rice and Tripe

RISO E TRIPPE

Ingredients	Metric/Imperial	American
boiled tripe	350 g/12 oz	$\frac{3}{4}$ pound
onion	1	1
carrot	1	1
celery stalk	1	1
garlic clove	1	1
sprig of rosemary	1	1
olive oil	4 tablespoons	$\frac{1}{3}$ cup
beef stock	1.5 litres/2$\frac{1}{2}$ pints	1$\frac{1}{2}$ quarts
salt and pepper		
bouquet garni	1	1
long-grain rice	250 g/9 oz	1$\frac{1}{3}$ cups
Asiago cheese	40 g/1$\frac{1}{2}$ oz	1$\frac{1}{2}$ ounces
chopped parsley	1 tablespoon	1 tablespoon

Wash the tripe, drain, dry and cut into strips.

Chop the cleaned vegetables together finely with the garlic and rosemary.

Heat the oil in a large pan over a low heat and cook the chopped mixture for 5 minutes until soft. Add the tripe, 600 ml/1 pint/2$\frac{1}{2}$ cups of stock, salt, pepper and bouquet garni.

Bring to the boil, cover with a lid and turn the heat down immediately so that the mixture simmers gently for 1$\frac{1}{2}$ hours, stirring frequently. If necessary add a little boiling stock during the cooking time. When the tripe is tender add the remaining hot stock and sprinkle in the rice.

Cook the mixture, stirring constantly, until the rice is *al dente*. Taste and adjust the seasoning, add the cheese, mix well and serve on heated plates sprinkled with parsley.

Time: 2$\frac{3}{4}$ hours   *Serves 4*

Rice with Onion Sauce

RISO CON SALSA DI CIPOLLE

Ingredients	Metric/Imperial	American
long-grain rice	350 g/12 oz	$1\frac{2}{3}$ cups
salt and pepper		
chicken stock	450 ml/$\frac{3}{4}$ pint	2 cups
medium-sized onions	4	4
butter	75 g/3 oz	6 tablespoons
dry white wine	2 tablespoons	3 tablespoons
plain (all-purpose) flour	1 tablespoon	1 tablespoon
single (thin) cream	6 tablespoons	$\frac{1}{2}$ cup
grated nutmeg	$\frac{1}{4}$ teaspoon	$\frac{1}{4}$ teaspoon
Parmesan cheese, grated	2 tablespoons	3 tablespoons

Cook the rice in boiling salted water. Place the stock in a pan over a low heat.

Chop the onions finely. Melt two-thirds of the butter in a large pan, add the onion and cook for a few minutes over medium heat until golden. Season with salt and pepper and add the wine. When the wine has evaporated sprinkle in the flour, stir and allow to colour slightly.

Gradually add the hot stock, stirring constantly, until the sauce is smooth and creamy. Leave to simmer gently for 15 minutes, then purée in a blender or food processor with the cream and nutmeg.

Mix the cooked rice with the sauce, put in a heated serving dish and stir in the remaining chopped butter and Parmesan cheese.

Time: 30 minutes   *Serves 4*

Baked Rice

RISO ARROSTO

Ingredients	Metric/Imperial	American
dried mushrooms	25 g/1 oz	1 ounce
artichoke	1	1
onion	$\frac{1}{2}$	$\frac{1}{2}$
frozen peas	200 g/7 oz	7 ounces
stock	1.25 litres/$2\frac{1}{4}$ pints	$1\frac{1}{4}$ quarts
canned plum tomatoes	150 g/5 oz	5 ounces
salt and pepper		
risotto rice	350 g/12 oz	$1\frac{2}{3}$ cups
Parmesan cheese, grated	25 g/1 oz	$\frac{1}{4}$ cup

Soak the mushrooms in warm water for 20 minutes.

Meanwhile remove the stalk and tough outer leaves from the artichoke. Cut the points off the inner leaves and remove the bristly choke. Chop the base and inner leaves. Chop the onion and put in a non-stick pan over a medium heat until golden. Add the peas, artichoke and a ladleful of the hot stock. Simmer for a few minutes.

Drain the mushrooms and chop finely. Add them to the other vegetables in the pan together with the chopped tomatoes. Season with salt and pepper, cover and cook over a very low heat for 10 minutes.

Trickle in the rice and add the remaining stock a ladleful at a time; cook, stirring frequently, until all the stock is absorbed and the rice is *al dente*.

Remove from the heat, put in a shallow flameproof serving dish, sprinkle with Parmesan cheese and put under a hot grill (broiler) for 3–4 minutes to brown the top. Serve at once.

Time: 50 minutes + 20 minutes: soaking   *Serves 4*

Creamy Rice with Vegetables

RISO CREMOSO ALLE VERDURE

Ingredients	Metric/Imperial	American
onion	$\frac{1}{2}$	$\frac{1}{2}$
celery stalk	1	1
medium-sized courgettes (zucchini)	2	2
carrot	1	1
tomato	1	1
oil	125 ml/4 fl oz	$\frac{1}{2}$ cup
risotto rice	350 g/12 oz	$1\frac{2}{3}$ cups
salt		
stock	1 litre/$1\frac{3}{4}$ pints	1 quart
Parmesan cheese, grated	25 g/1 oz	$\frac{1}{4}$ cup
chopped parsley	1 tablespoon	1 tablespoon
chopped basil	1 tablespoon	1 tablespoon

Finely chop the onion, celery, courgettes and carrot. Peel the tomato, deseed and chop. Heat the oil in a large heavy pan, add the vegetables and cook for a few minutes over a high heat.

Add the rice and a pinch of salt. Stir in a ladleful of the hot stock and cook, stirring, until the rice begins to swell and the stock has been absorbed. Continue adding stock, stirring constantly, until the rice is *al dente*.

Remove from the heat and add the Parmesan cheese, chopped parsley and basil. Stir well, cover and leave to rest for a few minutes before serving.

Time: 30 minutes   *Serves 6*

Party Rice

Party Rice

TIMBALLO DI RISO DELLA FESTA

Ingredients	Metric/Imperial	American
rice	450 g/1 lb	2⅓ cups
butter	120 g/4½ oz	½ cup + 1 tablespoon
grated nutmeg	¼ teaspoon	¼ teaspoon
Parmesan cheese, grated	50 g/2 oz	½ cup
eggs	2	2
Gruyère cheese, grated	25 g/1 oz	¼ cup
salt and pepper		
chopped basil	1 teaspoon	1 teaspoon
garlic clove	½	½
smoked cooked ham	150 g/5 oz	5 ounces
Mozzarella cheese	150 g/5 oz	5 ounces

Boil the rice in salted water until *al dente*, drain well, place in a bowl and dress with 75 g/3 oz/6 tablespoons melted butter, nutmeg and Parmesan cheese.

Preheat the oven to 180 C, 350 F, gas 4.

Beat the eggs in a bowl with the grated Gruyère cheese, salt and pepper, chopped basil and the crushed garlic, mix well.

Melt 25 g/1 oz/2 tablespoons of butter in a large shallow pan 23 cm/9 in in diameter and pour in the egg mixture. Allow to set like an omelette, turning once to cook on the other side.

Butter a round mould 25 cm/10 in in diameter. Line the bottom with rice, arrange half the ham on top and then place the omelette over this, followed by slices of Mozzarella and the remaining ham. Cover with the remaining rice.

Dot with butter and place in a moderate oven for 15 minutes. Serve immediately when piping hot.

Time: 45 minutes　　　　　　　　　　　　　　*Serves 6*

Rice with Mushrooms and Ham

GRATIN DI RISO CON FUNGHI E PROSCIUTTO COTTO

Ingredients	Metric/Imperial	American
mushrooms	450 g/1 lb	1 pound
lemon	½	½
butter	120 g/4½ oz	½ cup + 1 tablespoon
garlic clove	1	1
stock cubes	2	2
salt and pepper		
milk	50 ml/2 fl oz	¼ cup
chopped parsley	1 tablespoon	1 tablespoon
oil	2 tablespoons	3 tablespoons
onion	1	1
long-grain rice	450 g/1 lb	2⅓ cups
dry white wine	50 ml/2 fl oz	¼ cup
single (thin) cream	4 tablespoons	⅓ cup
Parmesan cheese, grated	50 g/2 oz	½ cup
cooked ham	150 g/5 oz	5 ounces

Wipe the mushrooms and steep in 225 ml/8 fl oz/1 cup of water with the juice of ½ lemon for 5 minutes. Drain, dry and slice finely.

Melt 50 g/2 oz/¼ cup of the butter in a heavy deep pan over a medium heat, add the crushed garlic and when golden add the sliced mushrooms. Crumble the stock cube into 1 litre/1¾ pints/1 quart of boiling water and add a little pepper. Pour over the mushrooms 225 ml/8 fl oz/1 cup of the stock and cook gently, adding a few spoons of milk from time to time. When the mushrooms are cooked sprinkle in the chopped parsley and remove from the heat.

Melt 25 g/1 oz/2 tablespoons butter over a medium heat with the oil, add the chopped onion and when golden sprinkle in the rice. Cook for a few minutes, then moisten with the wine. Allow to evaporate, then gradually add the hot stock until the rice is *al dente*. Add boiling water if necessary. Stir in 25 g/1 oz/2 tablespoons butter, the cream and half the Parmesan cheese.

Butter an ovenproof dish, put in a layer of risotto and cover with half the cooked ham cut into fine strips. Add half the mushrooms and cover with the remaining risotto. Arrange the remaining ham, mushrooms and remaining Parmesan cheese on the top. Dot with remaining butter and place in a moderately hot oven (200 C, 400 F, gas 6) until the top is crisp and golden.

Time: 1 hour and 10 minutes   *Serves 6*

Rice and Chicken Bake

TORTINO DI RISO E POLLO

Ingredients	Metric/Imperial	American
butter	75 g/3 oz	6 tablespoons
bacon	75 g/3 oz	3 ounces
lean veal	225 g/8 oz	½ pound
mushrooms	100 g/4 oz	¼ pound
canned plum tomatoes	400 g/14 oz	14 ounces
salt and pepper		
chicken livers	25 g/1 oz	1 ounce
onion	1	1
risotto rice	450 g/1 lb	1⅔ cups
stock	2 litres/3½ pints	2 quarts
Parmesan cheese, grated	50 g/2 oz	½ cup
oil	1½ tablespoons	2 tablespoons
chicken breast	600 g/1¼ lb	1¼ pounds
fresh breadcrumbs	2 tablespoons	3 tablespoons
cooked ham	225 g/8 oz	½ pound

Melt one-third of the butter in a large pan over a medium heat. Derind the bacon and cut into dice, cut the veal into tiny cubes and add both to the butter.

Wipe the mushrooms, dice finely, add to the meat and leave to cook for 10 minutes. Add the mashed plum tomatoes, salt and pepper and cook over a low heat with the lid on for 30 minutes. Add the washed, chopped chicken livers and continue cooking for a further 10 minutes.

Meanwhile melt the remaining butter in a large pan over a low heat, add the chopped onion and allow to soften for 4 minutes. Add the rice, then the stock a little at a time, stirring constantly until *al dente*. When cooked stir in the Parmesan cheese.

Preheat the oven to 200 C, 400 F, gas 6.

Slice the chicken breast thinly. Heat the oil over a medium heat in a shallow pan and fry the chicken on both sides.

Oil a large ovenproof dish, sprinkle with breadcrumbs and add half the risotto. Spread a little sauce over the top and cover with slices of chicken and cooked ham. Finish with the remaining risotto. Keep the remaining sauce hot.

Sprinkle the surface with breadcrumbs and place in a moderately hot oven for 15 minutes. Remove the dish from the oven, allow to rest for a few minutes and turn on to a large heated serving place. Cover the dish with the remaining sauce and serve hot.

Time: 1 hour   *Serves 8*

ing. Mix well until the ingredients are evenly distributed.

Butter an ovenproof bowl, sprinkle with breadcrumbs and pack in half the rice mixture. Add the ham cut into matchsticks, cover with the remaining rice and place in a moderate oven for 20 minutes.

Turn out on to a serving plate and serve immediately.

Time: 45 minutes   *Serves 4*

Savoury Rice Cake

TORTA SALATA DI RISO

Ingredients	Metric/Imperial	American
saffron	1 teaspoon	1 teaspoon
beef stock	2 litres/3½ pints	2 quarts
medium-sized onion	1	1
butter	75 g/3 oz	6 tablespoons
easy-cook rice	600 g/1¼ lb	scant 3 cups
dry white wine	125 ml/4 fl oz	½ cup
Parmesan cheese, grated	40 g/1½ oz	3 tablespoons
garlic clove	1	1
mushrooms	50 g/2 oz	2 ounces
canned plum tomatoes	400 g/14 oz	14 ounces
chopped parsley	1 tablespoon	1 tablespoon
Mozzarella cheese	350 g/12 oz	¾ pound

Soak the saffron in 50 ml/2 fl oz/¼ cup of the hot stock.

Chop the onion finely and place half in a large deep heavy pan with half the melted butter; cook over a low heat for 3 minutes. Raise the heat, add the rice and cook until golden, mixing with a wooden spoon. Moisten with the wine and when this has evaporated gradually add 225 ml/8 fl oz/1 cup of hot stock stirring until it is absorbed. Continue adding stock in this way, and at the end of the cooking time add the saffron mixture. Stir in the Parmesan cheese and seasoning.

Place the remaining onion and butter in a small pan with the crushed garlic. After 3 minutes add the chopped mushrooms and half the crushed tomatoes. Adjust the seasoning to taste and cook the sauce for about 15 minutes. Add the remaining crushed tomato, cook for a further 15 minutes, then add the chopped parsley at the end.

Grease an ovenproof cake pan and put in half the risotto; cover with mushroom mixture and Mozzarella slices. Cover with the remaining rice. Level off the surface and place in a hot oven (220 C, 425 F, gas 7) to brown for 15 minutes. Turn out and serve hot.

Time: 1 hour   *Serves 8*

Rice Mould with Eggs and Parsley

Rice Mould with Eggs and Parsley

BUDINO DI RISO CON UOVA E PREZZEMOLO

Ingredients	Metric/Imperial	American
long-grain rice	400 g/14 oz	2 cups
salt		
butter	50 g/2 oz	¼ cup
egg yolks	4	4
ground nutmeg	¼ teaspoon	¼ teaspoon
chopped parsley	2 tablespoons	2 tablespoons
Parmesan cheese, grated	25 g/1 oz	¼ cup
Gruyère cheese, grated	25 g/1 oz	¼ cup
freshly ground black pepper		
dried breadcrumbs	2 tablespoons	3 tablespoons
cooked smoked ham	100 g/4 oz	¼ pound

Preheat the oven to 180 C, 350 F, gas 4.

Cook the rice in salted boiling water until *al dente*, drain and tip into a bowl. Add the butter cut into small pieces, then stir in the egg yolks, nutmeg, chopped parsley, Parmesan cheese, Gruyère cheese and season-

Rice with Cumin

RISOTTO AL CUMO

Ingredients	Metric/Imperial	American
onion	1	1
butter	40 g/1½ oz	3 tablespoons
oil	3 tablespoons	scant ¼ cup
bunch of fresh cumin	1	1
dry white wine	125 ml/4 fl oz	½ cup
beef stock	1 litre/1¾ pints	1 quart
risotto rice	350 g/12 oz	1⅔ cups
salt and pepper		
Asiago cheese, grated	2 tablespoons	3 tablespoons

Finely chop the onion. Heat half the butter and the oil over a medium heat in a pan, cook the onion until golden, then add the chopped cumin. Moisten with wine and a little hot stock and leave the liquid to evaporate for a few minutes.

Sprinkle in the rice, stir with care, still on a medium heat, and allow to absorb the juices.

Continue cooking by adding more stock a little at a time. Adjust the seasoning and stir with a wooden spoon until the rice is *al dente*.

Add the remaining butter and the cheese. Stir well before serving.

Time: 30 minutes   *Serves 4*

Cumin is a herb the seeds of which are used to produce a liqueur called kümmel in Germany. It is widely used in confectionery. For the risotto the cumin leaves are used. This herb grows in the springtime on the high slopes of Asiago in northern Italy. If cumin is not available fennel can be used as a replacement, obviously changing the flavour of the dish. Alternatively use ¼ teaspoon of dried cumin.

White Rice with Eggs

RISO BIANCO CON UOVA

Ingredients	Metric/Imperial	American
long-grain rice	350 g/12 oz	1⅔ cups
salt		
eggs	4	4
chopped parsley	1 tablespoon	1 tablespoon
grated nutmeg	¼ teaspoon	¼ teaspoon
single (thin) cream	50 ml/2 fl oz	¼ cup
lemon	½	½

Cook the rice in salted boiling water until *al dente*. Drain and cool under running water, drain again and put in a serving dish.

Hard-boil (cook) the eggs for 8 minutes, shell and reserve 1 egg. Mash remaining eggs with a fork. Mix with the parsley and add to the rice.

Season with a little salt and nutmeg and add the cream mixed with lemon juice, stir well.

Sprinkle with sieved hard-boiled (cooked) egg and serve lightly chilled.

Time: 30 minutes   *Serves 4*

Country Rice

RISOTTO ALLA RUSTICA

Ingredients	Metric/Imperial	American
shallots	2	2
small onion	1	1
sprig of rosemary	1	1
chopped parsley	1 tablespoon	1 tablespoon
chopped marjoram	¼ teaspoon	¼ teaspoon
basil leaves	4	4
garlic clove	1	1
oil	2 tablespoons	3 tablespoons
butter	40 g/1½ oz	3 tablespoons
risotto rice	350 g/12 oz	1⅔ cups
dry white wine	50 ml/2 fl oz	¼ cup
plum tomatoes	4	4
stock	900 ml/1½ pints	3¾ cups
salt and freshly ground black pepper		
single (thin) cream	2 tablespoons	3 tablespoons

Clean and chop the vegetables and herbs; crush the garlic. Heat the oil and butter (reserving 1 teaspoon) in a large pan over a low heat, add the vegetables and herbs. Simmer for 5 minutes on a medium heat.

Sprinkle in the rice, allow to turn golden, moisten with the wine and allow the liquid to evaporate. Add the peeled plum tomatoes mashed with a fork.

Mix well and continue to cook by stirring and adding the boiling stock gradually. Taste and adjust the seasoning if necessary.

As the rice becomes *al dente*, add the butter, and plenty of pepper. Stir in the cream before serving hot.

Time: 30 minutes   *Serves 4*

Rice Salad with Green Mayonnaise

RISO IN INSALATA CON MAIONESE VERDE

Ingredients	Metric/Imperial	American
capers	2 tablespoons	3 tablespoons
pickled gherkins	25 g/1 oz	1 ounce
green olives	50 g/2 oz	$\frac{1}{3}$ cup
salt and pepper		
tuna in oil	100 g/4 oz	$\frac{1}{4}$ pound
long-grain rice	300 g/11 oz	$1\frac{1}{2}$ cups
cooked chopped spinach	100 g/4 oz	$\frac{1}{2}$ cup
basil	$\frac{1}{2}$ teaspoon	$\frac{1}{2}$ teaspoon
bunch of parsley	1	1
mayonnaise	225 ml/8 fl oz	1 cup
lemon	1	1
olive oil	6 tablespoons	$\frac{1}{2}$ cup
lettuce leaves		
sprigs of parsley		
slices of cucumber		

Rinse the capers and gherkins, chop with the olives and put in a bowl with a little salt and pepper. Mash the tuna fish and mix all the ingredients together in a bowl.

Boil the rice in salted water, drain when *al dente* and rinse under cold water. Drain well again and mix with the other ingredients.

Purée the spinach in a blender or food processor with the basil, half the parsley, mayonnaise, lemon juice, oil, salt and pepper.

Arrange the rice mixture on a bed of lettuce leaves in a serving dish and cover the top with the smooth green mayonnaise. Garnish with sprigs of parsley and cucumber slices.

Time: 1 hour　　　　　　　　　　　　　　*Serves 4*

Saffron Rice Ring

TIMBALLO DI RISO GIALLO

Ingredients	Metric/Imperial	American
For the sauce:		
shallot	1	1
butter	25 g/1 oz	2 tablespoons
cubed veal	350 g/12 oz	$\frac{3}{4}$ pound
mushrooms	225 g/8 oz	$\frac{1}{2}$ pound
salt and pepper		
stock cube	1	1
milk	4 tablespoons	$\frac{1}{3}$ cup
cream	100 ml/3½ fl oz	scant $\frac{1}{2}$ cup
saffron strands	1 teaspoon	1 teaspoon
onion	1	1
oil	2 tablespoons	3 tablespoons
butter	50 g/2 oz	$\frac{1}{4}$ cup
risotto rice	300 g/11 oz	$1\frac{1}{2}$ cups
dry white wine	50 ml/2 fl oz	$\frac{1}{4}$ cup
stock	900 ml/1½ pints	$3\frac{3}{4}$ cups
Parmesan cheese, grated	25 g/1 oz	$\frac{1}{4}$ cup
chopped parsley	1 tablespoon	1 tablespoon

First make the sauce: chop the shallot finely, heat half the butter in a pan over a medium heat, add the shallot and cook until golden. Add the cubed veal, allow to brown, turning from time to time, then add the sliced mushrooms. Stir to mix the ingredients for a few minutes, season well.

Crumble the stock cube into the milk and mix well with 600 ml/1 pint/2½ cups boiling water.

Add the milk and stock to the veal mixture and cook until the meat is tender. Add the cream.

Dissolve the saffron in 50 ml/2 fl oz/¼ cup of hot water.

Finely chop the onion, heat the oil and butter (reserving 1 tablespoon) in a deep pan and cook until golden on a medium heat.

Sprinkle in the rice, stir for a moment and allow to turn pale golden. Moisten with wine and allow to evaporate then add boiling stock a little at a time until the rice is *al dente*. A few minutes before turning off the heat add the saffron and the Parmesan cheese.

Butter a ring mould, add the prepared risotto, press down firmly with the back of a wet spoon, dot with a few knobs of butter and place in a moderate oven (180 c, 350 F, gas 4) for 15 minutes.

Turn the risotto on to a heated serving plate and fill the centre with the veal and mushroom sauce. Sprinkle with chopped parsley and serve immediately.

Time: 1¼ hours　　　　　　　　　　　　*Serves 4*

Saffron Rice Ring

Orange and White Rice Mould

Orange and White Rice Mould

TORTINO ARANCIONE E BIANCO

Ingredients	Metric/Imperial	American
stock	1 litre/2½ pints	1½ quarts
new carrots	600 g/1¼ lb	1¼ pounds
butter	120 g/4½ oz	½ cup + 1 tablespoon
oil	3 tablespoons	scant ¼ cup
garlic clove	1	1
bay leaves	2	2
salt and pepper		
Marsala wine	1½ tablespoons	2 tablespoons
milk	4 tablespoons	⅓ cup
onion	1	1
long-grain rice	450 g/1 lb	2⅓ cups
Parmesan cheese, grated	50 g/2 oz	½ cup
parsley sprigs	8	8

Put the stock in a pan over a medium heat.

Trim, scrub and dry the carrots. Melt half the butter with half the oil in a medium-sized pan, add the crushed garlic and fry over medium heat until golden. Discard the garlic and add the carrots and bay leaves. Leave for a few minutes to absorb flavour, then add a pinch of salt and pepper. Moisten with half the Marsala and when it has evaporated add a little of the hot stock and reduce the heat. Cook for about 10 minutes, adding more stock and milk at intervals to prevent the carrots from drying.

Melt 50 g/2 oz/¼ cup of the remaining butter with the remaining oil in a heavy pan. Add the chopped onion and fry over medium heat until golden. Mix in the rice, moisten with the remaining Marsala and leave until this has evaporated. Add the boiling stock a little at a time and cook, stirring frequently, until the rice is *al dente*.

Purèe half the carrots in a blender or food processor or sieve them (keep the remainder hot).

Add the Parmesan cheese to the cooked rice, mix together and divide into two equal portions. Add the carrot purée to one portion and mix until uniformly orange in colour.

Brush a ring mould with the remaining butter and put half the orange-coloured risotto in the base, followed by half the white risotto. Repeat the layers. Heat the mould in a moderately hot oven (200 C, 400 F, gas 6) for 10 minutes.

Turn the mould out on to a heated circular serving dish. Fill the centre with the hot carrots and cooking juices, discarding the bay leaves. Garnish with parsley.

Time: 1 hour 10 minutes　　　　　　　　　　*Serves 6*

PASTA

*Plain or with the addition of egg, spinach or
tomato flavouring, pasta is made into many
varied shapes and many of these shapes are
known by different names throughout the various
regions of Italy. Fresh pasta is not quite as
difficult to make as it may seem and most cooks
who can tackle pastry can make pasta.
However the convenience of dried pasta in the
store cupboard is a boon to every household.
Pasta is now considered to be an excellent food to
include in a healthy diet providing the sauces
served with it are made of fresh vegetables and
moderation is shown when adding cheese.
Pasta made from wholemeal flour is also
gaining popularity in many countries.
From this chapter you will learn to cook the
many traditional pasta dishes that are so typical
of Italian cooking.*

Pasta

Fresh pasta Making your own pasta is rather like making bread; with a little practice it is not difficult, and the results are immensely rewarding. A pasta machine makes the job quicker, but is by no means essential; all it takes is a long rolling pin (at least 70 cm/28 in) and a large clean work surface.

Good fresh pasta has a better flavour than dried, and is best served with plain or delicate sauces. It is possible to buy the most popular – ribbon pasta, ravioli and lasagne – from Italian food shops and large supermarkets. Fresh pasta cooks much more quickly than dried.

Dried pasta Commercially made dried pasta – *pasta asciutta* – has the advantage that it can be stored ready for use. It comes in an enormous variety of shapes and goes well with meat and sauces with a more robust flavour. Those enriched with egg are particularly good. All good pasta is made from hard durum wheat.

Pasta shapes If you cannot obtain exactly the pasta recommended in a recipe simply substitute another but make sure it is about the same size. Shell pasta is particularly good for holding sauces made with meat or chopped vegetables.

Quantities and cooking How much pasta to cook depends very much on appetite and occasion. Allow 75 g/3 oz/ounces per person as a basic amount for dried pasta; 125 g/4 oz/¼ pound for fresh.

Cook all types of pasta in a large pan. Fill two-thirds full with lightly salted water and bring to the boil. Add a few drops of oil to prevent the pasta from sticking together. Stir with a fork to separate the pieces. Keep the water at a good rolling boil, do not cover the pan, and drain when cooked.

With dried pasta this will be in about 6 minutes from the time the water returns to the boil for ribbon types such as fettucine, 12 minutes for spaghetti and 15 minutes for rigatoni or shells. With fresh pasta allow no more than 3–5 minutes for plain; 8–15 minutes for filled (such a ravioli).

The pasta will then be tender but still have some bite; this is known in Italy as *al dente* and the expression has been used throughout this book.

If the pasta is not needed straight away rinse in cold water to stop it continuing to cook.

Egg Tagliatelle

TAGLIATELLE

Ingredients	Metric/Imperial	American
plain (all-purpose) flour	400 g/14 oz	3½ cups
eggs	3	3
oil	1 tablespoon	1 tablespoon

Sift the flour in a heap on to a work surface, preferably of marble or wood. Make a well or indentation in the centre of the flour.

Break the eggs into the centre, add the oil, mix with a fork and work the dough with the hands until perfectly smooth and elastic. Roll out with a rolling pin, or use a pasta maker, until very thin.

Leave the pasta to dry, sprinkle with flour, then roll up the sheet of pasta gently. With a sharp knife cut into thin strips then shake the strips to loosen the tagliatelle. Sprinkle with flour and shake again.

Cook as required (see fresh pasta above).

Time: 30 minutes + 1 hour: drying　　　*Serves 4–6*

Green Tagliatelle

TAGLIATELLE VERDI

Ingredients	Metric/Imperial	American
plain (all-purpose) flour	400 g/14 oz	3½ cups
eggs	3	3
oil	1 tablespoon	1 tablespoon
spinach	150 g/5 oz	5 ounces

Cook the spinach (fresh or frozen) and squeeze out all the moisture by pressing in a sieve or colander with the back of a spoon. If possible purée in a vegetable mill, blender or food processor. (Drained, canned or puréed spinach can be used.)

Prepare the dough as for tagliatelle (see opposite), adding the eggs and oil together with the spinach, and roll out as instructed.

Tagliatelle are the most popular form of home-made pasta. In Rome the name often changes to fettucine.

Time: 30 minutes + 1 hour: drying　　　*Serves 4–6*

How to make fresh pasta

Sift the flour on to a work surface and make a large well in the centre. Break in the eggs, then take a fork and beat them lightly, gradually drawing in flour until the eggs are no longer liquid.

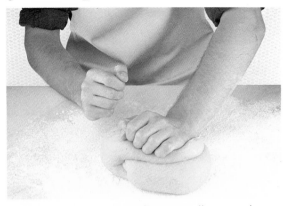

Continue mixing with the fingers until a smooth dough has formed. Knead it into a sausage shape using the heel of the hand, then fold in the ends and begin again. Continue for about 10 minutes until smooth and shiny. Leave to rest, covered.

Knead the dough into a sausage and divide in half. Knead one half into a ball. Roll it out thinly, using a long rolling pin and working away from you. Make sure it is of even thickness all over.

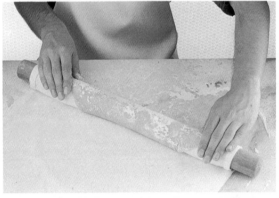

Continue rolling until the dough is so thin it is almost transparent. Put a clean warm tea towel or sheet of cling film on top and roll up both together. Leave to rest for 5 minutes, then unroll; remove the towel or film.

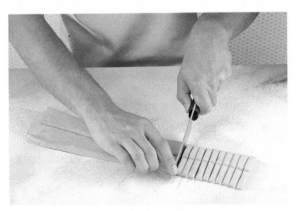

Roll the pasta in towards the centre from two opposite sides, working in 5 cm/2 in rolls. With a very sharp knife, cut across the rolls as shown to make thin strips – just under 1 cm/½ in wide.

Slide the knife blade under each strip, lift it up and the pasta will unfold down each side. Put the finished pasta on a clean tea towel, well spread out, and leave to dry for about 10 minutes. Repeat with the second piece of dough.

A selection of fresh home-made pasta: plain and spinach-flavoured tagliatelli in colander; from left to right fettucine, gnocchi, ravioli and tortellini

Tomato Tagliatelle

TAGLIATELLE ROSSE

Ingredients	Metric/Imperial	American
plain (all-purpose) flour	400 g/14 oz	3½ cups
eggs	3	3
oil	1 tablespoon	1 tablespoon
tomato paste	2 tablespoons	3 tablespoons

Sift the flour as for tagliatelle (see page 104).

Place the eggs, oil and tomato paste in the centre and continue to prepare and roll as for tagliatelle.

Time: 30 minutes + 1 hour: drying   Serves 4–6

Ravioli filled with Pumpkin

RAVIOLI DI ZUCCA

Ingredients	Metric/Imperial	American
For the pasta:		
plain (all-purpose) flour	450 g/1 lb	4 cups
eggs	3	3
water	4 tablespoons	6 tablespoons
oil	1 teaspoon	1 teaspoon
For the filling:		
pumpkin	2 kg/2 lb	2 pounds
salt		
eggs	2	2
Parmesan cheese, grated	75 g/3 oz	¾ cup
Amaretti biscuits	100 g/4 oz	¼ pound
fresh breadcrumbs	150 g/5 oz	2½ cups
sweet pickle	50 g/2 oz	2 ounces
grated nutmeg	¼ teaspoon	¼ teaspoon

Prepare the pasta (see tagliatelle recipe page 104). Roll out to obtain 2 large thin squares.

Prepare the filling: boil the pumpkin pieces with the skin in salted water. Quarter the cooked pieces and leave to cool down at room temperature. Remove the skin and leave to drain for 2 hours in a clean muslin cloth tied in a knot; squeeze after draining.

Pass the pumpkin through a sieve into a bowl, mix with the eggs, Parmesan cheese, crushed Amaretti, breadcrumbs, pickle, salt and nutmeg.

Arrange the mixture in tiny portions the size of a hazelnut on top of one square of pasta, brush round with a slightly dampened pastry brush and cover with the second. Seal around each knob with the fingers and cut with a pastry wheel.

Allow to dry for 1 hour at room temperature.

Cook in plenty of boiling salted water with a few drops of oil added for 8–12 minutes depending on size. Drain and serve.

Time: 35 minutes + 2 hours: draining;
1 hour: drying   Serves 4–6

Fresh Tagliatelle with Herbs

TAGLIATELLE ALL'UOVO CON ERBE AROMATICHE

Ingredients	Metric/Imperial	American
anchovy fillets	2	2
fresh tagliatelle pasta	450 g/1 lb	1 pound
salt and pepper		
sage leaves	2	2
chopped rosemary	¼ teaspoon	¼ teaspoon
chopped thyme	¼ teaspoon	¼ teaspoon
chopped marjoram	¼ teaspoon	¼ teaspoon
slice of onion	1	1
hard-boiled (cooked) eggs	2	2
butter	65 g/2½ oz	5 tablespoons
chopped oregano	¼ teaspoon	¼ teaspoon
Parmesan cheese, grated	2 tablespoons	3 tablespoons

Soak the anchovy fillets in a little milk to remove excess salt.

Cook the pasta in a large pan of lightly salted boiling water until just *al dente*.

Meanwhile finely chop the sage, rosemary, thyme and marjoram with the slice of onion and drained anchovies. Chop the eggs coarsely.

Put the butter in the top of a double boiler or in a bowl set over simmering water until softened. Add the chopped herb mixture and the eggs; season lightly with salt and pepper.

Drain the pasta, reserving a little of the cooking water. Combine with the herb sauce, add 2 tablespoons of the reserved water and a pinch of oregano; mix well. Serve with Parmesan cheese handed separately.

Time: 20 minutes   Serves 4

Tagliatelle with Broad Bean Sauce

Tagliatelle with Broad Bean Sauce

TAGLIATELLE CON SUGO DI FAVE

Ingredients	Metric/Imperial	American
spring onions	4	4
butter	65 g / 2½ oz	5 tablespoons
shelled broad (fava) beans	800 g / 1¾ lb	2⅓ cups
salt and pepper		
tagliatelle	350 g / 12 oz	¾ pound
Pecorino cheese	65 g / 2½ oz	2½ ounces
chopped parsley	1 tablespoon	1 tablespoon
smoked bacon	50 g / 2 oz	2 ounces

Chop the cleaned onions finely including the best of the green stems. Heat half the butter in a pan and cook the onions over a low heat for 3 minutes.

Add the peeled broad beans, allow to flavour for a few minutes, then add 225 ml / 8 fl oz / 1 cup of warm water and continue to cook for 25 minutes. Season well.

Bring a large pan with plenty of salted water to the boil. When the broad beans are cooked, place the pasta in the boiling water and leave to cook until *al dente* for approximately 8 minutes if dried and 4 minutes if using fresh pasta. Drain the pasta, dress with the remaining butter, crumbled Pecorino cheese and the parsley. Fry the bacon until crispy.

Divide into individual portions and top with bean sauce and crispy bacon pieces.

Time: 50 minutes   *Serves 4*

Tagliolini Flavoured with Cocoa

TAGLIOLINI AL GUSTO DI CACAO

Ingredients	Metric/Imperial	American
egg tagliolini	400 g / 14 oz	14 ounces
Ricotta cheese	200 g / 7 oz	7 ounces
butter	25 g / 1 oz	2 tablespoons
single (thin) cream	3 tablespoons	scant ¼ cup
cocoa powder	1 tablespoon	1 tablespoon
cinnamon	¼ teaspoon	¼ teaspoon
salt and pepper		

Place the tagliolini in plenty of boiling salted water. Pass the Ricotta cheese through a sieve.

Melt the butter in a double saucepan or heatproof bowl over a pan of water, then fold in the Ricotta and add the cream. Heat gently.

Drain the pasta and place in a serving dish; dress with the Ricotta mixture. Sprinkle the cocoa over the pasta with a pinch of cinnamon, salt and pepper. Mix and serve piping hot.

Time: 20 minutes   *Serves 4*

Tagliatelle with Borlotti Beans

TAGLIATELLE GUSTOSE CON FAGIOLI

Ingredients	Metric/Imperial	American
smoked bacon	75 g/3 oz	3 ounces
onion	1	1
oil	3 tablespoons	scant $\frac{1}{4}$ cup
sage leaves	5	5
canned borlotti beans	225 g/8 oz	$\frac{1}{2}$ pound
stock	2 tablespoons	3 tablespoons
flour	$\frac{1}{4}$ teaspoon	$\frac{1}{4}$ teaspoon
tomato paste	1 tablespoon	1 tablespoon
red wine	2 tablespoons	3 tablespoons
tagliatelle pasta	400 g/14 oz	14 ounces
salt and pepper		
Parmesan cheese, grated	2 tablespoons	3 tablespoons
Pecorino cheese, grated	1 tablespoon	1 tablespoon

Derind and cube the bacon; finely chop the onion. Heat the oil in a large heavy pan, add the bacon, onion and whole sage leaves; cook over a medium heat until golden.

Drain the borlotti beans, rinse and drain again, then add to the pan. Heat the stock.

Mix the flour and tomato paste in a small bowl; stir in the hot stock and the wine. Pour into the bean mixture, stir with a wooden spoon and simmer over a low heat until the sauce thickens.

Meanwhile cook the pasta in plenty of lightly salted boiling water until *al dente*.

Remove the sage leaves from the sauce, taste and adjust the seasoning. Drain the pasta, mix with the sauce and put in a large heated serving dish. Add the Parmesan and Pecorino cheese and serve hot.

Time: 30 minutes   *Serves 4*

Spicy Summer Pasta

TAGLIOLINI PRIMAVERILI

Ingredients	Metric/Imperial	American
head of lettuce	1	1
oil	4 tablespoons	6 tablespoons
fresh chilli	$\frac{1}{2}$	$\frac{1}{2}$
garlic cloves	2	2
plum tomatoes	350 g/12 oz	$\frac{3}{4}$ pound
salt and pepper		
tuna in oil	200 g/7 oz	7 ounces
fresh tagliolini	350 g/12 oz	$\frac{3}{4}$ pound
chopped parsley	1 tablespoon	1 tablespoon

Wash the lettuce, discarding any coarse or damaged leaves, drain well and cut into thin strips.

Heat the oil in a large shallow pan, add the chilli, deseeded and chopped, and the crushed garlic. Cook over medium heat until golden, then remove the chilli and garlic. Add the lettuce, and as soon as it wilts add the tomatoes, peeled if fresh, drained if canned and mashed with a fork. Season with salt and pepper and leave on a low heat until the sauce has thickened. Add the tuna, drained and chopped, at the very end of the cooking time.

Meanwhile cook the pasta in a large pan of lightly salted boiling water until *al dente*. Drain, cover with the sauce, sprinkle with parsley, mix and serve.

Time: 30 minutes   *Serves 4*

Tagliatelle with Borlotti Beans

cooking liquid and simmer for 10 minutes, then add the clams and the tomatoes, halved and deseeded. Cook for a further 10 minutes.

Add the prawns, followed in a few minutes by the fish pieces, and simmer until they are cooked through; about 15 minutes. Sprinkle with chives and keep hot.

Cook the fresh pasta in plenty of lightly salted boiling water for about 5 minutes or until *al dente*. Drain, mix with the seafood sauce and serve at once.

Time: 1 hour   *Serves 4–6*

Pappardelle with Seafood Sauce

Pappardelle with Seafood Sauce

FETTUCCE ALLA MARINARA

Ingredients	Metric/Imperial	American
clams	1 kg/2 lb	2 pounds
olive oil	5 tablespoons	⅓ cup
sole fillets	225 g/8 oz	½ pound
cod fillet	225 g/8 oz	½ pound
medium-sized onions	2	2
salt and pepper		
plum tomatoes	225 g/8 oz	½ pound
peeled prawns	225 g/8 oz	½ pound
bunch of chives	1	1
pappardelle or fettucine pasta	350 g/12 oz	¾ pound

Scrub the clams under running water, drain and put in a large shallow pan with 1 tablespoon of the oil. Raise the heat, cover with a lid and leave until the clam shells have opened. Remove the clams from the shells and put in a bowl. Strain the cooking liquid through a piece of muslin.

Cut the sole and cod fillets into bite-sized pieces.

Heat the remaining oil in a large pan, add the onions, chopped, and a little salt and pepper. Cook for a few minutes over medium heat until golden. Add the clam

Tagliatelle with Aubergine (Eggplant)

TAGLIATELLE ALLE MELANZANE

Ingredients	Metric/Imperial	American
large aubergines (eggplants)	2	2
salt and pepper		
medium-sized onion	1	1
bacon	25 g/1 oz	1 ounce
oil	2 tablespoons	3 tablespoons
butter	25 g/1 oz	2 tablespoons
dry white vermouth	1 tablespoon	1 tablespoon
plum tomatoes	4	4
chopped basil	1 tablespoon	1 tablespoon
garlic clove	1	1
tagliatelle	400 g/14 oz	14 ounces
Parmesan cheese, grated	1 tablespoon	1 tablespoon

Peel the aubergines and cut into cubes. Sprinkle with salt and leave for 30 minutes on an inclined chopping board or tray to drain off any excess liquid.

Chop the onion with the derinded bacon. Heat the oil with half the butter in a large deep pan; add the onion and bacon and cook over medium heat until golden. Rinse the aubergine, dry on paper towels and add to the pan. Mix together and simmer for about 30 minutes, moistening from time to time with a drop of vermouth.

Peel the tomatoes if using fresh ones, deseed and mash with a fork. Season with a little salt and add to the pan. Cook over high heat for 10 minutes, then add the basil, finely chopped along with the crushed garlic clove.

Meanwhile cook the pasta in plenty of lightly salted boiling water until *al dente*. Drain and add to the pan with the sauce. Add the remaining butter, diced, and sprinkle on the Parmesan cheese. Put in a large heated dish and serve at once.

Time: 1 hour + 30 minutes: resting   *Serves 6*

Melt half the butter in a large pan with the oil, add the chopped onion, diced carrot, parsley and finely sliced celery and cook over a low heat for 5 minutes.

Cut the rabbit into pieces, chop rindless bacon into cubes and add to the vegetables with the bay leaf. Cook for about 10 minutes on a medium heat. When the onion has turned golden, moisten with wine. Allow the wine to evaporate then sprinkle the contents of the pan with the flour. Blend in with a wooden spoon.

Dilute the tomato paste in the hot stock and pour into the pan. Mix well, adjust the seasoning, sprinkle with nutmeg and leave to simmer on a low heat until the liquid has almost completely reduced. Add a little more stock or water and leave to reduce to a good thick consistency.

When the rabbit is cooked, remove from the sauce and keep warm in a heated serving dish. Pass the sauce through a sieve or purée in a blender.

Cook the pasta in plenty of boiling salted water until *al dente*. Drain and place in a deep heated serving dish, dress with the remaining butter. Pour the sauce on to the pasta, mix and arrange the chopped rabbit on the top.

Time: 2 hours   *Serves 4*

Noodles with Rabbit

Noodles with Rabbit

PAPPARDELLE CON IL CONIGLIO

Ingredients	Metric/Imperial	American
butter	65 g/2½ oz	5 tablespoons
olive oil	3 tablespoons	scant ¼ cup
onion	½	½
carrot	1	1
chopped parsley	1 tablespoon	1 tablespoon
celery stalk	½	½
saddle of rabbit	1	1
bacon	50 g/2 oz	2 ounces
bay leaf	1	1
red wine	125 ml/4 fl oz	½ cup
plain (all-purpose) flour	1 tablespoon	1 tablespoon
tomato paste	1 tablespoon	1 tablespoon
stock	225 ml/8 fl oz	1 cup
salt and pepper		
grated nutmeg	¼ teaspoon	¼ teaspoon
wide fresh ribbon pasta	400 g/14 oz	14 ounces

Roman Tagliatelle

TAGLIATELLE ALLA ROMANA

Ingredients	Metric/Imperial	American
chopped parsley	1 tablespoon	1 tablespoon
shelled walnuts	40 g/1½ oz	¼ cup
marjoram	¼ teaspoon	¼ teaspoon
Ricotta cheese	225 g/8 oz	½ pound
Parmesan cheese, grated	2 tablespoons	3 tablespoons
salt and pepper		
tagliatelle	350 g/12 oz	¾ pound

Chop the parsley and walnuts. Place in a bowl with the marjoram, Ricotta and Parmesan cheese. Beat vigorously with a wooden spoon or an electric mixer until frothy and light.

Bring a large pan of salted water to the boil and cook the tagliatelle until *al dente*.

Just before draining the pasta, remove a few tablespoons of water from the pan and add to the Ricotta mixture. Mix well adding salt and pepper to taste.

Drain the pasta and place in a heated serving bowl, fold in the cheese mixture and serve.

Time: 20 minutes   *Serves 4*

Melt two-thirds of the butter in a large pan; add the asparagus and the ham cut into very fine slivers. Stir gently, season with salt and pepper and add the cream. Cook over a low heat for about 10 minutes, then add the Fontina cheese cut into slivers. Turn off the heat and leave the cheese to melt.

Cook the pasta in plenty of lightly salted boiling water until *al dente*. Drain and transfer to the pan with the sauce. Sprinkle with chopped basil, Parmesan cheese and the remaining butter, chopped. Mix and serve.

Time: 40 minutes   *Serves 4*

Pasta with Asparagus, Ham and Cheese

Pasta with Asparagus, Ham and Cheese

LINGUINE CON ASPARAGI, PROSCIUTTO E FORMAGGIO

Ingredients	Metric/Imperial	American
bundle of asparagus	1	1
salt and pepper		
butter	75 g/3 oz	6 tablespoons
cooked ham	75 g/3 oz	3 ounces
single (thin) cream	225 ml/8 fl oz	1 cup
Fontina cheese	75 g/3 oz	3 ounces
linguine pasta	350 g/12 oz	¾ pound
basil leaves	12	12
Parmesan cheese, grated	25 g/1 oz	¼ cup

Trim off woody ends and scrape tough skin from the asparagus. Rinse under cold running water. Tie into a bundle and stand in a tall pan with salted water two-thirds of the way up; cover the tips with a foil dome. Simmer for about 10 minutes, depending on the thickness of the asparagus. Drain, leave to cool, then remove the white part and cut remainder into pieces.

Pasta with Duck

FETTUCCINE ALL'ANATRA

Ingredients	Metric/Imperial	American
small onion	1	1
celery stalk	1	1
small carrot	1	1
garlic clove	1	1
bacon	40 g/1½ oz	1½ ounces
oil	4 tablespoons	6 tablespoons
butter	50 g/2 oz	¼ cup
duck giblets	225 g/8 oz	½ pound
duck meat	225 g/8 oz	½ pound
salt and pepper		
stock cube	1	1
brandy	2 tablespoons	3 tablespoons
clove	1	1
tomato paste	1 tablespoon	1 tablespoon
fettuccine	400 g/14 oz	14 ounces
single (thin) cream	2 tablespoons	3 tablespoons
Parmesan cheese, grated	25 g/1 oz	¼ cup

Prepare and finely chop the onion, celery, and carrot; crush the garlic; derind and chop the bacon. Heat the oil with half the butter in a large pan, add the chopped ingredients and cook over a low heat for 10 minutes.

Chop the giblets and duck meat and add to the pan. Mix and cook over a medium heat until golden. Season with salt and pepper and add the crumbled stock cube mixed with 225 ml/8 fl oz/1 cup hot water and cook for 10 minutes.

Turn up the heat, add the brandy and set it alight. When the flames have died down add the clove and tomato paste mixed with a little hot water and simmer very gently for a further 40 minutes, adding a very little extra stock if necessary; the sauce should be fairly dry.

Spaghetti with Eggs and Parsley

Pasta with Duck

Spaghetti with Egg and Parsley

VERMICELLI CON UOVA E PREZZEMOLO

Ingredients	Metric/Imperial	American
onion	$\frac{1}{4}$	$\frac{1}{4}$
stock	225 ml/8 fl oz	1 cup
eggs	2	2
salt and pepper		
chopped parsley	1 tablespoon	1 tablespoon
Pecorino cheese, grated	25 g/1 oz	$\frac{1}{4}$ cup
spaghetti	350 g/12 oz	$\frac{3}{4}$ pound

Finely chop the onion and put in a small pan with the stock; bring to the boil.

Beat the eggs in a bowl and season with salt and pepper; add the stock and onion. Return to the pan and continue to beat with a fork, until the liquid thickens slightly. Add the parsley and Pecorino cheese.

Cook the pasta in a large pan of lightly salted boiling water until *al dente*. Drain, combine with the egg mixture, stir well and serve.

If the dish appears too dry moisten with a little of the pasta cooking water.

Cook the pasta in plenty of lightly salted boiling water until *al dente* and drain well.

Add the cream to the duck mixture and stir well to make a smooth sauce. Remove the clove, then add the pasta and pour into a heated serving dish. Dot with the remaining butter and sprinkle with Parmesan cheese.

Time: 50 minutes   *Serves 4*

Time: 20 minutes   *Serves 4*

113

Green Ribbon Pasta

TAGLIATELLE VERDI PIU VERDE

Ingredients	Metric/Imperial	American
fresh green tagliatelle	450 g/1 lb	1 pound
salt and white pepper		
butter	50 g/2 oz	¼ cup
garlic clove	1	1
chopped parsley	1 tablespoon	1 tablespoon
chopped basil	1 tablespoon	1 tablespoon
Parmesan cheese, grated	25 g/1 oz	¼ cup

Cook the pasta in a large pan of lightly salted boiling water until just *al dente*. Drain well and transfer to a large flameproof casserole. Add the diced butter, crushed garlic, parsley and basil; season with salt and pepper.

Mix well and leave over a low heat for a few minutes for the flavours to mingle. Sprinkle with Parmesan cheese just before serving.

Time: 15 minutes   *Serves 4*

Spaghetti au Gratin

SPAGHETTI FILANTI

Ingredients	Metric/Imperial	American
spaghetti	350 g/12 oz	¾ pound
salt and pepper		
Parmesan cheese, grated	75 g/3 oz	¾ cup
butter	75 g/3 oz	6 tablespoons
grated nutmeg	¼ teaspoon	¼ teaspoon
Mozzarella cheese, cubed	100 g/4 oz	¼ pound
Gruyère cheese, grated	100 g/4 oz	1 cup

Cook the pasta in a large pan of lightly salted boiling water for 12 minutes. Add a ladleful of cold water, drain and quickly add half the Parmesan cheese, 60 g/2½ oz/5 tablespoons of the butter, salt, pepper and nutmeg. Mix well and put in a buttered ovenproof serving dish, alternating with layers of Mozzarella and Gruyère cheese. Sprinkle the remaining Parmesan cheese over the top and dot with the remaining butter.

Put in a hot oven (220 c, 425 f, gas 7), for about 10 minutes or until the top is crisp and golden. Serve at once.

Time: 35 minutes   *Serves 4*

Spaghetti with Tuna and Cauliflower

SPAGHETTI CON TONNO E CAVOLFIORE

Ingredients	Metric/Imperial	American
small cauliflower	1	1
salt and pepper		
white vinegar	2 tablespoons	3 tablespoons
medium-sized onion	1	1
garlic clove	1	1
oil	4 tablespoons	6 tablespoons
tuna in oil	200 g/7 oz	7 ounces
chopped parsley	1 tablespoon	1 tablespoon
spaghetti	350 g/12 oz	¾ pound
dried breadcrumbs	4 tablespoons	6 tablespoons

Remove the coarse stems surrounding the cauliflower, wash it and simmer for 10 minutes in a pan of water with a pinch of salt and the vinegar. Drain, allow to cool slightly, then divide into florets and slice, not too thinly.

Chop the onion finely and crush the garlic. Heat the oil in a large shallow pan, add the onion and garlic and cook over medium heat until golden. Add the sliced cauliflower, cook for a few minutes, then add the tuna, mashed with its oil, chopped parsley and plenty of pepper.

Cook the pasta in a large pan of lightly salted boiling water until *al dente*. Drain, transfer to the pan with the sauce, sprinkle with breadcrumbs, mix and serve.

Time: 30 minutes   *Serves 4*

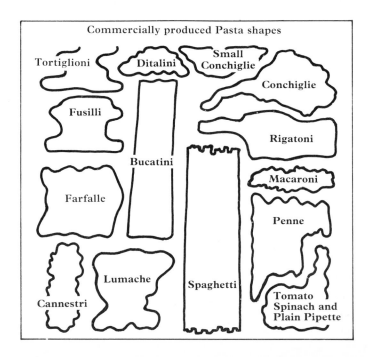

Commercially produced Pasta shapes

Tortiglioni, Ditalini, Small Conchiglie, Conchiglie, Fusilli, Bucatini, Rigatoni, Farfalle, Macaroni, Penne, Lumache, Spaghetti, Cannestri, Tomato Spinach and Plain Pipette

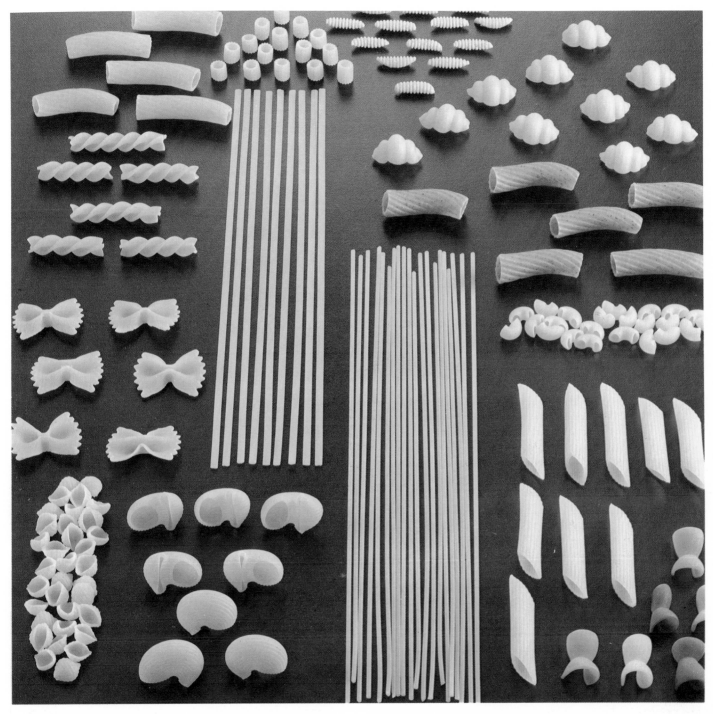

Saint Lucia Spaghetti

SPAGHETTI SANTA LUCIA

Ingredients	Metric/Imperial	American
baby squid	450 g / 1 lb	1 pound
olive oil	4 tablespoons	6 tablespoons
chopped parsley	1 tablespoon	1 tablespoon
garlic clove	1	1
spaghetti	400 g / 14 oz	14 ounces
salt and freshly ground black pepper		

Clean the squid by opening the bag with scissors and removing the interior. Remove the main bone, wash several times and drain. Cut into slices.

Heat the oil in a pan, add the parsley, crushed garlic and salt. Mix with a wooden spoon, then add the squid. Cover with a lid and cook for 30 minutes on a low heat.

Meanwhile cook the spaghetti in plenty of boiling salted water until *al dente*, drain and place in a heated bowl.

Dress with the hot squid and juices, sprinkled with plenty of pepper and serve. (Parmesan cheese is not required for this pasta dish.)

Time: 1 hour   *Serves 4*

Spaghetti Portofino-style

SPAGHETTI PORTOFINO

Ingredients	Metric/Imperial	American
oil	3 tablespoons	scant ¼ cup
garlic cloves	2	2
mushrooms	350 g/12 oz	¾ pound
bacon	75 g/3 oz	3 ounces
salt and pepper		
tuna in oil	100 g/4 oz	¼ pound
spaghetti	350 g/12 oz	¾ pound
beef ragu (page 30)	225 ml/8 fl oz	1 cup
Parmesan cheese, grated	25 g/1 oz	¼ cup

Heat the oil in a shallow pan; crush the garlic lightly, add to the pan and cook over a medium heat until golden, then remove.

Dice the mushrooms; derind and chop the bacon. Add to the pan, season with salt and pepper and cook for a few minutes, then add the tuna, drained and in large chunks. Simmer for 5 minutes then remove the pan from the heat.

Meanwhile cook the pasta in a large pan of lightly salted boiling water until *al dente*. Drain, pour over both the prepared sauce and the hot meat sauce and mix well. Divide between 4 individual dishes and sprinkle with Parmesan cheese.

Time: 20 minutes   *Serves 4*

Spaghetti Portofino-style

1 Heat the oil in a pan, add the garlic. After 1 minute add the mushrooms and bacon. Season well.
2 Add the tuna in chunks and cook for 5 minutes. Remove from the heat.
3 Cook the spaghetti in plenty of boiling salted water until *al dente*. Drain in a colander.
4 Mix the spaghetti with the tuna sauce and the beef ragu. Serve piping hot.

Spaghetti with Olive Oil and Garlic

SPAGHETTI ALL'AGLIO E OLIO

Ingredients	Metric/Imperial	American
fresh spaghetti	450 g/1 lb	1 pound
salt and freshly ground black pepper		
garlic cloves	2	2
olive oil	4 tablespoons	6 tablespoons
chopped parsley	2 tablespoons	3 tablespoons

Cook the pasta in a large pan of lightly salted boiling water until just *al dente*.

Meanwhile crush the garlic cloves and heat the oil in a small pan. Add the garlic, season with plenty of pepper and cook over medium heat until golden.

Drain the pasta thoroughly and put into a heated serving dish. Pour the oil and garlic sauce over, mix well and serve sprinkled with plenty of parsley.

Time: 15 minutes   *Serves 4*

Spaghetti Salad

SPAGHETTI IN INSALATA

Ingredients	Metric/Imperial	American
fresh tomatoes	450 g/1 lb	1 pound
garlic clove	1	1
basil leaves	6	6
anchovy fillets	2	2
capers	1 tablespoon	1 tablespoon
Gruyère cheese	75 g/3 oz	3 ounces
olive oil	4 tablespoons	6 tablespoons
oregano	$\frac{1}{4}$ teaspoon	$\frac{1}{4}$ teaspoon
salt and pepper		
spaghetti	350 g/12 oz	$\frac{3}{4}$ pound
black olives	25 g/1 oz	1 ounce
dried breadcrumbs	25 g/1 oz	$\frac{1}{4}$ cup
cheese, grated	2 tablespoons	3 tablespoons

Chop the peeled tomatoes and put in a large bowl with the crushed garlic, coarsely chopped basil, mashed anchovies, drained capers and cubed Gruyère cheese. Pour over the oil and season with oregano, salt and pepper. Mix well and put in the refrigerator.

Cook the pasta in a large pan of lightly salted boiling water until *al dente*. Drain and rinse under cold running water; drain again and transfer to the bowl containing the salad. Add the olives, halved and stoned, bread-crumbs and cheese. Mix well and serve.

Time: 45 minutes + 30 minutes: chilling   *Serves 4*

Spaghetti with Tuna, Anchovies and Onion

Spaghetti with Tuna, Anchovies and Onion

SPAGHETTI CON TONNO, ACCIUGHE E CIPOLLE

Ingredients	Metric/Imperial	American
anchovy fillets	4	4
oil	5 tablespoons	$\frac{1}{3}$ cup
large onions	2	2
salt and pepper		
stock	5 tablespoons	$\frac{1}{3}$ cup
tuna in oil	200 g/7 oz	7 ounces
single (thin) cream	2 tablespoons	3 tablespoons
spaghetti	350 g/12 oz	$\frac{3}{4}$ pound
chopped parsley	1 tablespoon	1 tablespoon

Soak the anchovy fillets in a little milk to remove excess salt.

Heat the oil in a large shallow pan. Chop the onions finely and add to the pan with the drained and chopped anchovies. Season with salt and pepper and simmer over a low heat, moistening from time to time with the stock, until the onion is transparent.

Drain and chop the tuna and add to the pan together with the cream. Mix well and simmer for another 5 minutes.

Meanwhile cook the pasta in a large pan of lightly salted boiling water until *al dente*.

Drain the pasta, mix with the sauce and serve sprinkled with parsley.

Time: 40 minutes   *Serves 4*

Spaghetti Baked in Foil

Spaghetti Baked in Foil

SPAGHETTI AL CARTOCCIO

Ingredients	Metric/Imperial	American
large leeks	5	5
butter	40 g/1½ oz	3 tablespoons
stock cube	1	1
milk	3 tablespoons	scant ¼ cup
salt and pepper		
tuna in oil	200 g/7 oz	7 ounces
Worcester sauce	¼ teaspoon	¼ teaspoon
single (thin) cream	4 tablespoons	6 tablespoons
spaghetti	350 g/12 oz	¾ pound
Parmesan cheese, grated	25 g/1 oz	¼ cup
chopped parsley	1 tablespoon	1 tablespoon

Trim the leeks and cut into fairly thick rings; rinse under running water and drain.

Melt the butter in a large deep pan, add the leeks and cook for a few minutes over a low heat. Crumble the stock cube into the milk, season with pepper, and pour over the leeks. Simmer until the leeks are tender, stirring occasionally.

Add the tuna, drained and chopped, Worcester sauce and cream; simmer for a further 5 minutes, then turn off the heat.

Cook the pasta in plenty of lightly salted boiling water until *al dente*. Drain, transfer to the pan with the sauce, add the Parmesan cheese and mix well.

Line a rectangular ovenproof dish with double-width foil, allowing plenty of overlap. Fill the dish with the pasta, sprinkle with parsley, fold over the foil and pinch the edges together. Cook in a moderate oven (180 C, 350 F, gas 4) for 10–15 minutes.

Time: 1 hour 10 minutes *Serves 4*

Spaghetti with Cooked Salami

SPAGHETTI AL SALAME COTTO

Ingredients	Metric/Imperial	American
spaghetti	350 g/12 oz	¾ pound
salt and pepper		
large onion	1	1
celery stalk	1	1
leeks	2	2
olive oil	2 tablespoons	3 tablespoons
butter	40 g/1½ oz	3 tablespoons
salami	150 g/5 oz	5 ounces
red wine	3 tablespoons	scant ¼ cup
plum tomatoes	6	6
Pecorino cheese, grated	2 tablespoons	3 tablespoons

Cook the pasta in a large pan of lightly salted boiling water until *al dente*.

Meanwhile finely chop the onion and celery. Wash the white part of the leeks thoroughly, drain and chop finely. Heat the oil and half the butter in a shallow pan, add the chopped vegetables and cook over a medium heat until golden.

Skin the salami and cut into cubes; add to the pan and cook for a few minutes. Sprinkle on the wine, reduce the heat and leave it to evaporate.

Peel the tomatoes if using fresh; drain if canned. Deseed and mash, then add to the pan. Season lightly with salt and pepper and leave to cook, uncovered, until the sauce has thickened and reduced.

Drain the spaghetti and put in a deep heated serving dish. Pour the sauce over, dot with the remaining butter and sprinkle with Pecorino cheese. Mix carefully and serve at once.

Time: 35 minutes *Serves 4*

Spaghetti with Cold Tomato Sauce

Plunge the tomatoes into boiling water for 1 minute, slide off the skins and dice the flesh. Put into a mixing bowl and add the chopped pepper mixture and the chopped basil. Mix well, remove the garlic and add the cheese. Work together with a wooden spoon, taste and adjust the seasoning and set aside.

Cook the pasta in plenty of boiling salted water until *al dente* drain well.

Mix with the cold sauce and serve at once.

Time: 40 minutes　　　　　　　　　　　　　*Serves 8*

Spaghetti with Cold Tomato Sauce

SPAGHETTI AL POMODORO FREDDO

Ingredients	Metric/Imperial	American
yellow (sweet) pepper	1	1
garlic clove	2	2
salt and pepper		
olive oil	2 tablespoons	3 tablespoons
fresh tomatoes	450 g/1 lb	1 pound
basil leaves	6	6
cream cheese	150 g/5 oz	5 ounces
spaghetti	700 g/1½ lb	1½ pounds

Put the pepper in a flame or under a hot grill (broiler) to char the skin all over. Remove the skin, cut open the pepper, remove the seeds and finely dice the flesh. Put in a small bowl with the lightly crushed garlic, a pinch of salt and pepper and the oil; mix well.

Spaghetti with Leeks, Spinach and Pine Nuts

SPAGHETTI CON SUGO FANTASIOSO

Ingredients	Metric/Imperial	American
leeks	3	3
onion	½	½
bacon	50 g/2 oz	2 ounces
pine nuts	2 tablespoons	3 tablespoons
butter	50 g/2 oz	¼ cup
oil	2 tablespoons	3 tablespoons
frozen spinach, thawed	100 g/4 oz	¼ pound
salt and pepper		
dry white wine	3 tablespoons	scant ¼ cup
plum tomatoes	200 g/7 oz	7 ounces
single (thin) cream	3 tablespoons	scant ¼ cup
spaghetti	350 g/12 oz	¾ pound
Parmesan cheese, grated	25 g/1 oz	¼ cup

Trim the roots, coarse outer leaves and green tops from the leeks; cut the white parts into rings, wash under running water and drain well. Chop the onion finely; dice the derinded bacon; chop the pine nuts coarsely.

Heat the butter and oil in a large pan over a low heat. Add the leeks, onion, bacon, and chopped pine nuts; cook until golden. Add the spinach, season with salt and pepper and sprinkle on the wine. Allow to evaporate then add the mashed tomatoes. Simmer until the sauce has reduced a little, add the cream. Stir and leave on a very low heat for about 10 minutes.

Meanwhile cook the pasta in a large pan of lightly salted boiling water until *al dente*. Drain, pour the sauce on top and mix well. Serve sprinkled with Parmesan cheese.

Time: 30 minutes　　　　　　　　　　　　　*Serves 4*

119

Spaghetti with Caper and Tuna Sauce

SPAGHETTI ALLA SALSA DI CAPPERI E TONNO

Ingredients	Metric/Imperial	American
yellow (sweet) pepper	$\frac{1}{2}$	$\frac{1}{2}$
medium-sized onion	1	1
capers	2 tablespoons	3 tablespoons
stock	125 ml/4 fl oz	$\frac{1}{2}$ cup
sprig of parsley	1	1
oil	5 tablespoons	$\frac{1}{3}$ cup
tuna in oil	65 g/2$\frac{1}{2}$ oz	2$\frac{1}{2}$ ounces
red wine	2 tablespoons	3 tablespoons
tomato paste	1 heaped tablespoon	1 heaped tablespoon
spaghetti	350 g/12 oz	$\frac{3}{4}$ pound

Deseed the pepper and chop both the onion and pepper into small dice with half the rinsed capers and the parsley. Heat the stock.

Heat the oil in a large deep pan, add the pepper and onion mixture and cook over a low heat until golden. Add the tuna, drained and chopped, and the remaining capers. Mix, cook for a few minutes, add the wine and leave until it has evaporated. Dilute the tomato paste with the hot stock, stir into the pan and simmer until thickened and reduced.

Meanwhile cook the pasta in a large pan of lightly salted boiling water until *al dente*. Drain and transfer to the pan containing the sauce. Mix quickly, leave for a few minutes for the flavours to mingle, then turn into a deep heated serving dish.

Time: 30 minutes   *Serves 4*

Bucatini with Anchovy and Tomato Sauce

BUCATINI AI RAGGI DEL SOLE

Ingredients	Metric/Imperial	American
anchovy fillets	5	5
milk		
large onion	1	1
garlic clove	1	1
celery stalks	2	2
bacon	50 g/2 oz	2 ounces
oil	4 tablespoons	6 tablespoons
plum tomatoes	400 g/14 oz	14 ounces
full-bodied red wine	2 tablespoons	3 tablespoons
salt and pepper		
bucatini pasta	350 g/12 oz	$\frac{3}{4}$ pound
black olives	2 tablespoons	3 tablespoons
large basil leaves	8	8

Soak the anchovy fillets in a little milk to remove excess salt.

Finely chop the onion together with the garlic, celery and derinded bacon. Heat the oil in a heavy pan, add the chopped onion mixture and cook over a low heat until golden. Drain and chop the anchovies, add to the pan and mash to a pulp with a wooden spoon.

Peel the tomatoes if fresh; drain if canned. Add to the pan, mash with a fork and cook over a medium heat until the mixture thickens, moistening at intervals with the wine.

Bring a large pan of lightly salted water to the boil, add the pasta and cook until *al dente*. Meanwhile stone the olives and add to the sauce, together with the basil leaves, torn into pieces. Season to taste.

Drain the pasta thoroughly, reserving some of the water. Mix the pasta with the sauce, add 2–3 table-spoons of the water. Mix well again and leave for a few minutes to allow the flavours to mingle, then transfer to a heated serving dish.

Time: 45 minutes   *Serves 4*

Bucatini with Anchovy and Tomato Sauce

Pasta Pie

PASTICCIO DI MACHERONI

Ingredients	Metric/Imperial	American
For the filling:		
pork	100 g/4 oz	$\frac{1}{4}$ pound
veal	100 g/4 oz	$\frac{1}{4}$ pound
chicken	100 g/4 oz	$\frac{1}{4}$ pound
oil	125 ml/4 fl oz	$\frac{1}{2}$ cup
cooked ham	100 g/4 oz	$\frac{1}{4}$ pound
salt and pepper		
grated nutmeg	$\frac{1}{4}$ teaspoon	$\frac{1}{4}$ teaspoon
egg yolks	2	2
Parmesan cheese, grated	40 g/1$\frac{1}{2}$ oz	3 tablespoons
large rigatoni	350 g/12 oz	$\frac{3}{4}$ pound
For the meat sauce:		
onion	1	1
carrot	1	1
celery	1	1
bacon	50 g/2 oz	2 ounces
olive oil	5 tablespoons	$\frac{1}{3}$ cup
minced (ground) veal	100 g/4 oz	$\frac{1}{4}$ pound
minced (ground) beef	100 g/4 oz	$\frac{1}{4}$ pound
dry red wine	3 tablespoons	scant $\frac{1}{4}$ cup
stock	350 ml/12 fl oz	1$\frac{1}{2}$ cups
tomato paste	1 tablespoon	1 tablespoon
pepper		
For the white sauce:		
butter	25 g/1 oz	2 tablespoons
plain (all-purpose) flour	25 g/1 oz	$\frac{1}{4}$ cup
milk	225 ml/8 fl oz	1 cup
salt and pepper		
grated nutmeg	$\frac{1}{4}$ teaspoon	$\frac{1}{4}$ teaspoon
For the pie:		
frozen puff pastry, thawed	450 g/1 lb	1 pound
egg	1	1

Prepare the filling by chopping the pork, veal and chicken into small cubes.

Heat the oil in a large pan over a medium heat and cook the meat for 15 minutes until golden, turning from time to time. Remove from the heat, drain and cool.

Mince (grind) all the meats together twice with the ham in a mincer or food processor and put in a bowl. Add salt, pepper, nutmeg, the egg yolks and the Parmesan cheese. Mix well with a wooden spoon.

Cook the pasta in a large pan with plenty of boiling salted water until just *al dente*. Before draining, run

Pasta Pie

cold water into the pan to stop the cooking process. Drain and fill each tube with the minced meat mixture.

To make the meat sauce chop the prepared onion, carrot, celery and derinded bacon. Heat the oil in a large pan on medium heat, add vegetables, until golden.

Add the minced veal and beef and continue to cook on a medium heat until the meat is golden. Moisten with wine and the stock, stirring until most of the liquid has been absorbed. Mix the tomato paste with 3–4 tablespoonfuls of hot water; add to the sauce with a sprinkling of pepper.

To make the white sauce, melt the butter in a pan, sprinkle in the sifted flour, mix well and cook for 1 minute, stirring constantly. Remove the pan from the heat and gradually add the hot milk, stirring vigorously; season well. Return to the heat and bring to the boil until the sauce thickens, add seasoning and nutmeg.

Roll out two large circular shapes of the thawed puff pastry to fit an ovenproof dish or large flan ring.

Place one layer of pastry in the base and up the sides of the dish or ring. Arrange a layer of filled pasta with a few tablespoonfuls of meat sauce and white sauce over the top. Continue to layer ingredients until used up.

Wet the edges of the pastry with a damp pastry brush and cover the dish with a pastry lid. Secure the edge firmly by pressing with the fingers; trim the edges. Make slits over the pie to allow steam to escape during cooking. Put in the refrigerator to rest for 15 minutes.

Pre-heat the oven to 230 C, 450 F, gas 8.

Brush the pie with lightly beaten egg, place in the hot oven and cook for 15 minutes until the pastry is golden. Reduce the heat to 180 C, 350 F, gas 4, continue cooking for a further 20 minutes and serve hot.

Time: 2$\frac{1}{2}$ hours + 15 minutes: resting   *Serves 6–8*

Rigatoni with Meat Balls

Shepherd's Macaroni

MACCHERONI ALLA PASTORA

Ingredients	Metric/Imperial	American
onions	2	2
stock	225 ml/8 fl oz	1 cup
salt and pepper		
fresh tomatoes	2	2
Parmesan cheese, grated	2 tablespoons	3 tablespoons
chopped parsley	1 tablespoon	1 tablespoon
macaroni	350 g/12 oz	¾ pound

Slice the onions with a sharp knife, as thinly as possible. Put in a large pan, add the stock and season with salt and pepper. Leave over a low heat until the stock has evaporated.

Peel and chop the tomatoes; add to the pan and continue cooking until the mixture is creamy. Add the Parmesan cheese and parsley, stir well and remove from the heat.

Cook the pasta in plenty of lightly salted boiling water. Drain, mix with the prepared sauce and serve hot.

Time: 40 minutes | *Serves 4*

Rigatoni with Meat Balls

MACCHERONI DEL CICLOPE

Ingredients	Metric/Imperial	American
bread roll	1	1
milk		
minced (ground) veal	225 g/8 oz	½ pound
fresh Italian sausages	100 g/4 oz	¼ pound
Mortadella sausage	25 g/1 oz	1 ounce
eggs	2	2
garlic clove	½	½
basil leaves	4–6	4–6
Parmesan cheese, grated	50 g/2 oz	½ cup
salt and pepper		
oil for frying		
plain (all-purpose) flour	2 tablespoons	3 tablespoons
butter	25 g/1 oz	2 tablespoons
oil	2 tablespoons	3 tablespoons
onion	1	1
canned plum tomatoes	400 g/14 oz	14 ounces
oregano	¼ teaspoon	¼ teaspoon
macaroni or rigatoni	350 g/12 oz	¾ pound

First prepare the meat balls: soak the centre of the bread roll in a little milk. Put the veal in a bowl, crumble in the skinned sausages and add the very finely chopped Mortadella, squeezed bread and eggs. Crush the garlic and mix with a few chopped basil leaves and 2–3 tablespoons of the Parmesan cheese. Add to the meat mixture, season with salt and pepper and mix well. Form into little balls; about the size of a cherry.

Heat plenty of oil in a large heavy pan, dip the meat balls lightly in flour and fry over medium heat until golden. Remove and drain on absorbent paper towels.

Heat the butter with the oil in a large deep pan, add the onion, very finely chopped, and cook over a low heat until transparent. Chop the tomatoes, add to the pan with a little salt and pepper and cook over medium heat until a thick sauce has formed. Before the end of the cooking time add the cooked meat balls, oregano and chopped basil leaves.

Cook the pasta in plenty of lightly salted boiling water until *al dente* and drain well. Pour into the pan with the sauce, mix well, sprinkle with the cheese.

Time: 1 hour | *Serves 4*

Ditali with Cauliflower

MACCHERONCINI CON CIME DI CAVOLFIORE

Ingredients	Metric/Imperial	American
anchovy fillets	2	2
small cauliflower	1	1
vinegar	2 tablespoons	3 tablespoons
oil	4 tablespoons	6 tablespoons
onion	1	1
garlic clove	1	1
plum tomatoes	4	4
salt and pepper		
macaroni or ditali	350 g/12 oz	$\frac{3}{4}$ pound
chopped parsley	1 tablespoon	1 tablespoon

Soak the anchovy fillets in a little milk to remove salt.

Remove the coarse stems from around the cauliflower, wash the head under running water and boil for 10 minutes in water acidulated with the vinegar. Drain, cool slightly, then divide into florets and slice.

Melt the oil in a large pan. Chop the onion finely and crush the garlic; add to the pan and cook for a few minutes over medium heat until golden.

Add the sliced cauliflower and the anchovies, drained and chopped. After a few minutes add the sliced tomatoes, and season with salt and pepper. Cook for about 10 minutes or until the cauliflower is tender.

Ditali with Cauliflower

Meanwhile cook the pasta in a large pan of lightly salted boiling water until *al dente*. Drain, mix with the sauce and sprinkle with parsley.

Time: 30 minutes — *Serves 4*

Bucatini with Chicken Giblets

BUCATINI CON RIGAGLIE DI POLLO

Ingredients	Metric/Imperial	American
small onion	1	1
small carrots	2	2
celery stalk	1	1
bacon	50 g/2 oz	2 ounces
sage leaves	4	4
sprig of rosemary	1	1
butter	50 g/2 oz	$\frac{1}{4}$ cup
oil	2 tablespoons	3 tablespoons
garlic clove	1	1
frozen peas	2 tablespoons	3 tablespoons
chicken giblets	225 g/8 oz	$\frac{1}{2}$ pound
salt and pepper		
Marsala wine	3 tablespoons	scant $\frac{1}{4}$ cup
tomato paste	1 tablespoon	1 tablespoon
stock	225 ml/8 fl oz	1 cup
bucatini pasta	400 g/14 oz	14 ounces
Pecorino cheese, grated	2 tablespoons	3 tablespoons

Finely chop the onion, carrot, celery, derinded bacon, sage leaves and rosemary. Heat half the butter in a large pan with the oil. Add the chopped ingredients and cook over a medium heat for a few minutes. Add the garlic, lightly crushed, and cook until golden.

Remove the garlic, increase the heat and add the frozen peas. Stir and leave to cook for 10 minutes. Meanwhile wash and coarsely chop the chicken giblets. Add them to the pan, lower the heat and simmer until cooked. Season with salt and pepper, add the Marsala and continue cooking for 5 minutes.

Mix the tomato paste with the hot stock and stir into the sauce.

Cook the pasta in plenty of lightly salted boiling water until *al dente*. Drain, tip back into the pan, mix with the sauce and leave for a few minutes to allow the pasta to absorb its flavour.

Sprinkle on the Pecorino cheese and the remaining butter, diced. Mix together with 2 large spoons and serve on individual plates.

Time: 20 minutes — *Serves 4*

Macaroni with Artichokes and Mozzarella Cheese

MACCHERONCINI AL CARCIOFI E MOZZARELLA

Ingredients	Metric/Imperial	American
artichokes	4	4
small onion	1	1
Parma ham	75 g/3 oz	3 ounces
butter	50 g/2 oz	$\frac{1}{4}$ cup
salt and pepper		
stock	125 ml/4 fl oz	$\frac{1}{2}$ cup
chopped parsley	1 tablespoon	1 tablespoon
macaroni or ditali	700 g/1½ lb	1½ pounds
Mozzarella cheese	350 g/12 oz	$\frac{3}{4}$ pound
oil	1 teaspoon	1 teaspoon
breadcrumbs	25 g/1 oz	$\frac{1}{4}$ cup
Parmesan cheese, grated	50 g/2 oz	$\frac{1}{2}$ cup
single (thin) cream	125 ml/4 fl oz	$\frac{1}{2}$ cup

Prepare the artichokes: remove the stalks and tough outer leaves, trim the points off the remaining leaves, cut in half and remove the bristly chokes from the centres. Wash well, dry and slice thinly.

Finely chop the onion and ham. Heat the butter in a large pan, add the onion and ham and cook over a medium heat until golden. Add the artichokes, season to taste and cook for a few more minutes.

Add the stock, lower the heat, cover and cook for about 40 minutes, stirring from time to time. When the artichokes are tender add the parsley.

Meanwhile cook the pasta in plenty of lightly salted boiling water until *al dente*.

Drain the pasta, mix with the artichoke sauce and add the cubed Mozzarella cheese; stir well. Oil a large shallow ovenproof dish. Pour in the pasta, add the cream, sprinkle with breadcrumbs and Parmesan cheese.

Put in a very hot oven (240 C, 475 F, gas 9) for about 15 minutes until the top has browned. Serve hot.

Time: 1½ hours   *Serves 8*

1 Prepare the artichokes. Chop the onion and the ham.
2 Heat the butter in a pan and cook the onion and ham mixture until golden brown. Add the sliced artichokes, season well; add the stock and cook for 40 minutes.
3 Add the artichoke sauce to the cooked, drained pasta.
4 Mix well with the Mozzarella cheese.
5 Arrange in an ovenproof dish, pour in the cream and spread over the top. Sprinkle with crumbs, cheese.

Macaroni with Tomato Sauce and Rosemary

MACCHERONCINI AL SUGO DI POMODORO E
ROSMARINO

Ingredients	Metric/Imperial	American
bacon	50 g/2 oz	2 ounces
garlic cloves	2	2
sprigs of rosemary	2	2
butter	50 g/2 oz	$\frac{1}{4}$ cup
oil	3 tablespoons	scant $\frac{1}{4}$ cup
minced (ground) beef	225 g/8 oz	1 cup
salt and pepper		
canned plum tomatoes	800 g/1$\frac{3}{4}$ lb	1$\frac{3}{4}$ pounds
beef stock cube	$\frac{1}{2}$	$\frac{1}{2}$
red wine	50 ml/2 fl oz	$\frac{1}{4}$ cup
tortiglioni (long macaroni)	350 g/12 oz	$\frac{3}{4}$ pound
Parmesan cheese, grated	25 g/1 oz	$\frac{1}{4}$ cup

Derind and finely chop the bacon with the garlic and
rosemary. Heat the oil in a heavy pan with half the
butter, add the bacon mixture and cook over a medium
heat until golden. Add the beef, mix to separate and
brown then reduce the heat. Season with salt and
pepper. Drain the tomatoes and add to the pan.

When the sauce has reduced pour in the stock and
add the wine. Simmer until it has reduced by half.
Cover with a lid and simmer very gently for a further 40
minutes, adding hot water if it dries out.

Cook the pasta in plenty of lightly salted boiling
water until *al dente*. Drain, put in a heated serving bowl
and add the prepared sauce, remaining butter, diced,
and the Parmesan cheese. Mix well and serve at once.

Time: 1 hour 10 minutes 　　　　　　　　　　*Serves 4*

3　　　　　　4　　　　　　5

Country-style Macaroni

MACCHERONI AL RUSTICA

Ingredients	Metric/Imperial	American
anchovy fillets	2	2
oil	4 tablespoons	6 tablespoons
garlic clove	1	1
smoked bacon	50 g/2 oz	2 ounces
canned plum tomatoes	400 g/14 oz	14 ounces
salt and pepper		
stoned black olives	50 g/2 oz	⅓ cup
chopped oregano	¼ teaspoon	¼ teaspoon
macaroni	350 g/12 oz	¾ pound
Pecorino cheese, grated	25 g/1 oz	¼ cup

Soak the anchovy fillets in a little milk to remove excess salt.

Heat the oil in a small pan; add the garlic and drained anchovies. Cook over medium heat for a few minutes, then remove the garlic and add the derinded and diced bacon.

Drain the tomatoes, cut into strips and add to the pan when the bacon is crisp. Season with salt and pepper and leave to cook on a low heat for about 20 minutes until a thick sauce has formed. Add the chopped olives and oregano halfway through the cooking time.

Cook the pasta in a large pan of lightly salted boiling water until *al dente*. Drain, transfer to a heated serving dish, pour on the sauce and sprinkle with Pecorino cheese. Mix well before serving.

Time: 40 minutes   *Serves 4*

Penne Provençale

PENNE ALLA PROVENZALE

Ingredients	Metric/Imperial	American
oil	2 tablespoons	3 tablespoons
butter	25 g/1 oz	2 tablespoons
onions	2	2
dry white wine	2 tablespoons	3 tablespoons
plum tomatoes	400 g/14 oz	14 ounces
stock cube	1	1
stoned black olives	50 g/2 oz	⅓ cup
mixed herbs	½ teaspoon	½ teaspoon
penne pasta	350 g/12 oz	¾ pound
salt and pepper		
Parmesan cheese, grated	25 g/1 oz	¼ cup

Heat the oil and butter together in a shallow pan. Slice the onions thinly, add to the pan and cook over a low heat for 10 minutes, moistening with the wine.

Drain and deseed the tomatoes; add to the pan along with the stock cube crumbled into 225 ml/8 fl oz/1 cup of boiling water. Add chopped olives and mixed herbs and cook for a further 15 minutes over medium heat.

Meanwhile cook the pasta in a large pan of lightly salted boiling water until *al dente*. Drain, put in a heated serving bowl and add the sauce, pepper and Parmesan cheese. Mix well and serve.

Time: 35 minutes   *Serves 4*

Penne au Gratin with Radicchio

PENNE GRATINATE CON RADICCHIO ROSSO

Ingredients	Metric/Imperial	American
heads of radicchio (red salad)	4	4
butter	50 g/2 oz	¼ cup
oil	2 tablespoons	3 tablespoons
garlic clove	1	1
anchovy fillets	4	4
salt and pepper		
Worcester sauce	¼ teaspoon	¼ teaspoon
single (thin) cream	2 tablespoons	3 tablespoons
penne pasta	400 g/14 oz	14 ounces
Parmesan cheese, grated	2 tablespoons	3 tablespoons
breadcrumbs	2 tablespoons	3 tablespoons

Wash the radicchio carefully, drain and slice coarsely. Heat half the butter with the oil in a large deep pan, add the crushed garlic and the drained anchovies. Mix well, add the radicchio and cook for a few minutes over a high heat. Season with a pinch of salt, a little pepper and a few drops of Worcester sauce. Turn the heat down and cook gently for 10 minutes. Add the cream, stir well and remove from the heat.

Cook the pasta in a large pan with plenty of boiling salted water until *al dente*, drain. Tip the pasta into the pan with the sauce, mix well and sprinkle with the Parmesan cheese.

Turn into an oiled ovenproof dish, sprinkle the surface with breadcrumbs and dot with the remaining butter. Place in a moderately hot oven (200 C, 400 F, gas 6) for 10 minutes. Serve piping hot.

Time: 30 minutes   *Serves 4*

Penne with Aubergine (Eggplant) and Walnuts

PENNE CON MELANZANE E NOCI

Ingredients	Metric/Imperial	American
medium-sized aubergine (eggplant)	2	2
salt		
oil	225 ml/8 fl oz	1 cup
shelled walnuts	16	16
garlic clove	1	1
large bunch of basil	1	1
Ricotta cheese	100 g/4 oz	¼ pound
Pecorino cheese, grated	2 tablespoons	3 tablespoons
olive oil	1 tablespoon	1 tablespoon
penne pasta	400 g/14 oz	14 ounces
freshly ground black pepper		

Wash and cut the aubergines into cubes. Arrange on a tilted tray, sprinkle with salt and leave to drain for 30 minutes. Pat dry with paper towels.

Penne Au Gratin with Radicchio

Heat the oil in a large shallow pan over a medium heat; fry the aubergines in batches until golden. Remove and keep warm.

Crush the walnuts roughly in a blender or food processor with the crushed garlic and basil leaves. Mix in a large serving dish with the Ricotta and grated Pecorino cheeses. Cream the nut and cheese mixture with a little olive oil and 2 tablespoons of hot water using a wooden spoon.

Cook the pasta in a large pan with plenty of boiling salted water until *al dente*. Drain and tip into the dish with the sauce, then add the aubergines. Mix with care and serve immediately with a good sprinkling of pepper on the top.

Time: 40 minutes + 30 minutes: resting   *Serves 4*

Soldier's Penne

PENNE ALLA BERSAGLIERA

Ingredients	Metric/Imperial	American
penne	350 g/12 oz	¾ pound
salt		
olive oil	5 tablespoons	⅓ cup
garlic clove	1	1
chilli	½	½
anchovy fillets	4	4
fresh breadcrumbs	50 g/2 oz	½ cup
pickled capers	1½ tablespoons	2 tablespoons
Pecorino cheese, grated	75 g/3 oz	¾ cup
freshly ground black pepper		
Worcester sauce	¼ teaspoon	¼ teaspoon
chopped parsley	1 tablespoon	1 tablespoon

Cook the pasta in a large pan with plenty of boiling salted water.

Meanwhile heat the oil in a large pan, add the crushed garlic with the chopped deseeded chilli.

Wash and drain the anchovies, add to the pan and mix over a medium heat with a fork. Stir in the breadcrumbs, mix and raise the heat to brown.

Add the capers with the grated Pecorino cheese, sprinkle with pepper and complete with a few drops of Worcester sauce.

Drain the pasta when *al dente*. Tip into the pan with the sauce, mix well and sprinkle with chopped parsley.

Time: 25 minutes   *Serves 4*

Bersagliere are specialised soldiers trained in accurate shooting. They wear a special helmet with plumes of long feathers.

Vegetarian Pasta

PENNE CON VERDURE SAPORITE

Penne with Black Olives

Ingredients	Metric/Imperial	American
green (sweet) pepper	1	1
onion	1	1
carrots	2	2
celery stalks	2	2
oil	4 tablespoons	6 tablespoons
butter	25 g/1 oz	2 tablespoons
garlic clove	1	1
fresh chilli	1	1
vegetable stock cube	1	1
dry white wine	125 ml/4 fl oz	½ cup
plum tomatoes	6	6
salt and pepper		
sprig of parsley	1	1
basil leaves	6	6
penne or other pasta	400 g/14 oz	14 ounces
Parmesan cheese, grated	40 g/1½ oz	3 tablespoons

Deseed the pepper, peel the onion, scrub and trim the carrots and celery. Cut all the vegetables into very fine slivers.

Heat three-quarters of the oil with the butter in a large heavy pan and add the lightly crushed garlic clove and the fresh chilli. Cook over medium heat until golden, then remove and discard. Add the prepared vegetables and simmer gently for a few minutes. Crumble in the stock cube, add the wine, raise the heat and cook until the liquid has reduced to three-quarters of its original amount.

If using fresh tomatoes plunge them briefly into boiling water and slide off the skins; deseed and finely chop. Add to the pan, season to taste and simmer for 10 minutes. Sprinkle with chopped parsley and basil, mix and turn off the heat.

Cook the pasta in plenty of lightly salted boiling water until *al dente*. Drain and put in a heated serving dish, add the vegetables along with the cooking juices, reserved oil and the Parmesan cheese. Mix well and serve at once.

Time: 50 minutes   *Serves 4*

Pasta with Black Olives

PENNE ALLE OLIVE NERE

Ingredients	Metric/Imperial	American
penne pasta	400 g/14 oz	14 ounces
salt		
small onion	1	1
celery stalk	1	1
red (sweet) pepper	1	1
oil	2 tablespoons	3 tablespoons
butter	50 g/2 oz	$\frac{1}{4}$ cup
dry white wine	2 tablespoons	3 tablespoons
black olive purée	2 tablespoons	3 tablespoons
black olives	50 g/2 oz	$\frac{1}{3}$ cup
single (thin) cream	6 tablespoons	$\frac{1}{2}$ cup
Gruyère cheese, grated	2 tablespoons	3 tablespoons
freshly ground black pepper		

Cook the pasta in plenty of lightly salted boiling water until *al dente*.

Meanwhile finely chop the onion, celery and the deseeded red pepper. Heat the oil with half the butter in a large pan, add the chopped vegetables and cook over a medium heat until golden.

Add the wine, simmer until it evaporates, then mix in the olive purée, stoned and chopped black olives and cream. Reserve a few whole olives for garnish.

Drain the pasta and pour into the pan with the sauce. Add the Gruyére cheese and remaining butter, diced; mix well. Season with plenty of pepper, leave on a low heat for a few minutes for the flavours to blend, then pour into a large heated serving dish.

Time: 30 minutes　　　　　*Serves 4*

Penne Carbonara

PENNE ALLA CARBONARA

Ingredients	Metric/Imperial	American
pig's cheek	100 g/4 oz	$\frac{1}{4}$ pound
garlic clove	1	1
olive oil	3 tablespoons	scant $\frac{1}{4}$ cup
stock	225 ml/8 fl oz	1 cup
pasta quills	350 g/12 oz	$\frac{3}{4}$ pound
salt and pepper		
eggs	3	3
Pecorino cheese, grated	4 tablespoons	6 tablespoons

Soak the pig's cheek in salted water for 1 hour; drain well.

Cut the pig's cheek into small cubes and crush the garlic. Heat the oil in a large heavy pan, add the meat and garlic and cook over a medium heat for about 10 minutes until the meat is cooked and the garlic is golden. Add the stock and cook for 30 minutes. Remove and discard the garlic.

Cook the pasta in plenty of lightly salted boiling water.

Meanwhile beat the eggs in a serving bowl with a pinch of salt and pepper and the Pecorino cheese. Put the bowl over a pan of boiling water and heat gently.

When the pasta is cooked *al dente* drain it and put in the pan with the meat. Mix quickly together with a wooden spoon, then turn into the bowl with the eggs. Mix until the eggs form a creamy sauce and serve at once.

Time: 55 minutes + 1 hour: soaking　　　*Serves 4*

Penne Carbonara

Penne with Sweet Peppers

MEZZE PENNE CON PEPERONI ALLA RUSTICA

Ingredients	Metric/Imperial	American
anchovy fillets	5	5
yellow (sweet) pepper	1	1
red (sweet) pepper	1	1
oil	125 ml/4 fl oz	½ cup
garlic cloves	2	2
salt and pepper		
dry white wine	3 tablespoons	scant ¼ cup
tomato paste	1 tablespoon	1 tablespoon
stock	225 ml/8 fl oz	1 cup
small penne pasta	350 g/12 oz	¾ pound
chopped parsley	1 tablespoon	1 tablespoon

Put the anchovy fillets to soak in a little milk to remove excess salt.

Wash both the peppers and place on an oiled baking tray. Put in a hot oven (220 C, 425 F, gas 7), turning occasionally, until the skins are burnt. Remove and carefully peel off the skins, remove the stems and the seeds, collecting the juices in a bowl. Using a knife and fork, cut into slivers 2.5 cm/1 in long and 5 mm/¼ in wide. Heat the stock.

Put the garlic and drained anchovies through a mincer (grinder) or food processor. Heat the oil in a large pan, add the anchovy and garlic mixture and cook over a low heat until softened. Add the slivers of pepper, stir, and moisten with the reserved juices. Season lightly, pour in the wine and allow it to evaporate slowly, then add the tomato paste diluted with the hot stock.

While the sauce is simmering cook the pasta in a large pan of lightly salted boiling water until *al dente*. Transfer to the pan with the sauce and mix well; pour into a deep heated serving dish and sprinkle with parsley.

Time: 50 minutes   *Serves 4*

Penne with Sweet Peppers

Penne with Sausage and Mixed Vegetables

PENNE UNA TIRA L'ALTRA

Ingredients	Metric/Imperial	American
onion	½	½
small shallot	1	1
small carrot	1	1
celery stalk	1	1
small yellow (sweet) pepper	1	1
oil	3 tablespoons	scant ¼ cup
butter	25 g/1 oz	2 tablespoons
Italian sausage	100 g/4 oz	¼ pound
basil leaves	4	4
dry red wine	50 ml/2 fl oz	¼ cup
plum tomatoes	400 g/14 oz	14 ounces
salt and pepper		
penne pasta	400 g/14 oz	14 ounces
Pecorino cheese, grated	2 tablespoons	3 tablespoons
Parmesan cheese, grated	2 tablespoons	3 tablespoons

Chop the onion and shallot, finely dice the carrot and slice the celery. Deseed the pepper, wash, dry and cut into small dice.

Heat the oil and butter in a flameproof casserole, add the chopped vegetables and cook on a low heat for 4 minutes.

Mix well and then add the crumbled sausage, diced pepper and chopped basil. Brown over a medium heat for 3–4 minutes; moisten with the red wine.

When the wine has evaporated, add the sieved plum tomatoes with a pinch of salt and plenty of pepper. Cook the sauce, covered with a lid, for 30 minutes, stirring from time to time.

Cook the pasta in plenty of boiling salted water until *al dente*, drain well. Tip into the casserole and mix well. Sprinkle with the grated cheeses and mix again before serving piping hot.

Time: 1 hour 10 minutes   *Serves 4*

Pasta with Sardines

PASTA CON LE SARDE

Ingredients	Metric/Imperial	American
fresh sardines	450 g/1 lb	1 pound
sultanas (seedless white raisins)	40 g/1½ oz	¼ cup
fennel heads	12	12
saffron	¼ teaspoon	¼ teaspoon
onion	1	1
olive oil	6 tablespoons	½ cup
pine nuts	25 g/1 oz	¼ cup
salt and pepper		
anchovies	3	3
macaroni	400 g/14 oz	14 ounces

Clean the sardines, discard the heads, remove the main bone and wash the fillets under running water.

Soak the sultanas in warm water. Clean the fennel and choose only the tender tops. Place in a pan with plenty of water and leave to boil for 10 minutes. Remove the fennel with a slotted spoon, reserving the cooking water to cook the pasta. Drain, chop and place the fennel on one side. Soak the saffron in 2 tablespoons of the fennel water.

Finely chop the onion. Heat two-thirds of the oil in a pan, add the onion and cook over a low heat for 4 minutes. Add the saffron, drained sultanas and pine nuts. Mix and allow to flavour, then stir in the sardine fillet and carefully allow to brown on all sides.

Add the chopped fennel, with a little salt and pepper, cover the pan for 10 minutes.

Heat the remaining oil in a small pan with the chopped rinsed anchovies, stirring with a wooden spoon until they are broken down. Add the anchovies to the pan with the sardines and mix gently, taking care not to break the sardines.

Bring the pan with fennel water back to the boil, sprinkle in the pasta and cook until *al dente*. Drain and place in a heated serving dish. Dress with the sardine sauce, mix and serve.

Time: 1 hour and 10 minutes   *Serves 4*

Pasta with Sardines

Pasta Maurizio

CONCHIGLIONI ALLA MAURIZIO

Ingredients	Metric/Imperial	American
chopped basil	½ teaspoon	½ teaspoon
garlic clove	1	1
canned plum tomatoes	400 g/14 oz	14 ounces
salt and pepper		
stock cube	½	½
anchovies	2	2
black olives	2 tablespoons	3 tablespoons
capers	1 tablespoon	1 tablespoon
large shell pasta	350 g/12 oz	¾ pound

Place the basil in a small saucepan with the crushed garlic and 2–3 tablespoons of water; leave to flavour for a few minutes. Add the tomatoes, a pinch of salt and pepper and the crumbled stock cube. Cook for 30 minutes on a low heat.

Rinse and drain the anchovies, remove the bone and chop into small pieces. Remove the stones from the olives and chop together with the capers. Halfway through the cooking time add the olives, capers and anchovies to the sauce.

Cook the pasta in plenty of boiling salted water, drain and place in a heated serving dish. Mix well with the sauce. Serve immediately.

Time: 30 minutes   *Serves 4*

Pasta Shells with Courgette (Zucchini)

CONCHIGLIONI CON ZUCCHINE

Ingredients	Metric/Imperial	American
butter	75 g/3 oz	6 tablespoons
courgettes (zucchini)	450 g/1 lb	1 pound
smoked bacon	100 g/4 oz	$\frac{1}{4}$ pound
chopped basil	$\frac{1}{2}$ teaspoon	$\frac{1}{2}$ teaspoon
salt and pepper		
large pasta shells	350 g/12 oz	$\frac{3}{4}$ pound
single (thin) cream	225 ml/8 fl oz	1 cup
Parmesan cheese, grated	25 g/1 oz	$\frac{1}{4}$ cup

Melt the butter in a heavy pan, add the diced courgettes and cook over medium heat until golden. Add the derinded bacon cut into cubes and the basil; season to taste.

Cook the pasta in a large pan of lightly salted boiling water until *al dente*. Mix with the courgettes, cream and Parmesan cheese. Serve at once.

Time: 30 minutes   *Serves 4*

Pasta Shells Gardener's-style

CONCHIGLIE ALLA GIARDINIERA

Ingredients	Metric/Imperial	American
medium-sized potatoes	2	2
French beans	225 g/8 oz	$\frac{1}{2}$ pound
salt and pepper		
medium-sized pasta shells	350 g/12 oz	$\frac{3}{4}$ pound
small onion	1	1
shallots	2	2
garlic clove	1	1
oil	4 tablespoons	6 tablespoons
tuna in oil	200 g/7 oz	7 ounces
capers	2 tablespoons	3 tablespoons
green olives, stoned	12	12
chopped parsley	1 tablespoon	1 tablespoon

Peel and cube the potatoes; top, tail and roughly chop the beans. Bring a large pan of salted water to the boil, add the potatoes and simmer for 10 minutes. Add the beans, cook for a further 15 minutes, then remove both vegetables with a slotted spoon. Return the water to the boil and cook the pasta.

Finely chop the onion and shallots; crush the garlic. Heat three-quarters of the oil in a large pan, add the onion, shallots and garlic and cook over medium heat until golden. Drain and chop the tuna, rinse the capers and chop the olives; add to the pan together with the parsley. Mix carefully, add the potatoes and beans, cover and continue cooking; adjust the seasoning if necessary.

When the pasta is cooked *al dente* drain thoroughly (reserve a little of the water) and put in a large heated serving bowl with the vegetable and tuna mixture. Add the remaining oil, pepper and a few drops of reserved cooking water. Mix well and serve.

Time: 45 minutes   *Serves 4*

Pasta Shells with Stuffed Olives

CONCHIGLIETTE ALLA OLIVE FARCITE

Ingredients	Metric/Imperial	American
small onion	1	1
garlic clove	1	1
celery stalk	1	1
oil	5 tablespoons	$\frac{1}{3}$ cup
tuna in oil	100 g/4 oz	$\frac{1}{4}$ pound
plum tomatoes	6	6
small pasta shells	350 g/12 oz	$\frac{3}{4}$ pound
salt and pepper		
stuffed green olives	100 g/4 oz	$\frac{1}{4}$ pound
coarsely chopped basil	1 tablespoon	1 tablespoon
Worcester sauce	$\frac{1}{2}$ teaspoon	$\frac{1}{2}$ teaspoon

Chop the onion, garlic and celery finely. Heat the oil in a heavy pan, add the chopped vegetables and tuna with its oil and cook for 15 minutes over a low heat. Deseed and chop the tomatoes, add to the pan and continue cooking until the sauce is well blended.

Meanwhile cook the pasta in plenty of lightly salted boiling water until *al dente*. Drain, pour into a heated bowl, add the sauce and mix well. Cut the olives horizontally into 3 and add to the sauce together with the basil, Worcester sauce and pepper to taste. Mix again and serve.

Time: 35 minutes   *Serves 4*

Chop the onion together with the celery, carrot and derinded bacon. Melt the butter in a large deep pan, add the rosemary and garlic and cook over a medium heat until golden. Remove the rosemary and garlic, add the chopped mixture and cook until golden brown. Add the lamb and cook it over a low heat, stirring occasionally and moistening with the brandy. If the sauce dries out too much add a few tablespoons of stock.

Cook the pasta in plenty of lightly salted boiling water until *al dente*. Meanwhile cut the cheese into strips and add to the sauce, stirring constantly.

Drain the pasta and add it to the sauce. Raise the heat and cook for a few minutes, stirring to mix the pasta and sauce together. Serve at once.

Time: 1 hour　　　　　　　　　　　　　　　*Serves 4*

Pasta Shells with Lamb Sauce

Pasta Shells with Lamb Sauce

CONCHIGLIE CON SUGO DI AGNELLO E SCAMORZA

Ingredients	Metric/Imperial	American
onion	1	1
celery stalk	1	1
carrot	1	1
bacon	40 g/1½ oz	1½ ounces
butter	40 g/1½ oz	3 tablespoons
sprig of rosemary	1	1
garlic clove	1	1
minced (ground) lamb	450 g/1 lb	1 pound
brandy	1 tablespoon	1 tablespoon
stock	3 tablespoons	scant ¼ cup
oil	1 tablespoon	1 tablespoon
pasta shells	350 g/12 oz	¾ pound
salt		
medium-sized unsmoked Scamorza cheese	1	1

Pasta Shells with Vodka Cheese Sauce

CONCHIGLIE AL CONDIMENTO BIANCO

Ingredients	Metric/Imperial	American
pasta shells	450 g/1 lb	1 pound
salt and pepper		
butter	40 g/1½ oz	3 tablespoons
garlic clove	1	1
vodka	1½ tablespoons	2 tablespoons
Crescenza (rindless fresh cheese)	75 g/3 oz	3 ounces
single (thin) cream	100 ml/3½ fl oz	scant ½ cup
Gruyère cheese, grated	50 g/2 oz	½ cup
grated nutmeg	¼ teaspoon	¼ teaspoon

Cook the pasta in plenty of lightly salted boiling water until *al dente*.

Melt half the butter in a large deep pan, add the garlic, cut in half, and the vodka. Allow the vodka to evaporate, then remove the garlic. Mash the Crescenza cheese with a fork and add to the pan; stir in the cream.

Dice the remaining butter and add to the pan a piece at a time, waiting for each one to melt and blend in before continuing. Whisk the sauce well and complete with half the Gruyère cheese, salt, pepper and nutmeg.

Drain the pasta, add to the sauce and mix well together with a spoon and fork. Stand for 2 minutes, then turn into a heated serving dish. Sprinkle with the remaining Gruyère cheese and serve at once.

Time: 25 minutes　　　　　　　　　　　　*Serves 4*

Buccaneer's Pasta

CONCHIGLIE DEL BUCANIERE

Ingredients	Metric/Imperial	American
onion	1	1
garlic clove	1	1
sprigs of parsley	2	2
basil leaves	6	6
oil	2 tablespoons	3 tablespoons
butter	40 g/1½ oz	3 tablespoons
cooked ham	50 g/2 oz	2 ounces
pork	100 g/4 oz	¼ pound
veal	100 g/4 oz	¼ pound
salt and pepper		
dry white wine	3 tablespoons	scant ¼ cup
canned plum tomatoes	400 g/14 oz	14 ounces
chopped thyme	¼ teaspoon	¼ teaspoon
pasta shells	350 g/12 oz	¾ pound
Parmesan cheese, grated	25 g/1 oz	¼ cup

Finely chop the onion, garlic, parsley and basil. Heat the oil with the butter in a heavy shallow pan, add the chopped ingredients and cook over a low heat until the onion is transparent.

Chop the ham, add to the pan and simmer for a few minutes, then add the pork and veal, finely diced. Cook over a medium heat, stirring, until lightly browned, then season with salt and pepper, moisten with the wine and leave until it has evaporated.

Chop the tomatoes, add to the pan with a pinch of salt and the thyme; leave the sauce to cook and thicken over a medium heat.

Meanwhile cook the pasta in plenty of lightly salted boiling water until *al dente*. Drain, mix with the sauce, sprinkle with Parmesan cheese and serve piping hot.

Time: 40 minutes　　　　　　　　　　　　　*Serves 4*

Pasta with Ham and Artichokes

RIGATONI CON PROSCIUTTO E CARCIOFI

Ingredients	Metric/Imperial	American
artichokes	4	4
lemon	1	1
shallots	2	2
butter	50 g/2 oz	¼ cup
oil	2 tablespoons	3 tablespoons
cooked ham	75 g/3 oz	3 ounces
stock cube	1	1
salt and pepper		
milk	125 ml/4 fl oz	½ cup
rigatoni pasta	350 g/12 oz	¾ pound
chopped parsley	1 tablespoon	1 tablespoon
Mozzarella cheese, cubed	1	1
Parmesan cheese, grated	25 g/1 oz	¼ cup

Rigatoni with Ham and Artichokes

Prepare the artichokes: remove the stalks and tough outer leaves, trim the points off the remainder. Blanch for 15 minutes in boiling water. Spread the leaves apart, pull out the soft inner leaves and scrape out the bristly choke with a spoon. Put in a bowl of water acidulated with the juice of a lemon to prevent discoloration.

Finely chop the shallots; heat half the butter with the oil in a large deep pan. Add the shallots and cook over medium heat until golden.

Rinse, drain and slice the artichokes and add to the pan together with the cubed ham. Stir together, cook for a few minutes over high heat, then switch to low, crumble in the stock cube, season with pepper, add the milk and leave to simmer.

Meanwhile cook the pasta in a large pan of lightly salted boiling water until *al dente*. Drain and transfer to the pan with the sauce. Mix in the remaining butter, parsley, Mozzarella and Parmesan cheeses. Mix again and serve.

Time: 40 minutes   *Serves 4*

Rigatoni Radicchio

RIGATONI ALLA MODA INSOLITA

Ingredients	Metric/Imperial	American
rigatoni	350 g/12 oz	¾ pound
salt and freshly ground black pepper		
heads of radicchio (red salad)	2	2
leeks	2	2
small onion	1	1
celery stalk	1	1
shallots	2	2
bacon	25 g/1 oz	1 ounce
sage leaves	2	2
oil	4 tablespoons	6 tablespoons
tuna in oil	100 g/4 oz	¼ pound
pickled capers	1 tablespoon	1 tablespoon
black olive purée	2 tablespoons	3 tablespoons
dry white wine	2 tablespoons	3 tablespoons
butter	25 g/1 oz	2 tablespoons

Cook the rigatoni in plenty of boiling salted water until *al dente*.

Wash, dry and thinly slice the radicchio.

Chop all the other cleaned vegetables finely with the derinded bacon and the sage leaves. Heat the oil in a large pan, add the chopped ingredients and gently cook for 10 minutes over a low heat. Add the slivers of radicchio, mix and after 5 minutes add the mashed tuna, the well-rinsed capers and the olive purée. (If olive purée is not available, purée stoned olives in the blender.)

Mix well and sprinkle in a little wine, allow to evaporate then add the butter in knobs. Beat with a fork to blend all the ingredients.

Drain the pasta when cooked and tip into the pan, mix and leave to flavour in the sauce. Sprinkle with pepper before serving piping hot.

Time: 35 minutes   *Serves 4*

Mrs Pia's Rigatoni

RIGATONI DELLA SORA PIA

Ingredients	Metric/Imperial	American
carrot	1	1
celery stalk	1	1
onion	½	½
bacon	50 g/2 oz	2 ounces
oil	4 tablespoons	6 tablespoons
butter	25 g/1 oz	2 tablespoons
minced (ground) beef	225 g/8 oz	1 cup
dry white wine	125 ml/4 fl oz	½ cup
salt and pepper		
grated nutmeg	¼ teaspoon	¼ teaspoon
fresh tomatoes	225 g/8 oz	½ pound
stock	300 ml/½ pint	1¼ cups
frozen peas	100 g/4 oz	¼ pound
rigatoni pasta	400 g/14 oz	14 ounces

Prepare and chop finely the carrot, celery, onion and derinded bacon. Heat the oil with the butter in a large casserole over a medium heat and add the vegetables. When they start to change colour, add the minced beef. Mix well for a few minutes until the meat is brown, then pour in the wine.

Allow to evaporate slightly, then season with salt, pepper and nutmeg.

Add the tomatoes, peeled, deseeded and chopped, pour in the stock and cook the sauce for 25 minutes. Add the peas and more stock from time to time if necessary. Make sure that the sauce is a good thick consistency after a further 30 minutes cooking.

Cook the pasta in plenty of boiling salted water until *al dente*. Drain, dress with the sauce and serve piping hot.

Time: 1 hour 10 minutes   *Serves 4*

Peasant's Pasta

Derind the bacon and dice. Chop the garlic, onion, carrot, celery and deseeded pepper into even-sized pieces. Heat the oil and butter in a large heavy pan, add the prepared vegetables and cook over medium heat until golden.

Add the peas and chopped tomatoes. Cook over a low heat until thick, crumble in the stock cube, season with salt, pepper and oregano, add the wine and simmer gently with no lid.

Meanwhile cook the pasta in plenty of lightly salted boiling water until *al dente*.

Drain the pasta, put in a deep serving dish and sprinkle with some of the Pecorino and Parmesan cheese. Pour over a little of the sauce, add a little more cheese, then the remaining sauce. Mix well and serve hot.

Time: 1 hour 10 minutes   *Serves 4*

The idea of the Italian title is to use up all the scraps left over at the end of the month.

Peasant's Pasta

BAVETTE DELL'ULTIMO DEL MESE

Ingredients	Metric/Imperial	American
bacon	50 g/2 oz	2 ounces
garlic clove	1	1
onion	1	1
carrot	1	1
celery	1	1
yellow (sweet) pepper	$\frac{1}{2}$	$\frac{1}{2}$
oil	3 tablespoons	scant $\frac{1}{4}$ cup
butter		
podded peas	4 tablespoons	6 tablespoons
plum tomatoes	225 g/8 oz	$\frac{1}{2}$ pound
stock cube	1	1
salt and pepper		
oregano	$\frac{1}{4}$ teaspoon	$\frac{1}{4}$ teaspoon
red wine	3 tablespoons	scant $\frac{1}{4}$ cup
bavette pasta	400 g/14 oz	14 ounces
Pecorino cheese, grated	2 tablespoons	3 tablespoons
Parmesan cheese, grated	1 tablespoon	2 tablespoons

Baked Pasta and Peppers

PASTA E PEPERONI AL FORNO

Ingredients	Metric/Imperial	American
large yellow (sweet) peppers	2	2
onion	$\frac{1}{2}$	$\frac{1}{2}$
plum tomatoes	6	6
salt and pepper		
stock	225 ml/8 fl oz	1 cup
penne pasta	350 g/12 oz	$\frac{3}{4}$ pound
chopped basil	$\frac{1}{2}$ teaspoon	$\frac{1}{2}$ teaspoon
Mozzarella cheese	200 g/7 oz	7 ounces
milk	3 tablespoons	scant $\frac{1}{4}$ cup

Remove the seeds from the peppers and rinse. Cut into strips and chop into fine dice. Put in a pan with the thinly sliced onion, peeled chopped tomatoes and a pinch of salt; cover and simmer for about 20 minutes, adding the stock after 5 minutes.

Meanwhile cook the pasta in plenty of lightly salted boiling water until *al dente*; drain well.

Sprinkle the sauce with basil and mix with the pasta and the diced Mozzarella cheese. Transfer to a large non-stick baking pan, pour over the milk and put in a moderately hot oven (200 C, 400 F, gas 6) for 15 minutes until golden and hot.

Time: 45 minutes   *Serves 4*

Pasta with Fennel and Smoked Ham

Pasta with Fennel and Smoked Ham

TORTIGLIONI ALLA DIVA

Ingredients	Metric/Imperial	American
tortiglioni pasta	400 g/14 oz	14 ounces
salt and pepper		
fennel heads	2	2
butter	60 g/2½ oz	5 tablespoons
small onion	1	1
cooked smoked ham	150 g/5 oz	5 ounces
dry white wine	1 tablespoon	1 tablespoon
milk	2 tablespoons	3 tablespoons
black olives	50 g/2 oz	2 ounces
cumin seeds	¼ teaspoon	¼ teaspoon
Parmesan cheese, grated	25 g/1 oz	¼ cup

Cook the pasta in plenty of lightly salted boiling water until *al dente*.

Meanwhile simmer the fennel heads in a small pan of boiling water for 10 minutes, then drain and slice thinly.

Heat half the butter in a large pan, add the finely chopped onion and cook over a low heat until transparent. Add the sliced fennel, simmer for 10 minutes and add the cubed ham. Mix together and cook until the ham is golden, then add the wine and leave until it evaporates.

Add the milk, cover and cook for a further 5 minutes. Finish with the olives, stoned and chopped, cumin seeds and a little pepper.

Drain the pasta, pour into the pan with the sauce and mix well. Add the Parmesan cheese and remaining butter, diced. Mix again, transfer to a large heated dish and serve at once.

Time: 30 minutes   *Serves 4*

Baked Pasta with Artichokes

PASTA AL FORNO CON CARCIOFI

Ingredients	Metric/Imperial	American
artichokes	4	4
small onion	1	1
stock	225 ml/8 fl oz	1 cup
salt and pepper		
macaroni	400 g/14 oz	14 ounces
Mozzarella cheese	1	1
milk	6 tablespoons	½ cup
Parmesan cheese, grated	25 g/1 oz	¼ cup
chopped parsley	1 tablespoon	1 tablespoon

Prepare the artichokes: remove the stems and hard outer leaves; trim the points off the remaining leaves and remove the hairy chokes from the centres. Rinse under running water and slice thinly.

Finely chop the onion and cook over medium heat in a non-stick pan until golden. Add the artichoke slices and stock, season and simmer until the liquid has reduced.

Cook the pasta in plenty of lightly salted boiling water until *al dente*. Drain and mix with the artichokes. Dice the Mozzarella cheese, add it to the mixture and put in a large ovenproof dish.

Mix the milk with the Parmesan cheese and parsley, pour over the pasta and put in a moderate oven (180 c, 350 f, gas 4) for about 5 minutes to brown the top. Serve at once.

Time: 40 minutes   *Serves 4*

Gourmet's Pasta

MEZZE MANICHE ALLA MODA DEL GOLOSO

Ingredients	Metric/Imperial	American
onion	1	1
garlic clove	1	1
celery stalk	1	1
carrot	1	1
butter	40 g/1½ oz	3 tablespoons
oil	2 tablespoons	3 tablespoons
minced (ground) veal	225 g/8 oz	½ pound
fresh Italian sausages	225 g/8 oz	½ pound
canned plum tomatoes	400 g/14 oz	14 ounces
tomato paste	2 tablespoons	3 tablespoons
salt and pepper		
aubergine (eggplant)	1	1
oil for frying		
mezze maniche pasta	350 g/12 oz	¾ pound
Parmesan cheese, grated	25 g/1 oz	¼ cup
bunch of basil	1	1

Finely chop the onion, garlic, celery and carrot. Heat three-quarters of the butter with the oil in a large pan, add the chopped vegetables and cook over a low heat until golden.

Add the veal together with the skinned and crumbled sausages and increase the heat to brown the mixture lightly. Chop the tomatoes and mix the tomato paste with a little hot water. Add both to the pan, season with a pinch of salt and pepper and leave over a low heat with the lid half on.

Meanwhile cut the aubergine into small cubes and fry in a little hot oil. Cook the pasta in plenty of lightly salted boiling water until *al dente*.

Drain the pasta, put into a heated serving bowl and mix with the sauce, remaining butter and fried aubergine cubes. Sprinkle with Parmesan cheese, mix and serve garnished with chopped basil.

Time: 40 minutes   *Serves 4*

Pasta with Pepper and Tuna Sauce

REGINETTE AL SUGO PRELIBATO

Ingredients	Metric/Imperial	American
anchovy fillets	2	2
leek	1	1
oil	4 tablespoons	6 tablespoons
yellow (sweet) pepper	1	1
plum tomatoes	350 g/12 oz	¾ pound
stock or white wine	225 ml/8 fl oz	1 cup
salt and pepper		
black stoned olives	12	12
tuna in oil	150 g/5 oz	5 ounces
reginette pasta	350 g/12 oz	¾ pound
Pecorino cheese, grated	2 tablespoons	3 tablespoons
bunch of basil	1	1

Soak the anchovy fillets in a little milk to remove excess salt.

Remove the root, coarse outer leaves and green top from the leek. Slice the white part into rings, rinse well and drain. Deseed the pepper, wash, dry and dice.

Heat the oil in a shallow pan, add the leeks and the anchovies, drained and chopped. Mix well, cook for a few minutes over a low heat, then add the chopped pepper. Peel the tomatoes if using fresh ones; drain if canned. Slice and add to the pan with the stock, wine or a mixture of both. Season with salt and pepper and

Gourmet's Pasta

Pasta with Pepper and Tuna Sauce

First prepare the tomato sauce: heat the butter with the oil over a medium heat and add the finely chopped onion and crushed garlic. When the onion is just turning golden add the beef and chopped Mortadella sausage. Stir until well mixed and lightly browned.

Add the wine, allow it to evaporate, then add the tomatoes, oregano, salt and pepper. Stir to break down the tomatoes and simmer for 30 minutes over a medium heat.

Meanwhile cook the sheets of lasagne, a few at a time, in plenty of boiling salted water in a large pan. Give each batch about 10 minutes. Remove with a slotted spoon, rinse in a colander with cold water and lay on a clean tea towel to dry.

Put a few tablespoons of the sauce in the bottom of an ovenproof dish. Arrange the first layer of lasagne, cover with a few tablespoons of Béchamel sauce, followed by a few tablespoons of tomato sauce. Arrange some slices of Mozzarella cheese on top, sprinkle with Parmesan cheese and then cover with a layer of lasagne. Continue in this way until all the ingredients are used up and top with breadcrumbs.

Put the dish in a moderate oven (180 c, 350 f, gas 4) for 20 minutes until the top is golden and crisp. Serve hot.

leave to simmer for 20 minutes. Just before the end of the cooking time add the chopped olives and the tuna, drained and chopped.

Cook the pasta in a large pan of lightly salted boiling water until *al dente*. Drain, put in a heated serving bowl, add the sauce and mix well. Sprinkle with Pecorino cheese and chopped basil and mix again before serving.

Time: 40 minutes   *Serves 4*

Time: 1 hour 10 minutes   *Serves 6*

Spicy Lasagne

Spicy Lasagne

LASAGNETTE ALLA MODA MIA

Ingredients	Metric/Imperial	American
butter	25 g/1 oz	2 tablespoons
oil	2 tablespoons	3 tablespoons
onion	1	1
garlic clove	1	1
minced (ground) beef	350 g/12 oz	$\frac{3}{4}$ pound
Mortadella sausage	75 g/3 oz	3 ounces
dry white wine	3 tablespoons	scant $\frac{1}{4}$ cup
canned plum tomatoes	400 g/14 oz	14 ounces
chopped oregano	$\frac{1}{4}$ teaspoon	$\frac{1}{4}$ teaspoon
salt and pepper		
fresh lasagne	450 g/1 lb	1 pound
Béchamel sauce (page 25)	600 ml/1 pint	$2\frac{1}{2}$ cups
Mozzarella cheese	225 g/8 oz	$\frac{1}{2}$ pound
Parmesan cheese, grated	75 g/3 oz	$\frac{1}{4}$ cup
dried breadcrumbs	2 tablespoons	3 tablespoons

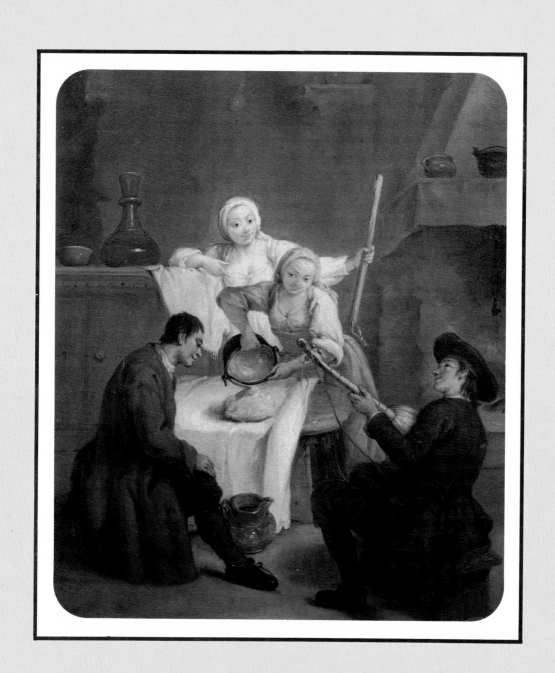

PIZZA
AND
POLENTA

*Pizza is said to have been invented by
the bakers in the back streets of Naples as a way
of making a little food stretch a long way.
However there are almost as many tales of pizza
as there are of the origins of pasta, some dating
back to Roman times.
The secret of the Italian pizza is in the baking
which takes place in the specially
built brick ovens.
Even so, home-made pizzas are fun to make
and are much loved by both young and old alike.
Polenta is another traditional recipe – prepared
from yellow maize flour, it is one of the
staple foods of northern Italy along with rice.
It is eaten in place of bread; fried or grilled to
accompany meat or poultry or it is eaten very
simply with tomato sauce.*

How to make pizza

1 Make up the yeast. Sift the flour and salt on to a board or into a bowl in a mound. Make a well in the centre; add the sugar, salt, oil and the measured water.

2 Mix into the flour with the finger tips and then start to add the yeast mixture. Mix well.

3 Flour the board and knead well using both hands. Lift the dough and beat on the table between kneading for about 10 minutes. Cover and leave to rise.

4 When the dough has doubled in size turn out on a floured board and knock back by kneading and rolling. Make into a ball again and leave covered for 15 minutes.

5 Turn out again, divide into 2 or 4 pieces and shape into a round. Place on an oiled baking, brush with oil and start adding the tomato base.

6 Complete the pizza by arranging the chosen fillings. The pizza here is quite thick; for a thin crispy base work the dough until it is half the thickness shown.

Homemade Pizza Dough

PASTA FATTA IN CASA

Ingredients	Metric/Imperial	American
fresh or dried yeast	25 g/1 oz	1 cake compressed
plain (all-purpose) flour	350 g/12 oz	3 cups
caster (fine granulated) sugar	1 teaspoon	1 teaspoon
salt	1 teaspoon	1 teaspoon
oil	3 tablespoons	4 tablespoons
extra flour for kneading	100 g/4 oz	1 cup

Put the fresh yeast in a cup and mix with a little lukewarm water; follow packet instructions if using dried yeast.

Sift the flour on to a large flat surface (wood, laminated plastic or marble) so that it forms a mound. Make a well in the centre and put in the sugar, salt, oil and 300 ml/½ pint/1¼ cups of lukewarm water. Mix together with the fingers. When the water is well blended with the flour incorporate the yeast a little at a time.

Knead the dough energetically with both hands, lifting it up and beating it on the work surface, for about 10 minutes or until smooth and elastic. Form into a ball, put in a lightly floured bowl and leave to rise in a slightly warm place (about 28 c/82 F) (not in an oven) for 30 minutes or until doubled in bulk.

Return the dough to the work surface and knead again for a few minutes, using the extra flour. Roll out several times with a rolling pin until soft. Reform into a ball and leave to rise for another 15 minutes.

Flatten the ball with the hands to obtain the required size round and put on an oiled baking tray. Press with the finger tips so that the pizza is thicker at the edges than in the centre.

Complete with the chosen topping and bake.

Time: 1½ hours
Makes 2 (30 cm/12 in) or 4 (20 cm/8 in) round pizza bases.

Note: liquid for yeast mixtures must be lukewarm (28 c/82 F; neither hot nor cold to the touch). If it is colder the rising will take longer, but if it is much warmer the action of the yeast will be killed.

This recipe will make just over 450 g/1 pound of dough.

Rustic Pizza

PIZZA RUSTICA

Ingredients	Metric/Imperial	American
For the dough:		
plain (all-purpose) flour	450 g/1 lb	4 cups
salt		
lard	25 g/1 oz	2 tablespoons
fresh yeast	25 g/1 oz	1 compressed cake
oil	2 tablespoons	3 tablespoons
milk	300 ml/½ pint	1¼ cups
egg yolk	1	1
For the topping:		
eggs	2	2
Pecorino cheese, grated	150 g/5 oz	5 ounces
Scamorza or Mozzarella cheese	2	2
fresh pork sausages	2	2
Italian salami	50 g/2 oz	2 ounces
Parma ham	50 g/2 oz	2 ounces

Prepare the dough as for basic pizza dough (see page 142): rub in the lard and mix the flour with egg yolk and milk.

While the dough is rising prepare the topping. Beat the eggs and mix with the Pecorino cheese. Slice the Scamorza cheese, skin the sausages and crumble.

Preheat the oven to 230 c, 450 f, gas 8.

Divide the dough in half and press one portion out into a 30 cm/12 in round. Grease a large baking tray with lard and put on the round of dough. Pinch up the edge so it is slightly raised. Spread with the egg mixture, then top with alternating layer of Scamorza cheese, crumbled sausage, salami and Parma ham, leaving a good border round the edge uncovered.

Press the second piece of dough out to the same size. Put on top of the first and fold the edges under inside the raised edge of the bottom piece. Pinch the edges firmly to seal in the filling. Brush the top with beaten egg and put in the hot oven for about 40 minutes.

Time: 1 hour + rising time   *Serves 6*

This is a regional dish from Teramo in the Abruzzo region.

Neapolitan Pizza

PIZZA NAPOLETANA

Making pizzas in a wood burning pizza oven.
Typical pizza ingredients are shown such as tomatoes, basil,
olives and cheese.

Ingredients	Metric/Imperial	American
made-up pizza dough (page 143)	450 g/1 lb	1 pound
canned plum tomatoes	400 g/14 oz	14 ounces
chopped oregano	¼ teaspoon	¼ teaspoon
salt and pepper		
olive oil	3 tablespoons	4 tablespoons
capers	1 tablespoon	1 tablespoon
anchovy fillets	4	4
basil leaves	4	4

Preheat the oven to 230 c, 450 f, gas 8.

Chop the tomatoes and put in a bowl with the oregano, a pinch of salt and the oil. Chop the drained capers and anchovies together with the basil leaves; add to the bowl and season to taste.

Divide the dough into four and press into rounds on greased baking trays, building up the edge of each one slightly to contain the filling. Spread with the tomato mixture and put in the hot oven for about 20 minutes, or until the pizzas are crisp and golden.

Time: 20 minutes + time for making dough
Makes 4 × 20 cm/8 in pizzas

Four Seasons Pizza

PIZZA 4 STAGIONI

Ingredients	Metric/Imperial	American
made-up pizza dough (page 143)	225 g/8 oz	½ pound
canned plum tomatoes	400 g/1 lb	1 pound
mushrooms	100 g/4 oz	¼ pound
salt and pepper		
oil	1 tablespoon	1 tablespoon
Mozzarella cheese	100 g/4 oz	¼ pound
canned artichoke hearts	8	8
tuna in oil	200 g/7 oz	7 ounces
garlic clove	1	1

Preheat the oven to 230 C, 450 F, gas 8. Drain, deseed and chop the tomatoes; wipe the mushrooms and slice evenly.

Press the dough out into a large round on an oiled baking tray. Spread with the tomatoes, season with salt and pepper and sprinkle with a little oil.

Divide the pizza into 4 equal parts, using the back of a knife to prevent cutting through the dough. Top one section with slices of Mozzarella cheese, the second with chopped artichokes, the third with mushrooms and the last with drained chopped tuna and slivers of garlic.

Put in the hot oven for about 20 minutes.

Time: 35 minutes + time for making dough   Serves 4

Roman Pizza

PIZZA ROMANA

Ingredients	Metric/Imperial	American
made-up pizza dough (page 143)	450 g/1 lb	1 pound
canned plum tomatoes	400 g/14 oz	14 ounces
salt and pepper		
Mozzarella cheese	225 g/8 oz	½ pound
anchovy fillets	4	4
chopped oregano	1 teaspoon	1 teaspoon
eggs	4	4
oil		

Preheat the oven to 230 C, 450 F, gas 8.

Drain the tomatoes, deseed, chop and season lightly with salt. Slice the Mozzarella cheese; rinse and chop the anchovies.

Divide the dough into four and press out into rounds on oiled baking trays. Trickle over a little oil and top with slices of cheese and the prepared tomatoes and anchovies. Sprinkle with oregano and put in the hot oven for 20 minutes.

Break an egg on top of each pizza, season with salt and pepper and return to the oven until the whites are just set. Serve at once.

Time: 40 minutes + time for making dough
Makes 4 (20 cm/8 in) pizzas

Ligurian Pizza

PIZZA LIGURE

Ingredients	Metric/Imperial	American
made-up pizza dough (page 143)	450 g/1 lb	1 pound
small onions	2	2
oil	50 ml/2 fl oz	¼ cup
basil leaves	4	4
fresh tomatoes	700 g/1½ lb	1½ pounds
salt		
anchovy fillets	8	8
garlic cloves	3	3
black olives	1 tablespoon	1 tablespoon
chopped oregano	1 teaspoon	1 teaspoon

Preheat the oven to 230 C, 450 F, gas 8.

Slice the onions thinly. Heat 2–3 tablespoons of the oil in a pan over a low heat, add the onions and cook gently for 5 minutes. Add the chopped basil leaves and peeled, deseeded and chopped tomatoes. Season lightly with salt and simmer for 30 minutes.

Remove the sauce from the heat and stir in the drained and chopped anchovies.

Divide the dough into four pieces and press out into rounds on oiled baking trays. Spread the prepared sauce over the top. Finish with slivers of garlic, stoned and halved olives and a sprinkling of oregano. Put in the hot oven for about 20 minutes; serve at once.

Time: 1 hour + time for making dough
Makes 4 (20 cm/8 in) pizzas

This pizza is a speciality of the region of Liguria in north-west Italy.

Cheese and Tomato Pizza

PIZZA MARGHERITA

Ingredients	Metric/Imperial	American
ready-prepared dough (page 143)	450 g/1 lb	1 pound
canned plum tomatoes	400 g/14 oz	14 ounces
salt and freshly ground black pepper		
Mozzarella cheese	225 g/8 oz	½ pound
oil		
basil leaves	6	6

Preheat the oven to 230 C, 450 F, gas 8.

Drain most of the juice from the tomatoes, deseed and chop, then season with a little salt. Slice the Mozzarella cheese thinly.

Divide the dough into 4 and press out into rounds on oiled baking trays. Sprinkle with a little oil, cover with the sliced Mozzarella cheese and top with tomatoes. Put in the very hot oven for 15 minutes, removing halfway through to add the basil leaves, dipped in oil.

Season with pepper and serve hot.

Time: 35 minutes + time for making dough.
Makes 4 (20 cm/8 in) pizzas

Tomato, Anchovy and Olive Pizza

PIZZA MARINARA

Ingredients	Metric/Imperial	American
ready-prepared dough (page 143)	450 g/1 lb	1 pound
canned plum tomatoes	400 g/14 oz	14 ounces
salt and freshly ground black pepper		
oil		
anchovy fillets	3	3
capers	1 tablespoon	1 tablespoon
black olives		

Preheat the oven to 230 C, 450 F, gas 8.

Drain most of the juice from the tomatoes, deseed and chop, then season with a little salt.

Divide the dough into 4 and press out into rounds on oiled baking trays.

Rinse and drain the anchovies and capers; chop roughly. Stone and chop the olives. Cover the rounds of dough with tomato and top with anchovies, capers and olives. Season with a little salt and sprinkle lightly with oil.

Put in the hot oven for 15–20 minutes. Season with pepper just before serving.

Time: 40 minutes + time for making dough.
Makes 4 (20 cm/8 in) pizzas

Onion Pizza

PIZZA CON CIPOLLE

Ingredients	Metric/Imperial	American
made-up pizza dough (page 143)	450 g/1 lb	1 pound
large onions	3	3
oil	50 ml/2 fl oz	¼ cup
eggs	2	2
milk	3 tablespoons	4 tablespoons
Parmesan cheese, grated	25 g/1 oz	¼ cup
salt and pepper		
black olives	16	16

Preheat the oven to 230 C, 450 F, gas 8.

Slice the onions very thinly. Heat the oil in a large deep pan, add the onions and cook over a low heat for about 10 minutes.

Remove from the heat and mix in the lightly beaten eggs, milk and Parmesan cheese. Season with salt and pepper.

Divide the dough into four and press out into rounds on oiled baking trays. Spread with the prepared topping and garnish with stoned halved olives. Put in the hot oven for 20 minutes or until crisp and golden.

Time: 45 minutes + time for making dough
Makes 4 (20 cm/8 in) pizzas

Bread sticks of varying lengths

Bread Sticks

GRISSINI

Ingredients	Metric/Imperial	American
plain (all-purpose) flour	450 g/1 lb	4 cups
dried yeast	25 g/1 oz	1 cake compressed
salt	1 teaspoon	1 teaspoon
oil	2 tablespoons	3 tablespoons
milk	300 ml/½ pint	1¼ cups

Sift 350 g/12 oz/3 cups of the flour into a large bowl (keep the remainder for kneading the dough). Add the yeast prepared according to packet instructions, salt, 2–3 tablespoons of oil and the milk. Knead energetically for 10 minutes, until smooth and elastic. Put in a warm place to rise for 1½ hours.

Preheat the oven to 230 c, 450 f, gas 8.

Divide the dough into pieces and roll into long thin sticks with floured hands. Cut the sticks into about 25 cm/10 in lengths. Put on oiled baking trays and put in the hot oven until crisp and golden; about 15 minutes.

Time: 2½ hours   Makes about 700 g/1½lbs/1½ pounds

Polenta

This basic dish from northern Italy is very nourishing and is often served in place of bread. If just boiled and left plain it is rather pudding-like and too stodgy for most tastes, but it is often allowed to cool and then fried in oil or browned under the grill or broiler. It can then be served with many savoury dishes, or it can be accompanied by a tomato or meat sauce, or eaten on its own with butter and cheese. Many of the dishes in this book are traditionally served with polenta.

Polenta is made from maize flour, which is similar to American cornmeal; the flour can be coarsely or finely ground according to regional preference.

Traditionally the dish is made in a *paioli*, a round-bottomed copper cauldron. A copper pan is the next best thing, but any heavy-based pan or casserole can be used, provided it is not lined with tin.

Polenta requires constant attention while it is cooking, so that it does not stick to the pan or turn lumpy, and this takes about 45 minutes to 1 hour. A double boiler can be used, but this increases the cooking time to over $1\frac{1}{2}$ hours. The water should be just at boiling poing when the polenta is added in a steady stream, and it must then be stirred with a wooden spoon throughout the cooking time, always in a clockwise direction.

Polenta

POLENTA

Ingredients	Metric/Imperial	American
boiling water	2 litres/3½ pints	2 quarts
coarsely ground maize flour		
(cornmeal)	450 g/1 lb	4 cups
salt	2 teaspoons	2 teaspoons

Make sure that the water has just started to bubble and come up to the boil. A kettle containing more boiling water will be needed later for topping up as the cornmeal absorbs the liquid.

Throw in the salt, then gradually sprinkle in half the meal, stirring constantly in a clockwise direction between each addition. Continue stirring until the mixture is smooth and free from lumps.

Gradually add the remaining meal, along with a little boiling water if the mixture becomes too stiff. Continue stirring in a clockwise direction, and add a few drops more water when necessary. After about 45 minutes the mixture will begin to leave the sides of the pan clean.

Turn the thick pudding mixture on to a board or marble slab and form into a dome shape. Use as required, hot or cold.

Alternatively cut the dome into 4 pieces when cooled, wrap in plastic film or foil and store in the refrigerator.

Time: 50 minutes–1½ hours   *Makes 12 slices*

The picture on page 148 shows strips of Polenta baked on top of a savoury dish
Below Hot Polenta served with small spit-roasted game birds

Variations
Hot polenta with butter and cheese
Cut one quarter of the mixture into slices while still steaming hot. Spread with softened butter and sprinkle with grated cheese or top with cheese slices. *Serves 4*

Hot polenta with sauce
Cut one quarter of the hot polenta into thick slices and accompany with 375 ml/12 fl oz/1½ cups of any favourite sauce. (See pages 22–37)   *Serves 4*

Fried polenta
Remove one quarter of the cold polenta from the refrigerator, unwrap and cut into slices. Heat 4–6 tablespoons of oil in a heavy-based shallow pan and fry over a medium heat, turning once, until golden brown and crisp. Serve with meat, poultry or game dishes, or with a sauce.   *Serves 4*

Grilled (Broiled) polenta
Cut one quarter of the cold polenta mixture into slices and brush lightly with olive oil. Place under a hot grill (broiler) until crisp and brown on each side. Serve as for fried polenta.   *Serves 4*

Baked polenta with cheese
Cut half of the cold polenta into slices. Butter a shallow ovenproof dish and arrange half the slices on the bottom. Slice 225 g/8 oz/½ pound of Fontina cheese and dice 50 g/2 oz/¼ cup of butter. Top the polenta with half the cheese slices and dot with half the butter. Cover with the remaining slices of polenta and finish with the remaining cheese and butter. Put in a hot oven (230 c, 450 f, gas 8) until the top is golden brown. Serve hot, either alone or accompanied by tomato sauce *Serves 4–6*

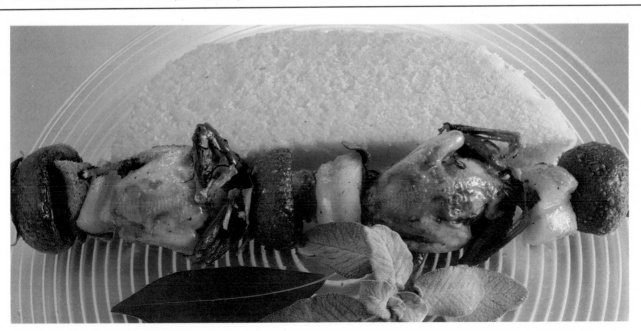

FISH

When travelling in Italy it is still worth
rising at dawn to visit the fish markets.
There are small markets around the coast with the
larger ones at Genoa, Naples, near Venice, Bari in
Puglia and the largest at San Benedetto del Tronto
in the south of the Marche region.
The varieties of fish to be found are quite amazing
but like most things the prices are
no longer very cheap.
The freshness of the fish has created little need
for complicated cooking methods, elaborate sauces
or garnishes. Fresh fried fish is nearly always
served with a simple green salad and fish soups
are as popular in Italy as they are
in the south of France.

Fish Stock
1 Chop the vegetables into even pieces. Put the washed and gutted fish or fish trimmings in a pan, season and add the vegetables.
2 Pour in enough water to cover the ingredients. Bring to the

boil, then reduce the heat and simmer for 10 minutes.
3 Add wine and simmer for a further 10 minutes.
4 Skim the stock while it is cooking. Cool, strain and use as required.

Fish Stock

BRODO DI PESCE

Ingredients	Metric/Imperial	American
onion	1	1
carrot	1	
celery stalk	1	1
fish trimmings*	1 kg/2 lb	2 pounds
parsley stalks	2	2
bay leaves	2	2
sprig of thyme	1	1
peppercorns	6	6

Prepare the vegetables and chop roughly into even-sized pieces.

Put into a pan with the fish trimmings and cover with about 1.2 litres/2¼ pints/1¼ quarts of cold water. Wash the parsley stalks and tie into a bundle with a piece of string along with the bay leaves and thyme. Add to the pan together with the lightly crushed peppercorns.

Bring to the boil over a low heat, skimming from time to time, then simmer for 25–30 minutes. Do not cook for longer or the flavour of the stock will be bitter and unpleasant.

Strain through a fine sieve to prevent any small bones from entering the stock.

Use as required in soups, sauces and for cooking fish. If a more strongly flavoured stock is required boil after straining to reduce the amount of liquid.

The stock can be frozen in small portions for use when required.

Time: 40 minutes	*Makes 1 litre/1¾ pints/1 quart*

*Use any of the following: skins, heads, tails, whole fresh fish if available. The shells of lobsters, crayfish, prawns and mussels can also be included.

Steamed Anchovies
1 Prepare the anchovies by removing the heads and backbones. Wash and pat dry with absorbent paper towels. Arrange some of the fish on a plate.
2 Sprinkle with chopped parsley and garlic, then with some

Parmesan cheese, seasoning and a little butter.
3 Continue layering the fish, parsley and garlic mixture with cheese, seasoning and butter until all the ingredients are used up. Cover with a second plate, put over a pan of boiling water and steam for at least 30 minutes.

Steamed Anchovies

ACCIUGHE AL VAPORE

Ingredients	Metric/Imperial	American
fresh anchovies	600 g/1¼ lb	1¼ pounds
bunch of parsley	1	1
garlic cloves	2	2
Parmesan or Pecorino cheese, grated	40 g/1½ oz	3 tablespoons
salt and pepper		
butter	60 g/2¼ oz	5 tablespoons

Prepare the anchovies: remove the heads and backbones, wash carefully under running water, dry and put some on a plate.

Chop the parsley and garlic cloves together. Sprinkle a little of the mixture over the anchovies together with some of the grated cheese, salt and pepper and a knob of butter. Continue these layers until all the ingredients are used up.

Cover with a second plate, inverted, and put over a pan of boiling water; steam for at least 30 minutes.

Time: 50 minutes   *Serves 4*

A very fresh anchovy is a beautiful green colour; this gradually changes to a darker and darker blue.

Stuffed Anchovies

ACCIUGHE RIPIENE

Ingredients	Metric/Imperial	American
fresh anchovies	600 g/1¼ lb	¼ pounds
bread rolls	2	2
milk		
eggs	3	3
Parmesan cheese, grated	50 g/2 oz	½ cup
salt and pepper		
chopped oregano	¼ teaspoon	¼ teaspoon
dried breadcrumbs	50 g/2 oz	½ cup
oil for deep frying		
lemon	1	1

Prepare the anchovies: cut off the heads, remove the insides, wash and drain. Slit open and cut out the backbones.

Soak the insides of the rolls in milk, squeeze and put in a small bowl with 1 egg, the Parmesan cheese, salt, pepper and oregano. Mix well. Fill the anchovies with this stuffing and close, securing with a cocktail stick (toothpick).

Beat the remaining eggs lightly and season with salt. Dip the anchovies first in beaten egg, then in breadcrumbs. Heat the oil in a deep fat fryer or deep pan to 190 C/350 F. Fry the anchovies in batches and drain on absorbent paper towels. Keep hot and serve with lemon wedges.

Time: 30 minutes   *Serves 4*

Baked Fresh Anchovies

TORTINO DI ALICI

Ingredients	Metric/Imperial	American
fresh anchovies	1 kg/2 lb	2 pounds
canned plum tomatoes	400 g/14 oz	14 ounces
onion	1	1
garlic cloves	2	2
oil	2 tablespoons	3 tablespoons
chopped parsley	1 tablespoon	1 tablespoon
Parmesan cheese, grated	50 g/2 oz	½ cup
salt and pepper		
dry breadcrumbs	50 g/2 oz	½ cup

Prepare the anchovies: remove the heads and backbones, wash under running water, drain and dry.

Drain the tomatoes and cut into strips; finely chop the onion and garlic.

Oil an ovenproof dish and put a layer of anchovies in the bottom. Cover with tomato, sprinkle with chopped onion, garlic, parsley, Parmesan cheese, salt and pepper. Repeat the layers until the ingredients are finished and cover with the breadcrumbs. Trickle the remaining oil on top.

Put in a very hot oven (240 C, 475 F, gas 9) for about 20 minutes until the top is golden brown.

Time: 45 minutes   *Serves 4*

Rolled Sardines in Tomato Sauce

ROTOLI DI SARDINE IN SALSA

Ingredients	Metric/Imperial	American
fresh sardines	450 g/1 lb	1 pound
Ricotta cheese	100 g/4 oz	¼ pound
Parmesan cheese, grated	50 g/2 oz	¼ cup
egg yolk	1	1
salt and pepper		
sprigs of parsley	2	2
garlic cloves	2	2
oil	125 ml/4 fl oz	½ cup
plum tomatoes	350 g/12 oz	¾ pound
basil leaves	4	4

Clean the sardines, remove the heads and tails, wash and dry. Cut open, remove the backbone and roll up.

Mix the Ricotta cheese in a bowl with the Parmesan cheese, egg yolk, a little salt and pepper and the parsley chopped with one of the garlic cloves.

Coat the sardine rolls with this mixture and thread them on to skewers. Brush an ovenproof dish with a little of the oil and put in the sardine rolls. Sprinkle each fish roll with a little oil.

Heat the remaining oil in a small pan. Add the remaining garlic clove, lightly crushed, and cook over a medium heat until golden. Add the tomatoes, peel if using fresh, drained if canned. Season with salt and pepper and the basil leaves and cook for 15 minutes.

Remove the garlic, pour the sauce over the sardine rolls and put in a moderately hot oven (200 C, 400 F, gas 6) for 20 minutes.

Time: 50 minutes   *Serves 4*

Baked Fresh Anchovies

1 Prepare the anchovies: remove heads and backbones, wash, drain and dry. (If fresh anchovies are unobtainable try the recipe with sprats.)

2 Oil an ovenproof dish and put in a layer of anchovies. Sprinkle with chopped onion, garlic and parsley mixed together.

3 Top with some tomato strips.

4 Sprinkle with salt, pepper and freshly grated Parmesan cheese.

5 Continue layering the ingredients until they are all used up. Top with breadcrumbs and sprinkle with oil before baking in a very hot oven.

155

Baked Sea Bass (Groper)

CERNIA AL FORNO

Ingredients	Metric/Imperial	American
sea bass (groper)	1 (1.5 kg/3 lb)	1 (3 pound)
butter	50 g/2 oz	$\frac{1}{4}$ cup
onion	1	1
dry white wine	125 ml/4 fl oz	$\frac{1}{2}$ cup
salt and pepper		

Clean the fish, descale, wash and dry. Make 2 or 3 oblique cuts on each side to make sure it cooks through. Melt half the butter in a large shallow pan, add the finely chopped onion, put in the fish and cook over a medium heat, turning once, until golden.

Pour in the wine and spread the remaining butter over the upper part of the fish. Season with salt and pepper. Increase the heat until the liquid boils, then remove from the heat. Wrap the fish and juices in a sheet of foil to make a parcel. Put in a moderate oven (180 C, 350 F, gas 4) for 15 minutes, turning the parcel from time to time carefully to make sure the fish is basted with the cooking juices.

Gently remove the fish from the wrapping and put on a heated serving dish. Transfer the cooking juices to a small pan and cook over a high heat until reduced and thickened. Pour over the fish and serve at once.

Time: 30 minutes   *Serves 4*

Baked Marinated Sea Bream

DENTICE MARINATO AL FORNO

Ingredients	Metric/Imperial	American
sea bream	1 (1 kg/2 lb)	1 (2 pound)
garlic clove	1	1
sprigs of rosemary	2	2
salt and pepper		
dry white wine	125 ml/4 fl oz	$\frac{1}{2}$ cup
oil	125 ml/4 fl oz	$\frac{1}{2}$ cup
dried breadcrumbs	1 tablespoon	2 tablespoons

Gut and scale the fish leaving the head and tail in place. Wash well and drain. Put the garlic clove inside along with a sprig of rosemary. Lay in a large shallow dish, season with salt and pepper and cover with the remaining rosemary leaves. Sprinkle with the wine and three-quarters of the oil. Marinate for 30 minutes.

Remove the fish, drain and dry. Coat with breadcrumbs and put in an ovenproof dish brushed with the remaining oil. Pour the marinade over and put in a moderately hot oven (200 C, 400 F, gas 6) for 20 minutes, baste from time to time until the fish is cooked through and golden. Serve hot.

Time: 1 hour   *Serves 4*

Sea Bream (Porgy) Italian-style

ORATA ALL'ITALIANA

Ingredients	Metric/Imperial	American
sea bream (porgy)	1 (1 kg/2 lb)	1 (2 pound)
small onion	1	1
garlic clove	1	1
bay leaf	1	1
salt and pepper		
dry vermouth	125 ml/4 fl oz	$\frac{1}{2}$ cup
butter	50 g/2 oz	$\frac{1}{4}$ cup
plain (all-purpose) flour	25 g/1 oz	$\frac{1}{4}$ cup
mushrooms	100 g/4 oz	$\frac{1}{4}$ pound
chopped parsley	1 tablespoon	1 tablespoon
single (thin) cream	2 tablespoons	3 tablespoons
Parmesan cheese, grated	25 g/1 oz	$\frac{1}{4}$ cup
dried breadcrumbs	25 g/1 oz	$\frac{1}{4}$ cup

Clean the fish, cut off the head and tail and divide the body into 4 steaks. Put the head and tail into a pan with the chopped onion and garlic, bay leaf and a little salt. Pour on 600 ml/1 pint/2$\frac{1}{2}$ cups of water and simmer for 30 minutes. Strain and reserve the liquid.

Meanwhile put the steaks in a non-stick pan, trickle in the vermouth mixed with 2 tablespoons of water and season lightly with salt. Cook over a low heat for 20 minutes. Take out the steaks, remove the skin and any bones and put the steaks in an ovenproof dish.

Melt half the butter in a small pan, add the flour, then pour in the vermouth juices and bring to the boil, stirring constantly. Gradually pour in 300 ml/$\frac{1}{2}$ pint/ $\frac{1}{4}$ cup of the reserved fish stock and mix well. Add the finely chopped mushrooms along with the parsley and a little salt and pepper. Finally stir in the cream and leave to cook for 10 minutes over a low heat.

Pour the sauce over the fish steaks. Sprinkle with Parmesan cheese and breadcrumbs and dot with the remaining butter. Put in a moderate oven (180 C, 350 F, gas 4) for 20 minutes and serve hot.

Time: 1 hour 10 minutes   *Serves 4*

Cod with Vegetables

MERLUZZO CON VERDURE

Ingredients	Metric/Imperial	American
saffron strands	½ teaspoon	½ teaspoon
yellow (sweet) peppers	2	2
tomatoes	2	2
small onion	1	1
garlic clove	1	1
cod fillet	600 g/1¼ lb	1¼ pounds
flour	1 tablespoon	2 tablespoons
oil	3 tablespoons	4 tablespoons
salt and pepper		
chopped parsley	1 tablespoon	1 tablespoon
polenta (optional)		

Put the saffron strands to soak in a little hot water.

Halve and deseed the peppers; cut into slivers. Quarter the tomatoes; finely chop the onion and garlic.

Cut the cod into even-sized pieces and dust with flour. Heat the oil in a large shallow pan, add the cod and cook over a medium heat for a few minutes, turning once, until golden. Season with salt and pepper, remove with a fish slice and keep warm.

Add the prepared vegetables to the pan and cook, stirring, until golden. Season with a pinch of salt, reduce the heat, cover with a lid and simmer for about 30 minutes. Stir in the saffron liquid halfway through.

When the vegetables are almost cooked add the pieces of cod and sprinkle with chopped parsley. Serve hot accompanied with slices of polenta if liked.

Time: 40 minutes   *Serves 4*

Cod with Vegetables
1 Cut sweet peppers into strips, chop tomatoes, onion and garlic.
2 Dust the cod lightly with flour and cook in hot oil until golden. Season and remove from the pan; keep warm.
3 Add the prepared vegetables to the pan, cover and cook over a low heat. After 15 minutes pour in the saffron.
4 Return the fish to the pan and sprinkle with parsley.

Cod Livorno-style

BACCALA ALLA LIVORNESE

Ingredients	Metric/Imperial	American
cod fillet	700 g/1½ lb	1½ pounds
oil	4 tablespoons	6 tablespoons
garlic clove	1	1
salt and pepper		
cinnamon	¼ teaspoon	¼ teaspoon
plum tomatoes	400 g/14 oz	14 ounces
chopped parsley	1 tablespoon	1 tablespoon
capers	1 tablespoon	1 tablespoon

Skin the fish and cut into bite-sized pieces. Heat the oil in a large pan, add the crushed garlic and cook over a medium heat until golden. Add the cod and cook for 2 minutes, turning to flavour with the oil. Season with salt, pepper and cinnamon.

Drain, deseed and coarsely chop the tomatoes. Put on top of the fish, cover with a lid and cook for 20 minutes, stirring from time to time and adding a little salted water if necessary.

Add the parsley and drained capers, mix and serve.

Time: 35 minutes   *Serves 4*

This is a regional dish from Livorno.

Baked Cod

BACCALA IN CASSERUOLA

Ingredients	Metric/Imperial	American
cod	600 g/1¼ lb	1¼ pounds
sprigs of parsley	4	4
small onion	1	1
anchovy fillets	50 g/2 oz	2 ounces
butter	25 g/1 oz	2 tablespoons
dry white wine	125 ml/4 fl oz	½ cup
salt and pepper		

Cut the cod into pieces and remove any bones. Chop the parsley and onion together. Mash the anchovies.

Grease a deep ovenproof casserole liberally with some of the butter. Put some of the cod on the bottom, sprinkle with onion and parsley and add a few pieces of anchovy. Dot with butter and continue in this way until all the ingredients are used up.

Pour over the wine mixed with an equal quantity of water, cover with a lid and put in a moderate oven (180 C, 350 F, gas 4) for 35 minutes or until the fish is cooked and the sauce well reduced. Taste and adjust the seasoning if necessary and serve hot.

Time: 45 minutes   *Serves 4*

Fillets of Halibut in Cream Sauce

FILETTI DI ROMBO IN SALSA AL GRATIN

Ingredients	Metric/Imperial	American
fish bones and heads	450 g/1 lb	1 pound
carrot	1	1
onion	1	1
lemon juice	1 tablespoon	1 tablespoon
sprigs of parsley	2	2
bay leaf	1	1
dry white wine	125 ml/4 fl oz	½ cup
garlic clove	1	1
single (thin cream)	5 tablespoons	7 tablespoons
butter	100 g/4 oz	½ cup
ripe tomatoes	2	2
chopped parsley	1 tablespoon	1 tablespoon
chopped thyme	1 teaspoon	1 teaspoon
chopped chives	2 teaspoons	2 teaspoons
salt and pepper		
fillets of halibut	700 g/1½ lb	1½ pounds

Prepare a fish stock: put the fish bones and heads in a saucepan with the sliced carrot and onion and the lemon juice. Pour in enough water to cover, add the parsley and bay leaf and bring slowly to the boil. Simmer for 20 minutes, skimming the surface from time to time.

Remove 225 ml/8 fl oz/1 cup of the stock and mix with the wine and finely chopped garlic. Put in a small pan over a medium heat and boil until reduced by half. Add the cream to the reduced stock. After a few minutes begin to add the diced butter, allowing each piece to melt before adding the next and stirring constantly. The resulting sauce should be thick and creamy. Finish with the peeled, deseeded and chopped tomatoes, chopped herbs and seasoning.

Strain the remaining stock into a large pan, add the fillets of halibut and cook over a low heat for 10 minutes. Drain and put in an ovenproof dish. Cover with the prepared sauce and put in a moderately hot oven (200 C, 400 F, gas 6) for 15 minutes or until the top is golden.

Time: 1½ hours   *Serves 4*

Fillets of Halibut in Cream Sauce
1 Make fish stock: put the fish trimmings in a pan with sliced carrot, onion, lemon juice, parsley and bay leaf. Cover with water and bring to the boil slowly.
2 Strain 225 ml/8 fl oz/1 cup of the stock into another pan, mix with wine and garlic; simmer until reduced. Gradually whisk in cream and butter to make a creamy sauce.
3 Strain the remaining stock into a large shallow pan. Add the fillets of halibut and poach gently over a low heat.
4 Transfer the fish to an ovenproof dish and pour over the prepared sauce. (Use the fish stock for soup or freeze for future use in another fish dish.)

159

Mackerel with Olives and Tomatoes

SGOMBRI ALLE OLIVE E POMODORO

Mackerel with Olives and Tomatoes

Ingredients	Metric/Imperial	American
flour	2 tablespoons	3 tablespoons
mackerel	4 (350 g/12 oz)	4 (¾ pound)
oil	4 tablespoons	6 tablespoons
garlic clove	1	1
anchovy fillets	3	3
plum tomatoes	225 g/8 oz	½ pound
black olives	24	24
fish stock	150 ml/¼ pint	⅔ cup
salt and pepper		
chopped parsley	1 tablespoon	1 tablespoon

Clean, dry and lightly flour the fish. Heat the oil in a large pan, add the crushed garlic and drained anchovies and cook over a medium heat until the garlic is lightly browned. Add the fish and cook for a few minutes, turning once.

Add the chopped drained tomatoes along with the halved stoned olives. Continue to cook, adding fish stock (see page 152) from time to time, for about 30 minutes, until the fish is cooked and the sauce well thickened. Season with salt and pepper and sprinkle with parsley a few minutes before the end of the cooking time.

Serve the fish with the sauce poured over. If liked accompany with bread rubbed with garlic, sprinkled with oil and toasted in the oven.

Time: 40 minutes   *Serves 4*

Grey Mullet in Garlic Breadcrumbs

PESCE ALLA ROMAGNOLA

Ingredients	Metric/Imperial	American
grey mullet or other firm white fish	1 kg/2 lb	2 pounds
egg	1	1
garlic cloves	2–3	2–3
sprig of rosemary	1	1
dried breadcrumbs	4 tablespoons	4 tablespoons
salt and pepper		
oil for frying		
lemon	1	1

Have the fish cleaned (head removed) and filleted. Wash under cold running water. Drain, dry and flatten out the fillets. Beat the egg with 3–4 tablespoons water on a flat plate.

Grey Mullet in Garlic Breadcrumbs

Finely chop the garlic with the rosemary spikes. Add to the breadcrumbs and season with salt and pepper. Coat the fish first in egg and then in the mixture, making sure it sticks well.

Heat the oil in a large shallow pan over a medium heat, add the fish and fry, turning once, until cooked through and golden; about 8 minutes.

Drain on absorbent kitchen paper and arrange on a heated plate. Serve accompanied with wedges of lemon.

Time: 30 minutes   *Serves 4*

This is a speciality of the Emilia-Romagna region.

Red Mullet Baked in Foil

TRIGLIE AL CARTOCCIO

Ingredients	Metric/Imperial	American
red mullet	4	4
salt and pepper		
butter	50 g/2 oz	¼ cup
plum tomatoes	225 g/8 oz	½ pound
capers	1 tablespoon	1 tablespoon
chopped basil	1 tablespoon	1 tablespoon
black olives	16	16

Clean and dry the fish and season with salt and pepper.

Brush a large sheet of foil with some of the butter. Put half the drained tomatoes in the centre along with half the drained capers. Sprinkle with half the basil, half the butter, diced and half the olives, stoned and chopped. Put the fish on top and cover with the remaining half of the ingredients.

Close the foil tightly, put on a baking sheet and bake in a moderately hot oven (200c, 400f, gas 6) for 35 minutes. Transfer the foil parcel to a serving dish and open it slightly.

Time: 40 minutes   *Serves 4*

Monkfish with Tomatoes and Capers

PESCATRICE AL POMODORO E CAPERI

Ingredients	Metric/Imperial	American
monkfish	1 (1 kg/2 lb)	1 (2 pound)
garlic clove	1	1
sprigs of parsley	4	4
oil	125 ml/4 fl oz	½ cup
dry white wine	200 ml/7 fl oz	¾ cup
red, green and yellow (sweet) peppers	1 each	1 each
ripe plum tomatoes	2	2
lemon	1	1
small onion	½	½
salt and pepper		
capers	1 tablespoon	1 tablespoon

Clean, wash and dry the fish. Crush the garlic and mix with half the parsley, chopped. Spread this mixture on the fish.

Heat half the oil in a large pan, add the fish and cook over a medium heat for 5–6 minutes on each side, until lightly browned. Moisten with the wine, cover with a lid and continue to cook for 15 minutes.

Meanwhile halve, deseed and chop the peppers. Purée in a blender or food processor along with the tomatoes, juice of the lemon, remaining oil, chopped onion, the remaining parsley and a little salt and pepper. Process until smooth and thick, then add the drained capers.

Put the fish on a heated serving dish and remove the bones. Pour over the sauce and leave to absorb flavour before serving cold.

Time: 50 minutes   *Serves 4*

Fish and Rice Balls

PALLINE DI PESCE E RISO

Ingredients	Metric/Imperial	American
salt and pepper		
monkfish or other firm white fish, cooked	350 g/12 oz	¾ pound
long-grain rice	350 g/12 oz	1⅔ cups
flour	1 tablespoon	1 tablespoon
eggs	2	2
lemon rind	½	½
chopped parsley	1 tablespoon	1 tablespoon
dried breadcrumbs	100 g/4 oz	1 cup
oil for frying		

Cook the rice in salted boiling water; drain and leave to cool.

Chop the fish and put in a bowl along with the cooked rice, flour, eggs, a little salt and grated lemon rind and the parsley. Mix well, adding some of the breadcrumbs if the mixture is too soft, and form into small even-sized balls. Flatten lightly, coat in breadcrumbs and leave to rest for a while in the refrigerator.

Heat plenty of oil in a shallow pan over a high heat, add the fish and rice balls and cook until golden. Drain on absorbent paper towels and serve hot.

Time: 30 minutes + 20 minutes: resting   *Serves 6*

Braised John Dory (Storer)

PESCE SAMPIETRO BRASATO

Ingredients	Metric/Imperial	American
John Dory	1 (1 kg/2 lb)	1 (2 pound)
celery stalk	1	1
carrot	1	1
small onion	1	1
lemon slices	2	2
sprig of parsley	1	1
garlic clove	1	1
butter	40 g/1½ oz	3 tablespoons
sage leaves	4	4
salt and pepper		
brandy	2 tablespoons	3 tablespoons
plum tomatoes	225 g/8 oz	½ pound

The fish should be gutted but left whole, descaled, washed and dried.

Prepare the celery, carrot and onion and chop coarsely along with the lemon slices. Finely chop the parsley and garlic together.

Braised John Dory (Storer)

Melt the butter in a large shallow pan, add the chopped sage leaves and cook over a medium heat for a few minutes. Add the fish and cook until golden, turning once. Then add the prepared vegetables, parsley and garlic mixture, season with a little salt and pour in the brandy.

When the brandy has evaporated add the tomatoes, drained and mashed with a fork, cover with a lid and leave over a low heat for 30 minutes.

Lift the fish out carefully and put on a heated serving plate. Cover with the strained cooking juices, season with pepper and serve with steamed new potatoes.

Time: 50 minutes   *Serves 4*

Sole Florentine

FILETTI DI SOGLIOLA GRATINATI ALLA
FIORENTINA

Ingredients	Metric/Imperial	American
sole	4	4
fresh spinach	450 g/1 lb	1 pound
butter	25 g/1 oz	2 tablespoons
oil	2 teaspoons	2 teaspoons
dry white wine	125 ml/4 fl oz	½ cup
salt and pepper		
Parmesan cheese, grated		
For the white sauce:		
butter	50 g/2 oz	¼ cup
milk	450 ml/¾ pint	2 cups
flour	50 g/2 oz	½ cup
salt and pepper		
grated nutmeg	¼ teaspoon	¼ teaspoon
single (thin) cream	2–3 tablespoons	3–4 tablespoons
Gruyère cheese, grated	50 g/2 oz	½ cup

Have the fishmonger fillet the fish and give back the heads and bones. Skin the fillets and put the skin in a small pan along with the trimmings. Cover with cold water, bring to the boil and simmer gently for about 20 minutes.

Meanwhile wash the spinach thoroughly, removing coarse stems, drain and cook in a deep pan for 5 minutes in the water remaining on the leaves. Drain and mix with the butter.

Put the sole fillets into an oiled flameproof dish, cover with the wine and 125 ml/4 fl oz/½ cup of the fish stock; season with salt and pepper. Put in a moderate oven (180 C, 350 F, gas 4) for about 15 minutes.

Remove the fish and keep hot. Put the dish over a high heat to reduce the cooking juices to about 2–3 tablespoons.

Prepare the white sauce: melt the butter in a small pan and heat the milk in a separate one. Stir the flour into the butter, then add the hot milk all at once. Season with salt, pepper and nutmeg; stir well over a low heat until thick and cooked.

Add the reduced fish juices and cream; cook for a further 5 minutes to reduce the sauce a little more, then add the Gruyère cheese.

Brush an ovenproof serving dish with oil and arrange the spinach on the bottom of the dish. Put the sole fillets on top; cover with the white sauce and top with Parmesan cheese. Put in a moderately hot oven (200 C, 400 F, gas 6) until the top is crisp and golden.

Time: 1 hour   *Serves 4*

Swordfish with Olives and Capers

PESCE SPADA ALLA MARINARA

Ingredients	Metric/Imperial	American
sprig of parsley	1	1
onion	1	1
butter	50 g/2 oz	¼ cup
garlic clove	1	1
plum tomatoes	4	4
salt and pepper		
swordfish or cod steaks	4	4
black olives	1 tablespoon	1 tablespoon
capers	1 tablespoon	1 tablespoon

Finely chop the parsley together with the onion. Melt the butter in a large shallow pan, add the lightly crushed garlic along with the chopped mixture and cook over a medium heat until lightly browned.

Peel the tomatoes if using fresh; drain if canned. Deseed, chop roughly and add to the pan. Season with salt and pepper and add the fish steaks.

Reduce the heat and cook for about 15 minutes, stirring from time to time. When the steaks are cooked through add the stoned chopped olives and drained capers. Leave for 2 minutes for the flavours to mingle.

Time: 30 minutes   *Serves 4*

Fresh Tuna with Creamy Sauce

TRANCE DI TONNO FRESCO IN FRICASSEA

Ingredients	Metric/Imperial	American
tuna steaks	4	4
flour	2 tablespoons	3 tablespoons
butter	65 g/2½ oz	5 tablespoons
slices of cob loaf	4	4
garlic clove	1	1
oil		
eggs	2	2
salt and pepper		
black olives	2 tablespoons	3 tablespoons
lemon juice	1 tablespoon	1 tablespoon
chopped parsley	1 tablespoon	1 tablespoon
small onion	1	1
single (thin) cream	2 tablespoons	3 tablespoons
Worcester sauce	¼ teaspoon	¼ teaspoon

Fresh Tuna with Creamy Sauce
1 Melt some butter in a pan and gently fry the floured tuna steaks until golden.
2 Rub the bread with garlic, brush with oil and toast.
3 Mix beaten egg with seasoning, chopped olives, lemon juice and parsley.
4 Cook onion in butter until golden, reduce the heat and add the egg mixture.
5 Stir until thick and creamy, then season with Worcester sauce.

Dust the tuna steaks with flour. Melt 50 g/2 oz/¼ cup of the butter in a shallow pan and fry the steaks over a medium heat for 8 minutes on each side, until golden.

Rub the bread with garlic and brush with a little oil, toast it, arrange on a serving plate and keep hot.

Break the eggs into a bowl, add salt and pepper, the stoned coarsely chopped olives, lemon juice and parsley. Beat well together.

Finely chop the onion and cook in a small pan in the remaining butter until golden. Reduce the heat, add the egg mixture and cook, stirring, until it begins to thicken. Add the cream and Worcester sauce and remove the pan from the heat. The sauce should be thick and creamy.

Put a tuna steak on each slice of toast and cover with the prepared sauce. Serve hot.

Time: 40 minutes *Serves 4*

Tuna Loaf

POLPETTONE DI TONNO

Ingredients	Metric/Imperial	American
fresh tuna	1 (600 g/1¼ lb)	1 (1¼ pound)
lemon	½	½
sprig of parsley	1	1
potatoes	2	2
salt		
Parmesan cheese, grated	50 g/2 oz	½ cup
eggs	4	4
mayonnaise		

Put the tuna in a deep pan with the juice of the ½ lemon, parsley, peeled and thinly sliced potatoes, a little salt and 600 ml/1 pint/2½ cups of water. Cover with a lid and cook over a medium heat for about 25 minutes until the fish and potatoes are tender.

Drain and sieve or blend along with the potatoes. Add the Parmesan cheese, eggs and a little salt; mix well and form into a large roll with the hands. Wrap in muslin and tie both ends.

Lower into a large pan of boiling water and cook over a low heat for 20 minutes. Drain and leave until cold before removing the muslin. Cut into thick slices and serve with mayonnaise.

Time: 1 hour + 2 hours: cooling   *Serves 4*

Tuna Livorno-style

TONNO ALLA LIVORNESE

Ingredients	Metric/Imperial	American
fresh tuna steaks	4	4
flour	50 g/2 oz	½ cup
small onion	1	1
sprigs of parsley	4	4
oil	4 tablespoons	6 tablespoons
salt and pepper		
dry white wine	125 ml/4 fl oz	½ cup
capers	1 tablespoon	1 tablespoon
bay leaf	1	1
cinnamon	¼ teaspoon	¼ teaspoon

Coat the tuna steaks in flour. Chop the onion and parsley together. Heat the oil in a heavy pan, add the onion mixture and cook on a medium heat, stirring, until just golden.

Add the tuna steaks and cook for 2 minutes on each side. Season with salt and pepper; pour over the wine. Leave until this has evaporated a little, then add the drained capers, crumbled bay leaf and the cinnamon. Cover with a lid and cook for about 15 minutes, adding a little water if necessary.

Serve the tuna steaks with the cooking juices pour over, accompanied with vegetables such as potatoes with parsley or a green salad.

Time: 30 minutes   *Serves 4*

This dish is a speciality of Livorno.

Stuffed Squid

CALAMARI FARCITI

Ingredients	Metric/Imperial	American
small squid	8	8
salt and pepper		
garlic cloves	2	2
sprig of parsley	1	1
Parmesan cheese	2 tablespoons	3 tablespoons
egg	1	1
frozen peas, thawed	225 g/8 oz	½ pound
oil	2 tablespoons	3 tablespoons
dry white wine	125 ml/4 fl oz	½ cup

Prepare the squid: remove the head, ink sac and transparent spine. Wash the body envelope and tentacles under running water. Chop off the tentacles and cook in salted boiling water for 15 minutes. Drain and chop finely along with the garlic and parsley.

Put the chopped mixture in a bowl, add the Parmesan cheese, egg, a little salt and pepper and mix well together. Finish with the peas. Stuff the squid with this mixture and sew with white cotton to ensure the stuffing remains in place during cooking.

Heat the oil in a large deep pan, add the squid and cook over a medium heat until golden all over. Pour in the wine; season with salt and pepper. Reduce the heat, cover with a lid and cook for 30 minutes. Serve hot.

Time: 1 hour   *Serves 4*

Stuffed Squid
1 Prepare the squid by removing the head, ink sac and spine. Wash the body, cut off the tentacles and chop finely. Mix with finely chopped parsley and garlic.
2 Put the chopped mixture in a bowl and add Parmesan cheese, egg and seasoning. Finally add peas.
3 Stuff this mixture into the body envelopes of the squid and sew up with fine string or thick white cotton. Fry until golden, then simmer in wine for 30 minutes.

Cuttlefish Stew

SEPPIE PROFUMATE

Ingredients	Metric/Imperial	American
cuttlefish	800 g/1¾ lb	1¾ pounds
small onion	1	1
oil	3 tablespoons	4 tablespoons
frozen peas, thawed	225 g/8 oz	½ pound
mushrooms	350 g/12 oz	¾ pound
tomato paste	1 tablespoon	1 tablespoon
dry white wine	125 ml/4 fl oz	½ cup
salt and pepper		
chopped parsley	1 tablespoon	1 tablespoon

Clean the cuttlefish by removing the beak, eyes and innards; wash thoroughly. Chop the body, head and arms into pieces.

Finely chop the onion. Heat the oil in a deep pan, add the onion and cook over medium heat until golden. Add the cuttlefish, leave for a while to absorb flavour, then add the peas and sliced mushrooms.

Mix the tomato paste with 125 ml/4 fl oz/½ cup of water. Add to the pan along with the wine and season to taste. Cover with a lid and cook for 30 minutes, then remove the lid to allow the sauce to thicken. Add the parsley and remove from the heat. Serve hot.

Time: 50 minutes   *Serves 4*

If a cuttlefish ink sac is used the dish will be black.

1   2   3

Pickled Whiting

NASELLI IN GUAZZETTO DI CIPOLLE

Ingredients	Metric/Imperial	American
whiting	2 (450 g/1 lb)	2 (1 pound)
large onion	1	1
garlic clove	1	1
celery stalk	1	1
olive oil	2 tablespoons	3 tablespoons
bay leaf	1	1
flour	1 tablespoon	1 tablespoon
salt and pepper		
white wine vinegar	2 tablespoons	3 tablespoons
vegetable stock	150 ml/¼ pint	⅔ cup
lemon	½	½
anchovy fillets	3	3
chopped parsley	1 tablespoon	1 tablespoon
slices of lemon or hard-boiled (cooked) egg		

Clean, wash and dry the whiting. Finely chop the onion along with the garlic and celery.

Heat the oil in a large deep pan, add the bay leaf and chopped onion mixture and cook over a medium heat until golden. Add 1 tablespoon of water and cook for a few more minutes.

Stir in the flour, season with salt and pepper and add the vinegar mixed with 150 ml/¼ pint/⅔ cup of water. Put in the whiting; if the liquid does not just cover it add a little more water. Reduce the heat, cover and simmer for about 10 minutes.

Add the hot stock and juice of ½ lemon along with the drained and chopped anchovies. Cook for a further 5 minutes, then remove the fish with a slotted spoon and put on a heated serving dish.

Increase the heat under the pan and reduce the cooking juices to make a thick sauce. Mix in the parsley and pour over the fish. Leave until cold, then garnish with slices of lemon or hard-boiled egg.

Time: 45 minutes   *Serves 4*

If preferred this dish can be prepared a day ahead and kept in the refrigerator.

Soused Eel

ANGUILLA IN SALSA

Ingredients	Metric/Imperial	American
onion	1	1
eel	1 kg/2 lb	2 pounds
oil	3 tablespoons	scant ¼ cup
bay leaf	1	1
wine vinegar	4 tablespoons	6 tablespoons
plum tomatoes	225 g/8 oz	½ pound
salt and pepper		

Chop the onion finely and cut the eel into 5 cm/2 in thick pieces.

Heat the oil in a large shallow pan, crumble in the bay leaf, then add the onion. Cook over a medium heat for a few minutes until golden.

Add the pieces of eel and cook for a few minutes. Then pour over the vinegar, add the tomatoes (peeled if they are fresh ones) and season to taste. Cover and cook for a further 20–25 minutes over a low heat until the eel is tender. Serve hot.

Time: 30 minutes   *Serves 4*

Eel Stewed in Wine

MURENA ALLA CAPRESE

Ingredients	Metric/Imperial	American
conger eel	1 kg/2 lb	2 pounds
bay leaf	1	1
cloves	3	3
salt and pepper		
dry white wine	225 ml/8 fl oz	1 cup
dried breadcrumbs	50 g/2 oz	½ cup
egg white	1	1
grated nutmeg	¼ teaspoon	¼ teaspoon
oil	2 tablespoons	3 tablespoons

The fish should be chopped into rounds and skinned. Wash and put in a large deep pan with the bay leaf, cloves, a little salt and pepper; cover with the wine. Bring to the boil, then simmer very gently for about 10 minutes. Drain immediately.

Dip the fish into stiffly beaten egg white, then into breadcrumbs. Season with salt, pepper and nutmeg.

Brush an ovenproof dish with oil, put in the fish, trickle over the remaining oil and put in a moderately hot oven (200 C, 400 F, gas 6) for about 15 minutes until crisp and golden.

Time: 30 minutes   *Serves 4*

Carp in Beer

Carp in Beer

CARPA IN UMIDO ALLA BIRRA

Ingredients	Metric/Imperial	American
dried mushrooms	15 g/½ oz	½ oz
carp	1 (1 kg/2 lb)	1 (2 pound)
butter	50 g/2 oz	¼ cup
small onion	1	1
garlic clove	1	1
fresh mushrooms	150 g/5 oz	5 ounces
salt and pepper		
beer or lager	450 ml/¾ pint	2 cups

Soak the dried mushrooms in warm water for 30 minutes.

Clean and descale the fish and cut the body into steaks. Melt the butter in a large pan. Add the chopped onion, crushed garlic and sliced mushrooms, along with the fish. Season with salt and pepper and cook over a medium heat until the onion is lightly browned.

Turn the steaks over, pour over the beer, add the drained mushrooms and cover with a lid. Leave over a low heat until the steaks are cooked through and the liquid reduced.

Transfer the steaks to a heated serving dish. Pour over the sauce and serve hot. (If the sauce is not thick enough put it over a high heat for a few mintues.)

Time: 35 minutes   *Serves 4*

169

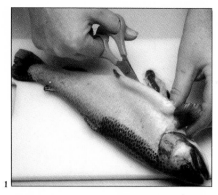

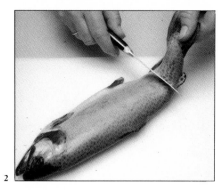

To Prepare Trout

1 Wash the fish under cold running water. Slit the stomach with scissors or a sharp knife. Hook a finger inside the throat and pull out the innards. Wash again under running water, removing any blood from inside.

2 Dry with absorbent paper towels. Hold the fish by the tail and run the blade of a knife up the body to remove the scales from both sides.

3 Cut off the dorsal and ventral fins close to the body.

4 Cut off the head fins and remove the eyes with a sharp-pointed knife.

Trout with Lemon

TROTELLE AL LIMONE

Ingredients	Metric/Imperial	American
trout	4 (350 g/12 oz)	4 ($\frac{3}{4}$ pound)
lemons	2	2
garlic clove	1	1
bay leaf	1	1
oil	4 tablespoons	6 tablespoons
Parma ham	50 g/2 oz	2 ounces
salt and pepper		
fish or vegetable stock	150 ml/$\frac{1}{4}$ pint	$\frac{2}{3}$ cup

Clean, wash and dry the trout. Peel the lemons and cut into thin slices with a sharp knife; remove the seeds.

Finely chop the garlic and put on a large baking tray with the crumbled bay leaf and 3–4 tablespoons of the oil. Arrange the lemon slices on the tray with the Parma ham and then the trout. Season lightly with salt and pepper, sprinkle on the remaining oil and put in a moderately hot oven (200 C, 400 F, gas 6). Cook for 30 minutes, basting from time to time with hot stock.

Remove the trout with a fish slice and put on a heated serving dish. Sieve or blend the remaining ingredients, reheat and serve separately.

Time: 45 minutes   *Serves 4*

Stuffed Trout

COTOLETTE DI TROTA

Ingredients	Metric/Imperial	American
trout	4 (350 g/12 oz)	4 ($\frac{3}{4}$ pound)
slices of Parma ham	4	4
Parmesan cheese, grated	1 tablespoon	1 tablespoon
egg	1	1
salt and pepper		
dried breadcrumbs	4 tablespoons	6 tablespoons
butter	75 g/3 oz	6 tablespoons
lemon	1	1

Clean the trout: remove the heads and open; remove backbones. Finely chop the ham, mix with the Parmesan cheese and stuff into the fish. Seal with a wooden cocktail stick (toothpick).

Dip the fish in lightly beaten egg seasoned with salt and pepper, then into breadcrumbs.

Melt the butter in a large shallow pan over a medium heat, add the fish and cook for 14 minutes until lightly browned and cooked through. Turn halfway through the cooking time and season with salt and pepper.

Remove and drain on absorbent paper towels, put on a heated serving dish and serve garnished with lemon wedges.

Time: 30 minutes   *Serves 4*

Stuffed Tench

TINCA RIPIENA

Ingredients	Metric/Imperial	American
tench	4 (225 g/8 oz)	4 (½ pound)
egg	1	1
fresh breadcrumbs	50 g/2 oz	½ cup
Parmesan cheese, grated	25 g/1 oz	¼ cup
garlic clove	1	1
sprig of parsley	1	1
salt and pepper		
lard	50 g/2 oz	¼ cup
bay leaves	2	2
sage leaves	16	16
oil	2 teaspoons	2 teaspoons
butter	25 g/1 oz	2 tablespoons
slices of polenta to serve (optional)		

Prepare the tench for cooking; remove the back bones carefully without breaking up the fish.

Make the stuffing: mix the egg with the breadcrumbs, Parmesan cheese, garlic and parsley finely chopped together and a little salt and pepper. Stuff each fish with this mixture and sew up with white cotton.

Grease a shallow ovenproof dish and cover the bottom with half the diced lard, 1 bay leaf and 8 sage leaves. Lay the fish on top, sprinkle with salt and pepper and cover with the remaining lard, bay leaf and sage. Sprinkle with a little oil, dot with butter and in a moderately hot oven (200 c, 400 f, gas 6) for 45 minutes.

Serve hot straight from the dish accompanied by slices of polenta if liked.

Time: 1 hour — — — — — *Serves 4*

Fried Scampi

FRITTO DI SCAMPI

Ingredients	Metric/Imperial	American
scampi tails	600 g/1¼ lb	1¼ pounds
plain (all-purpose) flour	50 g/2 oz	½ cup
oil for frying		
salt		
sprigs of parsley	4	4
lemon	1	1

Shell the scampi and coat liberally with flour.

Heat plenty of oil in a large shallow pan. Add the scampi and fry for 3–4 minutes. Drain on paper towels, arranged on a heated serving plate and sprinkle with salt.

Serve at once garnished with parsley and lemon wedges.

Time: 25 minutes — — — — — *Serves 4*

Cuttlefish and Shrimp Kebabs

SPIEDINI DI SEPPIOLINE E GAMBERETTI

Ingredients	Metric/Imperial	American
baby cuttlefish	450 g/1 lb	1 pound
shrimps	450 g/1 lb	1 pound
oil	125 ml/4 fl oz	½ cup
garlic clove	1	1
small onion	1	1
chopped parsley	1 tablespoon	1 tablespoon
chopped basil	1 tablespoon	1 tablespoon
salt and pepper		
sage leaves	12	12
bay leaves	12	12
dried breadcrumbs	25 g/1 oz	¼ cup
lemon	1	1

Prepare the cuttlefish (see page 167), cut into pieces. Shell the shrimps and put both into a bowl. Add most of the oil, the finely chopped garlic and onion, parsley, basil, salt and pepper. Marinate for about 1 hour.

Thread the shrimps and cuttlefish on to skewers, alternating with sage leaves and bay leaves. Coat with breadcrumbs, brush with remaining oil and cook under a hot grill (broiler) for 10 minutes, turning frequently.

Serve hot with lemon wedges.

Time: 30 minutes — — — — — *Serves 4*

Lobster in White Wine
1 To prepare the lobster first scrub the shell. Then cut off the legs and claws with a sharp knife and crush lightly. Cut through the body and tail sections to divide into pieces. Cut the head in half. Remove and reserve the intestines and coral; discard the bag containing sand.

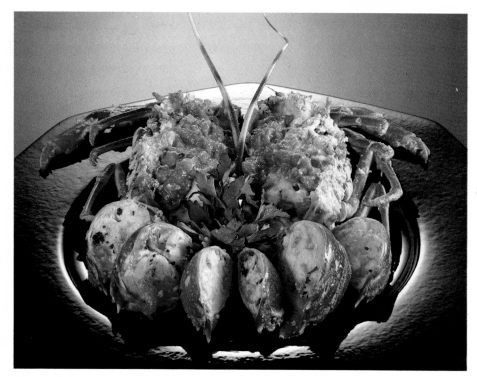

2 Put the lobster portions in a large pan on top of the vegetables. Season and brush with melted butter. Pour in wine, Marsala and cognac.
3 Transfer the cooked lobster to a heated serving dish. Reduce the cooking juices. Add the chopped intestines and coral, paprika and parsley. Simmer for 5 minutes.

Lobster in White Wine

ARAGOSTA ALLA BORGHESE

Ingredients	Metric/Imperial	American
cooked lobster	1 (1 kg/2 lb)	1 (2 pound)
butter	50 g/2 oz	$\frac{1}{4}$ cup
plum tomatoes	450 g/1 lb	1 pound
medium-sized onions	2	2
garlic clove	1	1
bay leaf	$\frac{1}{2}$	$\frac{1}{2}$
chopped thyme	$\frac{1}{4}$ teaspoon	$\frac{1}{4}$ teaspoon
chopped parsley	$1\frac{1}{2}$ tablespoons	2 tablespoons
salt and pepper		
dry white wine	125 ml/4 fl oz	$\frac{1}{2}$ cup
Marsala wine	50 ml/2 fl oz	$\frac{1}{4}$ cup
cognac	2 tablespoons	3 tablespoons
paprika	$\frac{1}{4}$ teaspoon	$\frac{1}{4}$ teaspoon

Scrub the shell and wash the lobster under cold running water. Cut off the legs and claws with a large sharp knife and crush lightly. Without removing the shell cut along the body (through the sections and the tail) to make into portions. Cut the head in half. Remove and reserve the intestines and the coral but discard the bag containing sand.

Grease a large flameproof dish with some of the butter, add the peeled, deseeded and chopped tomatoes along with the finely chopped onion and garlic, bay leaf, thyme and 1 tablespoon of parsley. Arrange the pieces of lobster in the pan, season with salt and pepper and brush with the remaining butter, melted. Pour in the white wine, Marsala and cognac and put in a moderate oven (180 c, 350 f, gas 4) for 25 minutes.

Transfer the lobster to a heated serving dish. Put the cooking dish over a high heat to thicken and reduce the cooking juices, stirring constantly. Add the finely chopped intestines and coral, remaining parsley and the paprika; cook for 5 minutes. Pour the sauce over the lobster and serve at once.

Time: 1 hour   *Serves 4*

Prawn Kebabs

Prawn Kebabs

SPIEDINI DI SCAMPI

Ingredients	Metric/Imperial	American
prawns	24	24
courgettes (zucchini)	3	3
large button mushrooms	16	16
oil	1 teaspoon	1 teaspoon
For the marinade:		
olive oil	225 ml/8 fl oz	1 cup
garlic clove, crushed	1	1
bay leaf	1	1
lemon juice	1 tablespoon	1 tablespoon
salt and pepper		

Shell the prawns if using fresh. Top, tail and wipe the courgettes and slice into thick rounds. Clean the mushrooms and remove the stems (use later in soup or stew). Put the caps along with the courgette rounds and prawns into a large bowl. Cover with the marinade and leave for about 1 hour, stir occasionally.

Drain off the marinade and thread the prawns, courgettes and mushrooms alternately on to metal skewers. Put on an oiled baking tray and cook in a moderately hot oven (190c, 370f, gas 5) for 20–25 minutes, basting from time to time with the cooking juices.

Serve hot with grilled or boiled vegetables.

Time: 30 minutes + 1 hour: marinating   *Serves 4*

173

POULTRY
AND
GAME

The varied recipes from the many regions in Italy can provide an adventurous cook with a wide repertoire when cooking chicken, poultry and game. Some of the combinations of poultry with ham and cheese may be rich but are delicious. Poultry and game are often marinated by Italian cooks and this adds subtle and interesting flavours to even a plain roast bird or a simple rabbit casserole.

To Joint Poultry

The term poultry covers chickens, guinea fowls, ducks, geese and turkeys. Insert the knife between the leg and body; cut through the skin to the thigh joint.

In the other hand grasp the leg firmly and dislocate the joint at the thigh by pressing the leg backwards. Put the knife into the ball and socket to separate the leg from the bird.

Divide the thigh and drumstick, if required, by cutting through the socket as above.

Remove the wing joints with scissors.

Cut along the rib cage with a knife or scissors on both sides of the bird to separate the breast from the back.

Divide the breast into two halves by cutting down one side of the breast bone.

To Stuff Poultry

Make up the stuffing according to the recipe.

Draw back the neck flap and pack the stuffing firmly over the breast. Replace the flap and close with a skewer or sew with fine string.

Spoon the remaining stuffing into the vent at the rear of the bird and close up with a skewer or sew with fine string.

It is essential to allow a longer cooking time for stuffed poultry and game to ensure that the bird is cooked through.

For frozen poultry and game always allow enough time for the bird to defrost completely before cooking. Remember that a 1.5 kg/3 pound bird will need 12 hours to defrost unless a microwave oven is used.

Chicken Breast Parcels

PETTI DI POLLO IN GRAN FESTA

Ingredients	Metric/Imperial	American
dried mushrooms	25 g/1 oz	1 ounce
large boned chicken breasts	2	2
bacon	50 g/2 oz	2 ounces
small onion	1	1
celery stalk	1	1
carrot	1	1
anchovy fillets	2	2
oil	2 tablespoons	3 tablespoons
salt and pepper		
paprika	$\frac{1}{4}$ teaspoon	$\frac{1}{4}$ teaspoon
brandy	2 tablespoons	3 tablespoons
plum tomatoes	2	2
Fontina cheese	50 g/2 oz	2 ounces

Soak the mushrooms in warm water for 30 minutes.

Meanwhile divide the chicken breasts in half and remove any sinews and fat. Flatten with a dampened meat mallet. Chop the derinded bacon with the vegetables and drained anchovies.

Heat the oil in a shallow pan over a medium heat. Add the chicken and fry for 1 minute. Turn over, season with salt, pepper and paprika; sprinkle on the brandy. When evaporated remove the chicken and set aside.

Add the chopped vegetable mixture to the pan, mix and cook over a low heat for 10 minutes. Squeeze the soaked mushrooms, chop coarsely and add to the pan along with the tomatoes, mashed with a fork. Mix well, taste and adjust the seasoning. Dice the Fontina cheese and stir into the pan.

Cut 4 large squares of foil and put a chicken breast on each one. Cover with one-quarter of the vegetable mixture and pinch the edges of the foil firmly together. Put on a baking tray and cook in a hot oven (220 c, 475 f, gas 7) for 20 minutes.

Serve in the foil parcels for each person to open.

Time: 50 minutes   *Serves 4*

Chicken Breast Parcels
1 Chop the bacon with the vegetables and the drained anchovies.
2 Heat the oil in a shallow pan over a medium heat. Add the flattened chicken breasts and fry for about 1 minute. Turn over and season. Sprinkle on the brandy and when it has evaporated remove the chicken from the pan.

3 Add the chopped vegetable and bacon mixture to the pan and cook for 10 minutes. Add the chopped mushrooms along with the tomatoes. Mix well, adjust the seasoning and add the diced Fontina cheese. Cook over a low heat for 3 minutes.
4 Arrange the chicken on 4 squares of foil or greaseproof (wax) paper. Divide the vegetable mixture amongst the chicken pieces and seal the parcels.

177

Tasty Chicken Livers

FEGATINI DI POLLO AL BUON SAPORE

Ingredients	Metric/Imperial	American
dried mushrooms	25 g/1 oz	1 ounce
small onion	1	1
carrot	$\frac{1}{2}$	$\frac{1}{2}$
celery stalk	1	1
garlic clove	$\frac{1}{2}$	$\frac{1}{2}$
sprig of parsley	1	1
butter	50 g/2 oz	$\frac{1}{4}$ cup
chicken livers	350 g/12 oz	$\frac{3}{4}$ pound
salt and pepper		
hard-boiled (cooked) eggs	2	2
dry white wine	50 ml/2 fl oz	$\frac{1}{4}$ cup
tomato paste	1 tablespoon	1 tablespoon
stock	3 tablespoons	4 tablespoons

Soak the mushrooms in warm water for 30 minutes.

Finely chop the onion, carrot, celery, garlic, parsley and drained mushrooms. Melt the butter in a heavy pan, add the chopped vegetables and cook over a low heat until softened. Add the washed and chopped chicken livers, increase the heat to medium and cook, stirring with a wooden spoon, until they change colour. Season with salt and pepper, then add the eggs, mashed with a fork. Pour in the wine and allow it to evaporate.

Mix the tomato paste with the hot stock, add to the pan and stir well. Simmer for a few minutes then transfer the livers to a serving plate and pour over the juices.

Time: 25 minutes   *Serves 4*

Chicken with Sweet Peppers

POLLO AI PEPERONI

Ingredients	Metric/Imperial	American
small onion	1	1
garlic clove	1	1
stock	225 ml/$\frac{1}{2}$ pint	1$\frac{1}{4}$ cups
chicken pieces	1.2 kg/2$\frac{1}{2}$ lb	2$\frac{1}{2}$ pounds
salt and pepper		
large yellow (sweet) peppers	3	3
plum tomatoes	150 g/5 oz	5 ounces
capers	1 tablespoon	1 tablespoon
chopped parsley	1 tablespoon	1 tablespoon
black olives	1 tablespoon	1 tablespoon

Finely chop the onion and garlic. Put in a large non-stick pan, add the stock and cook over a medium heat until transparent. Add the chicken pieces, season with a little salt and plenty of pepper, cover with a lid and simmer for about 1 hour over a low heat.

Meanwhile halve, deseed and chop the peppers. Add to the chicken about halfway through the cooking time, followed by the chopped tomatoes.

Five minutes before removing from the heat add the drained capers, chopped parsley and the olives, stoned and cut into rings.

Remove the chicken pieces from the pan and arrange on a heated serving plate. Continue cooking the sauce if necessary to reduce and thicken it, then pour over the chicken and serve at once.

Time: 1$\frac{1}{4}$ hours   *Serves 4*

Chicken Breasts with Mushrooms

PETTI DI POLLO AI FUNGHI

Ingredients	Metric/Imperial	American
boned chicken breasts	4	4
olive oil	2 tablespoons	3 tablespoons
butter	25 g/1 oz	2 tablespoons
onion	1	1
button mushrooms	225 g/8 oz	$\frac{1}{2}$ pound
stock	300 ml/$\frac{1}{2}$ pint	1$\frac{1}{4}$ cups
dry white wine	125 ml/4 fl oz	$\frac{1}{2}$ cup
salt and pepper		
chopped parsley	1 tablespoon	1 tablespoon

Divide the chicken breasts in half with a sharp knife, then halve again lengthways. Beat flat with a dampened meat mallet.

Heat the oil and butter in a large shallow pan. Add the finely sliced onion and cook over a medium heat until golden. Wipe and slice the mushrooms and add to the pan.

After a few minutes add the chicken and cook, turning, until golden on all sides. Pour in the stock, cover with a lid and continue cooking over a low heat for about 20 minutes, turning the chicken from time to time.

Add the wine and allow it to evaporate. Taste and adjust the seasoning.

When the chicken is tender sprinkle with chopped parsley and serve at once.

Time: 45 minutes   *Serves 4*

Friendship Chicken

POLLO DELL'AMICIZIA

Ingredients	Metric/Imperial	American
red and yellow (sweet) peppers	1	1
onions	2	2
garlic cloves	2	2
olive oil	125 ml/4 fl oz	½ cup
chicken pieces	1.2 kg/2½ lb	2½ pounds
red wine	50 ml/2 fl oz	¼ cup
plum tomatoes	400 g/14 oz	14 ounces
salt and pepper		
stock	125 ml/4 fl oz	½ cup
black olives	25 g/1 oz	1 ounce
chopped oregano	¼ teaspoon	¼ teaspoon

Cut open the peppers, remove pith and seeds, wash, dry and cut into tiny dice. Chop the onion and crush the garlic.

Heat the oil in a large casserole, add the chicken pieces and cook over a medium heat, turning until golden on all sides. Add the wine and leave it to evaporate. Then add the prepared peppers, onion and garlic, tomatoes, drained and mashed with a fork, salt and pepper. Pour in the stock, cover with a lid and leave over a low heat for about 1 hour, stirring occasionally. Alternatively cook in a moderate oven (180 C, 350 F, gas 4) for 1 hour.

Thirty minutes before the end of the cooking time add the olives, stoned and chopped. Leave the lid off so the sauce can reduce a little. Stir in the oregano at the very end.

Time: 1½ hours　　　　　　　　　　　　　　*Serves 4*

Friendship Chicken
1 Heat the oil in a large flameproof casserole over a medium heat, cook the chicken until golden on both sides. Add the wine and leave to evaporate.
2 Put the onion and garlic into the pan and cook for 2 minutes. Add the tomatoes and peppers. Season well and pour in the stock. Allow to cook for about 1 hour.
3 Half way through the cooking time add the stoned olives, cook without the lid if cooking on top of the stove to allow the sauce to reduce. Stir in the oregano at the end of the cooking time.

Terrine of Chicken
TERRINA DI POLLO IN GELATINA

Ingredients	Metric/Imperial	American
chicken breasts	600 g/1¼ lb	1¼ pounds
carrots	2	2
potato	1	1
celery stick	1	1
small onion	1	1
courgettes (zucchini)	2	2
salt		
frozen peas, thawed	225 g/8 oz	½ pound
green olives	24	24
pickled red pepper	1	1
mayonnaise	300 ml/½ pint	1¼ cups
hard-boiled (cooked) eggs	2	2
gelatine	1 envelope (sachet) or 5 teaspoons	1 envelope (sachet) or 5 teaspoons
lemon juice	3 tablespoons	4 tablespoons

Put the chicken breasts in a deep pan with the roughly chopped carrots, potato, celery, onion and courgettes. Season with salt, cover with cold water and bring to the boil over a high heat. Reduce the heat and simmer for 40 minutes, adding the peas after 30 minutes.

Remove the chicken with a slotted spoon and put on a chopping board. Drain the vegetables, discarding the celery and onion, and leave to cool. Dice the chicken finely, removing any bones, and put in a bowl along with the stoned sliced olives and strips of pepper.

Dice the carrot, potato and courgette finely, put in a separate bowl along with the peas and stir in the mayonnaise. Slice the eggs thinly.

Dissolve the gelatine in boiling water according to packet instructions, then add the lemon juice to make 600 ml/1 pint 2½ cups.

Pour enough of the gelatine to cover the bottom into a 450 g/1 pound rectangular dish or loaf pan. Put in the refrigerator or freezer until set; about 10 minutes.

Cover the set gelatine with a layer of chicken mixture, add more gelatine and allow to set. Follow this by a layer of sliced eggs and gelatine then a layer of mixed vegetables and gelatine. Allow to set between each layer. Top with a layer of gelatine. Repeat the layers until all the ingredients are used up, finishing with gelatine. Chill in the refrigerator for 2 hours.

Dip the dish briefly into hot water and invert on to a serving plate.

Time: 2 hours + 2 hours: chilling   *Serves 8*

Stuffed Chicken Breasts

INVOLTINI DI PETTO DI POLLO

Ingredients	Metric/Imperial	American
chicken breasts	4	4
cooked ham	100 g/4 oz	¼ pound
Mortadella sausage	50 g/2 oz	2 ounces
eggs	2	2
sage leaves	4	4
Gruyère cheese, grated	2 tablespoons	3 tablespoons
béchamel sauce (see page 25)	4 tablespoons	6 tablespoons
salt and pepper		
butter	25 g/1 oz	2 tablespoons
flour	2 tablespoons	3 tablespoons
stock cube	½	½
dry white wine	50 ml/2 fl oz	¼ cup
cheese slices	4	4

Remove any bones and fat from the chicken. Beat with a dampened meat mallet until large and flat. Cut in half before stuffing if very large.

Prepare the filling: finely chop the ham and Mortadella sausage. Put in a bowl with the eggs, chopped sage, Gruyère cheese and white sauce; season lightly with salt and pepper. Mix well. Divide between the chicken breasts and spread evenly with a spatula. Roll up tightly and secure with wooden cocktail sticks (toothpicks).

Melt the butter in a shallow pan. Dust the chicken rolls with flour, add to the pan and cook over a medium heat, turning until lightly browned all over. Add the crumbled stock cube and a little pepper, then sprinkle with the wine mixed with the same amount of water. Leave to evaporate, then cook on a low heat for another 15 minutes, add a little water if the chicken is drying out.

When the chicken is tender lay the cheese slices on top, cover with a lid, switch off the heat and leave until it melts. Serve at once.

Time: 50 minutes　　　　　　　　　　*Serves 4*

Terrine of Chicken
1 Poach the chicken, drain when cooked.
2 Drain the vegetables and allow to cool. Dice the cooked carrot, potato and courgettes.
3 Stir the vegetables into the mayonnaise with the peas.
4 Dice the chicken and mix with olives and peppers.
5 Coat the bottom of the pan with gelatine and set.
6 Place a layer of chicken mixture over the set gelatine.
7 Next arrange a layer of sliced eggs, cover with gelatine.
8 Allow to set and continue with the different layers.

Chicken Breasts with Pizzaiola Sauce

PETTI DI POLLO ALLA PIZZAIOLA

Ingredients	Metric/Imperial	American
canned plum tomatoes	200 g/7 oz	7 ounces
salt and pepper		
oil	2 tablespoons	3 tablespoons
capers	1 tablespoon	1 tablespoon
anchovy fillets	2	2
chopped oregano	$\frac{1}{4}$ teaspoon	$\frac{1}{4}$ teaspoon
boned chicken breasts	450 g/1 lb	1 pound
Fontina cheese slices	5	5
bacon slices	75 g/3 oz	3 ounces
milk if needed		

Put the tomatoes in a bowl along with the liquid. Mash with a fork, season with salt and pepper, then add the oil, drained chopped capers and anchovies and the oregano.

Flatten the chicken breasts with a meat mallet and lay in an oiled ovenproof dish. Season with salt and pepper; cover with the slices of cheese. Derind the bacon and lay the slices on top of the cheese. Top with the tomato mixture and cook in a moderately hot oven (190 C, 375 F, gas 5) for 40 minutes.

Time: 50 minutes   *Serves 4*

Roast Lemon Chicken

POLLO AGRO

Ingredients	Metric/Imperial	American
oven-ready chicken	1 (1.5 kg/3 lb)	1 (3 pound)
salt and pepper		
lemons	2	2
bay leaf	1	1
sage leaves	2	2
sprig of rosemary	1	1
stock cube	$\frac{1}{2}$	$\frac{1}{2}$

Season the chicken with salt and pepper. Stuff with 1 lemon, halved, and the herbs finely chopped and mixed together.

Lay the chicken in an ovenproof dish and put in a moderately hot oven (200 C, 400 F, gas 6). After about 15 minutes, when the skin begins to dry, prick all over with a fork to allow the juices to escape. Cook for 45 minutes, turning from time to time and basting halfway through with the juice of the remaining lemon and the stock cube dissolved in 150 ml/$\frac{1}{4}$ pint/$\frac{2}{3}$ cup of boiling water.

To serve remove the stuffing and dress with the cooking juices.

Time: 1 hour   *Serves 4*

Chicken Breasts with Pizzaiola Sauce
1 Mash the tomatoes into the juice with a fork, season well with salt and pepper. Add the oil, drained chopped capers and mash in the anchovies with the oregano using the fork.
2 Flatten the chicken breasts with a meat mallet and lay them in an oiled ovenproof dish.
3 Season well and cover with slices of cheese. Lay the bacon slices on top of the cheese.
4 Spread the tomato mixture evenly on top of the chicken, cheese and bacon before cooking.

Spring Chicken with Lemon

Spring Chicken with Lemon

POLLO DELICATO AL LIMONE

Ingredients	Metric/Imperial	American
bacon	40 g/1½ oz	1½ ounces
small celery stalks	5	5
large onion	1	1
garlic clove	1	1
oil	3 tablespoons	4 tablespoons
small spring chickens, cleaned and quartered	2	2
salt and pepper		
lemons	2	2
chicken stock	600 ml/1 pint	2½ cups
cornflour (cornstarch)	1 teaspoon	1 teaspoon
chopped parsley	1 tablespoon	1 tablespoon
lemon slices and parsley sprigs to garnish		

Derind the bacon and chop along with the celery, onion and garlic. Heat the oil in a large deep pan and stir in the chopped vegetables. Add the chicken quarters and cook over a medium heat, turning several times until lightly browned on both sides.

Season with salt and pepper and sprinkle on the grated rind of the lemons. Pour on the strained lemon juice, alternating with the stock. Cover and simmer over a low heat for 30 minutes, removing the lid for the last 15 minutes. Remove the chicken quarters and arrange on a heated serving dish.

Mix the cornflour with 3–4 tablespoons of the cooking juices, return to the pan and stir with a wooden spoon until the sauce has thickened slightly. Stir in the parsley and pour over the chicken.

Serve garnished with thin slices of lemon cut in half and tiny sprigs of parsley. Accompany with steamed new potatoes.

Time: 1 hour 20 minutes　　　　　　　　　*Serves 4*

183

Turkey Pieces with Mushrooms

SPEZZATO DI TACCHINO AI FUNGHI

Ingredients	Metric/Imperial	American
onion	1	1
butter	50 g/2 oz	¼ cup
oil	3 tablespoons	4 tablespoons
turkey pieces	900 g/2 lb	2 pounds
flour	2 tablespoons	3 tablespoons
Marsala wine	2 tablespoons	3 tablespoons
chicken stock	225 ml/8 fl oz	1 cup
mushrooms	350 g/12 oz	¾ pound
lemon	1	1
egg	1	1
chopped thyme	¼ teaspoon	¼ teaspoon
salt and pepper		

Finely chop the onion. Heat the butter and oil in a large deep pan, add the onion and cook over a medium heat until golden.

Coat the turkey pieces lightly in flour. Add to the pan, reduce the heat and simmer for about 25 minutes, turning now and then and adding the Marsala wine a little at a time and then half the stock.

Clean the mushrooms and put in a bowl. Cover with water acidulated with the juice of half the lemon. Leave for 10 minutes, then drain, dry and slice. Add to the pan with the turkey, mix well and continue cooking for another 20 minutes adding the remaining stock gradually.

Beat the egg lightly with the thyme and remaining lemon juice. Season the turkey with salt and pepper, pour over the egg mixture, mix quickly and transfer to a heated serving dish. Serve hot.

Time: 1¼ hours *Serves 4*

Turkey Escalopes with Yogurt

SCALOPPE DI TACCHINO ALLO YOGURT

Ingredients	Metric/Imperial	American
turkey escalopes	4 (100 g/4 oz)	4 (¼ pound)
butter	40 g/1½ oz	3 tablespoons
pepper		
stock cube	1	1
natural yogurt	150 g/5 oz	5 ounces
chopped parsley	1 tablespoon	1 tablespoon

Flatten the turkey escalopes with a dampened meat mallet. Heat the butter in a large shallow pan, add the escalopes and cook over a medium heat for 1 minute on each side until golden. Season with pepper and moisten with the stock cube dissolved in 225 ml/8 fl oz/1 cup of boiling water.

After a few minutes add the yogurt, cover and continue cooking for about 10 minutes. To serve pour the sauce over the escalopes and sprinkle with parsley.

Time: 15 minutes *Serves 4*

Turkey Fillets with Herbs

FESA DI TACCHINO AGLI AROMI

Ingredients	Metric/Imperial	American
turkey breast roast in one piece	900 g/2 lb	2 pounds
bacon	25 g/1 oz	1 ounce
mild mustard	2 tablespoons	3 tablespoons
sprigs of rosemary	2	2
sage leaves	4	4
garlic clove	1	1
butter	25 g/1 oz	2 tablespoons
olive oil	2 tablespoons	3 tablespoons
salt and pepper		
brandy	2 tablespoons	3 tablespoons
stock	300 ml/½ pint	1¼ cups

Make little slits in the turkey meat with a sharp knife. Derind and chop the bacon. Stuff the slits with bacon and cover the meat with mustard.

Finely chop the herbs together with the garlic. Heat the butter and oil in an open pressure coker, add the chopped mixture and cook over a medium heat for 2 minutes. Increase the heat, add the turkey and cook, turning, until lightly browned all over.

Season with salt and pepper, sprinkle with the brandy and set alight. When the flames have died down pour in the hot stock and seal the pressure cooker. Lower the heat when pressure is reached and cook at medium pressure for 30 minutes. Leave at room temperature for 10 minutes.

Depressurize and open the cooker. Remove the meat and leave the sauce over a low heat to thicken. Meanwhile slice the meat and arrange on a heated serving plate. Pour over the sauce and serve at once.

Time: 1 hour *Serves 4*

Alternatively cook in a casserole in a moderate oven (180 C, 350 F, gas 4) for 1 hour.

Turkey Fillets with Peas and Bacon
1 Heat the oil and butter in a pan, cook the shallots, add the bacon and cook for a few minutes. Stir in the peas.
2 Cut the turkey into strips and coat in flour.
3 Move the peas to one side, add the turkey and cook on each side until golden. Season and pour in the wine.
4 Stir in the tomato paste mixed with stock and cook for 15 minutes.

Turkey Fillets with Peas and Bacon

FILETTI DI TACCHINO CON PISELLI E PANCETTA

Ingredients	Metric/Imperial	American
shallots	2	2
smoked bacon	100 g/4 oz	$\frac{1}{4}$ pound
oil	2 tablespoons	3 tablespoons
butter	25 g/1 oz	2 tablespoons
frozen peas	450 g/1 lb	1 pound
turkey breast	600 g/1$\frac{1}{4}$ lb	1$\frac{1}{4}$ pounds
flour	2 tablespoons	3 tablespoons
salt and pepper		
dry white wine	50 ml/2 fl oz	$\frac{1}{4}$ cup
tomato paste	1 tablespoon	1 tablespoon
stock	125 ml/4 fl oz	$\frac{1}{2}$ cup
chopped parsley	1 tablespoon	1 tablespoon

Finely chop the shallots. Derind and dice the bacon. Heat the oil and butter in a large shallow pan, add the shallots and cook over a low heat until transparent. Add the bacon, cook until golden, then stir in the thawed peas. Simmer gently for another 15 minutes.

Meanwhile cut the turkey into strips, not too thinly, and coat in flour. Add to the pan with the peas, mix and cook, turning from time to time, until golden. Season with salt and pepper and pour in the wine.

When the wine has almost evaporated stir in the tomato paste mixed with the hot stock. Cover with a lid and cook for another 15 minutes. Sprinkle with parsley and serve at once.

Time: 1 hour   *Serves 4*

Rabbit with Peppers

CONIGLIO CON PEPERONI

Ingredients	Metric/Imperial	American
young rabbit	1 (1.2 kg/2½ lb)	1 (2½ pound)
butter	75 g/3 oz	6 tablespoons
large green (sweet) peppers	3	3
bacon	50 g/2 oz	2 ounces
sprig of rosemary	1	1
bay leaf	1	1
stock	600 ml/1 pint	2½ cups
oil	2 tablespoons	3 tablespoons
anchovy fillets	3	3
garlic clove	1	1
salt and pepper		
white wine vinegar	50 ml/2 fl oz	¼ cup

The rabbit should be cleaned and cut into pieces. Wash and dry; put one-third of the butter in a pan over a medium heat and add the rabbit pieces. Cook for a few minutes until golden on all sides.

Put the peppers under a hot grill (broiler) or hold in a flame for a few minutes to char the skins. Peel, halve, deseed and cut into slivers.

Derind the bacon and chop together with the rosemary leaves. Put in a separate pan with half the remaining butter, cook for 1 minute, then add the rabbit and bay leaf. Moisten with stock and cook for about 30 minutes on a low heat turning the pieces from time to time.

Heat the remaining butter in a deep pan along with the oil. Add the drained chopped anchovy fillets and crushed garlic; cook over a medium heat until the anchovies have melted. Add the pepper slivers, season with salt and pepper, cook until the pepper is tender, moistening from time to time with the vinegar.

Halfway through the rabbit's cooking time remove the bay leaf and add the peppers along with the cooking juices. Adjust the seasoning, mix and continue cooking until the rabbit is tender.

Time: 1½ hours *Serves 4*

Rabbit with Potatoes and Peppers

CONIGLIO ARROSTO CON PATATE E PEPERONI

Ingredients	Metric/Imperial	American
rabbit	1 (1.5 kg/3 lb)	1 (3 pound)
vinegar	50 ml/2 fl oz	¼ cup
flour	2 tablespoons	3 tablespoons
oil	50 ml/2 fl oz	¼ cup
garlic cloves	2	2
dry white wine	50 ml/2 fl oz	¼ cup
salt and pepper		
red (sweet) peppers	2	2
large potatoes	2	2
plum tomatoes	4	4
bay leaf	1	1
stock cube	1	1
chopped parsley	1 tablespoon	1 tablespoon

The rabbit should be cleaned and jointed. Wash, then put in a bowl of water acidulated with the vinegar and leave for 2 hours.

Drain the rabbit, rinse and dry on absorbent paper towels. Coat lightly with flour. Heat the oil in a large deep pan, add the chopped garlic and rabbit pieces and cook over a medium heat until golden, turning now and then. Moisten with the wine and leave to evaporate; season well.

Deseed and chop the peppers; chop the potatoes. Add to the pan, mix and cook until golden. Add the tomatoes mashed with a fork, the bay leaf and the stock cube dissolved in 150 ml/¼ pint/⅔ cup of boiling water.

Cover with a lid and cook until the rabbit is tender; about 30 minutes. Add more hot stock or water from time to time if necessary.

Transfer to a heated dish and serve hot sprinkled with parsley.

Time: 1¼ hours + 2 hours: soaking *Serves 4*

Rabbit with Potatoes and Peppers
1 Coat the drained rabbit with flour. Heat the oil in a pan and fry the garlic and rabbit until golden. Moisten with wine.
2 Add the peppers to the pan, stir round.
3 Tip the potatoes into the pan and cook until golden.
4 Add the tomatoes mashed with a fork, the bay leaf and the stock cube dissolved in water. Cover and cook adding a little more liquid from time to time, when necessary, to moisten.

Rabbit with Mixed Vegetables

Rabbit with Mixed Vegetables

CONIGLIO CON VERDURE IN SALSA

Ingredients	Metric/Imperial	American
rabbit	1 (1.5 kg/3 lb)	1 (3 pound)
garlic cloves	3	3
white peppercorns	4	4
white wine vinegar	225 ml/8 fl oz	1 cup
large onion	1	1
celery stalk	1	1
carrot	1	1
bacon	50 g/2 oz	2 ounces
oil	4 tablespoons	6 tablespoons
flour	2 tablespoons	3 tablespoons
salt and pepper		
red wine	50 ml/2 fl oz	$\frac{1}{4}$ cup
French beans	150 g/5 oz	5 ounces
medium-sized potatoes	3	3
plum tomatoes	400 g/14 oz	14 ounces
green olives	50 g/2 oz	2 ounces
bunch of basil	1	1

The rabbit should be cleaned and jointed. Put in a bowl with 1 chopped garlic clove, the peppercorns and vinegar. Cover and leave to marinate for 12 hours, turning the pieces from time to time. Then remove, rinse briefly under running water and dry on absorbent paper towels.

Chop the onion, celery, carrot and remaining garlic. Derind and chop the bacon. Heat the oil in a large deep pan, add the chopped ingredients and cook over a low heat until softened. Turn heat to medium.

Dust the rabbit pieces with flour, add to the pan and cook, turning from time to time, until golden on all sides. Season with salt and pepper, moisten with the wine and allow it to evaporate on a low heat.

Top and tail the beans and blanch in boiling water for 5 minutes. Drain and chop into small pieces. Add the chopped potatoes to the rabbit. After 5 minutes add the tomatoes, drained and chopped, and the stoned sliced olives. Cover the pan and simmer for 50 minutes. Add the beans and cook for 10 minutes.

Remove the lid, adjust the seasoning with salt, add 2–3 tablespoons of hot water and continue cooking over a moderate heat until the rabbit is tender; about 10 minutes. Shortly before the end of the cooking time mix in the chopped basil.

Transfer to a heated dish and serve hot.

Time: 2 hours + 12 hours: marinating　　　　*Serves 4*

Rabbit in Cream Sauce

CONIGLIO IN SALSA BIANCO

Ingredients	Metric/Imperial	American
rabbit, cleaned and jointed	1 (1.2 kg/2½ lb)	1 (2½ pound)
white wine vinegar	50 ml/2 fl oz	¼ cup
onions	2	2
garlic clove	1	1
celery stalk	1	1
lard	50 g/2 oz	2 ounces
oil	2 tablespoons	3 tablespoons
flour	2 tablespoons	3 tablespoons
salt and pepper		
dry white wine	50 ml/2 fl oz	¼ cup
milk	225 ml/8 fl oz	1 cup
stock cube	1	1
single (thin) cream	50 ml/2 fl oz	¼ cup
chopped parsley	1 tablespoon	1 tablespoon

Wash the rabbit pieces and put in a bowl. Cover with water acidulated with the vinegar and leave for 2 hours.

Finely chop the onions along with the garlic and celery. Heat the lard and oil in a flameproof casserole, add the chopped vegetables and cook over a low heat until softened.

Rinse and dry the pieces of rabbit and dust with flour. Add to the pan and cook, turning to brown evenly on all sides. Season with salt and pepper, then moisten with the wine and leave it to evaporate. Add the milk and when hot crumble in the stock cube. Cover with a lid and cook over a low heat until the rabbit is tender; about 30 minutes.

Just before the end of the cooking time stir in the cream and chopped parsley. Serve hot straight from the casserole.

Time: 1¾ hours + 2 hours: soaking   *Serves 4*

Hare Trentino-style

LEPRE ALLA TRENTINA

Ingredients	Metric/Imperial	American
hare with giblets	1 (1.5 kg/3 lb	1 (3 pound)
salt		
flour	3 tablespoons	4 tablespoons
small onion	1	1
bacon	50 g/2 oz	2 ounces
butter	50 g/2 oz	4 tablespoons
For the hare marinade:		
chopped rosemary	¼ teaspoon	¼ teaspoon
sage	½ teaspoon	½ teaspoon
bay leaf	1	1
juniper berries	6	6
black peppercorns	5	5
red wine	600 ml/1 pint	2½ cups
olive oil	125 ml/4 fl oz	½ cup
wine vinegar	3 tablespoons	4 tablespoons
For the giblet marinade:		
Grappa liqueur	2 tablespoons	3 tablespoons
red wine	300 ml/½ pint	1¼ cups
pine nuts	25 g/1 oz	1 ounce
sultanas	25 g/1 oz	1 ounce
cinnamon	¼ teaspoon	¼ teaspoon
cloves	2	2
sugar	1 tablespoon	1 tablespoon

The hare should be cleaned and cut into serving pieces. Wash and dry, rub with salt and put in a large bowl. Add all the ingredients for the hare marinade, cover and leave for at least 12 hours, stirring at intervals.

Also prepare the giblet marinade: wash the giblets, drain and chop. Put in a bowl and sprinkle with Grappa liqueur. Leave for 30 minutes, then add the remaining giblet marinade ingredients and leave for 12 hours.

Drain the pieces of hare, dry on absorbent paper towels and dip in flour. Chop the onion; derind and chop the bacon. Melt the butter in a large thick pan. Add the onion, bacon and hare pieces; cook over a medium heat until the hare pieces are golden.

Lower the heat, add 225 ml/8 fl oz/1 cup of the hare marinade, cover and simmer very gently for 1 hour. As the liquid reduces add more hare marinade, then the giblets with their marinade, including the pine nuts and sultanas. The finished sauce should be creamy.

Arrange the hare on a dish and keep warm. Sieve or blend the sauce, reheat and pour over the meat.

Time: 2½ hours + 12 hours: marinating   *Serves 6*

This dish is a speciality of Trento in the Trentino Alto Adige region of northern Italy; serve with polenta.

Stuffed Pigeons

PICCIONI FARCITI

Ingredients	Metric/Imperial	American
pigeons, cleaned with livers reserved	2	2
butter	50 g/2 oz	$\frac{1}{4}$ cup
salt and pepper		
brandy	2 tablespoons	3 tablespoons
fresh Italian sausage	75 g/3 oz	3 ounces
thin slices of bread	3	3
large mushrooms	4	4
garlic clove	1	1
sprig of parsley	1	1
small onion	1	1
egg yolk	1	1
Parmesan cheese, grated	2 tablespoons	3 tablespoons
shallot	1	1
Marsala wine	2 tablespoons	3 tablespoons
stock	225 ml/8 fl oz	1 cup
cornflour (cornstarch)	1 teaspoon	1 teaspoon

Wash and dry the pigeon livers. Melt half the butter in a small shallow pan, add the livers and cook over a low heat until the colour changes. Season with salt and pepper, add half the brandy and leave it to evaporate. Turn off the heat.

Mince (grind) the pigeon livers finely along with the skinned sausage, bread, cleaned mushrooms, garlic, parsley and onion. Transfer to a bowl, add the beaten egg yolk, Parmesan cheese and remaining brandy; mix well.

Stuff the pigeons with this mixture and sew up the openings with white cotton. Heat the remaining butter in a deep pan; add the pigeons along with the finely chopped shallot. Cook over a medium heat, turning until golden on all sides.

Season with salt and pepper, add the Marsala wine, cover with a lid, lower the heat and cook for 30 minutes, adding a tablespoon of hot stock and turning the birds from time to time. Remove the pigeons and keep hot.

Mix the cornflour with 2–3 tablespoons of the cooking juices, return to the pan and stir well to mix. Add the remaining stock and cook over a low heat until thick and creamy.

Remove the cotton from the pigeons, cut in half lengthways and serve with the sauce poured over.

Time: 1 hour   *Serves 4*

Guinea Fowl with Mushrooms and Onions

FARAONA CON FUNGHI E CIPOLLINE

Ingredients	Metric/Imperial	American
silver skin onions	12	12
salt and pepper		
fat bacon slices	4	4
oven-ready guinea fowl	1 (1.5 kg/3 lb)	1 (3 pound)
butter	50 g/2 oz	$\frac{1}{4}$ cup
stock	225 ml/8 fl oz	1 cup
brandy	2 tablespoons	3 tablespoons
mushrooms	225 g/8 oz	$\frac{1}{2}$ pound
cornflour (cornstarch)	1 teaspoon	1 teaspoon
egg yolk	1	1
sprig of parsley	1	1
garlic clove	$\frac{1}{2}$	$\frac{1}{2}$

Prepare the onions and cook in salted boiling water for 10 minutes.

Wrap the bacon over the breast of the guinea fowl and secure with kitchen string. Heat two-thirds of the butter in a heavy flameproof casserole. Add the bird along with the onions, drained and dried, and cook over a medium heat, turning to brown it lightly all over.

Moisten with a little stock, cover with a lid and cook over a medium heat for about 20 minutes, adding more stock from time to time. Then add the brandy and leave it to evaporate.

Clean the mushrooms and chop roughly. Add to the pan, season with salt and pepper and continue cooking for 15 minutes, turning the bird from time to time.

Meanwhile mix the remaining softened butter with the cornflour, egg yolk and the parsley, very finely chopped along with the garlic.

When the bird is tender remove from the sauce, take off the bacon, cut into portions and keep hot on a serving plate covered in foil. Put the casserole over a low heat, add the cornflour mixture and stir until the cooking juices have thickened. Pour over the guinea fowl and serve hot.

Time: 1$\frac{1}{4}$ hours   *Serves 4*

Guinea Fowl with Grapes

Guinea Fowl with Grapes

FARAONA ALL'UVA

Ingredients	Metric/Imperial	American
guinea fowl	1 (1.2 kg/2½ lb)	1 (2½ pound)
slices of fat bacon	4	4
butter	65 g/2½ oz	5 tablespoons
bay leaf	1	1
salt and pepper		
stock	4 tablespoons	6 tablespoons
gin	2 tablespoons	3 tablespoons
potato flour	1 teaspoon	1 teaspoon
white seedless grapes	24	24
beef extract	¼ teaspoon	¼ teaspoon
single (thin) cream	125 ml/4 fl oz	½ cup

Wash and dry the bird. Cover the breast with slices of bacon and tie with string. Put in an oval flameproof dish with high sides along with half the butter, diced. Put in a moderately hot oven (200 C, 400 F, gas 6) for 30 minutes, turning the bird twice.

Add the bay leaf to the dish, season the bird with salt and pepper and sprinkle with half the hot stock. Remove from the dish and carve into serving portions. Keep hot.

Put the dish over a medium heat, pour in the gin and set alight. When the flames have died down add the remaining butter, mixed with the potato flour, and the remaining stock. Stir until thickened, then add the washed grapes. Reduce the heat and simmer for 10 minutes, adding the beef extract dissolved in 2–3 tablespoons of hot water.

Return the pieces of guinea fowl to the dish. Turn until well covered in sauce, then stir in the cream. Cover with a lid and cook very gently for another 10 minutes. Remove the bay leaf and serve straight from the dish.

Time: 1 hour 10 minutes   *Serves 6*

Guinea Fowl with Mushrooms

Guinea Fowl with Mushrooms

FARAONA CON FUNGHI AL VERDE

Ingredients	Metric/Imperial	American
dried mushrooms	25 g/1 oz	1 ounce
young guinea fowl, prepared	1 (1.2 kg/2½ lb)	1 (2½ pound)
flour	2 tablespoons	3 tablespoons
silverskin onions	4	4
butter	50 g/2 oz	¼ cup
ham fat	25 g/1 oz	1 ounce
salt and pepper		
brandy	2 tablespoons	3 tablespoons
fresh mushrooms	225 g/8 oz	½ pound
sprig of parsley	1	1
garlic clove	1	1
stock cube	½	½
milk	125 ml/4 fl oz	½ cup
fried bread to serve		

Soak the dried mushrooms in warm water for 30 minutes.

Meanwhile cut the guinea fowl into serving portions and coat lightly with flour. Finely chop the onions. Heat the butter and chopped ham fat in a large deep pan, add the onion and cook over a medium heat until golden. Add the guinea fowl and cook, turning until lightly browned all over.

Season with salt and pepper, sprinkle on the brandy and set alight. When the flames have died down add the sliced fresh mushrooms and drained finely chopped dried mushrooms. Mix well and cook for 15 minutes.

Finely chop the parsley and garlic together. Add to the pan along with the crumbled stock cube and the milk. Cover with a lid, reduce the heat and cook until the guinea fowl is very tender and the sauce creamy. Alternatively cook in a moderate oven (180 C, 350 F, gas 4) for 1 hour.

Serve hot with little slices of bread fried in butter.

Time: 1¼ hours + 30 minutes: soaking　　　　*Serves 4*

Guinea Fowl in Wine Sauce

FARAONA IN SALMI

Ingredients	Metric/Imperial	American
guinea fowl	1	1
red wine	1 litre/1¾ pints	1 quart
carrot	1	1
celery stalk	1	1
garlic clove	1	1
chopped parsley	1 tablespoon	1 tablespoon
sage leaves	4	4
sprig of rosemary	1	1
juniper berries	4	4
cloves	2	2
peppercorns	6	6
onion	1	1
Parma ham	50 g/2 oz	2 ounces
stock	150 ml/¼ pint	⅔ cup
flour	3 tablespoons	4 tablespoons
salt		

The guinea fowl should be cleaned and cut into joints. Put them in a bowl with the wine, chopped carrot and celery, crushed garlic and all the herbs and spices. Cover and leave to marinate for 24 hours.

Slice the onion into thin rings with a sharp knife. Chop the Parma ham. Put both in a large deep pan, add the stock and cook over a low heat for 10 minutes.

Remove the pieces of guinea fowl from the marinade; drain, dry and dip in flour. Add to the pan and cook for a few minutes, then add the strained marinade. Bring to the boil; cover and simmer gently for about 1½ hours. Taste halfway through and add salt if necessary.

Arrange the portions on a heated serving plate. Sieve or blend the cooking juices, reheat and pour over the top. Serve hot.

Time: 2 hours + 24 hours: marinating *Serves 4*

In Italy this dish would be accompanied with polenta.

Wine Harvester's Partridge

PERNICI ALLA MODA DEL VENDEMMIATORE

Ingredients	Metric/Imperial	American
partridges, ready-cleaned with hearts and livers	6	6
butter	75 g/3 oz	6 tablespoons
salt and pepper		
brandy	2 tablespoons	3 tablespoons
thick slices of white bread	2	2
dry white wine, preferably sparkling	225 ml/8 fl oz	1 cup
Parmesan cheese, grated	2 tablespoons	3 tablespoons
sage leaves	8	8
garlic clove	½	½
vine leaves	6	6
slices of Parma ham	12	12
oil	4 tablespoons	6 tablespoons
bay leaves	2	2
seedless white grapes	36	36
potato flour	½ teaspoon	½ teaspoon

Wash and dry the hearts and livers. Heat one-third of the butter in a small shallow pan, add the hearts and livers and fry over a high heat for 2 minutes, turning to colour all over. Season with salt and pepper, moisten with the brandy and set alight, chop finely.

Remove the crusts from the bread and soak the crumb in half the wine. Squeeze and add to the giblet mixture. Pour over the cooking juices and add the Parmesan cheese. Mix well, then add half the sage leaves, finely chopped with the garlic.

Divide the mixture into 6 portions and stuff the partridges. Season and wrap each one in a vine leaf, then in 2 slices of Parma ham; secure with string.

Heat the remaining butter in a large deep pan along with the oil, bay leaves and remaining sage. When hot add the birds and cook for about 10 minutes over a medium heat, turning frequently. Wet with the remaining wine, cover and cook for a further 20 minutes.

Meanwhile wash and dry the grapes. Remove the birds from the pan and keep hot in a low oven. Stir in the potato flour, put 24 grapes in the cooking juices, and cook over a low heat for about 10 minutes.

Remove the ham and vine leaves from the birds and arrange the ham and birds on a hot serving plate. Pour over the sauce and garnish with the remaining grapes.

Time: 1 hour 20 minutes *Serves 6*

Pheasant Stuffed with Walnuts

FAGIANO FARCITO CON LE NOCI

Ingredients	Metric/Imperial	American
butter	75 g/3 oz	6 tablespoons
oven-ready pheasant with giblets	1 (1.5 kg/3 lb)	1 (3 pound)
salt and pepper		
long slices of bacon	2	2
carrot	1	1
onion	1	1
bouquet garni	1	1
brandy	1 tablespoon	1 tablespoon
For the stuffing:		
sage leaves	4	4
garlic clove	$\frac{1}{2}$	$\frac{1}{2}$
bread roll	1	1
single (thin) cream	50 ml/2 fl oz	$\frac{1}{4}$ cup
walnut kernels	225 g/8 oz	$\frac{1}{2}$ pound
egg	1	1
Parmesan cheese, grated	3 tablespoons	4 tablespoons
For the garnish:		
slices of bread	3	3
butter	100 g/4 oz	$\frac{1}{2}$ cup
walnut halves	12	12

Put a knob of the butter in a small pan, add the liver and heart of the pheasant and cook over a medium heat for a few minutes. Season with salt and pepper and put on a large chopping board along with the stuffing ingredients: sage, garlic, centre of the roll soaked in cream and squeezed, and the walnut kernels. Chop finely together. Put in a bowl with the egg, Parmesan cheese, seasoning and the cream left from the roll.

Stuff the pheasant with this mixture and sprinkle with salt. Wrap in bacon slices and secure with kitchen string. Melt the remaining butter in a large flameproof casserole, add the pheasant and cook over a medium heat, turning once or twice, until lightly browned all over. Add the finely chopped carrot, onion and bouquet garni. Put in a moderate oven (180 c, 350 f, gas 4). Remove after 10 minutes and cover with foil, then return for about 1 hour.

Remove the foil and bacon slices and put the pheasant on a heated serving dish. Garnish with triangles of fried bread and walnut halves. Pour over the cooking juices and finish by trickling on and lighting the brandy. Serve while still blazing.

Time: 2 hours　　　　　　　　　　　　　*Serves 6*

Pheasant with Truffles

FAGIANO TARTUFATO

Ingredients	Metric/Imperial	American
oven-ready pheasant	1 (1 kg/2 lb)	1 (2 pound)
salt and pepper		
flour	1 tablespoon	1 tablespoon
butter	65 g/2$\frac{1}{2}$ oz	5 tablespoons
onion	1	1
carrot	1	1
dry white wine (Riesling)	125 ml/4 fl oz	$\frac{1}{2}$ cup
stock	225 ml/8 fl oz	1 cup
white truffle	1	1

Cut the pheasant into pieces, sprinkle with salt and pepper inside and out and dust with flour.

Melt the butter in a heavy pan. Chop the onion and carrot, add to the pan and cook over a low heat until transparent. Add the pheasant pieces and cook over a medium heat, turning until golden on all sides. Moisten with the wine and leave it to evaporate.

Pour in half the hot stock, season with salt and pepper, cover with a lid and simmer for about 20 minutes. Stir from time to time and add more stock if the liquid is drying out. When the pheasant is tender remove and keep hot on a serving plate.

Add any remaining stock to the cooking juices and sieve or blend. Return to a low heat and cook, stirring, until thickened. Pour over the pheasant. Cut the truffle into very fine slivers, sprinkle over the dish and serve at once.

Time: 1$\frac{1}{4}$ hours　　　　　　　　　　　*Serves 4*

This is a regional dish from Asti in the Val D'Aosta.

Milanese Woodcock

BECCACCE AL MAMMOUTH

Ingredients	Metric/Imperial	American
woodcock	2	2
slices of fat bacon	100 g/4 oz	$\frac{1}{4}$ pound
butter	75 g/3 oz	6 tablespoons
salt and pepper		
Mammouth or Grand Marnier liqueur	125 ml/4 fl oz	$\frac{1}{2}$ cup
stock	300 ml/$\frac{1}{2}$ pint	1$\frac{1}{4}$ cups
liver pâté	1 tablespoon	1 tablespoon

Quail on a Bed of Almonds

Clean the woodcock, wrap in bacon and secure with kitchen string. Melt the butter in a flameproof casserole over a high heat, add the birds, season and cook until lightly browned on all sides. Reduce the heat to medium, sprinkle with the liqueur, stir and leave until evaporated.

Add the stock and cook until the birds are tender in a moderately hot oven (190 C, 375 F, gas 5) and the sauce well reduced; about 35 minutes.

Add the liver pâté to the juices and stir well adding 2–3 tablespoons of water if necessary. Remove the birds and keep warm.

Cut the string from the birds and carve in two, arrange on a heated serving dish and pour on the sauce from the casserole.

Serve hot accompanied by mashed potatoes or risotto with Parmesan cheese.

Time: 1¼ hours	*Serves 4*

This dish is a speciality of Milan; Mammouth liqueur is a speciality of the Lombardy region made in Milan. It bears some resemblance to Grand Marnier.

Quail on a Bed of Almonds

QUAGLIE SUL LETTO DI MANDORLE

Ingredients	Metric/Imperial	American
small oven-ready quail	8	8
sage leaves	8	8
slices of fat bacon	8	8
butter	40 g/1½ oz	3 tablespoons
almonds	2 tablespoons	3 tablespoons
salt and pepper		
stock	225 ml/8 fl oz	1 cup

Wash the quail carefully and dry on absorbent paper towels. Put a sage leaf on each one and wrap in a slice of bacon. Secure with kitchen string.

Melt the butter in a large shallow pan. Add the almonds and cook over a medium heat until golden. Put in the quail and cook, turning several times, until lightly browned on all sides. Season lightly with salt and pepper.

Cover with a lid, lower the heat and cook for about 30 minutes longer, moistening from time to time with a few tablespoons of hot stock. Serve at once, dividing the almonds into 4 portions.

Time: 45 minutes	*Serves 4*

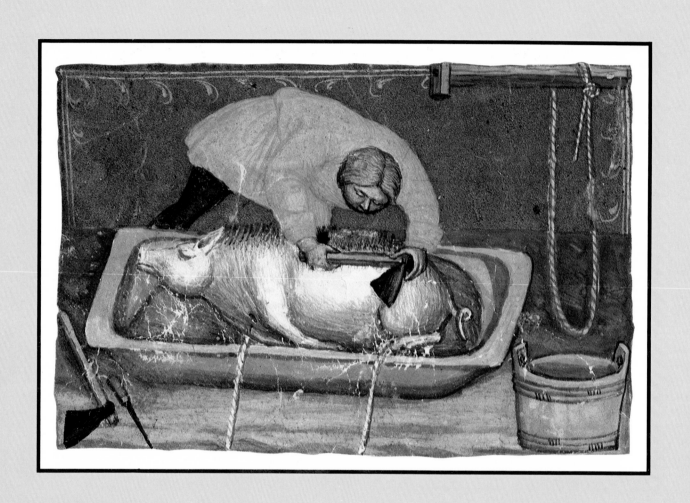

MEAT

*The quality of beef is most important in Italy.
In Tuscany the raw ingredients are considered to
play a major part in the cooking of the region.
A perfect beefsteak grilled over charcoal with only
the addition of salt and freshly ground pepper
and a few drops of olive oil indicates that the beef
must be of prime quality.
It is always advisable to become familiar with the
various cuts of beef, veal, lamb and pork to
produce the best results when cooking this
expensive commodity.
The Italians are renowned for their classic
recipes for offal and these economical variety
meats should be carefully considered when
planning family menus.*

Braised Beef with Endive
1 Stud the meat with herbed bacon fat.
2 Heat the oil and butter and fry the chopped onion, celery and endive.
3 Flour the meat, add to the pan and brown all over. Remove from the pan.
4 Add flour to the pan, pour in milk, half the wine and crumbled stock cube.
5 Transfer to the pressure cooker and add the meat.

Braised Beef with Endive

MANZO BRASATO ALL'INDIVIA

Ingredients	Metric/Imperial	American
large sprig of rosemary	1	1
garlic clove	1	1
mixed spice	¼ teaspoon	¼ teaspoon
salt and pepper		
bacon fat	100 g/4 oz	¼ pound
lean topside (tip) of beef	700 g/1½ lb	1½ pounds
small onion	1	1
celery stalk	1	1
endive (chicory) heads	2	2
oil	125 ml/4 fl oz	½ cup
butter	50 g/2 oz	¼ cup
flour		
milk	225 ml/8 fl oz	1 cup
beef stock cube	1	1
dry white wine	300 ml/½ pint	1¼ cups
stock	2 tablespoons	3 tablespoons
single (thin) cream	2 tablespoons	3 tablespoons

Finely chop the rosemary spikes with the garlic; mix with the mixed spice and a little pepper. Cut the bacon fat into small strips (1 cm/½ in × 4 cm/1½ in) and roll in the chopped mixture. Using a sharp-pointed knife make slits in the piece of meat and insert the strips of fat.

Finely chop the onion with the celery and endive. Heat the oil and butter in a flameproof casserole, add the chopped vegetables and cook over a very low heat for 10 minutes. Dust the meat with flour, add to the pan and brown lightly all over, stirring the vegetables with a wooden spoon to prevent burning. Season with a little salt, then remove the meat and put aside on a plate.

Add 1 tablespoon of flour to the pan, stir into the cooking juices and then add the milk, crumbled stock cube and half the wine. Stir until well mixed, then transfer to a pressure cooker, add the meat and leave on a low heat for a few minutes to blend the flavours. Add the remaining wine and the stock. Seal the cooker, bring to high pressure and cook for 20 minutes, lowering the heat when pressure is reached.

Leave the pressure cooker off the heat at room temperature for 15 minutes. Alternatively cook in a flameproof casserole on top of the stove over a low heat for 50 minutes, adding a little water from time to time.

Remove the meat, carve and keep warm. Put the sauce in a blender or food processor with the cream and process until smooth and creamy. Reheat gently and serve with the meat.

Time: 1¼ hours   *Serves 4*

Beef Braised in Barolo Wine

BUE BRASATO AL BAROLO

Ingredients	Metric/Imperial	American
celery stalks	2	2
carrots	2	2
onions	2	2
boned and rolled lean rib of beef	1.2 kg/2¼ lb	2¼ pounds
bay leaves	2	2
garlic clove	1	1
cloves	3–4	3–4
cinnamon	¼ teaspoon	¼ teaspoon
peppercorns	4–5	4–5
salt		
Barolo wine	300 ml/½ pint	1¼ cups
butter	25 g/1 oz	2 tablespoons

First prepare a marinade; trim and finely chop the celery, carrots and onions. Mix together and put half in a bowl. Add the meat, chopped bay leaves, crushed garlic, cloves, cinnamon and peppercorns. Cover with the remaining vegetable mixture, sprinkle with salt and pour in the wine. Leave to marinate in a cool place (not the refrigerator) for at least 6 hours, basting with the wine from time to time.

Remove and drain the meat. Melt the butter in a flameproof casserole, add the meat and cook over a high heat until lightly browned all over. Reduce the heat to low and strain in the marinade liquid. Add a little salt, cover and continue cooking in a moderate oven (180 c, 350 f, gas 4), basting with the liquid from time to time, for 1 hour.

Remove and slice the meat; keep hot. Strain the liquid into a small pan and cook until reduced and thickened. Serve poured over the meat or handed separately, as preferred.

Time: 1½ hours + 6 hours: marinating   *Serves 6*

Mustard Beef

FETTINE DI MANZO AL BUON SAPORE

Ingredients	Metric/Imperial	American
olive oil	150 ml/$\frac{1}{4}$ pint	$\frac{2}{3}$ cup
piece of topside (tip)	600 g/1$\frac{1}{4}$ lb	1$\frac{1}{4}$ pounds
salt		
black peppercorns	6	6
French mustard	1 teaspoon	1 teaspoon
garlic clove	1	1
young carrots, partly cooked	225 g/8 oz	$\frac{1}{2}$ pound
broccoli spears, partly cooked	225 g/8 oz	$\frac{1}{2}$ pound

Heat 2–3 tablespoons of the oil in a shallow pan over a high heat. Add the meat; fry for 2 minutes each side.

Remove to a chopping board, discard any fat and slice the meat medium thick. Arrange the slices in an oiled ovenproof dish; sprinkle with salt and the peppercorns. Mix 4–6 tablespoons of the remaining oil with the mustard and pour over the meat. Leave to marinate for 1 hour.

Heat the remaining oil in a shallow pan, add the crushed garlic and cook over a medium heat until softened. Add the carrots and broccoli and cook for 2 minutes, then add to the dish with the meat. Put, covered, in a moderate oven (180 C, 350 F, gas 4) for 25 minutes and serve hot.

Time: 40 minutes + 1 hour: marinating　　　*Serves 4*

Beef Braised in Beer

BOCCONCINI DI MANZO IN BIANCO

Ingredients	Metric/Imperial	American
onion	1	1
garlic clove	1	1
sage leaves	3	3
oil	2 tablespoons	3 tablespoons
butter	40 g/1$\frac{1}{2}$ oz	3 tablespoons
stewing beef	800 g/1$\frac{3}{4}$ lb	1$\frac{3}{4}$ pounds
flour	3 tablespoons	scant $\frac{1}{4}$ cup
salt and pepper		
grated nutmeg	$\frac{1}{4}$ teaspoon	$\frac{1}{4}$ teaspoon
lemon rind	1	1
lager (light beer)	225 ml/8 fl oz	1 cup
milk	175 ml/6 fl oz	$\frac{3}{4}$ cup
stock cube	$\frac{1}{2}$	$\frac{1}{2}$

Finely chop the onion with the garlic and sage leaves. Heat the oil and butter in a heavy flameproof casserole, add the chopped mixture and cook over a medium heat until golden.

Cube the meat, toss in flour and put in a sieve to shake out the excess. Add to the pan and cook, stirring, until lightly browned all over. Season with salt, pepper, nutmeg and grated lemon rind. Sprinkle on 2–3 tablespoons of the lager and allow it to evaporate, then reduce the heat.

Heat the milk in a small pan and dissolve the stock cube in it. Add two-thirds of the milk to the pan with the meat, and when this has been absorbed add 2–3 tablespoons of the lager. Continue in this way until all the milk and lager has been used.

Cover and cook in a moderate oven (180 C, 350 F, gas 4) until the meat is tender and the sauce is smooth. Serve with puréed potatoes.

Time: 1 hour 40 minutes　　　*Serves 4*

Countryman's Roast Beef

ARROSTO DI MANZO DEL CONTADINO

Ingredients	Metric/Imperial	American
bunch of basil	1	1
garlic clove	1	1
eggs	2	2
salt and pepper		
Parmesan cheese, grated	2 tablespoons	3 tablespoons
oil	4 tablespoons	6 tablespoons
red (sweet) peppers	2	2
thick slice of sirloin	700 g/1$\frac{1}{2}$ lb	1$\frac{1}{2}$ pounds
bacon slices	75 g/3 oz	3 ounces
butter	25 g/1 oz	2 tablespoons
shallot	1	1
stock cube	1	1
dry white wine	50 ml/2 fl oz	$\frac{1}{4}$ cup
stock	125 ml/4 fl oz	$\frac{1}{2}$ cup

Finely chop the basil leaves with the garlic. Beat the eggs lightly, add a little salt and pepper and stir in the chopped mixture along with the Parmesan cheese.

Heat half the oil in a 20 cm/8 in shallow pan over a medium heat. Pour in the egg mixture, allow to set on one side, then with the help of a lid turn the omelette over and cook the other side.

Countryman's Roast Beef

Char the skin of the pepper under a hot grill (broiler) or in a flame. Peel, deseed and cut into strips.

Spread the meat out on a work surface and sprinkle lightly with salt. Cover with slices of derinded bacon and put the prepared omelette on top. Add the peppers, roll up tightly and secure with kitchen string.

Heat the remaining oil with the butter in a flame-proof casserole, add the chopped shallot and cook over a medium heat until golden. Then add the meat roll and brown it lightly all over. Crumble the stock cube into the pan, season with pepper and moisten with the wine. Continue cooking until the wine has evaporated, then add the stock. Cover and cook in a moderately hot oven (190 c, 375 f, gas 5) for 25 minutes or until the meat is tender.

Slice the meat roll, arrange on a heated dish and serve with the cooking juices poured over, accompanied by creamed potatoes.

Time: 1 hour 20 minutes   *Serves 6*

Beef Steaks with Mozzarella

1 Cut the courgettes and pepper into matchstick strips. Trim the aubergine and dice.

2 Melt the butter over a medium heat and brown the steaks on each side. Remove and keep warm.

3 Add the oil to the meat pan and cook the chopped onion and crushed garlic until golden. Add the prepared vegetables and cook for a few minutes.

4 Add the tomatoes to the pan; season and sprinkle with chopped basil.

5 Cut 4 pieces of foil large enough to wrap up the steaks. Put a steak in the centre of each one and cover with a good portion of the vegetable mixture.

6 Top with 2 slices of Mozzarella cheese. Pinch the edges of the foil together. Cook in a moderate oven for 15 minutes until the cheese has melted.

1

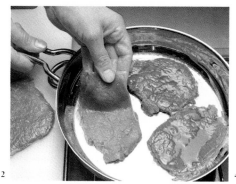

3

4

2

5

6

Inebriated Steaks

BISTECCHINE UBRIACHE

Ingredients	Metric/Imperial	American
full-bodied red wine	125 ml/4 fl oz	½ cup
clove	1	1
garlic clove	1	1
lemon rind	½	½
butter	25 g/1 oz	2 tablespoons
small steaks	8	8
flour	2 tablespoons	3 tablespoons
salt and freshly ground black pepper		
beef stock cube	¼	¼

Put the wine in a small pan with the clove, crushed garlic and a piece of lemon rind. Leave over a medium heat until reduced by half.

Melt the butter in a large shallow pan. Coat the steaks lightly in flour, add to the pan and cook over a medium heat for 2 minutes on each side until golden. Strain the wine into the pan and add the stock cube dissolved in 4–6 tablespoons of hot water. Continue to cook for 10 minutes.

Season generously with pepper and serve with the cooking juices poured over.

Time: 25 minutes   *Serves 4*

Beef Steaks with Mozzarella

BISTECCHE DEL BUON TEMPO

Ingredients	Metric/Imperial	American
courgette (zucchini)	1	1
yellow (sweet) pepper	1	1
aubergine (eggplant)	1	1
butter	25 g/1 oz	2 tablespoons
beef steaks	4	4
salt and pepper		
oil	2 tablespoons	3 tablespoons
onion	1	1
garlic clove	1	1
plum tomatoes	6	6
basil leaves	10	10
Mozzarella cheese	8 slices	8 slices

Top and tail the courgette and cut into matchstick strips. Deseed the pepper and cut into thin strips. Trim the aubergine and dice.

Melt the butter in a shallow pan over a medium heat, put in the steaks and cook for 2–4 minutes on each side according to taste. Season, remove from the pan and keep warm.

Add the oil to the same pan and cook the finely chopped onion and crushed garlic until golden. Add the prepared vegetables and cook for a few minutes. Peel the tomatoes if using fresh; drain if canned. Chop and add to the pan along with a little salt and pepper; sprinkle with chopped basil.

Cut 4 pieces of foil large enough to wrap round the steaks with room to spare. Put a steak in the centre of each and top with a portion of the vegetable mixture and 2 slices of Mozzarella cheese. Pinch the edges of the foil together and put in a moderate oven (180 c, 350 f, gas 4) for 15 minutes to melt the cheese. Serve at once.

Time: 50 minutes   *Serves 4*

Steak with Pesto Sauce

BISTECCHINE AL PESTO

Ingredients	Metric/Imperial	American
beef steaks	8 (75 g/3 oz)	8 (3 ounce)
basil leaves	24	24
garlic clove	1	1
Pecorino cheese, grated	1 tablespoon	1 tablespoon
Parmesan cheese, grated	1 tablespoon	1 tablespoon
pine nuts	1 tablespoon	1 tablespoon
olive oil	50 ml/2 fl oz	¼ cup
salt and pepper		
butter	25 g/1 oz	2 tablespoons

Trim the steaks into regular shapes and flatten with a dampened meat mallet.

Wash and dry the basil leaves, then purée in a blender or food processor along with the garlic, Pecorino and Parmesan cheeses, pine nuts and 2–3 tablespoons of the oil. Process into a thick sauce, adding more oil if necessary. Season lightly with salt.

Melt the butter in a heavy shallow pan, add the steaks and cook for 1 minute on each side over a high heat. Reduce the heat to low and season with salt and pepper. Spread the pesto sauce over the steaks and put some in the cooking juices. Cover with a lid and cook gently for about 10 minutes until the steaks are well flavoured with the sauce.

Time: 30 minutes   *Serves 4*

Mixed Meat Loaf

POLPETTONE MISTO

Ingredients	Metric/Imperial	American
boiled potatoes	2	2
cooked spinach	225 g/8 oz	½ pound
cooked ham	100 g/4 oz	¼ pound
minced (ground) beef	450 g/1 lb	1 pound
Parmesan cheese, grated	25 g/1 oz	2 tablespoons
eggs	2	2
salt and pepper		
dried breadcrumbs	2 tablespoons	3 tablespoons
ripe tomatoes	2	2
lemon juice	2 tablespoons	3 tablespoons
chopped chives	1 teaspoon	1 teaspoon

Mash or sieve the potatoes in a bowl, add the chopped spinach and ham, beef, Parmesan cheese and eggs; season lightly with salt and pepper. Mix well with a fork and form into a loaf shape with the hands. Coat with breadcrumbs.

Wrap the loaf in muslin, knot the ends and cook in boiling salted water for about 1 hour. Drain and leave until cold.

Remove the muslin, slice the meat and arrange on a serving dish. Dice the tomatoes, sprinkle with salt, pepper, lemon juice and chives. Scatter over the meat and serve.

Time: 1½ hours *Serves 4*

Fantasy Beef

FETTINE DI MANZO FANTASIA

Ingredients	Metric/Imperial	American
slices of bread	4	4
milk		
Mortadella sausage	150 g/5 oz	5 ounces
sprigs of rosemary	2	2
garlic clove	1	1
salt		
olive oil	3 tablespoons	4 tablespoons
lean topside (tip) beef	600 g/1¼ lb	1¼ pounds
stock	200 ml/7 fl oz	¾ cup

Remove the crusts from the bread and soak the crumb in a little milk. Finely chop the Mortadella sausage with a few rosemary spikes and the garlic. Add the squeezed breadcrumbs and a little salt if necessary.

Pour the oil into a small tall pan. Slice the meat to the same size as the bottom of the pan. Put in one slice, cover with some of the prepared mixture, follow with another slice and continue in this way until all the ingredients are used up.

Pour in a few tablespoons of the hot stock, cover with a lid and leave to cook over a low heat for about 1 hour, 6adding more stock when necessary. Serve hot with mashed potatoes.

Time: 1½ hours *Serves 4*

Beef Stew with Mushrooms

BOCCONCINI DI MANZO AI FUNGHI

Ingredients	Metric/Imperial	American
leek	1	1
carrot	1	1
onion	1	1
celery stalk	1	1
oil	3 tablespoons	4 tablespoons
bacon fat	25 g/1 oz	1 ounce
yellow (sweet) pepper	1	1
mushrooms	150 g/5 oz	5 ounces
braising steak	600 g/1¼ lb	1¼ pounds
flour	2 tablespoons	3 tablespoons
salt and pepper		
red wine	50 ml/2 fl oz	¼ cup
tomato paste	2 tablespoons	3 tablespoons
stock	600 ml/1 pint	2½ cups
chopped parsley	1 tablespoon	1 tablespoon

Trim the leek, discarding the green part, wash well and drain. Chop finely along with the carrot, onion and celery.

Heat the oil and diced bacon fat in a large deep pan. Add the chopped vegetables and cook over a low heat until softened.

Deseed and dice the pepper; wipe and slice the mushrooms. Add to the other vegetables, mix and leave for a few minutes until golden. Trim and cube the steak, season, coat lightly with flour and add to the pan. Cook, turning, until lightly and evenly browned. Pour in the wine and allow it to evaporate completely. Mix the tomato paste with the hot stock and pour into the pan. Cover with a lid and leave over a low heat for about 1 hour. (If the stew dries out too much add more stock.) Serve sprinkled with parsley.

Time: 1½ hours *Serves 4*

Chef's Beef Rolls

Chef's Beef Rolls

FETTE DI MANZO ALLA MODA DELLO CHEF

Ingredients	Metric/Imperial	American
butter	50 g/2 oz	¼ cup
oil	4 tablespoons	6 tablespoons
garlic clove	1	1
mushrooms	225 g/8 oz	½ pound
salt and pepper		
Marsala wine	2 tablespoons	3 tablespoons
béchamel sauce	4 tablespoons	6 tablespoons
cooked ham	75 g/3 oz	3 ounces
truffle paste	1 teaspoon	1 teaspoon
Parmesan cheese, grated	25 g/1 oz	¼ cup
eggs	2	2
thin slices of topside (tip)	4	4
flour	2 tablespoons	3 tablespoons
dry white wine	50 ml/2 fl oz	¼ cup
beef stock	225 ml/8 fl oz	1 cup
double (thick) cream	2 tablespoons	2 tablespoons

Melt half the butter with half the oil in a large shallow pan, add the lightly crushed garlic and cook over a medium heat until golden. Remove the garlic and add the wiped sliced mushrooms. Cook over a high heat for 1 minute, stirring, then reduce to low, season with salt and pepper, sprinkle with the Marsala wine and simmer for 10 minutes.

Stir the mushrooms into the béchamel sauce (see page 25), add the chopped ham, truffle paste, Parmesan cheese and eggs; mix well.

Lay the slices of meat out on a work surface, beat with a dampened meat mallet and spread with the mushroom mixture. Roll up and secure each with a wooden cocktail stick (toothpick). Coat lightly with flour.

Heat the remaining butter and oil in a heavy shallow pan over a medium heat, add the beef rolls and cook for a few minutes, turning to brown evenly on all sides. Season with salt and pepper, then add wine and stock.

Reduce the heat and leave for about 20 minutes until cooked. Remove the rolls with a slotted spoon, discard the sticks and slice each one into 3 or 4 pieces. Arrange on a heated serving dish. Stir the cream into the pan juices and pour over the meat.

Time: 1 hour   *Serves 4*

Veal Escalopes Livorno

SCALLOPINE ALLA LIVORNESE

Ingredients	Metric/Imperial	American
small escalopes of veal	8	8
plain (all-purpose) flour	50 g/2 oz	$\frac{1}{2}$ cup
ripe tomatoes	2	2
garlic clove	1	1
salt		
black olives	16	16
dry white wine	50 ml/2 fl oz	$\frac{1}{4}$ cup
stock	125 ml/4 fl oz	$\frac{1}{2}$ cup
chopped parsley	1 tablespoon	1 tablespoon

Dip each escalope in flour. Peel and finely chop the tomatoes; put them in a large shallow pan with the lightly crushed garlic clove, a pinch of salt and the stoned chopped olives. Pour in the wine and simmer gently for about 15 minutes, then mash with a fork.

Put in the escalopes, raise the heat and cook for 10 minutes, adding enough hot stock to stop the sauce from drying out. Turning the escalopes over halfway through.

Sprinkle with parsley and serve hot.

Time: 30 minutes   *Serves 4*

A regional dish from Livorno.

Veal Escalopes Bolognese

SCALLOPPE ALLA BOLOGNESE

Ingredients	Metric/Imperial	American
veal escalopes	4 (100 g/4 oz)	4 ($\frac{1}{4}$ pound)
plain (all-purpose) flour	1 tablespoon	1 tablespoon
egg	1	1
butter	40 g/1$\frac{1}{2}$ oz	3 tablespoons
slices of cooked ham	4	4
fresh Parmesan cheese in slices	100 g/4 oz	$\frac{1}{4}$ pound
dry white wine	50 ml/2 fl oz	$\frac{1}{4}$ cup
stock	50 ml/2 fl oz	$\frac{1}{4}$ cup
salt and pepper		
grated nutmeg	$\frac{1}{4}$ teaspoon	$\frac{1}{4}$ teaspoon

Flatten the escalopes with a meat mallet to make them really thin and trim off any fat. Coat in flour, then in lightly beaten egg.

Melt the butter in a large shallow pan and when it is foaming add the escalopes and fry for 3 minutes on each side.

Butter an ovenproof dish large enough to take all the escalopes in a single layer. Put in the escalopes and top each one with a slice of ham, then slices of cheese.

Pour the wine and stock into the pan used to fry the escalopes. Season with salt, pepper and nutmeg and cook over a medium heat, stirring with a wooden spoon to incorporate the pan juices, until the liquid has reduced by half. Pour the liquid over the meat, cover and put in a moderate oven (180 c, 350 f, gas 4) for 15 minutes. Serve straight from the dish.

Time: 40 minutes   *Serves 4*

A regional dish from Bologna.

Veal Chops with Fontina Cheese

COSTOLETTE ALLA FONTINA

Ingredients	Metric/Imperial	American
thick veal chops on the bone	4	4
Fontina cheese	100 g/4 oz	$\frac{1}{4}$ pound
salt and pepper		
plain (all-purpose) flour	25 g/1 oz	$\frac{1}{4}$ cup
eggs	2	2
dried breadcrumbs	4 tablespoons	6 tablespoons
butter	75 g/3 oz	6 tablespoons

Slit the chops horizontally with a sharp knife, stopping just short of the bone. Put a few slices of cheese inside each chop, then beat with a meat mallet to stick the meat and cheese together. Secure with wooden cocktail sticks (toothpicks). Season lightly with salt and pepper, dust with flour and dip first in beaten egg, then in breadcrumbs. Press firmly with the palm of one hand to make sure the breadcrumbs stick on.

Melt the butter in a heavy shallow pan over medium heat. When foaming add the chops and brown lightly on each side. Lower the heat and cook until the meat is tender and the cheese melted.

Time: 45 minutes   *Serves 4*

A regional dish from Aosta, sometimes made even richer by the addition of slivers of truffle along with the cheese.

Veal Escalopes with Basil

SCALOPPINE AL BASILICO

Ingredients	Metric/Imperial	American
small veal escalopes	16	16
flour	3 tablespoons	4 tablespoons
sprig of basil	1	1
garlic cloves	2	2
butter	75 g/3 oz	6 tablespoons
salt and pepper		
dry white wine	125 ml/4 fl oz	$\frac{1}{2}$ cup

Flatten the escalopes with a dampened meat mallet and coat lightly in flour. Strip the leaves from the basil and chop finely together with the garlic cloves.

Melt two-thirds of the butter in a large shallow pan over a medium heat until foaming. Add the veal and cook for 1 minute on each side. Season with salt and pepper; add the wine along with 125 ml/4 fl oz/$\frac{1}{2}$ cup of water. Reduce the heat and cook until the sauce is thick and smooth; about 10 minutes.

Transfer the escalopes to a heated serving dish. Add the remaining butter to the pan, then the basil and garlic mixture. Cook, stirring, for about 1 minute, then pour over the veal. Serve accompanied by a salad or creamed potatoes.

Time: 20 minutes   *Serves 8*

1 Strip the leaves from the basil and chop together with the garlic cloves.
2 Cook the veal escalopes in two-thirds of the butter and the wine.
3 Fry the basil and garlic mixture. Pour over the veal and garnish with tomato wedges and basil leaves if liked.

Veal and Mortadella Burgers
1 Heat the oil and butter in a shallow pan. Cook the sliced mushrooms over a medium heat until golden on each side.
2 Lower the heat and add the mashed tomatoes. Crumble the stock cube into the pan, stir well and cook until the mixture is the consistency of sauce. Add the chopped parsley.
3 Put the veal into a bowl with the chopped Mortadella sausage and season with salt and pepper. Mix well and shape into four rounds.
4 Cook under a hot grill (broiler) for 5 minutes on each side.
5 Put the cooked burgers on a heatproof dish and spoon a portion of the mushroom mixture over each one.
6 Top each burger with a slice of Mozzarella cheese and grill (broil) until the cheese has melted. Garnish with sprigs of herbs such as thyme, basil or parsley.

Veal and Mortadella Burgers

HAMBURGER DI VITELLO E MORTADELLA ALLA MODA DEL PASTORE

Ingredients	Metric/Imperial	American
oil	4 tablespoons	6 tablespoons
butter	25 g/1 oz	2 tablespoons
mushrooms	150 g/5 oz	5 ounces
plum tomatoes	400 g/14 oz	14 ounces
stock cube	$\frac{1}{2}$	$\frac{1}{2}$
chopped parsley	1 tablespoon	1 tablespoon
minced (ground) veal	450 g/1 lb	1 pound
Mortadella sausage	100 g/4 oz	$\frac{1}{4}$ pound
salt and pepper		
slices of Mozzarella cheese	4	4

Heat the oil and butter in a shallow pan. Wipe and slice the mushrooms; add to the pan and cook over a medium heat for a few minutes. Lower the heat and add the tomatoes, mashed with a fork. Crumble in the stock cube, stir and leave until reduced to a sauce-like consistency. Finish with chopped parsley.

Put the veal in a bowl with the chopped Mortadella sausage; season lightly with salt and pepper. Form into 4 burgers and cook under a hot grill (broiler) for 5 minutes on each side.

Arrange the burgers in a long ovenproof dish, pour a portion of mushroom sauce over each one and top with a slice of Mozzarella cheese. Put under the grill (broiler) until the cheese has completely melted. Serve at once.

Time: 50 minutes   *Serves 4*

Saltimbocca with Sage

SALTIMBOCCA ALLA SALVIA

Ingredients	Metric/Imperial	American
veal escalopes	8	8
slices of Parma ham	8	8
sage leaves	8	8
flour	2 tablespoons	3 tablespoons
lemon	$\frac{1}{2}$	$\frac{1}{2}$
garlic clove	1	1
salt and pepper		
milk	125 ml/4 fl oz	$\frac{1}{2}$ cup
stock cube	$\frac{1}{2}$	$\frac{1}{2}$

Flatten the escalopes with a dampened meat mallet. Trim off any fat from the Parma ham and lay a slice on top of each escalope; finish with a sage leaf. Form into the traditional *saltimbocca* shape by bringing the 4 corners into the centre and securing with a wooden cocktail stick (toothpick). Coat lightly in flour.

Pour the juice of the $\frac{1}{2}$ lemon into a non-stick pan, add the crushed garlic and cook over a medium heat until golden. Add the *saltimbocca*, season with salt and pepper, then add the milk mixed with the crumbled stock cube.

Reduce the heat and cook for a further 10 minutes, turning from time to time. Serve hot with the cooking juices poured over.

Time: 25 minutes   *Serves 4*

Veal Stew with Baby Onions and Cream

DADI DI CARNE CON CIPOLLE ALLA CREMA

Ingredients	Metric/Imperial	American
onions	1 kg/2 lb	2 pounds
oil	2 tablespoons	3 tablespoons
butter	50 g/2 oz	$\frac{1}{4}$ cup
garlic cloves	2	2
pie veal	1.2 kg/2$\frac{1}{4}$ lb	2$\frac{1}{4}$ pounds
salt and pepper		
Marsala wine	50 ml/2 fl oz	$\frac{1}{4}$ cup
stock	300 ml/$\frac{1}{2}$ pint	1$\frac{1}{4}$ cups
single (thin) cream	300 ml/$\frac{1}{2}$ pint	1$\frac{1}{4}$ cups
chopped parsley	1 tablespoon	1 tablespoon

Drop the onions in boiling water and peel; cut off the roots.

Heat the oil and butter in a large deep pan, add the lightly crushed garlic and cook over a medium heat until golden. Add the onions and cook for 5 minutes, shaking the pan from time to time to brown evenly.

Discard the garlic and put in the diced veal; stir round for 5 minutes. Season to taste with salt and pepper and pour over the Marsala wine. When this has evaporated add the stock, lower the heat, cover with a lid and simmer gently for 1 hour. Stir in the cream. Sprinkle with parsley and serve hot.

Time: 1$\frac{1}{4}$ hours   *Serves 8*

Roast Veal with Lemon

ARROSTO DI VITELLO AL PROFUMO DI LIMONE

Ingredients	Metric/Imperial	American
butter	40 g/1½ oz	3 tablespoons
piece of veal fillet	800 g/1¾ lb	1¾ pounds
medium-sized onion	1	1
lemon	1	1
dry white wine	125 ml/4 fl oz	½ cup
beef stock	225 ml/8 fl oz	1 cup
salt and pepper		

Dice the butter and put in a roasting pan. Add the veal, finely chopped onion and the lemon, cut into wedges, deseeded and chopped. Pour over the wine and most of the stock. Put in a moderately hot oven (200 C, 400 F, gas 6). Cook for about 40 minutes or until tender, removing regularly to turn the veal over and baste with the cooking juices; season lightly with salt. Add more stock if the liquid dries out.

Remove the veal and pass the cooking juices through a sieve into a small pan; reheat gently. Slice the veal and arrange on a heated serving plate; dress with the seasoned cooking juices and serve.

Time: 1 hour 20 minutes　　　　　　　　*Serves 4*

Veal Stew with Mushrooms

BOCCONCINI DI VITELLO CON PATATE, FUNGHI E CIPOLLE

Ingredients	Metric/Imperial	American
large potatoes	2	2
carrot	1	1
celery stalk	1	1
onions	2	2
oil	4 tablespoons	6 tablespoons
butter	25 g/1 oz	2 tablespoons
mushrooms	350 g/12 oz	¾ pound
braising veal	800 g/1¾ lb	1¾ pounds
salt and pepper		
bay leaves	2	2
dry white wine	50 ml/2 fl oz	¼ cup
stock	600 ml/1 pint	2½ cups
chopped parsley	1 tablespoon	1 tablespoon
single (thin) cream	4 tablespoons	6 tablespoons

Cube the potatoes and carrot; finely chop the celery and onions.

Heat the oil and butter in a deep heavy pan, add the carrot, celery and onions and cook on a medium heat for 5 minutes.

Add the potatoes along with the sliced mushrooms and continue cooking until golden. Trim and cube the meat; add to the pan and season with salt and pepper. Add the bay leaves and wine; when the wine has evaporated turn the heat to low, add a little of the hot stock and cover the pan. Cook for about 1 hour or until the veal is tender, adding more stock from time to time.

Stir in the parsley and cream, transfer to a heated dish and serve at once.

Time: 1 hour 45 minutes　　　　　　　　*Serves 4*

Osso Bucco with Lemon

OSSIBUCHI IN GREMOLATA

Ingredients	Metric/Imperial	American
dried mushrooms	50 g/2 oz	2 ounces
veal knuckles	4	4
plain (all-purpose) flour	50 g/2 oz	½ cup
salt and pepper		
olive oil	3 tablespoons	scant ¼ cup
carrot	1	1
onion	1	1
celery stalk	1	1
butter	100 g/4 oz	½ cup
red wine	225 ml/8 fl oz	1 cup
canned plum tomatoes	225 g/8 oz	½ pound
stock	225 ml/8 fl oz	1 cup
chopped parsley	1 tablespoon	1 tablespoon
lemon rind	½	½

Soak the mushrooms in warm water for 30 minutes; drain and dry.

Coat the veal knuckles in flour and season with salt. Heat the oil in a heavy pan over a medium heat, add the meat and cook until golden on all sides. Remove and drain on absorbent paper towels.

Finely chop the carrot, onion, celery and mushrooms all together. Melt the butter in a flameproof casserole, add the vegetable mixture and cook over a medium heat

Osso Bucco with Lemon

until golden. Add the veal, cook for a few minutes, then add the wine. Cover with a lid and put in a moderate oven (180 C, 350 F, gas 4) for 30 minutes until the wine has completely evaporated. Remove and turn the oven down to 160 C, 325 F, gas 3.

Mash the tomatoes with a fork and add with the juice to the casserole along with the stock. Return to the oven and cook for a further 2 hours, until the meat is very tender.

Taste and adjust the seasoning. Sprinkle with parsley and grated lemon rind and serve hot.

Time: 3 hours   *Serves 4*

Cold Veal with Avocado Sauce
1 Slice cold veal evenly. Arrange on a plate, overlapping the slices.

2 Mash an egg in a bowl, add mustard and lemon juice; mix well.
3 Mix mashed avocado with the

egg and lemon juice sauce. Stir in chopped parsley. Serve the meat covered with this sauce.

Cold Veal with Avocado Sauce

VITELLO FREDDO ALL'AVOCADO

Ingredients	Metric/Imperial	American
piece of veal leg	1.5 kg/3 lb	3 pounds
small onion	1	1
carrot	1	1
celery stalk	1	1
salt and pepper	1	1
bouquet garni	1	1
hard-boiled (cooked) egg	1	1
mild mustard	2 teaspoons	3 teaspoons
oil	1 tablespoon	1 tablespoon
lemon juice	2 tablespoons	3 tablespoons
ripe avocado	1	1
chopped parsley	1 tablespoon	1 tablespoon

Put the veal in a deep pan with the quartered onion, roughly chopped carrot and halved celery stalk. Just cover with cold water, season with salt, pepper and bouquet garni and bring to the boil. Reduce the heat to low, cover the pan and cook for about 1 hour until the veal is tender.

Drain, leave until cold, then carve and arrange the slices on a serving plate, overlapping them slightly. Use the stock for soup.

Put the egg in a small bowl and mash with a fork. Work in the mustard, oil and half of the lemon juice; season with salt and pepper.

Peel the avocado, cut in half and remove the stone. Mash the flesh with the remaining lemon juice until creamy. Add the egg sauce and chopped parsley and mix well. Cover the meat with this sauce and serve.

Time: 2 hours *Serves 8*

Veal Nests with Egg

NIDI DI CARNE DI VITELLO ALL'UOVO

Ingredients	Metric/Imperial	American
minced (ground) veal	600 g/1¼ lb	1¼ pounds
small eggs	10	10
bread roll	1	1
chopped parsley	1 tablespoon	1 tablespoon
Parmesan cheese, grated	3 tablespoons	4 tablespoons
mashed potato	225 g/8 oz	½ pound
Mortadella sausage	75 g/3 oz	3 ounces
salt and pepper		
butter, melted	5 tablespoons	7 tablespoons
milk		

Put the veal in a bowl with 2 of the eggs, lightly beaten; the centre of the roll, soaked in milk and squeezed; the parsley, Parmesan cheese, potato and chopped Mortadella. Mix well and season with salt and pepper.

Make the nests by forming the mixture into 8 balls, flattening them and making a depression in the centre with the back of a spoon.

Brush a shallow ovenproof dish with a little of the melted butter. Put in the nests and brush with the remaining butter. Cook in a moderate oven (180 c, 350 f, gas 4) for 35 minutes, adding a little milk to each nest halfway through.

Remove from the oven, crack an egg into each nest and sprinkle with salt. Return to the oven for 10 minutes until the whites are just set and the yolks still soft.

Time: 1 hour *Serves 4*

Veal Nests with Egg
1 Put the veal into a bowl with 2 eggs, a soaked bread roll and chopped parsley. Add chopped Mortadella sausage.
2 Stir in grated Parmesan cheese and mashed potato, mix well and season with salt and pepper.
3 Form the mixture into 8 balls. Flatten and form into nests by making a neat indentation with the back of a soup spoon.
4 Brush an ovenproof dish with melted butter. Put in the nests and brush the insides with more butter. Cook for 35 minutes, adding a little milk halfway through.
5 Crack an egg into each nest, sprinkle with salt, return to the oven and cook until the eggs are just set. Garnish with parsley and serve with matchstick carrots if liked.

Veal Olives with Mozzarella and Anchovy

INVOLTINI DI VITELLO SAPORITI

Ingredients	Metric/Imperial	American
small veal escalopes	8	8
slices of cooked ham	4	4
Mozzarella cheeses	2	2
anchovy fillets	4	4
salt and pepper		
chopped oregano	$\frac{1}{4}$ teaspoon	$\frac{1}{4}$ teaspoon
small onion	1	1
celery stalk	1	1
carrot	1	1
butter	50 g/2 oz	$\frac{1}{4}$ cup
flour	2 tablespoons	3 tablespoons
Marsala wine	2 tablespoons	3 tablespoons
tomato paste	1 tablespoon	1 tablespoon
stock	150 ml/1$\frac{1}{4}$ pint	$\frac{2}{3}$ cup
bay leaf	1	1

Beat the escalopes lightly with a dampened meat mallet. Put half a slice of ham on top of each one, followed by a thin slice of Mozzarella cheese and half a drained anchovy fillet. Season with pepper and oregano. Roll up tightly and secure with wooden cocktail sticks (toothpicks).

Finely chop the onion with the celery and carrot. Melt the butter in a shallow pan, add the vegetables and cook over a medium heat until golden.

Dust the veal olives with flour, add to the pan and cook for a few minutes, turning to brown lightly on all sides. Season with a little salt and pepper and sprinkle on the Marsala. Leave for a few minutes, then add the tomato paste dissolved in the hot stock along with the bay leaf.

Reduce the heat and simmer gently until the sauce has thickened. Remove the bay leaf and serve the veal olives with the sauce poured over.

Time: 1 hour 20 minutes   *Serves 4*

Veal and Rice Salad

INSALATA DI RISO CAPRICCIOSA

Ingredients	Metric/Imperial	American
long-grain white rice	450 g/1 lb	2$\frac{1}{3}$ cups
salt and pepper		
carrot	1	1
onion	$\frac{1}{2}$	$\frac{1}{2}$
celery stalk	1	1
loin of veal	450 g/1 lb	1 pound
lemon	1	1
garlic clove	1	1
oil	125 ml/4 fl oz	$\frac{1}{2}$ cup
basil leaves	6	6
large yellow (sweet) peppers	2	2
French beans	350 g/12 oz	$\frac{3}{4}$ pound
Mozzarella cheese	350 g/12 oz	$\frac{3}{4}$ pound
ripe tomatoes	5	5
chopped parsley	1 tablespoon	1 tablespoon

Cook the rice in lightly salted boiling water until tender but still firm; rinse under running cold water, drain well and put in a large salad bowl.

Prepare and roughly chop the carrot, onion and celery. Put them in a deep pan with the veal, a pinch of salt and enough cold water to cover the meat. Bring to the boil and simmer for 1$\frac{1}{2}$ hours.

Drain the meat, cut into cubes and put in a separate bowl with the juice of the lemon, crushed garlic clove, 2–3 tablespoons of oil and the chopped basil leaves; marinate for 1 hour.

Wash the peppers and put under a hot grill (broiler) or in a flame to char the skins. Remove the skins and deseed. Cut the flesh into thin strips. Add these to the meat in the marinade. Stir well and allow the flavours to mingle.

Meanwhile cook the French beans in a little lightly salted boiling water for 8 minutes or until tender. Drain, cut into 5 cm/2 in lengths and add to the marinade.

Cube the Mozzarella cheese and the peeled tomatoes. Put them into the salad bowl with the rice; discard the garlic from the marinade and add the meat to the bowl of rice and cheese. Sprinkle in the parsley and season with salt, pepper and the remaining oil. Stir well before serving.

Time: 2 hours + 1 hour: marinating   *Serves 8*

Veal Chops with Savoury Butter

BRACIOLINE DI VITELLO CON BURRO
PICCANTE

Ingredients	Metric/Imperial	American
anchovies	3	3
garlic cloves	2	2
butter	150 g/5 oz	½ cup + 2 tablespoons
chopped parsley	1 tablespoon	1 tablespoon
lemon	1	1
salt and pepper		
veal chops	12	12
dry white wine	125 ml/4 fl oz	½ cup
oil	6 tablespoons	8 tablespoons
chopped rosemary	½ teaspoon	½ teaspoon
lettuce leaves		

Finely chop the anchovies and 1 garlic clove; dice the butter. Put in a small bowl with the chopped parsley; season with a squeeze of lemon juice and pepper to taste. Work the mixture together and form it into a 2 cm/¾ in diameter cylinder. Wrap in foil and put in the refrigerator to harden.

Flatten the veal with a meat mallet. Make a marinade using the wine, half the oil, rosemary, crushed garlic clove, remaining lemon juice and salt and pepper. Marinate the veal for 3 hours.

Drain the chops and cook under a hot grill (broiler) or on a hot plate, using the remaining oil. Serve on individual plates, topped with thick slices of anchovy butter and garnished with lettuce leaves.

Time: 30 minutes + 3 hours: marinating   *Serves 6*

Veal Chops with Savoury Butter

Saddle of Lamb with Rice

Lamb with Olives

AGNELLO ALLE OLIVE

Ingredients	Metric/Imperial	American
boned shoulder of lamb	1 kg/2 lb	2 pounds
plain (all-purpose) flour	50 g/2 oz	$\frac{1}{2}$ cup
olive oil	5 tablespoons	$\frac{1}{3}$ cup
salt		
black olives	100 g/4 oz	$\frac{1}{4}$ pound
fresh chilli	$\frac{1}{2}$	$\frac{1}{2}$
chopped oregano	$\frac{1}{2}$ teaspoon	$\frac{1}{2}$ teaspoon
lemon	1	1

Dust the lamb with flour and put it in a flameproof casserole along with the olive oil. Cook over a high heat until lightly browned, then season with salt, turn over and brown the other side. Turn the heat down low, cover and cook for 30 minutes in a moderate oven (180 c, 350 f, gas 4).

Stone and chop the olives, sprinkle over the meat and add the deseeded and chopped chilli and the oregano. Cook for a further 30 minutes or until the meat is tender.

Stir in the juice of half the lemon before the end of the cooking time. Serve hot, decorated with lemon slices.

Time: 1$\frac{1}{2}$ hours　　　　　　　　　　　　　　*Serves 4*

This dish from Aquila can be made using other cuts of lamb, as shown above. It is traditionally accompanied with cubed potatoes baked with olive oil and oregano.

Saddle of Lamb with Rice

SELLA DI AGNELLO AL GUSTO DELICATO

Ingredients	Metric/Imperial	American
leeks	2	2
shallots	2	2
small onion	1	1
ham fat	40 g/1$\frac{1}{2}$ oz	1$\frac{1}{2}$ ounces
butter	175 g/6 oz	$\frac{3}{4}$ cup
oil	2 tablespoons	3 tablespoons
bouquet garni	1	1
salt and pepper		
dry white wine	50 ml/2 fl oz	$\frac{1}{4}$ cup
stock	300 ml/$\frac{1}{2}$ pint	1$\frac{1}{4}$ cups
cornflour (cornstarch)	1 teaspoon	1 teaspoon
single (thin) cream	300 ml/$\frac{1}{2}$ pint	1$\frac{1}{4}$ cups
boned saddle of lamb	1.5 kg/3 lb	3 pounds
fat bacon	100 g/4 oz	$\frac{1}{4}$ pound
carrots	6	6
courgettes	6	6
chopped parsley	1 tablespoon	1 tablespoon
long-grain rice	350 g/12 oz	1$\frac{2}{3}$ cups
Parmesan cheese, grated	3 tablespoons	scant $\frac{1}{4}$ cup

First prepare the sauce: trim and wash the leeks and chop the white part along with the shallots, onion and ham fat. Melt 50 g/2 oz/¼ cup of the butter with half the oil in a deep pan over a low heat, add the chopped mixture and bouquet garni and cook until golden. Season with salt and pepper and moisten with the wine. When this has evaporated add one-quarter of the stock, mix and cook until reduced by half.

Purée in a blender or food processor. Stir the cornflour into the cream in a deep pan, add the sauce and mix well. Put over a very low heat and cook, stirring constantly, until thickened. Remove from the heat.

Next prepare the lamb: wrap it in strips of fat bacon and tie up with kitchen string. Put in an oval ovenproof casserole, brush with oil and season with salt and pepper. Put in a moderately hot oven (200 c, 400 f, gas 6) for about 40 minutes.

While the lamb is cooking prepare the vegetables: trim and wash the carrot and courgettes, cut into matchstick strips and mix together. Melt 50 g/2 oz/¼ cup of the remaining butter in a deep pan over a low heat. Add the vegetable mixture, turn in the butter for a few minutes, then moisten with a few tablespoons of hot stock from time to time. Cover and simmer gently until tender; about 25 minutes. Season with a little salt, sprinkle with chopped parsley and keep hot.

Also cook the rice in salted boiling water until *al dente*. Drain well and dress with the remaining butter, beaten until creamy with the Parmesan cheese. Mix well to ensure that every grain of rice is coated, then divide between 6 oiled ramekins. Level and firm the tops with a damp spoon and put in the oven along with the lamb for the last ten minutes of the cooking time. Turn out around the edges of a large heated serving plate. Reheat the sauce over hot water.

Remove the lamb from the oven, discard the bacon and string and carve it into fairly thick slices. Put the slices on the mounds of rice and top with a little of the sauce. Pile the vegetables in the centre of the dish and in between the rice mounds.

Time: 1 hour   *Serves 6*

1 Make the sauce. Stir the cornflour into the cream in a jug. Mix with the sauce and transfer into a deep pan. Cook until thickened over a low heat.
2 Prepare the lamb by wrapping in bacon strips. Brush with oil and season before cooking.
3 Prepare the vegetables into matchstick strips and cook.
4 Cook the rice and divide amongst oiled ramekin dishes.
5 Remove the lamb from the oven; discard the bacon. Carve into thick slices.

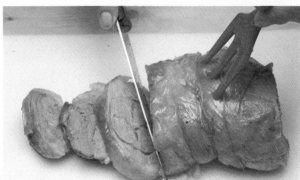

217

Lamb Stew with Potatoes

Lamb Stew with Potatoes

SPEZZATINO DI AGNELLO CON PATATE

Ingredients	Metric/Imperial	American
oil	50 ml/2 fl oz	¼ cup
lean lamb, cubed	1 kg/2 lb	2 pounds
garlic clove	1	1
salt and pepper		
potatoes	4	4
stock	600 ml/1 pint	2½ cups
sprig of thyme	1	1
sprig of rosemary	1	1
black olives	50 g/2 oz	2 ounces

Heat the oil in a deep pan over a medium heat, add the lamb and cook, stirring, until lightly browned on all sides. Add the crushed garlic and season with salt and pepper.

Peel, wash and cube the potatoes; add to the pan and mix with the meat. Simmer for a few minutes, then add the stock, thyme and rosemary. Cover and cook over moderate heat for about 1 hour or until the lamb is tender. Stone and chop the olives and add to the pan about 10 minutes before the end of the cooking time.

Transfer to a heated dish and serve hot.

Time: 1¼ hours   *Serves 4*

Lamb in Piquant Sauce

AGNELLO IN SALSA PICCANTE

Ingredients	Metric/Imperial	American
fresh spinach	225 g/8 oz	½ pound
lean lamb, cubed	1 kg/2 lb	2 pounds
flour	2 tablespoons	3 tablespoons
oil	2 tablespoons	3 tablespoons
butter	50 g/2 oz	¼ cup
salt and pepper		
medium-sized onion	1	1
garlic clove	1	1
capers	1 tablespoon	1 tablespoon
anchovy fillets	3	3
black olives	50 g/2 oz	2 ounces
chopped parsley	1 tablespoon	1 tablespoon
stock	225 ml/8 fl oz	1 cup
natural yogurt	125 ml/4 fl oz	½ cup

Rinse the spinach throughly, drain well and chop coarsely.

Coat the lamb in flour. Heat the oil and butter in a deep pan, add the lamb and cook over a medium heat until golden. Season with salt and pepper, remove from the pan and keep on one side.

Chop the onion and garlic finely together, add to the pan and cook until golden. Add the drained and chopped capers and anchovy fillets, stoned and chopped olives and the parsley. Mix well, leave for a few minutes, then add the prepared spinach.

Replace the lamb, add two-thirds of the stock, cover with a lid and leave over a low heat for just over 1 hour, adding more stock if the sauce dries out too much.

Add the yogurt during the last 10 minutes. Mix well and turn on to a heated serving dish.

Time: 1 hour 40 minutes　　　　　　　　*Serves 4*

Lamb Stew

ABBACCHIO BRODETTATO

Ingredients	Metric/Imperial	American
leg of lamb	1.2 kg/2½ lb	2½ pounds
lemons	1½	1½
salt and pepper		
olive oil	50 ml/2 fl oz	¼ cup
bacon	50 g/2 oz	2 ounces
onion	½	½
dry white wine	125 ml/4 fl oz	½ cup
stock	225 ml/8 fl oz	1 cup
egg yolks	4	4
chopped parsley	1 tablespoon	1 tablespoon

Rub the lamb with the lemon half, chop into even-sized cubes. Season with salt and pepper and put in a large deep pan with the heated oil, derinded and chopped bacon and finely chopped onion. Cook over a medium heat until lightly browned on all sides.

Pour in the wine and continue cooking, adding a few tablespoons of stock from time to time, until the meat is tender; about 1 hour.

Just before the end of the cooking time beat the egg yolks and add to the pan along with the parsley and a little grated lemon rind. Taste and adjust the seasoning and dilute the cooking juices with lemon juice.

Turn the heat right down and stir vigorously to create a soft creamy sauce. Remove the pieces of lamb, arrange on a heated serving plate and pour the sauce over.

Time: 1¼ hours　　　　　　　　*Serves 6*

A regional dish from Viterbo in the Lazio region.

Lamb Cutlets with Egg and Lemon Sauce

FRICCO DI AGNELLO

Ingredients	Metric/Imperial	American
loin of lamb	1 kg/2 lb	2 pounds
ham fat	150 g/5 oz	5 ounces
carrot	1	1
celery stalk	1	1
medium-sized onion	1	1
garlic clove	1	1
butter	50 g/2 oz	¼ cup
dry white wine	125 ml/4 fl oz	½ cup
plum tomatoes	225 g/8 oz	½ pound
salt and pepper		
stock	225 ml/8 fl oz	1 cup
egg yolks	2	2
lemon	1	1

Wash and dry the lamb; chop into cutlets or have the butcher prepare these. Finely chop the ham fat with the carrot, celery, onion and garlic. Melt the butter in a large deep pan over medium heat, add the chopped mixture and fry until golden. Then add the lamb, cover and leave until lightly browned, stirring occasionally.

Pour in the wine and leave it to evaporate. Sieve the tomatoes, stir them into the pan, season with salt and pepper and add the stock. Continue cooking over a medium heat for about 20 minutes or until the meat is tender.

Transfer the lamb to a heated serving dish and keep warm. Sieve the cooking juices into a small bowl and add the egg yolks along with the juice of the lemon; mix well. Put the bowl over a pan of gently boiling water and cook for 5 minutes, stirring constantly. Pour over the lamb and serve hot

Time: 1 hour　　　　　　　　*Serves 4*

A regional dish from Perugia in Umbria.

Marinated Lamb Chops

1 Prepare the marinade 12 hours ahead. Crush the garlic, add finely chopped onion and celery to the marinade bowl. Deseed and chop the chilli and add to the bowl with the bay leaf, parsley, thyme, oregano, peppercorns, salt and the clove. Add the olive oil and the lamb chops, pour over the red wine and mix well. Turn the meat in the marinade several times during the last two hours.

2 Drain the chops from the marinade and coat in flour while still damp. Spread on absorbent paper towels and season lightly.

3 Heat the oil and butter in a large heavy pan and cook the finely chopped onion until golden. Add the chops and turn once to brown one side then add the spinach. Mix well.

4 Strain 150 ml/¼ pint/⅔ cups of the marinade over the chops. Cover and cook on a low heat turning the chops from time to time.

5 10 minutes before the end of the cooking time, gradually stir in the yogurt. Serve garnished with parsley and, if liked, a sprig of bay leaves. Plain boiled rice makes an excellent accompaniment for this dish.

Marinated Lamb Chops

AGNELLO IN MARINATA

Ingredients	Metric/Imperial	American
For the marinade:		
garlic cloves	2	2
onion	1	1
celery stalk	1	1
fresh chilli	$\frac{1}{2}$	$\frac{1}{2}$
bay leaf	1	1
sprigs of parsley	2	2
chopped thyme	$\frac{1}{4}$ teaspoon	$\frac{1}{4}$ teaspoon
chopped oregano	$\frac{1}{4}$ teaspoon	$\frac{1}{4}$ teaspoon
peppercorns	3	3
salt		
clove	1	1
olive oil	2 tablespoons	3 tablespoons
red wine	450 ml/$\frac{3}{4}$ pint	2 cups
thin lamb chops	1.2 kg/2$\frac{1}{2}$ lb	2$\frac{1}{2}$ pounds
flour	2 tablespoons	3 tablespoons
salt and pepper		
large onion	1	1
fresh spinach	350 g/12 oz	$\frac{3}{4}$ pound
oil	3 tablespoons	4 tablespoons
butter	40 g/1$\frac{1}{2}$ oz	3 tablespoons
natural yogurt	225 ml/8 fl oz	1 cup
chopped parsley	1 tablespoon	1 tablespoon

Prepare the marinade 12 hours ahead: crush the garlic, finely chop the onion and celery, deseed and chop the chilli. Put in a large dish, add the remaining marinade ingredients and mix well. Add the chops, cover and leave overnight. During the last 2 hours stir from time to time to ensure the chops are well impregnated with the marinade.

When ready to cook remove the chops and coat in flour while still damp. Put on paper towels and season lightly with salt.

Finely chop the onion; wash the spinach, drain and chop coarsely. Heat the oil and butter in a large heavy pan, add the onion and cook over a medium heat until golden. Add the chops and spinach and mix well.

Strain in 150 ml/$\frac{1}{4}$ pint/$\frac{2}{3}$ cup of the marinade, cover and cook over a low heat, turning the chops from time to time, for 30 minutes. Strain in sufficient marinade to end up with a thick sauce.

Stir in the yogurt 10 minutes before the end of the cooking time and serve hot garnished with parsley.

Time: 1 hour 20 minutes + 12 hours: marinating Serves 6

Breadcrumbed Lamb Chops

COSTOLETTE IMPANATE AGRE

Ingredients	Metric/Imperial	American
onions	3	3
wine vingear	225 ml/8 fl oz	1 cup
oil	125 ml/4 fl oz	$\frac{1}{2}$ cup
sprigs of rosemary	2	2
sage leaves	4	4
salt		
peppercorns	8	8
small loin chops	32	32
plain (all-purpose) flour	50 g/2 oz	$\frac{1}{2}$ cup
eggs	3	3
milk	4 tablespoons	6 tablespoons
dried breadcrumbs	100 g/4 oz	1 cup
butter	40 g/1$\frac{1}{2}$ oz	3 tablespoons
oil	2 tablespoons	3 tablespoons

Chop the onions very finely, put in a mortar and crush with a pestle until juice begins to come out; or purée in a blender. Transfer to a large shallow dish. Add the vinegar, oil, rosemary and sage leaves, a sprinkling of salt and the peppercorns. Stir well and add the chops; turn to ensure they are well coated. Cover and marinate for 24 hours.

Remove the chops and dip first in flour, then into the eggs lightly beaten with the milk, and finally into the breadcrumbs.

Put the butter and oil in a large heavy pan over a high heat. When very hot add the chops in batches and cook until lightly browned on both sides. Remove and drain on absorbent paper towels. Keep hot until ready to serve.

Time: 30 minutes + 24 hours: marinating Serves 8

Roast Pork with Prunes

ARROSTO DI MAIALE CON PRUGNE

Ingredients	Metric/Imperial	American
prunes, soaked overnight	12	12
pork fillet (tenderloin)	600 g/1¼ lb	1¼ pounds
butter	25 g/1 oz	2 tablespoons
salt		
stock	225 ml/8 fl oz	1 cup

Drain the prunes and remove the stones. Slit the meat partway through lengthways and pack with prunes using a wooden spoon.

Melt the butter in a deep heavy pan or flameproof casserole, add the meat and cook over a medium heat for a few minutes, turning to brown all sides. Season with salt, pour in the stock, cover and cook for about 1 hour. Baste with the cooking juices from time to time and add more stock if necessary.

Time: 1¼ hours + 12 hours: soaking   *Serves 4*

This dish can be made with other cuts of pork suitable for stuffing. It can also be cooked in a moderate oven, adding 4 apples, cored and filled with knobs of butter, halfway through the cooking time.

Roast Pork Loin

ARISTA DI MAIALE ARROSTO

Ingredients	Metric/Imperial	American
rolled loin of pork	1 kg/2 lb	2 pounds
garlic cloves	2	2
sprigs of rosemary	3	3
cloves	3	3
salt and pepper		
oil	1 tablespoon	1 tablespoon

Make slits in the pork rind with a sharp pointed knife. Fill these with slivers of garlic and pieces of rosemary. Stud with the cloves. Sprinkle with salt and pepper and brush with oil.

Put in an oiled baking pan and cook in a moderate oven (180 C, 350 F, gas 4) for about 1 hour, turning and basting from time to time.

Remove the string. To serve hot, cut into slices, arrange on a heated serving dish and accompany with vegetables to taste. To serve cold, allow to cool before carving and accompany with salads.

Time: 1 hour 10 minutes   *Serves 4*

Marinated Loin of Pork

ARISTA MARINATA

Ingredients	Metric/Imperial	American
sprig of rosemary	1	1
garlic cloves	2	2
salt and pepper		
pork loin	1.5 kg/3 lb	3 pounds
onion	1	1
celery stalk	1	1
carrot	1	1
sage leaves		
fennel seeds	¼ teaspoon	¼ teaspoon
clove	1	1
white peppercorns	3	3
dry white wine	450 ml/¾ pint	2 cups
oil	125 ml/4 fl oz	½ cup
potato flour	1 teaspoon	1 teaspoon
tomato paste	1 teaspoon	1 teaspoon
small red cabbage	1	1

Finely chop the rosemary leaves along with 1 of the garlic cloves; season with salt and pepper. Make slits in the pork and stud with this mixture. Put the pork in a bowl.

Prepare and finely chop the onion, celery and carrot. Add to the bowl along with the sage leaves, fennel seeds, clove, remaining garlic clove, crushed, the peppercorns and a little salt. Cover with the wine and leave to marinate for 12 hours, turning the meat occasionally.

Remove the meat from the marinade and dry on absorbent paper towels. Heat the oil in a heavy pan over a medium heat, add the meat and brown it lightly all over.

Remove the garlic from the marinade and pass the rest through a blender or food processor along with the potato flour. Season the meat with salt and pepper and slowly pour in the marinade purée. Finish with the tomato paste, mixed with a little hot water, mix well, cover and cook over a low heat for about 1 hour.

Trim, wash and dry the red cabbage, shred finely and add to the pan. Leave to cook for another 40 minutes. The liquid should reduce down to a thick smooth dark sauce.

Remove the meat and cut into slices. Return to the pan with the sauce and cabbage, put on a heated serving dish and serve at once.

Time: 2 hours + 12 hours: marinating   *Serves 4*

Marinated Loin of Pork

1 Chop rosemary finely with 1 clove of garlic. Season the mixture with salt and pepper. Make slits in the pork and stud with the herb and garlic mixture.

2 Prepare the vegetable for the marinade. Chop the onion, celery and carrot and put into the bowl with the meat. Add the sage, fennel seeds, clove and remaining crushed garlic clove. Sprinkle on the peppercorns and the salt. Pour in the wine and turn the meat in the mixture. Leave to marinate for 12 hours turning the meat from time to time.

3 Remove the meat from the marinade, drain and dry on absorbent paper towels. Heat the oil in a thick pan and brown the meat on all sides.

4 Remove the garlic from the marinade and pass through a blender or food processor, mix with the potato flour in the machine. Season the meat and gradually pour on the puréed marinade.

5 Mix the tomato paste with a little hot water. Pour on to the meat and mix well. Cover and cook over a low heat for 1 hour.

6 Trim and wash the red cabbage. Cut into fine shreds and add to the pan. Allow to cook for a further 40 minutes to make a thick dark sauce.

Pork Chops with Borlotti Beans

Pork in Marsala Wine

FETTINE DI MAIALE ALLA FRANCESE

Ingredients	Metric/Imperial	American
leek	1	1
onion	$\frac{1}{2}$	$\frac{1}{2}$
celery stalk	1	1
garlic clove	1	1
sprig of rosemary	1	1
peppercorns	2	2
slices of pork fillet (tenderloin)	8	8
oil	4 tablespoons	$\frac{1}{3}$ cup
Marsala wine	3 tablespoons	scant $\frac{1}{4}$ cup
flour	2 tablespoons	3 tablespoons
butter	25 g/1 oz	2 tablespoons
salt		
tomato paste	1 teaspoon	1 teaspoon
stock cube	$\frac{1}{2}$	$\frac{1}{2}$

Trim, wash and drain the leek and chop finely with the onion, celery and garlic. Mix with the rosemary leaves and crushed peppercorns.

Beat the pork slices lightly with a meat mallet and put on a large plate. Cover with the chopped mixture, trickle over half the oil and 1 tablespoon of the Marsala wine. Cover and leave to marinate for 2 hours.

Remove and reserve all traces of the chopped mixture and coat the pork slices with flour. Heat the remaining

Pork Chops with Borlotti Beans

BRACIOLE CON FAGIOLE

Ingredients	Metric/Imperial	American
pork chops	4	4
flour	2 tablespoons	3 tablespoons
stock	150 ml/$\frac{1}{4}$ pint	$\frac{2}{3}$ cup
salt and pepper		
white wine	125 ml/4 fl oz	$\frac{1}{2}$ cup
sage leaves	4	4
plum tomatoes	225 g/8 oz	$\frac{1}{2}$ pound
cans of borlotti beans	2 (400 g/14 oz)	2 (14 ounce)

Coat the chops with flour, then put in a heavy pan with the hot stock and sage leaves. Cook for a few minutes over a medium heat, stirring from time to time, then season with salt and pepper, add the wine and allow it to evaporate.

Add the drained and chopped tomatoes and continue to cook over a low heat for about 20 minutes. Add the drained beans halfway through.

Remove the chops with a slotted spoon and arrange on a heated serving plate. Cover with the beans and cooking juices and serve at once.

Time: 30 minutes   *Serves 4*

oil with the butter in a large heavy pan over a low heat. Strain the marinade, reserving the liquid, and put the chopped mixture in the pan. Cook for a few minutes until golden, then add the pork slices, season with salt and raise the heat to brown on both sides.

Mix the tomato paste with 3 tablespoons/scant ¼ cup of hot water, pour into the pan with the pork and crumble in the piece of stock cube. Add the remaining Marsala, and reserved marinade. Cover and cook for 30 minutes, stirring from time to time.

Taste and adjust the seasoning; if the sauce is too thick add 1–2 tablespoons of hot water. Arrange the pork slices on a heated serving plate, cover with the sauce and serve at once.

Time: 40 minutes + 2 hours: marinating   *Serves 4*

Pork Spare Ribs with Sauerkraut

COSTINE DI MAIALE CON CRAUTI

Ingredients	Metric/Imperial	American
butter	75 g/3 oz	6 tablespoons
pork spare ribs	1.2 kg/2¼ lb	2¼ pounds
dry white wine	125 ml/4 fl oz	½ cup
salt and pepper		
stock	1 litre/1¾ pints	1 quart
white cabbage	1	1
onion	1	1
bacon	50 g/2 oz	2 ounces
wine vinegar	50 ml/2 fl oz	¼ cup

Melt one-third of the butter in a large deep pan or flameproof casserole, add the ribs and brown them lightly all over. Drain off all the fat, pour in the wine and allow it to evaporate, then season with salt and pepper. Add 600 ml/1 pint/2½ cups of stock, cover and leave over a low heat for 1 hour.

Shred the cabbage, wash and drain. Put in a pan, cover with boiling water and drain after 10 minutes.

Meanwhile melt the remaining butter in a large deep pan. Finely chop the onion, derind and chop the bacon. Add to the pan and cook over a medium heat until golden. Add the cabbage with 300 ml/½ pint/1¼ cups of stock and cook without a lid until all the liquid has reduced. Season with salt and pepper, cover and cook for a further 20 minutes, adding more stock.

Ten minutes before the end of the cooking time add the vinegar and increase the heat to high so that it evaporates. Transfer the cabbage to the pan with the ribs and cook together for a further 10 minutes.

Time: 2 hours   *Serves 4–6*

Pork Fillet on a Bed of Vegetables

FILETTO DI MAIALE SU LETTO DI VERDURE

Ingredients	Metric/Imperial	American
pork fillet (tenderloin)	800 g/1¾ lb	1¾ pounds
bay leaves	2	2
garlic clove	1	1
oil	3 tablespoons	scant ¼ cup
butter	50 g/2 oz	¼ cup
salt and pepper		
brandy	2 tablespoons	3 tablespoons
large onion	1	1
carrots	2	2
turnip	1	1
celery stalks	3	3
courgettes (zucchini)	3	3
thin green beans	100 g/4 oz	¼ pound
stock cube	½	½
single (thin) cream	4 tablespoons	6 tablespoons
Worcester sauce	¼ teaspoon	¼ teaspoon
chopped parsley	1 tablespoon	1 tablespoon

Tie the pork up with kitchen string so that it keeps its shape during cooking, trapping the bay leaves underneath the string.

Crush the garlic. Heat the oil and butter in a large flameproof casserole, add the garlic and cook over a medium heat until golden. Put in the pork, increase the heat slightly and turn it with a wooden spoon until lightly browned all over. Season with a little salt and plenty of pepper. Pour in the brandy and set alight, then remove the pork and keep covered.

Prepare all the vegetables, wash, dry and cut into short strips the same thickness as the green beans. Put in the pan with the meat juices and cook, covered, over a low heat for a few minutes. Then crumble in the piece of stock cube and moisten with cream from time to time. When the vegetables are almost tender lay the pork on top, sprinkle in the Worcester sauce and moisten with a little hot water. Cover and cook in a moderate oven (180 C, 350 F, gas 4) for 15 minutes, turning the pork over at least once.

When ready to serve remove the string and bay leaves; slice the pork fairly thickly. Pile the vegetables on a heated serving plate, using a slotted spoon. Arrange the slices on top, pour the cooking juices over and sprinkle with parsley.

Time: 1 hour   *Serves 4*

Tripe à la Mode de Reggio

TRIPPA ALLA REGGIANA

Ingredients	Metric/Imperial	American
precooked beef tripe	1 kg/2 lb	2 pounds
bacon	50 g/2 oz	2 ounces
celery stalk	1	1
carrot	1	1
small onion	1	1
garlic clove	1	1
oil	5 tablespoons	$\frac{1}{3}$ cup
salt and pepper		
dry white wine	50 ml/2 fl oz	$\frac{1}{4}$ cup
stock cube	1	1
bay leaf	1	1
eggs	2	2
Parmesan cheese, grated	3 tablespoons	scant $\frac{1}{4}$ cup
chopped parsley	1 tablespoon	1 tablespoon

Wash the tripe carefully under running water, drain and dry on paper towels.

Derind the bacon and chop finely with the celery, carrot, onion and garlic. Heat the oil in a large deep pan over a low heat, add the prepared bacon and vegetables and cook for a few minutes until softened.

Cut the tripe into very thin strips, add to the pan and mix well. Leave to simmer for a few minutes, then season with salt and pepper.

Pour in the wine and when it has evaporated add the stock cube dissolved in 225 ml/8 fl oz/1 cup of hot water, along with the bay leaf. Cover with a lid and simmer very gently for 1½ hours, adding a tablespoon of hot water from time to time if the mixture gets too dry.

At the end of the cooking time beat the eggs in a bowl with 2–3 tablespoons of the Parmesan cheese and the parsley. Pour the mixture over the tripe, whisking vigorously with a fork. Leave on a very low heat for a few minutes, then turn into a serving dish and sprinkle with the remaining Parmesan cheese.

Time: 1 hour 50 minutes　　　　　*Serves 4*

A regional dish from Reggio Emilia.

Tripe with Tomatoes and Basil

TRIPPA CON POMODORO E BASILICO

Ingredients	Metric/Imperial	American
tripe	1 kg/2 lb	2 pounds
onion	1	1
garlic clove	1	1
celery stalk	1	1
carrot	1	1
butter	25 g/1 oz	2 tablespoons
salt and pepper		
dry white wine	50 ml/2 fl oz	$\frac{1}{4}$ cup
plum tomatoes	400 g/14 oz	14 ounces
bay leaf	1	1
cooked haricot (navy) beans	225 g/8 oz	$\frac{1}{2}$ pound
bunch of basil	1	1
Parmesan cheese, grated	25 g/1 oz	$\frac{1}{4}$ cup

Wash the tripe under cold running water, drain and cut into strips 4 cm/1½ in long. Prepare and finely chop the onion, garlic, celery and carrot.

Melt the butter in a deep pan, add the chopped vegetables and cook over a medium heat until golden. Add the tripe, increase the heat to high and cook for a few minutes, stirring. Season lightly with salt and pepper, pour in the wine and allow it to evaporate.

Add the tomatoes, mashed with a fork, the bay leaf and a little more salt. Reduce the heat to low, cover and cook for 2½ hours, adding a little hot water if it dries out too much.

About 15 minutes before the end of the cooking time add the cooked beans and chopped basil. Serve hot sprinkled with Parmesan cheese.

Time: 2 hours 50 minutes　　　　　*Serves 4*

Liver and Anchovy Rolls

INVOLTINI DI FEGATO

Ingredients	Metric/Imperial	American
anchovy fillets	4	4
sage leaves	3	3
butter	50 g/2 oz	$\frac{1}{4}$ cup
fresh breadcrumbs	2 tablespoons	3 tablespoons
egg	1	1
salt and pepper		
slices of liver	8	8
brandy	2 tablespoons	3 tablespoons

Liver and Anchovy Rolls
1 Melt half the butter in a small pan. Drain and chop anchovies with the sage leaves and add to the melted butter. Add breadcrumbs and cook until crisp.
2 Mix in the egg and seasoning. Spread the liver on a clean board. Arrange a portion of breadcrumb mixture on each slice.
3 Roll up the liver slices and secure each with a cocktail stick (toothpick).
4 Melt the remaining butter in a pan over a low heat. Add the liver rolls and cook until lightly browned all over. Trickle in the brandy, allow to evaporate and season with salt and pepper. Serve with new potatoes arranged on radicchio and garnish with sage leaves if liked.

Drain the anchovies and chop finely along with the sage leaves. Melt half the butter in a small pan, add the breadcrumbs and cook over a medium heat until crisp and golden.

Put the anchovies in a bowl with the breadcrumbs, add the egg and season with salt and pepper. Mix well and spread a portion on each slice of liver. Roll up and secure with wooden cocktail sticks (toothpicks).

Melt the remaining butter in a shallow pan, add the liver rolls and cook over a low heat until lightly browned. Trickle in the brandy and when it has completely evaporated, season lightly with salt and pepper.

Arrange on a heated dish and serve at once.

Time: 30 minutes　　　　　　　　　　　　　*Serves 4*

Kidneys Flavoured with Juniper

ROGNONI DI VITELLO AL PROFUMO DI GINEPRO

Ingredients	Metric/Imperial	American
lamb's kidneys	800 g/1¾ lb	1¾ pounds
wine vinegar	4 tablespoons	6 tablespoons
salt and pepper		
butter	50 g/2 oz	¼ cup
brandy	2 tablespoons	3 tablespoons
juniper berries	10	10
stock	4 tablespoons	6 tablespoons
slices of French bread	24	24
butter for frying		

Core and skin the kidneys; slice lengthways and put in a bowl of water acidulated with the vinegar for about 2 hours. Drain well, dry and season with salt and pepper.

Melt the butter in a large shallow pan, add the kidneys and cook over a medium heat until lightly browned. Add the brandy and set alight. When the flames have died down add the coarsely chopped juniper berries and the stock. Cover with a lid and simmer for about 20 minutes.

Serve the kidneys accompanied with slices of French bread fried in butter until crisp and golden.

Time: 45 minutes + 2 hours: soaking	*Serves 4*

Liver with Courgettes (Zucchini) and Onions

FEGATO SALTATO CON ZUCCHINE E CIPOLLE

Ingredients	Metric/Imperial	American
medium-sized onions	3	3
large slices of liver	4 (125 g/4 oz)	4 (¼ pound)
flour	2 tablespoons	3 tablespoons
butter	25 g/1 oz	2 tablespoons
beef extract	1 teaspoon	1 teaspoon
lemon	½	½
courgettes (zucchini)	450 g/1 lb	1 pound
oil	125 ml/4 fl oz	½ cup
salt and pepper		
chopped parsley	1 tablespoon	1 tablespoon

Peel the onions, cut into quarters and soak in cold water for about 20 minutes.

Meanwhile coat the slices of liver in flour and heat the butter in a large shallow pan. Add the liver and cook over a high heat for 3 minutes on each side. Dissolve the beef extract in 125 ml/4 fl oz/½ cup of hot water and the lemon juice. Add to the pan, stir, cook for a few minutes and turn off the heat. Keep warm in a covered bowl placed over a pan of boiling water.

Wash and dry the courgettes; cut into rounds. Drain and dry the onions; chop finely.

Heat the oil in another shallow pan, add the onions and cook over a medium heat until golden. Add the courgettes, lower the heat and cook until tender. Season to taste with salt and pepper, add the chopped parsley and liver and serve hot.

Time: 45 minutes	*Serves 4*

Ox Heart with Vegetables

CUORE DI BUE STUFATO CON VERDURE

Ingredients	Metric/Imperial	American
carrots	2	2
celery stalk	1	1
large onion	1	1
garlic clove	1	1
butter	25 g/1 oz	2 tablespoons
oil	2 tablespoons	3 tablespoons
ox heart	600 g/1¼ lb	1¼ pounds
flour	2 tablespoons	3 tablespoons
red wine	50 ml/2 fl oz	¼ cup
plum tomatoes	400 g/14 oz	14 ounces
salt and pepper		
stock	300 ml/½ pint	1¼ cups
basil leaves	10	10

Prepare and finely chop the carrots, celery, onion and garlic; mix together.

Heat the butter and oil in a deep pan, add the chopped mixture; cook over a low heat until soft.

Slice the heart, trim, wash and drain. Coat with flour, add to the pan with the vegetables, raise the heat and cook for a few minutes until lightly browned on both sides. Add the wine and allow it to evaporate.

Add the tomatoes, mashed with a fork, season lightly with salt and pepper, cover with a lid and simmer over a medium heat for about 30 minutes or until the heart is tender, adding a little stock from time to time.

When ready to serve chop the basil leaves finely. Sprinkle over the dish and stir in.

Time: 1 hour 40 minutes	*Serves 4*

Calf's Tongue
LINGUA DI VITELLO ALL'ORTORLANA

Ingredients	Metric/Imperial	American
calf's tongue	1	1
celery stalk	1	1
carrot	1	1
bay leaves	2	2
sprigs of parsley	3	3
white peppercorns	2	2
salt and pepper		
flat mushrooms	225 g/8 oz	½ pound
button mushrooms	225 g/8 oz	½ pound
butter	100 g/4 oz	½ cup
onion	1	1
garlic clove	1	1
milk	300 ml/½ pint	1¼ cups
dry white wine	50 ml/2 fl oz	¼ cup

Clean the tongue and put in a deep pan along with the chopped celery and carrot, bay leaves, 1 sprig of parsley and the peppercorns. Cover with cold water, season with salt and bring to the boil. Reduce the heat to low and simmer for 2 hours, then drain and cool.

Meanwhile clean the two types of mushroom and chop finely, keeping them separate. Melt three-quarters of the butter in a deep pan, add the finely chopped onion and garlic and cook over a medium heat until golden. Add the button mushrooms, followed by the open ones a few minutes later. Mix well and season with salt and pepper. Reduce the heat and cook for 5 minutes, adding the milk a little at a time. Sprinkle with chopped parsley, remove the mushrooms with a slotted spoon and arrange around the edge of a heated ovenproof serving dish.

Skin the tongue, cut into slices and heat through in the mushroom cooking juices. Add the wine and cook until it has evaporated. Lay the slices down the centre of the dish, pour over the remaining butter, melted, and put in a moderate oven (180 c, 350 f, gas 4) for 10 minutes.

Time: 2 hours 20 minutes   *Serves 4*

Sweetbreads with Parma Ham and Spinach
ANIMELLE DI VITELLO CON PROSCIUTTO E SPINACI

Ingredients	Metric/Imperial	American
sweetbreads	600 g/1¼ lb	1¼ pounds
vinegar	1 teaspoon	1 teaspoon
salt and pepper		
spinach	450 g/1 lb	1 pound
butter	50 g/2 oz	¼ cup
small onion	1	1
Parma ham	100 g/4 oz	¼ pound
stock	125 ml/4 fl oz	½ cup
Parmesan cheese, grated	2 tablespoons	3 tablespoons
single (thin) cream	3 tablespoons	4 tablespoons

Trim and wash the sweetbreads. Put in a bowl and cover with cold water acidulated with the vinegar. Leave to soak for 2 hours, renewing the water from time to time so that the sweetbreads become white.

Bring a deep pan of salted water to the boil, add the sweetbreads and simmer for a few minutes. Drain, rinse under cold running water and cut into bite-sized pieces.

Wash the spinach thoroughly in cold water, removing any stalks and coarse ribs. Drain and cook for 5 minutes in a deep pan in the water still clinging to the leaves. Drain and squeeze.

Melt the butter in a large deep pan, add the chopped onion and diced Parma ham and cook over a low heat until golden. Add the prepared sweetbreads and simmer for about 10 minutes, stirring gently. Moisten with the stock.

Coarsely chop the spinach, add to the pan and mix very carefully into the other ingredients. Season lightly with salt and pepper and cook for a further 10 minutes.

Sprinkle on the Parmesan cheese, remix carefully, then add the cream and wait for it to be absorbed. Transfer to a heated dish and serve at once.

Time: 50 minutes   *Serves 4*

VEGETABLES
AND
SALADS

*The Italian cook expects the best quality when
buying vegetables and salad ingredients.
Serve vegetables raw whenever possible as they
taste so much better and are a valuable
source of fibre in the diet.
Cook vegetables for the minimum time
in a small amount of water to
preserve the nutrients. Use the cooking liquid in
soups, stews and sauces. The combinations
of vegetables in Italian cookery are
an inspiration to any cook and
a boon to vegetarians.*

Vegetables

Fresh vegetables play an important part in the cookery of Italy and great care is taken in the selection and preparation. Many vegetable dishes are interesting combinations of several types. Vegetables which are grown above the ground such as peas, beans and cabbages are cooked in boiling water. The root vegetables or those which grow under the ground such as potatoes, carrots and turnips are put into cold water and brought to the boil. It is wasteful to cook vegetables in large amounts of water as much of the nutritive value is lost. Vegetables are best cooked in a covered pan with the minimum of water; the vegetable water can then be used in soups and sauces. The only exceptions to this rule are green beans which need a reasonable amount of water to help retain their colour.

Globe artichoke Wash well and steep in water which has been acidulated with vinegar or lemon juice for at least 10 minutes. Trimming the leaves is optional as it in no way alters the taste. Cook in enough boiling water to cover. Time will depend on the age and size of the artichoke – they are cooked when an outside leaf pulls away easily. Drain upside down to allow the water to run out.

Jerusalem artichoke Peel and cover with acidulated water to prevent discoloration. Put in cold salted water and bring to the boil as for potatoes. If cut into even-sized pieces they will take about 15 minutes to cook if freshly picked.

Asparagus Cut off woody ends of stalks; scrape or peel the rest of white part. Rinse, tie in bundles and stand in a tall pan of simmering salted water; cover the tips with a foil dome. Cook for 8–25 minutes depending on thickness.

Aubergine (eggplant) Cut off the stem and wash the skins. Slice or halve, sprinkle with salt and put on a tilted tray to drain off excess bitter juices. Wipe dry with paper towels. Fry in oil until golden or blanch the halves for 3 minutes before stuffing.

Broad beans Remove from the pod unless young enough to eat whole. Cook for 7–10 minutes depending on age and size.

Green beans Top and tail. Leave whole if small, string and slice if large. Cook for 5–10 minutes.

Broccoli Remove outer leaves and trim thick stalks. Cook whole heads for 8 minutes.

Brussel sprouts Trim stalks, remove damaged leaves. Cook for 8–15 minutes depending on size.

Cabbage Remove coarse or damaged outer leaves. Shred only before cooking. Cook for 8–12 minutes depending on quantity.

Cauliflower Remove outer leaves; leave whole or break into florets. Cook for 8–15 minutes.

Celery Wash well and remove strings with a potato peeler. Slice and use as required.

Celeriac Remove root and cut into pieces. Drop into acidulated water to prevent discolouration. Cook as for celery. For both braising is better.

Chillies Remove stem, deseed and rinse. Wash hands afterwards to avoid skin irritation.

Courgettes (zucchini) Trim the ends, slice, sprinkle with lemon juice and stand for 15 minutes if time allows. Fry or steam.

Leeks Remove coarse green tops, roots and damaged leaves. Make a cross cut in the leafy part and wash. Braise whole; sauté if halved or sliced.

Mushrooms Peel only if wild; wipe cultivated ones on a clean damp cloth. Sauté or use raw.

Onions Peel, slice or dice. Peel small onions and use whole.

Peppers (sweet peppers) Wash, halve, deseed, rinse and char or blanch, then slice. May also be stuffed and cooked in the oven.

Potatoes Wash, then cook in their skins to retain both texture and nutrients. Peel when cooked.

Spinach Remove thick stalks, wash well and cook in the water that remains on the leaves until limp.

Turnip and swede (rutabagas) Top and tail, peel thinly if young, more thickly if older. Dice or slice and use as required.

Tomatoes If the recipe calls for peeled tomatoes plunge briefly into boiling water; slide off skins. Many of the recipes use plum tomatoes; if these are not available it is probably better to use canned ones in cooked dishes as the English/Dutch tomatoes have less flavour and are expensive.

Salad Vegetables

Salad vegetables should be prepared as near to the serving time as possible. Store green salad vegetables such as cabbage, lettuce and endive in the vegetable compartment of the refrigerator. If storing lettuces for several days leave whole and pack in plastic bags. Do not cut lettuce with a knife or the edges will turn black; tear the leaves instead. Dry well on absorbent paper towels, otherwise the leaves will not take the dressing.

Spring onions should be firm; remove any damaged leaves and store in a sealed box or bag to avoid flavouring other foods.

Cucumbers should be firm and fresh. Store in a cool larder or in the salad drawer of a refrigerator for a short period only. If the refrigerator is too cold the cucumber will quickly turn to ice.

Dried peas and beans (pulses)

These are cheap and nutritious but require long soaking before being cooked.

Use plenty of cold water; overnight soaking is best for most types, but small ones only need 4–5 hours, while split peas and lentils can be soaked briefly or not at all. Drain and discard the soaking water; rinse the beans.

Put in a deep pan with plenty of cold water; do not add salt as this toughens the beans and prolongs cooking time. Bring to the boil and cook rapidly for the first 10 minutes; this is especially important with red kidney beans to kill off indigestible toxins. Simmer gently until tender: allow up to 1 hour for small pulses, 1½ hours for medium-sized ones and 2 hours for large ones. Chick peas and soya beans may take even longer.

Some packaged pulses are part-cooked; follow the cooking instructions given.

Pancakes with Asparagus and Cheese

CREPES AGLI ASPARAGI

Ingredients	Metric/Imperial	American
For the pancakes:		
eggs	2	2
plain (all-purpose) flour	200 g/7 oz	1¾ cups
salt		
milk	275 ml/9 fl oz	scant 1¼ cups
oil	2 tablespoons	3 tablespoons
For the filling:		
asparagus	1 kg/2 lb	2 pounds
salt and pepper		
butter	50 g/2 oz	¼ cup
garlic clove	1	1
cooked ham	150 g/5 oz	5 ounces
chopped parsley	1 tablespoon	1 tablespoon
Parmesan cheese, grated	50 g/2 oz	½ cup
For the white sauce:		
butter	50 g/2 oz	¼ cup
plain (all-purpose) flour	50 g/2 oz	½ cup
milk	600 ml/1 pint	2½ cups
salt and pepper		
grated nutmeg	¼ teaspoon	¼ teaspoon
egg yolk	1	1
Emmental cheese, grated	50 g/2 oz	½ cup

Prepare the pancake mixture; beat the eggs in a bowl with the flour and ½ teaspoon of salt until well mixed. Add the milk a little at a time, stir with a whisk, taking care not to make any lumps. Allow the mixture to rest for 1 hour before using.

Clean the asparagus, removing the woody stalks, wash and tie together in a bundle. Cook in salted water for 15 minutes ensuring the tips cook outside the water. Drain, remove any tough parts and divide into pieces 2.5 cm/1 in long.

Heat the butter in a pan on a low heat, stir in the crushed garlic and the chopped ham and cook for 2 minutes. Add the cooked asparagus. Adjust the seasoning, sprinkle in the chopped parsley and remove from the heat.

To make the pancakes: put a non-stick pan on a high heat and grease with a few drops of oil. Pour in 2 tablespoons of batter, tipping the pan to cover the bottom with a thin layer. Use a spatula to turn the pancakes over to cook on the other side. Oil the pan between batches. Pile on a plate.

Fill each pancake with a little asparagus and sprinkle with Parmesan cheese. Roll them up and place in an oiled ovenproof dish.

Prepare the white sauce: melt the butter in a small pan, add the flour, mix with a wooden spoon to form a roux and pour in the milk gradually, mixing well. Bring to the boil stirring constantly, add salt, pepper and grated nutmeg. When the sauce is cooked, remove from the heat, add the egg yolk and grated Emmental cheese. Pour over the pancakes.

Place in a moderate oven (180 C, 350 F, gas 4) to heat for 10 minutes. Remove from the oven and place under the grill (broiler) to brown. Serve piping hot.

Time: 1½ hours + 1 hour: resting   *Serves 6*

Artichokes Pizzaiola

Artichokes Pizzaiola

CARCIOFI ALLA PIZZAIOLA

Ingredients	Metric/Imperial	American
artichokes	8	8
lemon	1	1
olive oil	4 tablespoons	$\frac{1}{3}$ cup
garlic clove	1	1
canned plum tomatoes	400 g/14 oz	14 ounces
Parmesan cheese, grated	25 g/1 oz	$\frac{1}{4}$ cup
chopped oregano	$\frac{1}{4}$ teaspoon	$\frac{1}{4}$ teaspoon
chopped parsley	1 tablespoon	1 tablespoon
salt and pepper		
stock	2 tablespoons	3 tablespoons

Prepare the artichokes; discard the hard outer leaves, trim the points off the rest, divide into wedges and remove the soft inner leaves and bristly chokes. Drop into water acidulated with the juice of a lemon.

Heat the oil in a deep pan, add the lightly crushed garlic and cook over medium heat until golden. Discard the garlic and put in the drained artichokes.

Add the tomatoes, mashed with a fork, Parmesan cheese, oregano and parsley. Season with salt and pepper and simmer gently until the artichokes are done, moistening now and then with hot stock. Serve hot.

Time: 40 minutes   *Serves 4*

Asparagus au Gratin

ASPARAGI AL GRATIN

Ingredients	Metric/Imperial	American
asparagus	1.5 kg/3 lb	3 pounds
salt and white pepper		
butter	75 g/3 oz	6 tablespoons
plain (all-purpose) flour	50 g/2 oz	$\frac{1}{2}$ cup
milk	475 ml/16 fl oz	2 cups
grated nutmeg	$\frac{1}{4}$ teaspoon	$\frac{1}{4}$ teaspoon
Parmesan cheese, grated	25 g/1 oz	$\frac{1}{4}$ cup
hard-boiled (cooked) egg yolks	2	2

Prepare the asparagus: scrape the stalks, rinse under cold running water and trim the ends to ensure that all are the same length. Tie into bundles and stand in a tall pan containing enough boiling salted water to come two-thirds of the way up the stems; cover the tips with a foil dome. Simmer for about 10–15 minutes until just tender.

Meanwhile prepare the sauce: melt two-thirds of the butter in a small pan, stir in the flour, then gradually add the milk. Stir well to prevent lumps from forming and cook over a low heat until smooth and thick. Season with salt, pepper and nutmeg.

Drain the asparagus, untie the bundles and cut off the white parts (reserve for later use). Arrange the green

tips in a buttered ovenproof dish and cover with the prepared sauce. Sprinkle with Parmesan cheese, dot with the remaining butter and put in a moderate oven (180 c, 350 f, gas 4) until the top is crisp and golden.

Sieve the egg yolks over the top just before serving.

Time: 40 minutes   _Serves 4_

Asparagus au Gratin
1 Drain the cooked asparagus. Untie the bundles and cut off the green tips (use the remaining stalks for soup). Arrange the tips in a buttered ovenproof dish in a dome shape.
2 Pour the sauce over the asparagus leaving the tip of the dome showing. Sprinkle with grated Parmesan cheese and dot with butter. Brown in the oven or under a medium grill (broiler). Cover the top with the sieved egg yolks just before serving.

Asparagus in Tarragon Sauce

ASPARAGI CON SALSA AL DRAGONCELLO

Ingredients	Metric/Imperial	American
asparagus	1.5 kg/3 lb	3 pounds
salt and white pepper		
tuna in oil	40 g/1½ oz	1½ ounces
anchovy fillets	2	2
olive oil	200 ml/7 fl oz	¾ cup
dry white wine	2 tablespoons	3 tablespoons
chopped tarragon	2 teaspoons	3 teaspoons
hard-boiled (cooked) eggs	2	2
lemon	½	½

Trim off the woody ends from the asparagus and scrape off tough skin at the lower ends. Rinse under cold running water. Divide into bundles and tie up with string. Stand in a tall pan containing enough boiling salted water to come two-thirds of the way up; cover the tips with a foil dome. Simmer for 8–18 minutes depending on the thickness of the asparagus.

Meanwhile prepare the sauce: drain and chop the tuna and anchovies. Put in a blender or food processor with 2–3 tablespoons of the oil, the wine and the tarragon.

Sieve the hard-boiled egg yolks into a bowl and beat with a wooden spoon. Add a pinch of salt, then slowly trickle in a few drops of oil. Stir in one direction and add more oil once the first has been absorbed. Continue until all the oil has been used up and the mixture is thick and smooth.

Add the mixture to the blender with the lemon juice, season with a pinch of salt if necessary, and a little pepper. Blend briefly to mix the ingredients.

Drain the asparagus, and cut off the white ends (reserve for soup or stock). Arrange the tips in a ring on a heated serving plate and pour the sauce over. Sieve the hard-boiled egg whites over the asparagus before serving.

Time: 30 minutes   _Serves 4_

Stuffed Aubergine

Stuffed Aubergines (Eggplants)

MELANZANE RIPIENE

Ingredients	Metric/Imperial	American
small round aubergines (eggplants)	600 g / 1¼ lb	1¼ pounds
salt and pepper		
plum tomatoes	600 g / 1¼ lb	1¼ pounds
onion	1	1
capers	1 heaped tablespoon	1 heaped tablespoon
anchovy fillets	4	4
oil	125 ml / 4 fl oz	½ cup
basil leaves	6	6
Pecorino cheese, grated	50 g / 2 oz	½ cup

Wash and dry the aubergines, then cut the tops off. Slit the flesh in wedge shapes from the top 2½ cm / 1 in down the sides with a sharp knife. Sprinkle with salt and leave upside down on an inclined chopping board for 30 minutes to drain off bitter juices; rinse well.

Meanwhile peel the tomatoes if using fresh, deseed and chop finely. Also finely chop the onion, capers and drained anchovy fillets.

Heat one-third of the oil in a shallow pan, add the onion and cook over a medium heat until golden. Add the drained anchovies and cook until softened. Stir in the tomatoes, capers and chopped basil leaves; season with pepper. Continue cooking until the sauce has thickened. Remove from the heat and add the Pecorino cheese.

Dry the aubergines on paper towels and put them in a pie pan. Fill with the prepared sauce; trickle over the remaining oil and put in a moderate oven (180 C, 350 F, gas 4) for about 30 minutes.

Time: 1¼ hours + 30 minutes: resting   *Serves 4*

Aubergine Cubes in Herb Sauce

CUBETTI DI MELANZANE AL SUGHETTO PROFUMATO

Ingredients	Metric/Imperial	American
large aubergines	4	4
salt and pepper		
fresh tomatoes	450 g/1 lb	1 pound
garlic clove	1	1
small onion	1	1
sprig of parsley	1	1
anchovy fillets	3	3
butter	25 g/1 oz	2 tablespoons
oil	4 tablespoons	6 tablespoons
chopped thyme	$\frac{1}{4}$ teaspoon	$\frac{1}{4}$ teaspoon
chopped marjoram	$\frac{1}{4}$ teaspoon	$\frac{1}{4}$ teaspoon

Wash and dry the aubergines and cut into cubes about 2.5 cm/1 in square. Put in a colander, sprinkle with salt, cover with a weighted plate and leave for 30 minutes to drain off excess juices.

Drop the tomatoes briefly into boiling water, then peel, deseed and cut into strips. Finely chop the garlic together with the onion and parsley. Drain and chop the anchovies.

Heat the butter and oil in a large shallow pan over a low heat. Add the anchovies and mash with a fork.

Squeeze the aubergines, rinse under cold running water and dry on absorbent paper towels. Add to the pan, raise the heat and fry, stirring from time to time. After a few minutes add the tomatoes, chopped garlic mixture, thyme and marjoram. Season with salt and pepper, cover and continue cooking over medium heat for 15 minutes, stirring occasionally.

Transfer to a heated dish and serve at once.

Time: 30 minutes + 30 minutes: resting   *Serves 4*

Mediterranean Mixed Vegetables

MISTO DI VERDURE ALLA MEDITERRANEA

Ingredients	Metric/Imperial	American
plum tomatoes	450 g/1 lb	1 pound
yellow, red and green (sweet) peppers	1 of each	1 of each
aubergines (eggplants)	2	2
courgettes (zucchini)	2	2
onions	2	2
garlic clove	1	1
olive oil	125 ml/4 fl oz	$\frac{1}{2}$ cup
salt and freshly ground black pepper		
basil leaves	4	4
chopped parsley	1 tablespoon	1 tablespoon
chopped thyme	$\frac{1}{4}$ teaspoon	$\frac{1}{4}$ teaspoon
chopped marjoram	$\frac{1}{4}$ teaspoon	$\frac{1}{4}$ teaspoon

If using fresh tomatoes drop briefly into boiling water, then remove and slide off the skins. Drain canned tomatoes. Cut in half lengthways, deseed and cut into strips.

Wash and dry the peppers and put under a hot grill (broiler) or hold in a flame to char the skin and make it easier to remove. Deseed and cut into small pieces.

Trim, wash and dry the aubergines and courgettes; cube the aubergines and slice the courgettes lengthways. Finely chop the onions with the garlic.

Heat the oil in a large pan over a medium heat, add the onion and garlic and cook until golden. Add all the other vegetables except tomatoes, increase the heat slightly and cook for 20 minutes, stirring occasionally. Add the strips of tomato along with 125 ml/4 fl oz/$\frac{1}{2}$ cup of water and a little salt. Reduce the heat to low and cook for a further 20 minutes.

Turn off the heat, add the chopped herbs and season with plenty of pepper. Serve hot.

Time: 1 hour   *Serves 4–6*

Stuffed Avocados

AVOCADO RIPIENI

Ingredients	Metric/Imperial	American
walnuts in shells	100 g/4 oz	¼ pound
hazelnuts in shells	100 g/4 oz	¼ pound
ripe avocados	4	4
celery stalk	1	1
tomato ketchup or paste	2 tablespoons	3 tablespoons
white wine vinegar	1 tablespoon	1 tablespoon
salt and pepper		

Shell the walnuts and dip in boiling water for a few minutes; drain, and chop finely, leaving a few whole ones for garnishing. Prepare the hazelnuts in the same way.

Cut 3 of the avocados in half lengthways, remove the stones and arrange the avocados on a serving dish.

Open the remaining avocado, scoop out the flesh and put in a bowl. Mash with a fork and add the chopped nuts; celery, trimmed and cut into matchstick strips; tomato ketchup, vinegar, salt and pepper. Mix well.

Fill the centres of the halved avocados with this mixture and serve garnished with reserved nuts.

Time: 40 minutes   *Serves 4*

French Beans in Soy Sauce

FAGIOLINI IN SALSA DI SOIA

Ingredients	Metric/Imperial	American
French beans	1 kg/2 lb	2 pounds
salt and pepper		
oil	2 tablespoons	3 tablespoons
garlic clove	1	1
butter	50 g/2 oz	¼ cup
cornflour (cornstarch)	½ teaspoon	½ teaspoon
soy sauce	2 teaspoons	3 teaspoons
white wine vinegar	1 tablespoon	1 tablespoon
sugar	¼ teaspoon	¼ teaspoon
stock	3 tablespoons	4 tablespoons
chopped parsley	1 tablespoon	1 tablespoon

Top and tail the beans, rinse and cook in salted boiling water for 10 minutes. Rinse immediately under cold running water.

Heat the oil in a large shallow pan, add the lightly crushed garlic and cook over medium heat until golden. Discard the garlic and put in the beans. Lower the heat and cook gently.

Meanwhile beat the butter in a small bowl with the cornflour, soy sauce, vinegar and sugar. Pour the mixture over the beans, add the hot stock and heat gently for a few minutes.

Transfer to a heated serving dish, sprinkle with parsley and serve hot.

Time: 45 minutes   *Serves 4*

This dish also makes an excellent cold summer antipasto.

French Beans in Tomato Sauce

FAGIOLINI ALL'UCCELLETTO

Ingredients	Metric/Imperial	American
medium-sized onion	1	1
garlic clove	1	1
oil	2 tablespoons	3 tablespoons
butter	25 g/1 oz	2 tablespoons
canned plum tomatoes	225 g/8 oz	½ pound
salt and pepper		
French beans	600 g/1¼ lb	1¼ pounds
stock	3 tablespoons	scant ¼ cup
tuna in oil	65 g/2½ oz	2½ ounces
chopped basil	1 tablespoon	1 tablespoon

Finely chop the onion with the garlic. Heat the oil and butter in a heavy pan, add the onion and garlic and cook over a medium heat for a few minutes until golden.

Drain and chop the tomatoes. Stir into the pan, season with salt and pepper and continue cooking for about 10 minutes until the sauce has thickened.

Top and tail the beans, then cook in boiling salted water for 6 minutes. Drain, cut in half and add to the tomato sauce. Mix well and continue cooking until the beans are tender, adding a little stock from time to time.

Add the chopped drained tuna and the basil a few minutes before the end of the cooking time. Mix well and serve hot. Garnish with basil leaves if available.

Time: 40 minutes   *Serves 4*

Stuffed Avocados

French Beans in Tomato Sauce

French Beans with Potatoes

French Beans Farmer's Style

FAGIOLINI DEL CONTADINO

Ingredients	Metric/Imperial	American
French beans	450 g / 1 lb	1 pound
salt and pepper		
garlic clove	1	1
shallots	2	2
oil	125 ml / 4 fl oz	½ cup
anchovy fillets	2	2
egg yolks	2	2
wine vinegar	2 tablespoons	3 tablespoons
chopped parsley	1 tablespoon	1 tablespoon
basil leaves	4	4

Top and tail the beans, wash and cook in lightly salted water until just cooked but firm.

Meanwhile finely chop the garlic with the shallots. Heat the oil in a shallow pan, add the chopped mixture and cook over a medium heat until golden.

Drain the beans, cut into pieces and add to the pan with the shallots. Drain and chop the anchovies, add to the pan and simmer until cooked down.

Beat the egg yolks with the vinegar, chopped parsley and basil. Pour over the beans and cook, stirring gently, until the egg is just set. Taste and adjust the seasoning; serve hot.

Time: 40 minutes   *Serves 4*

French Beans with Potatoes

PATATE E FAGIOLINI AL PREZZEMOLO

Ingredients	Metric/Imperial	American
medium-sized potatoes	4	4
salt and pepper		
French beans	600 g / 1¼ lb	1¼ pounds
olive oil	2 tablespoons	3 tablespoons
butter	40 g / 1½ oz	3 tablespoons
small onion	1	1
garlic clove	1	1
stock	2 tablespoons	3 tablespoons
wine vinegar	1 tablespoon	1 tablespoon
chopped parsley	1 tablespoon	1 tablespoon

Cook the potatoes, without peeling, in salted water for 15 minutes. Drain, peel and cut into large dice.

Top and tail the French beans and blanch in boiling salted water for a few minutes. Rinse immediately under cold running water and cut into pieces the same length as the potato chunks.

Heat the oil and butter in a large pan. Finely chop the onion and crush the garlic, add to the pan and cook over a low heat for a few minutes until transparent.

Add the potatoes and beans, mix together and season with pepper. Sprinkle on the stock, cover and simmer for 15 minutes. Then stir in the vinegar, wait until this evaporates and sprinkle on the parsley.

Mix and turn into a heated serving dish.

Time: 50 minutes   *Serves 4*

Herbed French Beans

FAGIOLINI VERDI PROFUMATI

Ingredients	Metric/Imperial	American
tiny French beans	700 g/1½ lb	1½ pounds
salt and pepper		
bunch of basil	1	1
sprig of parsley	1	1
garlic clove	1	1
anchovy fillets	4	4
oil	50 ml/2 fl oz	¼ cup
wine vinegar	2 tablespoons	3 tablespoons

Top and tail the beans, wash and cook in boiling salted water until just tender.

Meanwhile wash the basil and parsley and chop finely together with the garlic and drained anchovy fillets.

Heat the oil in a large pan, add the chopped mixture, leave for a moment then add the drained beans. Mix and cook for a few minutes over medium heat.

Season with pepper, add the vinegar and leave until it has evaporated. Cook for a few minutes and serve hot.

Time: 40 minutes   *Serves 4*

Braised Broad (Fava) Beans

FAVE STUFATE

Ingredients	Metric/Imperial	American
fresh broad (fava) beans	1 kg/2 lb	2 pounds
onion	1	1
garlic clove	1	1
chilli	½	½
olive oil	2 tablespoons	3 tablespoons
lard	40 g/1½ oz	1½ oz
stock	225 ml/8 fl oz	1 cup
salt and pepper		
chopped parsley	1 tablespoon	1 tablespoon

Shell the beans and put in a bowl of cold water. Leave for 15 minutes to soften.

Meanwhile chop the onion finely along with the garlic. Deseed and finely chop the chilli. Heat the oil and lard in a deep pan, add the chopped ingredients and cook over medium heat for a few minutes.

Pour in the stock and add the drained beans. Cover with a lid and cook, stirring from time to time, until the beans are tender; about 20 minutes.

Taste and adjust the seasoning and serve hot sprinkled with parsley.

Time: 1 hour   *Serves 4*

French Beans with Tomatoes

FAGIOLINI DI SANT'ANNA AL POMODORO

Ingredients	Metric/Imperial	American
small thin French beans	450 g/1 lb	1 pound
salt		
olive oil	125 ml/4 fl oz	½ cup
garlic clove	1	1
pine nuts	1 tablespoon	1 tablespoon
chopped parsley	1 tablespoon	1 tablespoon
stock	225 ml/8 fl oz	1 cup
ripe tomatoes	225 g/8 oz	½ pound
anchovy fillets	2	2
slices of cob loaf	4	4

Top, tail and wash the beans; cook in boiling salted water until just tender; drain and chop.

Heat 4–5 tablespoons of the oil in a shallow pan, add the crushed garlic, chopped pine nuts and parsley along with a little of the stock. Cook over a medium heat until golden.

Peel the tomatoes if using fresh; drain if canned. Chop and add to the pan along with the drained and chopped anchovies. Simmer for about 10 minutes, then add the beans, mix well and season with salt if necessary.

Meanwhile cube the bread and fry in the remaining oil until golden. Drain on absorbent paper towels.

Oil an ovenproof dish and fill with layers of bean and tomato mixture, alternating with fried bread cubes and finishing with bean and tomato. Put in a moderately hot oven (180 C, 350 F, gas 4) for 10 minutes to thicken the sauce. Serve hot.

Time: 1½ hours   *Serves 4*

This is a regional dish from Florence.

Cannellini Beans Farmer's-style

FAGIOLI ALLA MODA DEL FATTORE

Ingredients	Metric/Imperial	American
dried cannellini beans, soaked overnight	450 g/1 lb	1 pound
celery stalk	1	1
bay leaves	2	2
bacon	100 g/4 oz	$\frac{1}{4}$ pound
bacon fat	50 g/2 oz	2 ounces
oil	3 tablespoons	4 tablespoons
onion	$\frac{1}{2}$	$\frac{1}{2}$
chopped sage leaves	1 tablespoon	1 tablespoon
sprig of rosemary	1	1
garlic clove	1	1
ripe plum tomatoes	3	3
stock cube	$\frac{1}{2}$	$\frac{1}{2}$
red wine	2 tablespoons	3 tablespoons

Put the beans in a large pan with 2 litres/3½ pints/2 quarts of water, the chopped celery and the bay leaves. Bring to the boil and simmer for at least 2 hours until tender.

Derind the bacon, put in a small pan with enough water to cover and boil for 10 minutes. Remove with a slotted spoon and cut into bite-sized pieces.

Chop the bacon fat and put in a shallow pan with the oil. Add the chopped onion, herbs and crushed garlic; cook over a medium heat until the onion is golden.

Add the drained cooked beans, mix together, season with salt and plenty of pepper and leave for 10 minutes to allow the flavours to mingle.

Peel the tomatoes if using fresh; drain if canned. Deseed, chop and add to the pan. Then add the boiled bacon, crumble in the stock cube and stir in the wine.

Leave the sauce to thicken a little, then adjust the seasoning and serve hot.

Time: 3 hours + 8 hours: soaking　　　　*Serves 4*

Broccoli with Olives

BROCCOLI CON OLIVE NERE AL PROFUMO DI AGLIO

Ingredients	Metric/Imperial	American
broccoli spears	1 kg/2 lb	2 pounds
salt		
large garlic cloves	2	2
chilli	$\frac{1}{2}$	$\frac{1}{2}$
oil	50 ml/2 fl oz	$\frac{1}{4}$ cup
anchovy fillets	2	2
plum tomatoes	350 g/12 oz	$\frac{3}{4}$ pound
black olives	150 g/5 oz	5 ounces

Trim and wash the broccoli; cook in boiling salted water for 8 minutes and drain immediately.

Crush the garlic; deseed and chop the chilli. Heat the oil in a deep pan, add the garlic, chilli and drained anchovies. Cook over a low heat until the anchovy has blended into the other ingredients.

Meanwhile peel the tomatoes if using fresh, drain if canned, and chop roughly. Add to the pan, mix and leave to cook for about 10 minutes, then add the broccoli.

Mix carefully with a wooden spoon and simmer gently for 8 minutes, adding a few tablespoons of hot water if the mixture gets too dry.

Just before the end of the cooking time add the stoned and halved olives. Mix and serve hot.

Time: 25 minutes　　　　*Serves 4*

Tri-colour Calabrese

BROCCOLETTI AL TRICOLORE

Ingredients	Metric/Imperial	American
large onion	1	1
bacon	75 g/3 oz	3 ounces
oil	4 tablespoons	6 tablespoons
medium-sized potatoes	3	3
calabrese	600 g/1¼ lb	1¼ pounds
plum tomatoes	5	5
chopped parsley	1 tablespoon	1 tablespoon
salt and pepper		
red wine	50 ml/2 fl oz	$\frac{1}{4}$ cup
stock	2 tablespoons	3 tablespoons

Chop the onion finely; derind and chop the bacon. Heat the oil in a casserole, add the onion and bacon and cook over a low heat until the onion is transparent.

Peel and cube the potatoes, add to the pan and cook for 5 minutes turning from time to time. Divide the calabrese into pieces, wash, dry and add to the pan.

Mix well and cook over a medium heat for 20 minutes. Peel the tomatoes if using fresh, drain if canned and chop. Add to the pan along with the parsley, salt and pepper. Pour in the wine and allow it to evaporate, then add the stock.

Cover with a lid and simmer gently for about 20 minutes. Serve hot straight from the casserole.

Time: 1 hour   *Serves 4*

Matchstick Carrots

Matchstick Carrots

CAROTE A FIAMMIFERO

Ingredients	Metric/Imperial	American
carrots	1 kg / 2 lb	2 pounds
butter	75 g / 3 oz	6 tablespoons
onion	1	1
stock cube	1	1
bay leaf	1	1
salt and pepper		
single (thin) cream	2 tablespoons	3 tablespoons
bay leaves	2	2

Top and tail the carrots and scrape or scrub. Wash and dry, then cut into matchstick strips.

Heat the butter in a deep pan over a medium heat. Add the finely chopped onion and cook until golden. Add the carrots and stir well.

Dissolve the stock cube in 125 ml/4 fl oz/$\frac{1}{2}$ cup of hot water and add to the pan along with the bay leaf. Reduce the heat and simmer until the carrots are tender, stirring from time to time.

Season with salt and pepper and stir in the cream immediately before serving. Garnish with 2 bay leaves.

Time: 50 minutes   *Serves 4*

Braised Courgettes

Braised Courgettes (Zucchini)

ZUCCHINE IN TEGLIA

Ingredients	Metric/Imperial	American
courgettes (zucchini)	6	6
oil	2 tablespoons	3 tablespoons
butter	25 g/1 oz	2 tablespoons
shallot	1	1
canned plum tomatoes	350 g/12 oz	$\frac{3}{4}$ pound
salt and pepper		
stock	2 tablespoons	3 tablespoons
black olives	20	20
chopped oregano	$\frac{1}{4}$ teaspoon	$\frac{1}{4}$ teaspoon
chopped parsley	1 tablespoon	1 tablespoon
Mozzarella cheese	1	1

Top and tail the courgettes, wash, dry and cut into sticks 5 cm/2 in long.

Heat the oil and butter in a large shallow pan, add the chopped shallot and cook over a low heat until softened. Add the courgettes and cook for a few minutes over a high heat, then reduce it to medium. Add the tomatoes, mashed with a fork, season with salt and pepper and leave to cook until the courgettes are tender, adding a little stock if necessary.

Add the halved and stoned olives, oregano and parsley; cube the Mozzarella cheese and scatter over the top. Cover the pan, switch off the heat and leave to rest for a few minutes before serving.

Time: 40 minutes   *Serves 4*

Courgettes (Zucchini) with Eggs

ZUCCHINE IN VESTE GIALLA

Ingredients	Metric/Imperial	American
courgettes (zucchini)	600 g/1¼ lb	1¼ pounds
butter	25 g/1 oz	2 tablespoons
oil	2 tablespoons	3 tablespoons
garlic clove	1	1
salt and pepper		
eggs	2	2
lemon	1	1
chopped chives	1 tablespoon	1 tablespoon

Wash, trim and thinly slice the courgettes.

Melt the butter and oil in a large shallow pan, add the lightly crushed garlic and cook over a medium heat for a few minutes until golden. Discard the garlic and stir in the courgettes. After 6–8 minutes season with salt and pepper.

Beat the eggs in a bowl with the juice of a lemon, the chives and a pinch of salt and pepper. Pour over the courgettes and mix together. Remove from the heat as soon as the egg mixture has set and serve at once.

Time: 30 minutes   *Serves 4*

Mixed Fried Vegetables

FRITTO MISTO DI VERDURE

Ingredients	Metric/Imperial	American
courgettes (zucchini)	2	2
carrots	2	2
turnip	1	1
potatoes	2	2
plain (all-purpose) flour	2 tablespoons	3 tablespoons
oil for frying		
salt and pepper		
basil leaves	4	4

Prepare the vegetables: trim the courgettes, trim and scrape the carrots; peel the turnip and potatoes. Wash, drain and cut into tiny cubes. Coat in flour and put into a sieve to shake off the excess.

Heat plenty of oil in a large heavy shallow pan over medium heat. When the oil is quite hot add the vegetables and cook until golden. Remove with a slotted spoon and drain on absorbent paper towels.

Season with salt and pepper, sprinkle with chopped basil and serve piping hot.

Time: 30 minutes   *Serves 4*

Baked Mixed Vegetables

MISTO DI VERDURE IN FORNO

Ingredients	Metric/Imperial	American
medium-sized onions	3	3
olive oil	225 ml/8 fl oz	1 cup
salt and pepper		
medium-sized potatoes	4	4
courgettes (zucchini)	450 g/1 lb	1 pound
plum tomatoes	6	6
chopped oregano	½ teaspoon	½ teaspoon
cheese, grated	3 tablespoons	4 tablespoons

Peel the onions and slice thinly. Heat half the oil in a shallow pan over a medium heat. Add the onions and a

pinch of salt and cook for 3 minutes; remove the pan from the heat before they turn golden.

Simmer the washed potatoes for 10 minutes in salted boiling water. Drain, peel and cut into fairly thick slices.

Trim, wash and slice the courgettes. Peel the tomatoes or drain if using canned, cut into strips.

Brush a deep ovenproof dish with some of the remaining oil and put a layer of potatoes on the bottom. Sprinkle with a little oil and season with salt, pepper and oregano. Cover with half the onions and then a layer of courgettes; season with salt and pepper and sprinkle with some more oil and a little cheese. Top with a layer of tomato strips and continue in this way until all the ingredients are used up, ending with a layer of tomato.

Cover the dish with foil and put in a moderate oven (180 C, 350 F, gas 4) for 30 minutes. Serve hot.

Time: 1 hour   *Serves 4*

Baked Spring Vegetables

ARCOBALENO VEGETARIANO IN FORNO

Ingredients	Metric/Imperial	American
new potatoes	4	4
new carrots	4	4
baby onions	6	6
leeks	2	2
small courgettes (zucchini)	5	5
garlic clove	1	1
oil	4 tablespoons	⅓ cup
salt and pepper		
chopped oregano	¼ teaspoon	¼ teaspoon
stock	125 ml/4 fl oz	½ cup
fresh peas	2 tablespoons	3 tablespoons
Mozzarella cheese	1	1

Prepare all the vegetables: scrape the potatoes, wash and cube. Trim and scrub the carrots and cut up evenly. Divide the onions into quarters. Trim the leeks, discarding the green parts; cut the white parts into rings, wash and drain. Cut the courgettes in half lengthways and dice. Crush the garlic.

Heat the oil in a medium-sized ovenproof dish and put in all the prepared vegetables. Sprinkle with salt and pepper and add the garlic and oregano. Mix well, cover with foil and put in a moderate oven (180 C, 350 F, gas 4). After 20 minutes remove the foil and stir in the stock and peas. Replace the foil and cook for 30 minutes.

Remove the foil just before the end of the cooking time, put the cubed cheese on top. Return to the oven to melt the cheese.

Time: 1¼ hours   *Serves 4*

Chick Peas with Butter and Sage

CECI AL BURRO E SALVIA

Ingredients	Metric/Imperial	American
smoked bacon	50 g/2 oz	2 ounces
onion	½	½
dry white wine	50 ml/2 fl oz	¼ cup
stock cube	½	½
peppercorns	4	4
butter	60 g/2½ oz	5 tablespoons
canned chick peas	400 g/14 oz	14 ounces
garlic clove	1	1
sage leaves	4	4

Derind and finely chop the bacon with the onion. Dry-fry in a small pan, then sprinkle in the wine, crumble in the stock cube, add the peppercorns and simmer until the liquid has reduced by one quarter.

Melt the butter in a pan, then add the drained chick peas, crushed garlic and chopped sage. Mix well, add the bacon mixture and simmer for about 20 minutes over a low heat.

Discard the garlic and peppercorns; serve hot.

Time: 40 minutes   *Serves 4*

Chick Peas in Savoury Sauce

CECI IN SALSA GUSTOSA

Ingredients	Metric/Imperial	American
canned chick peas	400 g/14 oz	14 ounces
small sprig of parsley	1	1
onion	¼	¼
anchovy fillets	2	2
capers	1 tablespoon	1 tablespoon
mustard	1 teaspoon	1 teaspoon
hard-boiled (cooked) egg	1	1
olive oil	5 tablespoons	7 tablespoons
wine vinegar	2 tablespoons	3 tablespoons
salt and pepper		

Drain the chick peas and drop into a pan of boiling water. Remove immediately, drain again and put in a heatproof bowl.

Finely chop the parsley with the onion, drained anchovies and capers. Put in a bowl and stir in the mustard, then the egg, mashed with a fork. Put the oil and vinegar in a small screw-top jar, season with salt and pepper and shake to mix. Stir into the chopped mixture a little at a time.

Pour this dressing over the chick peas and mix thoroughly. Cover the bowl and leave for at least 1 hour.

Put the bowl over a pan of simmering water, cover and leave until warmed through. Serve at once.

Time: 20 minutes + 1 hour: resting   *Serves 4*

If using dried chick peas soak them overnight in warm water, then cook for 2½ hours in boiling water flavoured with a few sage leaves, a chopped celery stalk, a chopped onion and 2/3 tablespoons of oil. Do not add salt until the peas are cooked.

Fantasy Chicory

CICORIA FANTASIA

Ingredients	Metric/Imperial	American
chicory (Belgian endive)	1 kg/2 lb	2 pounds
salt and pepper		
olive oil	4 tablespoons	6 tablespoons
small onion	1	1
eggs, beaten	2	2
Parmesan cheese, grated	3 tablespoons	4 tablespoons
Pecorino cheese, grated	2 tablespoons	3 tablespoons

Trim the chicory and wash in plenty of cold running water. Cook in boiling salted water until just tender; about 6 minutes. Drain well.

Heat the oil in a shallow pan. Chop the onion finely, add to the pan and cook over a medium heat until golden. Add the chicory, then season with salt and pepper.

Pour in the eggs and stir continuously with a fork to blend into the vegetables. Remove from the heat as soon as the egg has set.

Sprinkle with the two cheeses, mix and serve.

Time: 30 minutes   *Serves 4*

Spring Greens on Toast with Bacon

CROSTONI DI ERBETTE CON PANCETTA

1 Cook the garlic and greens in the butter.
2 Cook the diced bacon in oil separately with sage leaves.
3 Remove crusts and toast bread in the oven.
4 Cover each slice of bread with the greens.
5 Top with cubes of cheese and the cooked bacon.

Ingredients	Metric/Imperial	American
spring greens	450 g / 1 lb	1 pound
salt and pepper		
butter	60 g / 2½ oz	5 tablespoons
garlic clove	1	1
smoked bacon	75 g / 3 oz	3 ounces
oil	1 tablespoon	1 tablespoon
sage leaves	10	10
thick slices of bread	4	4
Fontina cheese	100 g / 4 oz	¼ pound

Wash the greens under cold running water, drain and cook in a very little lightly salted boiling water. Drain and squeeze well.

Heat two-thirds of the butter in a small pan, add the crushed garlic and the greens and cook over medium heat for a few minutes. Derind and dice the bacon; heat the oil in a separate small pan. Add the bacon with 2 whole sage leaves and cook until golden.

Cut the crusts from the bread and arrange the slices in a buttered ovenproof dish. Put in a moderate oven (180 C, 350 F, gas 4) for 8 minutes to toast.

Cover each piece of toast with a layer of greens, cubes of Fontina cheese and the bacon (discard the sage leaves). Put the dish back into the oven for about 10 minutes until the cheese has melted and the bacon is lightly browned. Decorate with sage leaves.

Time: 40 minutes   *Serves 4*

Eggs in Pink Sauce

UOVA IN SALSA ROSA

Ingredients	Metric/Imperial	American
salt		
white wine vinegar	4 tablespoons	6 tablespoons
lemon	$\frac{1}{2}$	$\frac{1}{2}$
eggs	8	8
red cabbage leaves	8	8
chopped parsley	1 tablespoon	1 tablespoon
For the sauce:		
mayonnaise	225 ml/8 fl oz	1 cup
tomato ketchup	3 tablespoons	scant $\frac{1}{4}$ cup
salt and white pepper		
Worcester sauce	1 teaspoon	1 teaspoon
brandy	$1\frac{1}{2}$ tablespoons	2 tablespoons
whipped cream	225 ml/8 fl oz	1 cup

Put a large pan with plenty of salted water on the heat. Add the vinegar and lemon juice and bring to the boil. Put in the eggs one at a time; lower the heat and leave to cook for 3 minutes. Remove with a slotted spoon, then place the eggs on a damp tea-towel.

Prepare the sauce: put the mayonnaise in a bowl with the tomato ketchup, a pinch of salt, pepper, a few drops of Worcester sauce and mix together with a whisk. Add the brandy a little at a time mixing continuously; finally add the whipped cream to obtain a smooth soft sauce.

Cover a serving dish with the red cabbage leaves, well washed and dried, place an egg on each leaf and pour over the sauce. Garnish the centre with parsley.

Time: 35 minutes   *Serves 4–8*

1 Prepare the artichokes and cook until tender. Remove the tough outer leaves. Cut in half and remove the choke. Keep fresh in water with lemon juice added.
2 Drain the artichokes when ready to serve. Slice thinly and arrange in a salad bowl. Add the oil and mix well.
3 Pour over the lemon juice and snip some of the chives into the bowl. Stir again and allow to stand for 5 minutes.
4 Drain the tuna fish and flake. Add the tuna to the bowl and mix again.
5 Mix in the cubed cheese and top with the remaining snipped chives.
To serve as individual salads, retain some of the cubed cheese and chives from the main salad. Divide amongst the individual dishes and garnish the centre of each with cubes of cheese and chives.

Artichoke, Cheese and Tuna Salad

ANTIPASTO DEL BUONGUSTAIO

Ingredients	Metric/Imperial	American
artichokes, cooked	4	4
lemons	2	2
olive oil	3 tablespoons	scant $\frac{1}{4}$ cup
salt and pepper		
bunch of parsley or chives	1	1
tuna in oil	200 g/7 oz	7 ounces
Gruyère or other hard cheese	225 g/8 oz	$\frac{1}{2}$ pound

Remove the stalks and tough outer leaves from the artichokes; trim the points from the tender light-coloured leaves. Cut in half and remove the bristly chokes from the centres. Put into cold water acidulated with the juice of 1 lemon to prevent discoloration.

When ready to serve drain the artichokes, slice thinly and put into a salad bowl. Add the oil, juice of the remaining lemon, salt and pepper and the chopped parsley or chives. Stir well and allow to stand for a few minutes.

Drain the tuna, chop the fish and add to the bowl along wtih the cubed Gruyère cheese. Mix well and serve.

Time: 30 minutes   *Serves 8*

Artichoke, Cheese and Tuna Salad

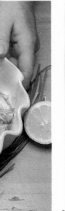

Spinach, Ricotta and Avocado Salad

Spinach, Ricotta and Avocado Salad

INSALATA DI SPINACI CRUDI CON RICOTTA
E SALSA DI AVOCADO

Ingredients	Metric/Imperial	American
fresh spinach	450 g/1 lb	1 pound
avocado	1	1
Ricotta cheese	225 g/8 oz	½ pound
olive oil	6 tablespoons	½ cup
lemon juice	2 tablespoons	3 tablespoons
salt and pepper		

Remove any damaged leaves and coarse stems from the spinach, wash well under cold running water, drain, dry and chop coarsely.

Cut the avocado in half, remove the stone, then scoop out the flesh with a teaspoon. Put in a blender or food processor with the Ricotta cheese, oil, lemon juice and a little salt and pepper. Blend for a few minutes until smooth and creamy.

Put the spinach in a salad bowl, pour the dressing over and serve.

Time: 20 minutes   *Serves 4*

Tuna, Carrot and Black Olive Salad

INSALATA DI TONNO, CAROTE E OLIVE NERE

Ingredients	Metric/Imperial	American
carrots	6	6
potatotes	2	2
salt and pepper		
tuna in oil	450 g/1 lb	1 pound
black olives	4 tablespoons	6 tablespoons
wine vinegar	2 tablespoons	3 tablespoons
basil leaves	4	4

Scrape or peel the carrots and potatoes and cook together in lightly salted boiling water.

Dice the potatoes, slice the carrots thinly and put in a salad bowl. Drain and chop the tuna and add to the bowl along with the stoned and halved olives.

Mix the tuna oil and vinegar in a screwtop jar, season with salt and pepper; shake well to mix.

Pour the dressing over the salad, mix gently and serve sprinkled with chopped basil leaves.

Time: 30 minutes   *Serves 4*

Queen of Salads

INSALATA REGINA

Ingredients	Metric/Imperial	American
lettuce	225 g/8 oz	$\frac{1}{2}$ pound
honeydew melon	$\frac{1}{2}$	$\frac{1}{2}$
white grapes	12	12
small strawberries	6	6
shelled walnuts	12	12
celery stalks	2	2
olive oil	4 tablespoons	6 tablespoons
wine vinegar	2 tablespoons	3 tablespoons
salt and pepper		

Wash and dry the lettuce, chop finely and put into a salad bowl.

Add the cubed melon, halved and deseeded grapes, hulled and sliced strawberries, finely chopped walnuts and celery.

Put the oil in a small screwtop jar with the vinegar, season with salt and pepper; shake well to mix.

Pour the dressing over the salad, mix and serve.

Time: 25 minutes   *Serves 4*

Fennel, Orange and Olive Salad

INSALATA DI FINOCCHI, ARANCE E OLIVE

Ingredients	Metric/Imperial	American
medium-sized fennel heads	4	4
oranges	2	2
black olives	100 g/4 oz	$\frac{1}{4}$ pound
olive oil	5 tablespoons	7 tablespoons
lemon	$\frac{1}{2}$	$\frac{1}{2}$
salt and pepper		
cumin seeds	$\frac{1}{4}$ teaspoon	$\frac{1}{4}$ teaspoon

Wash the fennel heads, dry and cut in half lengthways. Slice thinly and put in a large salad bowl.

Peel the oranges and slice thinly (crossways); remove pith and seeds and cut each slice into 4. Add to the bowl, along with the stoned and chopped olives.

Mix the oil with the juice of the half lemon in a small bowl; season with a little salt and plenty of pepper. Pour this dressing over the salad and sprinkle on the cumin seeds. Mix together and leave to rest in a cool place (not the refrigerator) for 1 hour before serving.

Time: 20 minutes + 1 hour: resting   *Serves 4*

Mushroom and Parmesan Cheese Salad

INSALATA DI FUNGHI E GRANA

Ingredients	Metric/Imperial	American
mushrooms	450 g/1 lb	1 pound
olive oil	6 tablespoons	$\frac{1}{2}$ cup
lemon	1	1
salt and pepper		
Parmesan cheese, in a piece	100 g/4 oz	$\frac{1}{4}$ pound
chopped parsley	1 tablespoon	1 tablespoon

Wipe the mushrooms with a clean damp cloth and slice thinly into a salad bowl.

Next prepare the dressing: put the oil in a small bowl with the strained juice of the lemon and a pinch of salt and pepper. Beat well to mix.

Finely chop or coarsely grate the Parmesan cheese and add to the mushrooms. Pour on the dressing, mix gently and sprinkle with the parsley.

Time: 20 minutes   *Serves 4*

Apple and Celery Salad

INSALATA DI MELE E SEDANO 'SQUISITEZZA'

Ingredients	Metric/Imperial	American
celery stalks	9	9
dessert apples	2	2
lemon	1	1
shelled walnuts	12	12
cottage cheese	225 g/8 oz	$\frac{1}{2}$ pound
basil leaves	6	6
garlic clove	$\frac{1}{2}$	$\frac{1}{2}$
salt and pepper		
olive oil	5 tablespoons	7 tablespoons
lettuce leaves	4	4

Scrub and trim the celery, remove any coarse strings and cut into matchstick strips. Put in a salad bowl.

Peel, core and dice the apples and squeeze lemon juice over to prevent discoloration. Add to the salad bowl along with the chopped walnuts.

Process the cheese in a blender or food processor for a few minutes. Add the finely chopped basil and garlic, salt, pepper and oil and process again until smooth and creamy.

Put a lettuce leaf in the bottom of each of 4 small goblets, arrange the apple and celery salad on top and finish with the dressing. Serve at once.

Time: 20 minutes   *Serves 4*

Hot Pepper Salad with Stuffed Olives

INSALATA DI PEPERONI PICCANTI ALLE OLIVE FARCITE

Ingredients	Metric/Imperial	American
red (sweet) peppers	4	4
sprig of parsley	1	1
garlic clove	1	1
tuna in oil	75 g/3 oz	3 ounces
hard-boiled (cooked) eggs	2	2
fresh chilli	$\frac{1}{2}$	$\frac{1}{2}$
shallots	2	2
mustard	2 teaspoons	2 teaspoons
olive oil	150 ml/$\frac{1}{4}$ pint	$\frac{2}{3}$ cup
salt		
wine vinegar	2 tablespoons	3 tablespoons
stuffed green olives	12	12

Wash and dry the pepper, put on a foil-lined baking tray and cook in a moderately hot oven (200 C, 400 F, gas 6) for 10 minutes until the skin peels off easily. Cool under running water, peel, deseed and cut into slivers 4 cm/1½ in long by 2 cm/½ in wide. Put the slivers in a deep dish.

Finely chop the parsley along with the garlic, drained tuna, chopped eggs and deseeded chilli.

Finely chop the shallots and mix with the mustard in a small bowl.

Gradually add the oil, mix well, add a pinch of salt and the vinegar, mix again and pour over the pepper strips.

Garnish with the olives, cover with foil and leave to rest in a cool place for 2 hours before serving.

Time: 35 minutes + resting: 2 hours   *Serves 4*

Beetroot with Tuna Sauce

BARBABIETOLE CON SALSA TONNATA

Ingredients	Metric/Imperial	American
medium-sized cooked beetroot	2	2
pickled silverskin onions	2 tablespoons	3 tablespoons
hard-boiled (cooked) egg	1	1
tuna in oil	100 g/4 oz	$\frac{1}{4}$ pound
olive oil	200 ml/7 fl oz	$\frac{3}{4}$ cup
salt and white pepper		
lemon	$\frac{1}{2}$	$\frac{1}{2}$
capers	1 tablespoon	1 tablespoon
chopped parsley	1 tablespoon	1 tablespoon

Trim and peel the beetroot, slice thinly and put in a glass bowl.

Purée the onions in a blender or food processor with the egg and drained tuna. Trickle in the olive oil and blend again. Season with salt and pepper, add the juice of the half lemon and blend until smooth.

Transfer to a bowl, add the well-drained capers and chopped parsley, then pour over the beetroot. Cover and leave to rest in a cool place for 1 hour before serving.

Time: 15 minutes + 1 hour: resting   *Serves 4*

This salad is an ideal accompaniment to cold cuts of meat.

Spring French Bean Salad

INSALATA DI FAGIOLINI PRIMAVERILE

Ingredients	Metric/Imperial	American
new potatoes	12	12
salt and pepper		
tiny French beans	1 kg/2 lb	2 pounds
hard-boiled (cooked) eggs	2	2
pickled gherkins	6	6
watercress	½ bunch	½ bunch
Ricotta cheese	40 g/1½ oz	1½ ounces
tuna in oil	200 g/7 oz	7 ounces
olive oil	5 tablespoons	7 tablespoons
mustard	1 teaspoon	1 teaspoon
wine vinegar	2 tablespoons	3 tablespoons

Scrape the new potatoes and cook in lightly salted boiling water. Top and tail the beans and cook in a separate pan. Drain both vegetables well, slice and put in a salad bowl.

Chop the eggs and add to the bowl along with the sliced gherkins.

Put the watercress in a blender or food processor with the Ricotta cheese, drained tuna, oil, mustard, vinegar and a pinch of salt and pepper. Process until smooth and creamy.

Pour on top of the salad, and leave to rest for 1 hour at room temperature; mix well before serving.

Time: 30 minutes + 1 hour: resting   *Serves 4*

Spring Fresh Bean Salad
1 Slice the cooked potatoes into rounds. Arrange the cooked beans in a bowl cutting any long ones in half.
2 Chop up the hard-boiled (cooked) eggs and mix with the beans and potatoes. Slice the gherkins and add to the salad bowl.
3 Purée the watercress, cheese, tuna with the oil, vinegar and seasonings until smooth and creamy. Arrange on top of salad.

Potato Salad with Pizzaiola

Potato Salad with Pizzaiola Sauce

INSALATA DI PATATE ALLA PIZZAIOLA

Ingredients	Metric/Imperial	American
potatoes	1 kg/2 lb	2 pounds
salt and pepper		
small onion	1	1
anchovy fillets	3	3
olive oil	5 tablespoons	7 tablespoons
plum tomatoes	5	5
green (sweet) pepper	½	½
black olives	50 g/2 oz	½ cup
wine vinegar	2 tablespoons	3 tablespoons
chopped oregano	¼ teaspoon	¼ teaspoon

Peel the potatoes and cook in salted boiling water until just tender.

Meanwhile finely chop the onion; drain and chop the anchovies. Put 2 tablespoons of the oil in a shallow pan over a medium heat, add the onion and anchovy and cook until the onion is golden. Drop the tomatoes briefly into boiling water to loosen the skins; peel and slice, then add to the pan.

Put the pepper under a hot grill (broiler) or hold it in a flame to char the skin; peel, deseed and dice. Add to the pan with the tomato mixture, stir briefly, then add half the stoned and chopped olives. Moisten with the

vinegar, leave for a few seconds, then turn off the heat but keep the pan warm.

Drain the potatoes and cut into slices while still hot. Put in a large salad bowl and pour the prepared sauce over. Add the remaining oil, the oregano, a little salt and plenty of pepper. Mix well and serve while still warm. Garnish with a few whole olives.

Time: 1 hour   *Serves 4*

Cooked Vegetable Salad

INSALATA APPETITOSA DI VERDURE COTTE

Ingredients	Metric/Imperial	American
shelled peas	225 g/8 oz	½ pound
potatoes	225 g/8 oz	½ pound
French beans	225 g/8 oz	½ pound
carrots	4	4
salt and pepper		
black olives	100 g/4 oz	¼ pound
capers	1 tablespoon	1 tablespoon
tomato paste	1 tablespoon	1 tablespoon
mustard	1 teaspoon	1 teaspoon
olive oil	5 tablespoons	7 tablespoons
wine vinegar	2 tablespoons	3 tablespoons
hard-boiled (cooked) eggs	2	2

Prepare all 4 vegetables and cook separately in salted boiling water until just tender. Drain well.

Dice the potatoes and carrots; chop the beans into short lengths. Put in a large salad bowl along with the peas. Add halved stoned olives and drained capers.

Put the tomato paste in a small bowl with the mustard and beat with a fork. Trickle in the olive oil, beating constantly, then add the vinegar and season with salt and pepper.

Dress the salad with this mixture and mix gently but thoroughly to ensure that the vegetables are evenly coated. Garnish with thinly sliced egg.

Time: 30 minutes   *Serves 4*

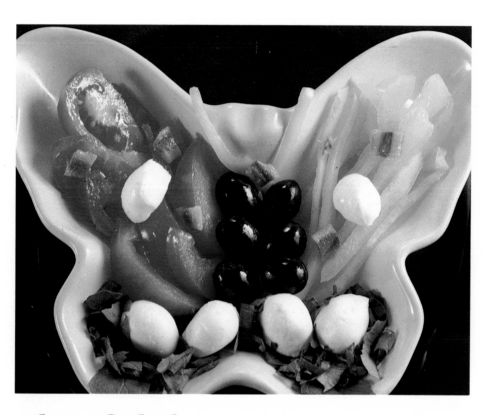

Six-colour Salad

Six-colour Salad

INSALATA AI SEI COLORI

Ingredients	Metric/Imperial	American
large ripe tomatoes	4	4
rocket or sorrel leaves	16	16
yellow (sweet) pepper	1	1
tuna in oil	200 g/7 oz	7 ounces
anchovy fillets	4	4
black olives	75 g/3 oz	⅔ cup
Mozzarella cheese	100 g/4 oz	¼ pound
olive oil	4 tablespoons	6 tablespoons
wine vinegar	2 tablespoons	3 tablespoons
salt and white pepper		

Wash, dry and quarter the tomatoes; wash, dry and finely slice the rocket leaves. Put in a salad bowl. Remove the stones from half the olives.

Prepare the pepper: wipe with a damp cloth, cut in half, remove seeds and pith, then slice into matchstick strips.

Add to the bowl along with the drained and chopped tuna and anchovies, stoned black olives and chopped Mozzarella cheese.

Beat the oil and vinegar together in a small bowl with a seasoning of salt and pepper. Pour over the salad, mix well and serve. Garnish with whole black olives.

Time: 20 minutes   *Serves 4*

PUDDINGS
AND
CAKES

*The Italians usually eat fresh fruit at the end of
a meal and the special desserts and cakes are kept
for important occasions like birthdays, Saints'
days, Christmas and Easter.
There are many delicious puddings and cakes;
some of the most interesting flavours being a
blend of the soft cheeses such as ricotta and
mascarpone cheese with fruits. Delicious ice
creams and sorbets are often eaten in the heat of
the day as well as at meal times.*

Crispy Apricot Cream

GRATIN DI ALBICOCCHE

Ingredients	Metric/Imperial	American
icing (confectioners') sugar	75 g/3 oz	$\frac{3}{4}$ cup
fresh apricots	18	18
rum	2 tablespoons	3 tablespoons
potato flour	2 tablespoons	2 tablespoons
milk	400 ml/14 fl oz	$1\frac{3}{4}$ cups
vanilla pod (bean)	1	1
eggs, separated	3	3
dark brown sugar	2 tablespoons	3 tablespoons
cinnamon	$\frac{1}{2}$ teaspoon	$\frac{1}{2}$ teaspoon
hazelnuts	25 g/1 oz	1 ounce
single (thin) or double (thick) cream	300 ml/$\frac{1}{2}$ pint	$1\frac{1}{4}$ cups

Put one-third of the icing sugar in a heavy-based pan, add 125 ml/4 fl oz/$\frac{1}{2}$ cup of water, mix and put over a low heat until dissolved.

Blanch the apricots in boiling water for a few minutes, cool under running water, peel, halve and remove the stones. Put into the prepared syrup, add the rum and baste each piece with syrup. Cook over a low heat for 10 minutes; remove and leave to cool.

Mix the potato flour with a little of the milk. Meanwhile boil the remaining milk with the vanilla pod. Turn off the heat and leave to infuse for 5 minutes covered with a lid.

Beat the egg yolks with the remaining icing sugar in another pan. When light and fluffy add the potato flour mixture, whisking constantly, then gradually trickle in the hot milk, including the vanilla pod. Put over a low heat, bring slowly to the boil and cook for 2 minutes. Turn off the heat and remove the vanilla pod.

When the vanilla cream is cool whip the egg whites until standing in soft peaks and fold them in.

Put the apricot halves in a round ovenproof glass dish, cut sides uppermost. Cover with the vanilla cream and sprinkle with brown sugar mixed with cinnamon. Put in a moderately hot oven (200 c, 400 f, gas 6) for 15 minutes, then grill (broil) until the top is golden.

Sprinkle with finely chopped hazelnuts and serve at once, handing the cream separately in a jug.

Time: 1 hour   *Serves 6*

Peach Upside-down Cake

DOLCE DI PESCHE IN BELLAVISTA

Ingredients	Metric/Imperial	American
For the topping:		
canned peach halves	12	12
ripe banana	1	1
lemon juice	1 tablespoon	1 tablespoon
sugar	1 tablespoon	1 tablespoon
butter	1 teaspoon	1 teaspoon
preserving sugar	2 tablespoons	3 tablespoons
glacé (candied) cherries	16	16
Maraschino liqueur	2 tablespoons	2 tablespoons
For the cake:		
butter, softened	100 g/4 oz	$\frac{1}{2}$ cup
caster (fine granulated) sugar	100 g/4 oz	$\frac{1}{2}$ cup
vanilla flavouring	$\frac{1}{4}$ teaspoon	$\frac{1}{4}$ teaspoon
eggs	2	2
plain (all-purpose) flour	100 g/4 oz	1 cup
baking powder (soda)	2 teaspoons	2 teaspoons
brandy	1 tablespoons	1 tablespoon
whipped cream to decorate	125 ml/4 fl oz	$\frac{1}{2}$ cup

Drain the peaches. Peel and mash the banana with a fork, add lemon juice and 1 tablespoon of sugar.

Butter a 23–25 cm/9–10 in cake pan and sprinkle with preserving sugar crystals. Fill 8 of the peach halves with the banana mixture and top with a cherry. Arrange in the pan upside down, ensuring that the cherries are in contact with the cake pan and will turn out on top of the cake when cooked. Soak the remaining 4 peach halves in the Maraschino.

Preheat the oven to 180 c, 350 f, gas 4. Cream the butter with the sugar and vanilla flavouring until light and fluffy. Beat in the eggs one at a time, then fold in the sifted flour and baking powder. Stir in the brandy.

Stir well with a spoon, then gently spread the mixture over the peaches. Put the pan in the moderate oven for 40 minutes. When cooked remove and leave to cool for 15 minutes before inverting on to a serving dish.

Decorate with the liqueur-flavoured peaches cut into wedges, alternating with the remaining cherries and rosettes of whipped cream. If time allows leave until cold before serving.

Time: 1 hour 25 minutes   *Serves 6*

Almond Cream Cups
1 Beat the egg yolks and sugar until light and fluffy. Add the toasted chopped almonds to the hot milk.
2 Trickle the almond and milk mixture into the egg mixture, mixing as each addition is made.
3 Return to the pan and cook until thick, add the liqueur. Allow to cool.
4 Gently fold in the whipped cream. Whip the egg whites and fold these into the mixture.

Almond Cream Cups

COPPETTE DI CREMA DI MANDORLE

Ingredients	Metric/Imperial	American
milk	600 ml/1 pint	2½ cups
vanilla flavouring	¼ teaspoon	¼ teaspoon
eggs, separated	3	3
caster (fine granulated) sugar	75 g/3 oz	⅓ cup
potato flour	50 g/2 oz	½ cup
blanched almonds	175 g/6 oz	1½ cups
Amaretto liqueur	2 tablespoons	3 tablespoons
whipped cream	300 ml/½ pint	1¼ cups

First prepare the cream: heat the milk in a small pan over a low heat with the vanilla. Beat the egg yolks with the sugar until light and fluffy, then fold in the sifted potato flour.

Finely chop the almonds and toast in a non-stick pan or under a hot grill (broiler). Retain a few nuts for decoration. Add to the hot milk and trickle into the egg mixture. Pour into a heavy pan.

Return the pan to a moderate heat and cook, stirring continuously in one direction only, until the cream is smooth and thick.

Remove from the heat and trickle in the liqueur. Leave at room temperature until cool, then gently fold in the whipped cream. Whip the egg whites until standing in soft peaks and fold into the cream mixture.

Divide the cream between individual glass goblets and chill in the refrigerator for 2 hours before serving. Decorate with nuts.

Time: 20 minutes + 2 hours: chilling   *Serves 6*

Golden Pears in Marsala

PERE DORATE IN MARSALA

Ingredients	Metric/Imperial	American
sugar	100 g/4 oz	½ cup
lemon	1	1
Marsala wine	125 ml/4 fl oz	½ cup
dessert pears	6	6
redcurrant jelly	2 teaspoons	2 teaspoons
pieces of crystallized (candied) ginger	4	4
angelica or mint leaves to decorate		

Make a syrup by dissolving the sugar in 300 ml/½ pint/1¼ cups of water in a small pan over a low heat, stirring from time to time.

Add 2 slices of lemon to the pan along with half the juice. Cook for a further 3 minutes, then remove from the heat. Stir in the Marsala wine and set aside.

Peel the pears carefully, leaving the stems in place. Stand them in a deep pan, pour over the syrup, put over a medium heat and bring the liquid to simmering point. Reduce the heat to minimum and poach the pears gently for 8 minutes or until tender. Baste with the syrup and allow to cool for 10 minutes.

Lift the pears out carefully with a slotted spoon and put in a serving dish. Strain the syrup into a clean pan, add the redcurrant jelly and bring to the boil over a high heat. Boil rapidly until reduced by half.

Cut the ginger into 12 slices and arrange 2 beside each pear in the serving dish. Pour over the syrup and decorate with leaves made from angelica, or fresh mint leaves.

Time: 45 minutes   *Serves 6*

Raspberries in Red Wine

SCIROPPO DI LAMPONE

Ingredients	Metric/Imperial	American
raspberries	700 g/1½ lb	1½ pounds
red wine	600 ml/1 pint	2½ cups
sugar	1.2 kg/2½ lb	5 cups

Clean and prepare the raspberries and put in a large bowl. Pour in the wine, cover and leave at a cool room temperature for 12 hours.

Strain the juice through a piece of muslin. Set the raspberries aside. Put the sugar in a large pan, add the juice and cook over a low heat, stirring constantly, until boiling, then boil hard for 2–3 minutes. Switch off the heat and leave to cool.

Strain again, using the muslin or a funnel and coffee filter paper. Put the raspberries into heat-sterilized jars and pour the juice on top. Seal with lids or plastic wrap. Use in fruit salad or with ice-cream.

Time: 35 minutes + 12 hours: steeping   *Serves 6*

Lemon Bavarois with Blackcurrant Sauce

BAVARESE AL LIMONE CON SALSA DI MIRTILLE

Ingredients	Metric/Imperial	American
powdered gelatine	5 teaspoons	5 teaspoons
egg yolks	4	4
caster (fine granulated) sugar	175 g/6 oz	¾ cup
lemon juice	175 ml/6 fl oz	¾ cup
grated lemon rind	1 tablespoon	1 tablespoon
vanilla flavouring	¼ teaspoon	¼ teaspoon
whipped cream	600 ml/1 pint	2½ cups
egg whites	2	2
oil	1 teaspoon	1 teaspoon
For the sauce:		
blackcurrants	450 g/1 lb	1 pound
Moscato wine	300 ml/½ pint	1¼ cups
caster (fine granulated) sugar	150 g/5 oz	⅔ cup
cinnamon	¼ teaspoon	¼ teaspoon
butter	15 g/½ oz	1 tablespoon
potato flour	1 tablespoon	1 tablespoon
brandy	2 tablespoons	3 tablespoons
candied lemon slices to decorate	6	6

Sprinkle the gelatine powder on to 150 ml/¼ pint/⅓ cup of very hot water and stir until dissolved.

Beat the egg yolks with the sugar in a heatproof bowl. When light and fluffy pour in the strained lemon juice mixed with 175 ml/6 fl oz/¾ cup of water, stirring constantly with a wooden spoon. Put the bowl over a pan of hot water, or the mixture into a thick pan, and cook over a low heat, stirring, until creamy. Add the gelatine mixture and stir to mix thoroughly. Remove from the heat and stir in the lemon rind and vanilla.

Fold the whipped cream into the mixture with a metal spoon. Whip the egg whites until they form soft peaks and fold into the mixture.

Line a 450 g/1 pound loaf pan with oiled greaseproof paper, ensuring that it stands 4 cm/1½ in above the sides. Pour in the prepared mixture and freeze for at least 2 hours, stirring twice during the first hour.

Meanwhile prepare the sauce: wash and drain the blackcurrants. Reserve 1 tablespoon for decoration and steep the remainder in the wine, sugar and cinnamon for 1 hour. Transfer to a heavy pan and bring to the boil over a low heat. Mix the butter with the potato flour and add to the sauce along with the brandy. Stir well and leave to boil for 10 minutes. Remove from the heat and pass through a sieve.

Remove the lemon custard from the freezer. Take a firm grip of the greaseproof paper and turn out on to an oval dish. Cover with the warm sauce and decorate with lemon slices and reserve blackcurrants. Serve at once.

Time: 40 minutes + 2–3 hours: freezing   *Serves 6*

Lemon Bavarois with Blackcurrant Sauce
1 Pour the lemon juice into the beaten egg yolk and sugar mixture.
2 Add the gelatine and then the lemon rind.
3 Fold in the whipped cream and then the whipped egg whites.
4 Pour the mixture into the lined pan.
5 While the lemon mixture is in the freezer, prepare the sauce. Add the brandy to the blackcurrant mixture and boil for 10 minutes.

Stuffed Baked Apples

Stuffed Baked Apples
MELE ALLA NOCE DI COCCO

Ingredients	Metric/Imperial	American
ripe bananas	2	2
sugar	2 tablespoons	3 tablespoons
Dutch toasts	8	8
honey	1 tablespoon	1 tablespoon
rum	2 tablespoons	2 tablespoons
dessert apples	6	6
butter, melted	65 g/2½ oz	5 tablespoons
desiccated coconut	3 tablespoons	4 tablespoons
dry white wine	2 tablespoons	3 tablespoons
raspberry jam (jelly to decorate)		

First prepare the stuffing: mash the bananas in a bowl with the sugar and crumble in 4 of the toast biscuits. Add the honey and rum and mix well.

Peel the apples and remove the cores, leaving the apples whole. Brush with some of the butter and fill with the stuffing. Brush the apples with some of the butter. Crumble the remaining toasts, mix with the coconut; spread over the outside of the apples.

Brush a deep baking pan with the remainder of the butter. Put in the apples, close together. Pour in 2–3 tablespoons of water with the wine and put in a moderate oven (180 C, 350 F, gas 4) for 30 minutes, until the apples are cooked. Top each apple with a teaspoon of jam and cool slightly before serving.

Time: 50 minutes *Serves 6*

Green Apple Mousse
MOUSSE DI MELE VERDE

Ingredients	Metric/Imperial	American
green dessert apples	800 g/1¾ lb	1¾ pounds
caster (fine granulated) sugar	200 g/7 oz	scant 1 cup
butter	25 g/1 oz	2 tablespoons
lemon rind	1	1
nutmeg	⅛ teaspoon	⅛ teaspoon
grapefruit	1	1
powdered gelatine	5 teaspoons	5 teaspoons
vanilla flavouring	¼ teaspoon	¼ teaspoon
Kirsch	125 ml/4 fl oz	½ cup
Ricotta cheese	225 g/8 oz	½ pound
egg whites	2	2
salt		
sultanas (seedless white raisins)	25 g/1 oz	1 tablespoon

Peel the apples, cut into wedges, remove the cores and slice the wedges roughly. Put in a pan along with the sugar, butter, grated lemon rind, nutmeg and juice of the grapefruit. Cover with a lid and cook over a low heat for 10 minutes.

Meanwhile sprinkle the gelatine on to 150 ml/¼ pint/ ⅔ cup of very hot water and stir until dissolved.

1

2

3

Green Apple Mousse
1 Peel the apples and cut into quarters. Remove the cores and slice roughly. Put the apples into a pan with the sugar, butter, grated lemon rind, nutmeg and grapefruit juice. Cover and poach gently for 10 minutes.
2 Remove the apples with a slotted spoon and purée in a blender or food processor. Add the prepared gelatine to the juice in the pan with the vanilla and two-thirds of the Kirsch. Add this liquid to the apples and process again to mix well. Sieve the Ricotta cheese into a bowl and add the puréed apple mixture. Fold in gently until the mixture is evenly mixed.
3 Whip the egg whites until they stand in stiff peaks and fold into the apple and Ricotta cheese mixture. Put the mixture into a large piping bag with a plain or fluted vegetable nozzle. Pipe onto a serving dish in a mound shape and freeze for 2 hours. Decorate with sultanas which have been steeped in the remaining Kirsch.

Remove the apples with a slotted spoon and purée in a blender or food processor. Add the gelatine mixture to the pan used to cook the apples and mix well. Pour into the blender along with the vanilla and two-thirds of the Kirsch; process until mixed together. Sieve the Ricotta cheese into a bowl; add the apple mixture and fold in carefully with a whisk.

Whip the egg whites with a pinch of salt until they stand in stiff peaks and fold carefully into the apple mixture.

When all the ingredients are well blended together put the mixture in a piping bag fitted with a large plain or fluted vegetable nozzle and pipe on to a serving dish in the shape of a mound. Put in the freezer for 2 hours. Meanwhile steep the sultanas in the remaining Kirsch.

Serve the mousse straight from the freezer, sprinkled with the sultanas.

Time: 45 minutes + 2 hours: freezing   *Serves 6*

Chocolate Nut Gâteau

CASSATA AL CENTERBE

Ingredients	Metric/Imperial	American
torrone (Italian hazelnut chocolate)	200 g/7 oz	7 ounces
plain (semi-sweet) chocolate	100 g/4 oz	$\frac{1}{4}$ pound
butter	200 g/7 oz	scant cup
icing (confectioners') sugar	225 g/8 oz	2 cups
egg yolks	5	5
cocoa powder	50 g/2 oz	$\frac{1}{4}$ cup
blanched almonds, chopped and toasted	50 g/2 oz	2 ounces
fresh sponge cake	2 (20 cm/8 in)	2 (8 in)
brandy	2 tablespoons	3 tablespoons
glacé (candied) cherries	8	8

Put both the hazelnut and plain chocolate in a blender and reduce to crumbs.

Soften the butter and put in a bowl with the icing sugar. Beat until thick, creamy and soft. Add the egg yolks, beating until each one is absorbed before adding the next.

Divide this mixture into 3 equal portions and put in separate bowls. Add the cocoa powder to the first, the chopped almonds to the second and the blended chocolate to the third. Mix well.

Remove one-third from each of these mixtures, put in a fourth bowl and mix well together.

Divide the sponge cakes horizontally in half. Put one on a round serving plate. Sprinkle with some of the brandy, cover with the cocoa mixture and level the top. Cover with a second layer of sponge cake, sprinkle with more brandy and cover with the almond mixture. Repeat the operation using the chocolate mixture.

Cover with the final layer of sponge cake and sprinkle with the remaining brandy. Spread the combined mixture from the fourth bowl all over the top and sides of the cake, smoothing with a spatula. Carefully cover with a foil dome and chill in the refrigerator for at least 2 hours, preferably overnight.

Serve decorated with glacé cherries.

Time: 1$\frac{1}{2}$ hours + 2–12 hours: chilling   *Serves 8*

This is a regional dessert from Aquila.

Chocolate Nut Gâteau

Apricots with Zabaglione

ALBICOCCHE ALLO ZABAIONE

Ingredients	Metric/Imperial	American
large ripe apricots	24	24
sugar	4 tablespoons	6 tablespoons
ground cinnamon	¼ teaspoon	¼ teaspoon
butter	50 g/2 oz	¼ cup
vanilla pod (bean)	½	½
blanched almonds to decorate	100 g/4 oz	¼ pound
For the zabaglione:		
eggs	4	4
caster (fine granulated) sugar	2 tablespoons	3 tablespoons
dry Marsala wine	2 tablespoons	3 tablespoons
white wine	1 tablespoon	1 tablespoon

Wash the apricots, cut in half and remove the stones. Put in a large deep pan and sprinkle with the sugar, cinnamon and diced butter. Add the vanilla pod, pour in 125 ml/4 fl oz/½ cup of water, cover and cook over a low heat until the liquid is syrupy and the apricots just tender. Remove from the heat and arrange in an ovenproof serving dish.

Apricots with Zabaglione
1 Wash the apricots, cut in half and arrange in a flameproof dish. Sprinkle with the sugar, cinnamon and diced butter. Add the water and cook. Drain and arrange in an ovenproof serving dish.
2 Prepare the zabaglione by beating the egg yolks with sugar in a bowl set over hot water. Whisk until light and fluffy.
3 When the mixture is thick add the Marsala and the wine and continue to whisk away from the heat until well mixed.
4 Spoon the zabaglione into the apricot halves. Cook in the oven.
5 Remove from the oven and allow to cool slightly. Sprinkle the zabaglione with chopped almonds before serving.

Meanwhile prepare the zabaglione: beat the egg yolks with the sugar in a heatproof bowl set over a pan of hot water on a low heat (make sure that the water does not touch the bottom of the bowl). When the mixture is soft and well whipped add the Marsala and the wine. Continue to beat lightly with a whisk and cook over the hot water until the mixture increases in volume and begins to thicken. Turn off the heat and continue to whisk for a few minutes.

Spoon the zabaglione into the apricot halves. Put in a moderately hot oven (200 c, 400 f, gas 6) for 15 minutes. Remove from the oven and allow to cool – this dish should be served lukewarm. Decorate with coarsely chopped almonds lightly toasted in a non-stick pan.

Time: 50 minutes   *Serves 6*

Deep-fried Amaretti Cakes

Deep-fried Amaretti Cakes

FRITTELLINE DI PANTALONE AGLI AMARETTI

Ingredients	Metric/Imperial	American
plain (all-purpose) flour	175 g/6 oz	1½ cups
Ricotta cheese	225 g/8 oz	½ pound
Amaretti biscuits	100 g/4 oz	¼ pound
drinking chocolate	50 g/2 oz	½ cup
caster (fine granulated) sugar	4 tablespoons	6 tablespoons
Amaretto liqueur	1½ tablespoons	2 tablespoons
eggs	3	3
egg yolk	1	1
fine dried breadcrumbs	50 g/2 oz	½ cup
oil for frying		
extra caster sugar to decorate		

Work the sifted flour into the sieved Ricotta cheese. Add the crushed Amaretti biscuits along with the drinking chocolate, sugar and liqueur. Mix in 2 whole eggs and egg yolk – this stage can be done in a food processor.

When a thick paste is obtained (if the mixture is too wet add a little more flour) form into little flattened rounds. Dip in beaten egg, mixed with 2–3 tablespoons cold water, and then in breadcrumbs.

Heat plenty of oil in a large deep pan. When very hot add the little cakes in batches and fry until golden on both sides. Remove with a slotted spoon and drain on absorbent paper towels.

Cover a serving plate with a doily and pile the cakes on it in the shape of a pyramid. Sprinkle with caster sugar and serve hot.

Time: 45 minutes   *Serves 6*

Queen of Grapefruits

POMPELMI DELLA REGINA

Ingredients	Metric/Imperial	American
grapefruit	6	6
icing sugar	225 g/8 oz	2 cups
Kirsch	2 tablespoons	3 tablespoons
egg whites	3	3
Maraschino cherries	6	6

Wash and dry the grapefruit. Cut off the tops about a quarter of the way down and scoop out the flesh, taking care to preserve the skins intact. Remove and discard the membranes and seeds; dice the flesh. Put in a large bowl, cover with the sugar, pour over the Kirsch and leave to rest for 30 minutes.

Meanwhile beat the egg whites until standing in stiff peaks.

Drain the grapefruit pieces and use to fill the grapefruit skins to within 3 cm/1¼ in of the top. Cover with egg white, forming a peak, and put on a baking tray. Put the tray under the grill (broiler), as close as possible to the heat. Switch on to high and leave until the egg whites have set (about 5 minutes).

Decorate each grapefruit with a cherry and serve at once.

Time: 40 minutes + 30 minutes: resting   *Serves 6*

Tips for making successful ice creams

1 Put all the tools and containers to be used for both making and serving the ice cream in the refrigerator for at least 30 minutes beforehand so that they are well chilled. Turn the freezer setting to its highest setting (lowest temperature).
2 Pass fruit to be made into a sorbet through a nylon or stainless steel sieve and immediately mix with lemon juice to prevent discoloration.
3 If using an ice cream scoop stand it in a jug filled with cold water and ice cubes. This will ensure that the ice cream leaves the scoop cleanly and forms a perfect shape.
4 To release ice cream from a mould without spoiling its shape simply apply a cloth soaked in hot water to the outside of the container; do not dip into hot water.
5 Accompany the ice cream with crisp wafers or biscuits to contrast with its smooth creamy texture. In Italy ice cream served as the final course of the meal is often accompanied by liqueurs or cordials. The best combinations are:
With fruit sorbets: vodka, grappa or gin.
With vanilla or fruit-flavoured ice creams: whisky, port, Marsala or brandy.
With chocolate ice cream: whisky or crème de menthe.

Coffee Ice Cream
GELATO DI CAFFE

Ingredients	Metric/Imperial	American
instant coffee granules	50 g/2 oz	scant cup
egg yolks	4	4
caster (fine granulated) sugar	150 g/5 oz	⅔ cup
milk	225 ml/8 fl oz	1 cup

Put 255 ml/8 fl oz/1 cup of water in a small pan and bring to the boil. Stir in the coffee, remove from the heat, cover and leave to stand for 30 minutes.

Meanwhile beat the egg yolks and sugar in a bowl until light and fluffy. Put the milk into a small pan and heat until just about to boil. Pour slowly over the egg mixture, stirring constantly. Gradually add the cooled black coffee.

Put the mixture in a heavy-based pan over a very low heat and cook, stirring constantly, until it thickens. Do not allow to boil. Remove from the heat and leave until cold, stirring occasionally to prevent lumps and a skin forming.

Pour into a tray and put in the freezer with the thermostat at the highest setting until firm; about 2 hours.

Transfer to a chilled bowl and beat until foamy, first with a wooden spoon and then with a beater. Return to the tray and freeze for a further 2 hours or more.

Time: 35 minutes + 30 minutes: resting and 4 hours: chilling   *Serves 4–6*

Lemon Ice
GELATO DIL LIMONE

Ingredients	Metric/Imperial	American
caster (fine granulated) sugar	225 g/8 oz	1 cup
salt		
milk	125 ml/4 fl oz	½ cup
lemons	3–4	3–4
egg whites	2	2

Put three-quarters of the sugar in a pan along with a pinch of salt and 225 ml/8 fl oz/1 cup of water. Heat gently for 5 minutes, then remove from the heat and allow to cool. Add the milk and the juice of the lemons; mix well.

Pour the mixture into a tray, put in the freezer with the thermostat at its highest setting and leave until firm; about 2 hours.

Meanwhile beat the egg whites until standing in stiff peaks and gently fold in the remaining sugar.

Break up the semi-frozen mixture with a wooden spoon and put in a chilled bowl. Beat until creamy, then fold in the egg white mixture. Quickly pour into the tray and return to the freezer for a further 2 hours or more.

Time: 35 minutes + 4 hours: freezing   *Serves 4–6*

Fruit Sorbet

SORBETTO DI FRUTTA

Ingredients	Metric/Imperial	American
caster (fine granulated) sugar	450 g/1 lb	2 cups
ripe fruit (peaches, apricots, bananas, raspberries, strawberries, blackcurrants etc)	225 g/8 oz	½ pound
lemon	1	1
orange rind	1	1

Put the sugar in a pan with 450 ml/¾ pint/2 cups of water and heat gently for 5 minutes. Strain through muslin and leave to cool.

Prepare the fruit and pass through a fine nylon or stainless steel sieve into a bowl. Add the juice and grated rind of the lemon, grated orange rind and the prepared sugar syrup. Leave to rest for 30 minutes.

Strain throuth muslin, pour into refrigerator trays and put in the freezer with the thermostat turned to its maximum setting. Leave until firm; about 3 hours.

Time: 40 minutes + 30 minutes: resting and 3 hours: freezing   *Serves 4–6*

Flaming Ice Cream

COPPA DELLO SCAPOLO

Ingredients	Metric/Imperial	American
shelled hazelnuts	150 g/5 oz	1 cup
plain (semi-sweet) chocolate	150 g/5 oz	5 ounces
block of vanilla ice cream	1 (600 ml/1 pint)	1 (1 pint)
honey	4 tablespoons	6 tablespoons
cinnamon	¼ teaspoon	¼ teaspoon
brandy	125 ml/4 fl oz	½ cup

Chop the hazelnuts coarsely and toast in a hot oven, or in a non-stick pan set over medium heat.

Grate the chocolate into a bowl, add 4–6 tablespoons of water and set over a pan of simmering water until melted.

Divide the ice cream between 6 goblets. Brush with honey and sprinkle with hazelnuts. Top with hot chocolate flavoured with cinnamon.

When ready to serve trickle a little brandy over the top of each ice cream and set alight.

Time: 25 minutes   *Serves 6*

Whipped Chocolate Cream

SPUMONE

Ingredients	Metric/Imperial	American
double (thick) cream	450 ml/¾ pint	2 cups
caster (fine granulated) sugar	100 g/4 oz	½ cup
plain (semi-sweet) chocolate	100 g/4 oz	¼ pound
crystallized (candied) fruit	50 g/2 oz	¼ cup
toasted hazelnuts	25 g/1 oz	¼ cup

Whip the cream straight from the refrigerator while very cold. Gradually add the sugar, stirring constantly. Pour into refrigerator trays and put in the freezer with the thermostat set on maximum for about 2 hours.

Turn the frozen cream into a chilled bowl and beat while adding the grated chocolate along with the finely chopped fruit and nuts. Return to the freezer for a further 2–3 hours or until completely frozen.

Time: 15 minutes + 3 hours: freezing   *Serves 4–6*

Strawberry Ice Cream

GELATO DI FRAGOLA

Ingredients	Metric/Imperial	American
single (thin) cream	1 litre/1¾ pints	1 quart
caster (fine granulated) sugar	225 g/8 oz	1 cup
fresh strawberries	1 kg/2 lb	2 pounds

Put one quarter of the cream in a heavy-based pan and scald (heat until just about to boil). Add the sugar, reserving 2–3 tablespoons, stir to dissolve and leave the mixture to cool.

Meanwhile hull, wash and drain the strawberries. Put in a large bowl and mash with a fork (if they are small a few can be left whole). Sweeten with the reserved sugar.

Add the remaining cream and cooled sweetened cream. Beat well and pour into trays. Freeze with the thermostat on its highest setting until firm; about 2 hours.

Transfer to a large chilled bowl and beat until foamy. Return to the trays and freeze for a further 2 hours or more.

Time: 35 minutes + 4 hours: freezing   *Serves 4–6*

A selection of shaped pans and moulds which make attractive cakes, puddings and ice creams

Vanilla and Chocolate Ice Cream

GELATO DI VANIGLIA E CIOCCOLATO

Ingredients	Metric/Imperial	American
egg yolks	4	4
caster (fine granulated) sugar	175 g/6 oz	¾ cup
double (thick) cream	200 ml/7 fl oz	¾ cup
milk	450 ml/¾ pint	2 cups
vanilla pods (beans)	1½	1½
plain (semi-sweet) chocolate	75 g/3 oz	3 ounces

Beat the egg yolks and sugar until light and fluffy. Gradually add the cream, then the milk. Put into a heavy-based pan along with the vanilla pods and cook over a very low heat, stirring constantly, until the mixture thickens. Strain into a bowl and allow to cool, stirring occasionally to prevent a skin forming on the surface.

Divide the mixture in half. Set one half aside and put the other in a bowl set over a pan of gently simmering water. Add the finely grated chocolate and 2–3 tablespoons of water; stir well to mix. Remove from the heat and allow to cool.

Pour the vanilla and chocolate mixtures into separate trays and put in the freezer, thermostat at the highest setting, until firm; about 2 hours.

Put into separate chilled bowls and beat until foamy. Return to the trays and freeze for a further 2 hours or more. Serve the two flavours together.

Time: 35 minutes + 4 hours: chilling   *Serves 4–6*

269

Chocolate and Coffee Cake

TORTA DI CIOCCOLATO E CAFFE

Ingredients	Metric/Imperial	American
eggs, separated	9	9
caster (fine granulated) sugar	200 g/7 oz	scant cup
vanilla flavouring	½ teaspoon	½ teaspoon
plain (semi-sweet) chocolate	225 g/8 oz	½ pound
strong black coffee	125 ml/4 fl oz	½ cup
rum	2 tablespoons	3 tablespoons
salt		
butter	15 g/½ oz	2 teaspoons
very fine dried breadcrumbs	3 tablespoons	4 tablespoons
For the decoration:		
sweetened whipped cream	225 ml/8 fl oz	1 cup
coffee essence	1 tablespoon	1 tablespoon
curls of chocolate	12	12

Preheat the oven to 180 C, 350 F, gas 4. Beat the egg yolks in a bowl with the sugar and vanilla flavouring until light and fluffy.

Grate the chocolate coarsely, put in a bowl along with the hot coffee and set over hot water until melted. Mix into the egg yolk mixture, then add the rum.

Whip the egg whites with a pinch of salt until stiff but not dry and fold into the egg yolk mixture.

Butter a shallow 20 cm/8 in cake pan and sprinkle with breadcrumbs. Pour in the cake mixture and cook in the moderate oven for about 45 minutes.

Leave to cool, then turn out on to a serving plate. Decorate the top with coffee-flavoured cream and chocolate curls.

Time: 1¼ hours *Serves 6*

Mimosa Cake

TORTA MIMOSA

Ingredients	Metric/Imperial	American
large sponge cake	1 (450 g/1 lb)	1 (1 pound)
Strega liqueur	3 tablespoons	4 tablespoons
milk	300 ml/½ pint	1¼ cups
For the filling:		
egg yolks	4	4
caster (fine granulated) sugar	4 tablespoons	⅓ cup
plain (all-purpose) flour	3 tablespoons	4 tablespoons
milk	450 ml/¾ pint	2 cups
large lemon rinds	3	3
whipping cream	450 ml/¾ pint	2 cups
icing (confectioners') sugar	1 tablespoon	1 tablespoon

Using a bread knife slice a 2 cm/¾ in layer off the top of the sponge cake; set aside. Take a pointed knife and mark a 2 cm/¾ in border round the top of the cake; cut down and scoop out the centre so as to form an empty shell, reserving the pieces in a bowl.

Mix the liqueur and milk together in a small bowl. Sprinkle half this mixture over the hollowed out centre of the cake.

Prepare the filling: beat the egg yolks and caster sugar in a deep pan until light and fluffy. Fold in the flour, then gradually add the milk, stirring constantly, followed by the grated lemon rinds. Put the pan on a medium heat and stir until the sauce is cooked. It should be thick and coat the back of the spoon. Remove from the heat, transfer to a small bowl and leave to cool.

Whip the cream and sweeten it with the icing sugar. Add to the sauce a little at a time, folding it in with a spatula.

Put a good half of this mixture into the cake shell. Cover with the lid, crust side down. Sprinkle the top and sides with the remaining liqueur mixture and spread the remaining cream mixture evenly over the top. Sprinkle with crumbs made from the reserved pieces of cake.

Chill in the refrigerator for at least 4 hours before serving.

Time: 1 hour + 4 hours: chilling *Serves 6*

Mimosa Cake
1 Cut the top layer off the cake with a bread knife.
2 With a sharp knife mark a 2 cm/¾ in border round the bottom part of the cake. Cut down, without going through the bottom, and scoop out the centre to form a shell.
3 Reserve the crumbs from the cake by removing with a spoon into a bowl.
4 Mix the liqueur and milk together and brush half over the scooped out shell.

5 Make the filling and allow to cool. Add the sweetened cream and fold in.
6 Pour half the filling into the shell.
7 Cover with the lid, crust side down, and brush the sides and top with the remaining liqueur mixture.
8 Spread the top with the remaining cream and top with sponge crumbs.

Chocolate Walnut Cake

TORTA MARGARETH

Ingredients	Metric/Imperial	American
butter	225 g/8 oz	1 cup
icing (confectioners') sugar	275 g/10 oz	2¼ cups
eggs, separated	8	8
plain chocolate	225 g/8 oz	½ pound
shelled walnuts	275 g/10 oz	2½ cups
Amaretto liqueur	2 tablespoons	3 tablespoons
plain (all-purpose) flour	275 g/10 oz	2½ cups
icing sugar and walnut halves to decorate		

Preheat the oven to 160 c, 325 f, gas 3.

Have the butter at room temperature. Put in a bowl with the sugar and cream until light and fluffy. Add the egg yolks one at a time, then beat for a few minutes more. Add the grated chocolate, finely chopped walnuts and the liqueur. Stir in the sifted flour.

Beat the egg whites until standing in stiff peaks. Fold them gently into the mixture. Grease and flour a 25 cm/10 in round cake pan. Pour in the cake mixture and bake in the moderate oven for 1 hour. Leave to cool.

Turn out and serve sprinkled with icing sugar and decorated with walnut halves.

Time: 1½ hours   *Serves 6–8*

Chocolate Walnut Cake

Marble Cake

TORTA VARIEGATA

Ingredients	Metric/Imperial	American
butter	175 g/6 oz	¾ cup
caster (fine granulated) sugar	275 g/10 oz	1¼ cups
eggs, separated	4	4
plain (all-purpose) flour	175 g/6 oz	1½ cups
potato flour	150 g/5 oz	1¼ cups
salt		
baking powder	4 teaspoons	4 teaspoons
milk	3 tablespoons	4 tablespoons
rum	2 tablespoons	3 tablespoons
cocoa powder	75 g/3 oz	¾ cup
icing (confectioners') sugar	2 tablespoons	3 tablespoons

Dice the butter, put in a bowl and allow to soften at room temperature. Add 25 g/8 oz/1 cup of sugar and cream until light and fluffy. Mix in the egg yolks one at a time.

Sift the flours with a pinch of salt, then fold into the creamed mixture. Mix the baking powder with the milk and add to the mixture along with the rum, stirring constantly.

Beat the egg whites until standing in stiff peaks, then gently fold into the flour mixture.

Preheat the oven to 180C, 350F, gas 4. Butter a deep 25 cm/10 in round cake pan, coat with flour and shake out the excess.

Divide the cake mixture into two equal portions. Colour the first with the cocoa powder mixed with the remaining sugar. Fill the cake pan with portions of plain cake mixture alternating with portions of chocolate cake mixture to give the marbled effect when cooked.

Bake in the moderate oven for 45 minutes. Allow to cool before turning out on to a wire rack. Sprinkle with icing sugar just before serving.

Time: 1¼ hours   *Serves 6–8*

Grandmama's Cakes

TORTA DELLA NONNA

Ingredients	Metric/Imperial	American
plain (all-purpose) flour	350 g/12 oz	3 cups
caster (fine granulated) sugar	100 g/4 oz	½ cup
orange rind	1	1
candied orange peel, diced	50 g/2 oz	2 ounces
butter, melted	225 g/8 oz	1 cup
Grand Marnier	1 tablespoon	1 tablespoon
milk	125 ml/4 fl oz	½ cup
butter for greasing		
orange jelly marmalade	8 tablespoons	10 tablespoons

Preheat the oven to 180C, 350F, gas 4.

Sift the flour into a bowl. Add the sugar, grated orange rind and candied peel. Add the melted butter, liqueur and milk and mix quickly with the hands to form a batter. Grease a square shallow 20 cm/8 in cake pan and pour in the mixture. Press the surface down with the finger tips.

Put in the moderate oven until cooked but still soft; 20–25 minutes. Leave to cool.

Cut the cake into diamond shapes. Put the marmalade in a small pan with 3–4 tablespoons of water; cook over a low heat for a few minutes until dissolved. Spread over the top of the cake.

Time: 45 minutes   *Serves 6*

Honeyed Nut Cake

PANFORTE CASERECCIO

Ingredients	Metric/Imperial	American
shelled walnuts	150 g/5 oz	1¼ cups
blanched almonds	150 g/5 oz	1 cup
candied peel	100 g/4 oz	¼ pound
candied orange peel	150 g/5 oz	5 ounces
coriander seeds	2 teaspoons	2 teaspoons
ground cinnamon	¼ teaspoon	¼ teaspoon
ground nutmeg	¼ teaspoon	¼ teaspoon
plain (all-purpose) flour	175 g/6 oz	1½ cups
icing (confectioners') sugar	225 g/8 oz	2 cups
honey	150 g/5 oz	5 ounces
rice paper		
icing (confectioners') sugar	1 tablespoon	1 tablespoon

Toast the walnuts and almonds in a moderately hot oven (200C, 400F, gas 6) for 7 minutes. Chop finely and mix in a bowl with the candied peels cut into thin strips. Add the coriander, cinnamon, nutmeg and sifted flour (reserve 2–3 tablespoons of flour for later use). Lower the oven setting to cool (150C, 300F, gas 2).

Put the icing sugar in a deep pan, reserving 1 tablespoon. Add 1 tablespoon of water and the honey. Put over a very low heat and stir continuously with a wooden spatula. When the mixture begins to boil drop a little into a saucer of ice-cold water to see if it will form a ball. If so remove from the heat and pour into the bowl with the fruit and flour. Otherwise continue cooking until it does.

Stir the combined mixtures with a wooden spoon until all the ingredients are well blended. Coat the hands with flour and form it into a ball, then flatten to 2 cm/¾ in thick.

Line a baking pan with rice paper, then add the dough. Level the top with a dampened palette knife. Sprinkle with the reserved sugar and flour. Put in the cool oven and cook for 30 minutes.

Trim the rice paper with scissors from the edge of the cake and sprinkle the top with icing sugar. Leave to cool completely before serving.

Time: 1¼ hours   *Serves 6–8*

This is a regional speciality from Siena.

Orange Cake

DOLCE ALLE ARANCE

Ingredients	Metric/Imperial	American
For the cake:		
shelled almonds	50 g/2 oz	scant $\frac{1}{2}$ cup
caster (fine granulated) sugar	100 g/4 oz	$\frac{1}{2}$ cup
eggs	3	3
plain (all-purpose) flour	200 g/7 oz	$1\frac{3}{4}$ cups
milk	4 tablespoons	6 tablespoons
butter, melted	50 g/2 oz	$\frac{1}{4}$ cup
baking powder	2 teaspoons	2 teaspoons
For the filling:		
milk	200 ml/7 fl oz	scant cup
lemon rind	$\frac{1}{2}$	$\frac{1}{2}$
egg yolks	2	2
sugar	50 g/2 oz	$\frac{1}{2}$ cup
plain (all-purpose) flour	25 g/1 oz	$\frac{1}{4}$ cup
rum	125 ml/4 fl oz	$\frac{1}{2}$ cup
orange marmalade	2 tablespoons	3 tablespoons
oranges	2	2

Preheat the oven to 200 c, 400 f, gas 6.

Drop the almonds into boiling water for 1 minute, then remove the skins, dry well and chop finely. Put the sugar in a bowl, add the eggs and beat for 5 minutes until light and fluffy.

Add the chopped almonds, then gradually incorporate the sifted flour, along with the milk and melted butter. Work for 5 minutes, using a wooden spoon or electric mixture at low speed, then stir in the baking powder.

Grease and flour a 20 cm/8 in cake pan. Pour in the cake mixture and bake in the moderately hot oven for 30 minutes. Leave to cool and turn out on to a plate.

Meanwhile prepare the filling: put the milk in a small pan with the lemon rind and heat gently. Beat the egg yolks with the sugar in another pan, then add the flour and hot milk. Cook the cream over a medium heat, stirring constantly, until thick. Boil for a few minutes, then remove from the heat and allow to cool. Stir in 3–4 tablespoons of the rum.

Melt the marmalade in a small pan along with the remaining rum; remove from the heat and set aside. Peel the oranges and slice thinly.

Cut the cake horizontally into three equal layers. Spread each layer with one-third of the cream and sandwich together. Decorate the top with orange slices and pour over the melted marmalade mixture.

Time: 1½ hours   *Serves 8*

Coconut Cake
1 Sift the flour, baking powder and sugar into a large bowl. In a separate bowl beat together the egg, milk and melted butter. Make a well in the centre of the flour and pour in the egg mixture.
2 Sprinkle in the coconut and the lemon rind; beat the mixture well to form a thick batter.
3 Coat a pastry brush with any butter remaining in the pan used for melting. Brush over a cake pan with the butter and tip in the cake batter.

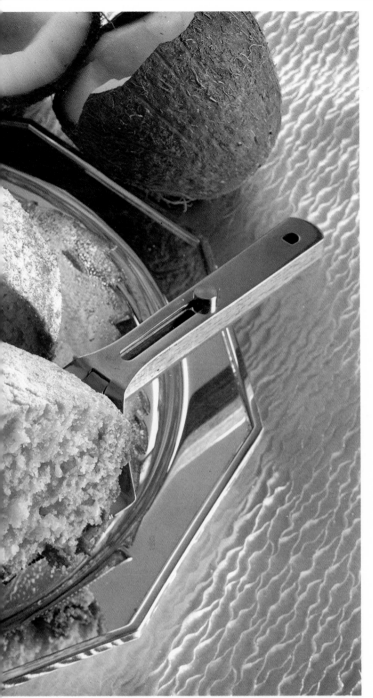

Coconut Cake

DOLCE DI COCCO

Ingredients	Metric/Imperial	American
plain (all-purpose) flour	175 g/6 oz	1½ cups
baking powder	4 teaspoons	4 teaspoons
caster (fine granulated) sugar	175 g/6 oz	¾ cup
egg	1	1
milk	125 ml/4 fl oz	½ cup
melted butter	4 tablespoons	6 tablespoons
lemon rind	½	½
desiccated coconut	50 g/2 oz	⅔ cup
icing (confectioners') sugar		
single (thin) cream	300 ml/½ pint	1¼ cups
cinnamon	¼ teaspoon	¼ teaspoon

Preheat the oven to 180 c, 350 f, gas 4.

Sift the flour into a large bowl with the baking powder and sugar. Beat the egg in a bowl with the milk and melted butter and pour into the centre of the flour mixture. Add the finely grated lemon rind and coconut. Beat well together to form a thick elastic batter.

Butter a 20 cm/8 in cake pan. Pour in the batter and cook in a moderate oven for about 35 minutes or until the cake is crisp and golden.

Remove from the oven, leave for a few minutes, then turn out on to a wire rack and allow to cool completely.

Sift icing sugar over the top and transfer to a serving plate. Mix the cream with the cinnamon and pour over the cake immediately before serving.

Time: 1 hour 10 minutes　　　　　　　　*Serves 8*

MENUS FOR SPECIAL OCCASIONS

These specially selected Italian menus can be used to plan a superb meal for the important dinner party, birthday or anniversary celebration. The menus have the preparation time carefully planned to help the hostess to enjoy the party. For a less formal occasion one or two courses can be omitted to suit the time available for preparation.

Menu

Avocado and Crab Salad

ANTIPASTO IN INSALATA

Cream of Tomato Soup with Basil

CREMA DI POMODORO CON BASILICO

Loin of Pork with Citrus Fruit

LONZA DI MAIALE AGLI AGRUMI

Stuffed Peaches

PESCHE RIPIENE

Preparation

One day ahead
Prepare the stuffed peaches, leave to cool and stand in the refrigerator.

Three hours ahead
Take the stuffed peaches out of the refrigerator to come back to room temperature. Cook the cream of tomato soup but do not garnish it yet.

Two hours ahead
Prepare the avocado and crab salad and begin to cook the loin of pork.

One hour ahead
Prepare the herb cream garnish for the soup.

Half an hour ahead
Complete the loin of pork and heat up the soup.

Avocado and Crab Salad

ANTIPASTO IN INSALATA

Ingredients	Metric/Imperial	American
avocado	1	1
lemon juice	1 tablespoon	1 tablespoon
canned sweet corn	200 g/7 oz	7 ounces
canned crabmeat	200 g/7 oz	7 ounces
mayonnaise	125 ml/4 fl oz	$\frac{1}{2}$ cup
tomato ketchup	1 teaspoon	1 teaspoon
Worcester sauce	1 teaspoon	1 teaspoon
red cabbage	$\frac{1}{2}$	$\frac{1}{2}$
black olives	2 tablespoons	3 tablespoons

Peel the avocado and remove the stone. Cut the flesh into cubes and brush with lemon juice to stop them going black; place in a bowl. Drain the sweet corn and add the kernels to the bowl. Drain the crabmeat, reserving the liquid, and add the meat to the bowl.

In a separate bowl mix the mayonnaise, crab liquid, tomato ketchup and Worcester sauce thoroughly together. Pour on to the avocado mixture and stir well.

Remove the core and thick ribs from the cabbage and cut the leaves into very thin strips. Divide these between 6 individual serving dishes. Pile the avocado mixture on top. Purée the stoned black olives in a blender or food processor. Garnish the salads with the purée and put on the lowest refrigerator shelf for 30 minutes before serving.

Time: 15 minutes + 30 minutes: chilling   *Serves 6*

1 Mix avocado with sweetcorn and crabmeat.
2 Mix mayonnaise, liquid and sauces together.
3 Pour this sauce on to the avocado mixture and stir well.
4 Remove the core from the cabbage and cut into thin strips. Pile the avocado mixture on the cabbage. Arrange the puréed olives on top of the mixture. Chill in the refrigerator before serving.

Cream of Tomato Soup with Basil

CREMA DI POMODORO CON BASILICO

Ingredients	Metric/Imperial	American
plum tomatoes	1.2 kg/2¾ lb	2¾ pounds
onion	1	1
potatoes	2	2
carrot	1	1
celery stalk	1	1
butter	50 g/2 oz	¼ cup
stock	1 litre/1¾ pints	1 quart
whipping cream	300 ml/½ pint	1¼ cups
sugar	1 teaspoon	1 teaspoon
salt and pepper		
basil leaves	12	12

Prepare the vegetables: chop the tomatoes, peeling first if fresh. Finely chop the onion, dice the potatoes, carrot and celery.

Melt the butter in a large pan over a low heat, add all the vegetables and simmer for a few minutes. Cover with the stock and cook very gently for about 1 hour.

Sieve or blend the soup and return it to the heat. Add half the cream, a pinch of sugar and season to taste. Stir until boiling and remove from the heat.

Whip the remaining cream and stir in the chopped basil. Serve the soup in individual bowls topped with a spoon of basil cream.

Time: 1½ hours   *Serves 6*

Cream of Tomato Soup with Basil

Loin of Pork with Citrus Fruit

LONZA DI MAIALE AGLI AGRUMI

Ingredients	Metric/Imperial	American
small onion	1	1
butter	50 g/2 oz	¼ cup
loin of pork	1.2 kg/2¾ lb	2¾ pounds
Marsala wine	1½ tablespoons	2 tablespoons
orange	1	1
lemon	1	1
salt and pepper		
stock	125 ml/4 fl oz	½ cup
black olives	12	12

Chop the onion finely. Melt the butter in a large heavy pan over medium heat, add the onion and cook until golden. Add the loin of pork and brown it on all sides.

Add the Marsala and, when this has evaporated, the juice from the orange and lemon. Season with salt and pepper, cover and cook over a low heat for about 1½ hours. Add a little stock from time to time to make sure it does not dry out.

Halfway through the cooking time stone and chop the olives and add them to the pork with a little pepper.

Serve the pork thinly sliced with the cooking juices poured over, accompanied with roast or mashed potatoes.

Time: 1½ hours   *Serves 6*

Loin of Pork with Citrus Fruit
1 Brown loin of pork on all sides, add the wine.
2 Allow to evaporate then add citrus juices.
3 After half the cooking time add olives.

Stuffed Peaches

PESCHE RIPIENE

Stuffed Peaches

Ingredients	Metric/Imperial	American
large yellow peaches	6	6
Amaretti biscuits	100 g/4 oz	¼ pound
Amaretto or other liqueur	2 tablespoons	3 tablespoons
egg yolks	2	2
sugar	75 g/3 oz	9 tablespoons
chopped blanched almonds	40 g/1½ oz	Scant ⅓ cup
butter	50 g/2 oz	¼ cup
icing (confectioners') sugar		

Cut the peaches in half and remove the stones. With a teaspoon, remove some of the flesh from the centres. Chop this and place in a bowl with the crushed biscuits, liqueur, egg yolks, sugar, almonds and most of the butter; mix well.

Stuff each peach half with this mixture and top with a knob of butter. Put them on an oiled baking tray and cook in a moderately hot oven (200 C, 400 F, gas 6) for 35–40 minutes.

Arrange the peaches on a serving dish and sprinkle with icing sugar. Serve warm or cold.

Time: 1 hour   *Serves 6*

Menu

Soup with Ricotta Cubes
DADINI DI RICOTTA IN BRODO

John Dory (Storer) in Tomato Sauce
ORATA CON GUAZZETTO DI POMODORO

Leg of Veal
NOCE DI VITELLO STECCATA

Cognac Soufflé
SOUFFLE AL COGNAC

Preparation

One day ahead
Prepare the soup up to the end of the second stage where it is cleared with egg white. Cool and then store in a sealed container in the refrigerator.

Three hours ahead
Remove the soup from the refrigerator and prepare the ricotta cubes. Begin to cook the veal.

Two hours ahead
Prepare the mixture for the soufflé and clean the fish.

One hour ahead
Cook the fish. Finish cooking the veal and carve it. Reheat the soup.

Half an hour ahead
Complete all the dishes and place the soufflé in the oven.

Soup with Ricotta Cubes

DADINI DI RICOTTA IN BRODO

Ingredients	Metric/Imperial	American
stewing beef and veal, mixed	800 g/1¾ lb	1¾ pounds
beef bone	1	1
chicken wings	2	2
salt and pepper		
carrot	1	1
celery stalk	1	1
onion	1	1
chopped parsley	1 tablespoon	1 tablespoon
egg white, beaten	1	1
Ricotta cheese, cubed	350 g/12 oz	¾ pound
eggs, separated	2	2
Parmesan cheese, grated	75 g/3 oz	¾ cup

Put the beef and veal, beef bone and chicken wings in a large pan. Season with salt and cover with 3 litres/5¼ pints/3 quarts of water. Bring to the boil over medium heat, removing the scum with a slotted spoon as it rises to the surface.

Meanwhile chop the carrot, celery and onion. Add them to the pan, together with the parsley, as soon as the water boils. Cover and cook very gently for about 3 hours.

Pour the soup through a sieve and leave until cold. Remove all fat from the surface. Return to the rinsed out pan and reheat. When boiling rapidly add the beaten egg white. Leave to boil for 30 minutes and sieve once more, preferably through muslin. Cool and refrigerate until required.

To make the ricotta cubes put the ricotta cheese in a bowl and carefully blend in the egg yolks. Beat the egg whites until standing in peaks and gently fold them into the ricotta mixture, along with the grated Parmesan cheese and a pinch of salt and pepper. Spread the mixture on to a foil-lined tray, levelling the top. Bake in a moderately hot oven (200 C, 400 F, gas 6) until the top is crusty and golden. Cool and cut into small cubes.

To serve put the ricotta cubes into a soup tureen and cover them with boiling soup. Allow to stand for 2–3 minutes for the flavours to blend before serving.

Time: 4 hours   *Serves 6*

Soup with Ricotta Cubes
1 Put the Ricotta cheese in a bowl and mix with a wooden spoon. Gradually beat the egg yolks into the cheese. Fold in the stiffly beaten egg whites with the Parmesan cheese and seasoning.
2 Spread the mixture on a baking tray lined with foil and bake until golden.
3 Allow to cool and cut into small cubes. Serve in the tureen and pour the hot soup over the cubes.

John Dory in Tomato Sauce

John Dory (Storer) in Tomato Sauce

ORATA CON GUAZZETTO DI POMODORO

Ingredients	Metric/Imperial	American
John Dory (storer)	1 (1.8 kg/3¾ lb)	1 (3¾ pound)
butter	75 g/3 oz	6 tablespoons
bay leaf	1	1
chopped parsley	1 tablespoon	1 tablespoon
salt and pepper		
dry white wine	125 ml/4 fl oz	½ cup
ripe tomatoes	600 g/1¼ lb	1¼ pounds
small onion	½	½

If the fish has not already been cleaned, scrape it to remove the scales, slit it open down the belly to remove the intestines and cut off the fins. Wash well under running water and pat dry with paper towels.

Melt 40 g/1½ oz/3 tablespoons of the butter in a large oval pan. Add the bay leaf, whole fish, chopped parsley, a little salt and pepper, the wine and a ladleful of water. Cover and cook on a medium heat for 40 minutes.

Meanwhile prepare the tomato sauce. Drop the tomatoes into boiling water for 1 minute so the skins can be removed easily and chop them finely. Peel and chop the onion. Melt the remaining butter in a small pan and fry the onion until golden. Add the tomato and season with salt and pepper. Simmer for 30 minutes.

Remove the fish carefully from the pan and put it on a warmed serving dish. Boil the cooking liquid to reduce it slightly and add it to the tomato sauce. Cook the sauce for a further 10 minutes or so until thickened.

Remove the bay leaf from the sauce and pour it over the fish. Keep hot until ready to serve, accompanied with boiled potatoes.

Time: 50 minutes   *Serves 6*

Leg of Veal

NOCE DI VITELLO STECCATA

Ingredients	Metric/Imperial	American
garlic clove	1	1
chopped rosemary	1 teaspoon	1 teaspoon
chopped sage leaves	$\frac{1}{2}$ teaspoon	$\frac{1}{2}$ teaspoon
salt and pepper		
thick slice smoked gammon	1 (100 g/4 oz)	1 ($\frac{1}{4}$ pound)
leg of veal	1.8 kg/3¾ lb	3¾ pounds
butter	50 g/2 oz	$\frac{1}{4}$ cup
dry white wine	125 ml/4 fl oz	$\frac{1}{2}$ cup
stock	125 ml/4 fl oz	$\frac{1}{2}$ cup
chopped parsley	1 tablespoon	1 tablespoon

Chop or crush the garlic clove finely, mix it with the chopped rosemary and sage and season with a pinch of salt and pepper. Cut the gammon into small cubes and sprinkle them with the herb mixture.

Make slits all over the veal with a sharp-pointed knife and push a piece of gammon into each one. Melt the butter in a large pan over a medium heat and brown the veal all over. Add the wine, lower the heat and simmer for about 2 hours, moistening with a little stock.

Remove the meat from the pan and cut it into slices. Arrange them on a warmed serving plate. Add the chopped parsley to the cooking juices in the pan and reheat for a minute. Pour over the meat and serve.

Time: 2¼ hours   *Serves 6*

Leg of Veal
1 Sprinkle the gammon with the chopped herbs.
2 Push gammon into slits made in the veal.
3 Brown the meat all over and add the wine.

Cognac Soufflé

SOUFFLE AL COGNAC

Ingredients	Metric/Imperial	American
butter	75 g/3 oz	6 tablespoons
plain (all-purpose) flour	50 g/2 oz	½ cup
milk	700 ml/1¼ pints	3 scant cups
sugar	90 g/3½ oz	scant ½ cup
potato flour	4 tablespoons	6 tablespoons
cognac	4 tablespoons	6 tablespoons
eggs, separated	6	6
lemon juice	¼ teaspoon	¼ teaspoon
salt		

Cognac Soufflé

Melt the butter in a small pan over a low heat and stir in the flour. When thoroughly mixed gradually add the milk and bring to the boil, stirring constantly. When the mixture has thickened remove it from the heat and add the sugar, potato flour and cognac. Stir well and leave to cool.

Preheat the oven to 200 C, 400 F, gas 6. Brush a 20 cm/8 in soufflé dish with oil and coat the inside with sugar.

Beat the egg whites until they form very stiff peaks, adding a pinch of salt and 2–3 drops of lemon juice to maintain the peaks. Stir the yolks into the cooled mixture, then fold in the whites. Bake in the moderately hot oven for 15 minutes, then increase the heat to 220 C, 425 F, gas 7 for another 15 minutes or until the soufflé is well risen and golden. Do not open the oven during cooking, or the soufflé will sink, and serve at once straight from the dish.

Time: 1¼ hours *Serves 6*

Menu

Gruyère Croquettes
CROCCHETTE DI GRUYERE

Macaroni Cheese with Courgettes (Zucchini)
MACCHERONCINI GRATINATI ALLE ZUCCHINE

Beef with Pizzaiola Sauce
COSTATA DI BUE ALLA PIZZAIOLA

Fruit Salad Cake
MACEDONIA IN TORTA

Preparation

One day ahead
Prepare the sauce for the macaroni, and the fruit salad cake; store in a cool place.

Two hours ahead
Prepare the macaroni cheese ready for browning during the last half hour.

One hour ahead
Make the gruyère croquettes ready for reheating a few minutes before serving.

Half an hour ahead
Prepare the beef with pizzaiola sauce.

Gruyère Croquettes

CROCCHETTE DI GRUYERE

Ingredients	Metric/Imperial	American
Gruyère cheese	225 g/8 oz	½ pound
butter	40 g/1½ oz	3 tablespoons
fresh breadcrumbs	100 g/4 oz	2 cups
eggs	3	3
salt and pepper		
dried breadcrumbs	50 g/2 oz	¾ cup
oil for frying		

Remove the rind from the Gruyère and grate the cheese finely. Melt the butter in a small pan over a low heat.

In a small bowl, mix together the breadcrumbs, melted butter, grated cheese, 2 eggs and seasoning. Mix well with a fork, then form into small balls the size of a walnut. Coat completely in the remaining egg and dried breadcrumbs.

Fry the croquettes in oil, a few at a time, until golden. Remove with a slotted spoon and place on paper towels to absorb excess oil. Serve hot.

Time: 30 minutes   *Serves 6*

Gruyère Croquettes

Macaroni Cheese with Courgettes (Zucchini)

MACCHERONCINI GRATINATI ALLE ZUCCHINE

Ingredients	Metric/Imperial	American
butter	50 g / 2 oz	¼ cup
plain (all-purpose) flour	25 g / 1 oz	¼ cup
salt and pepper		
milk	600 ml / 1 pint	2½ cups
egg yolk	1	1
onion	½	½
small carrot	1	1
celery stalk	1	1
courgettes (zucchini)	450 g / 1 lb	1 pound
stock	225 ml / 8 fl oz	1 cup
macaroni	450 g / 1 lb	1 pound
chopped basil	½ teaspoon	½ teaspoon
Mozzarella cheese	225 g / 8 oz	½ pound
oil	1 teaspoon	1 teaspoon
dried breadcrumbs	1 tablespoon	1 tablespoon

Melt half the butter in a small pan, stir in the flour and season with a pinch of salt and pepper. Gradually add the milk and bring to the boil, stirring constantly, to obtain a thick white sauce. Allow to cool slightly and stir in the egg yolk.

Chop the onion, carrot and celery finely. Melt the remaining butter in a large heavy pan over a medium heat and cook until golden. Meanwhile slice the courgettes thinly. Add them to the pan along with a pinch of salt and pepper and the stock. Cook for about 30 minutes, reducing the heat if the mixture becomes too dry.

Cook the macaroni in plenty of salted boiling water. Drain well, mix with the cooked vegetables and sprinkle with chopped basil.

Cube the Mozzarella cheese and stir into the pasta. Brush an ovenproof casserole with oil and sprinkle with breadcrumbs. Pour in the pasta, cover with the white sauce and put in a hot oven (200 C, 425 F, gas 7) for about 15 minutes to reheat the sauce and brown the top. Serve hot.

Time: 1 hour   *Serves 6*

Macaroni Cheese with Courgettes
1 Prepare the vegetables and slice courgettes.
2 Heat the butter and cook vegetables.
3 Cook the macaroni in boiling salted water.
4 Mix the drained macaroni with vegetables, basil and cheese. Pour into a dish and cover with white sauce.

Beef with Pizzaiola Sauce

Beef with Pizzaiola Sauce

COSTATA DI BUE ALLA PIZZAIOLA

Ingredients	Metric/Imperial	American
plum tomatoes	400 g/14 oz	14 ounces
oil	2 tablespoons	3 tablespoons
T-bone beef steaks	6	6
salt and pepper		
garlic cloves	2	2
oregano	$\frac{1}{4}$ teaspoon	$\frac{1}{4}$ teaspoon

Peel the tomatoes if using fresh, and slice thickly. Heat the oil in a large heavy pan over a high heat, add the steaks and brown on both sides. Remove with a slotted spoon, season with salt and pepper and keep warm on a heated serving dish.

Crush the garlic cloves and brown them lightly in the cooking juices left in the pan. Add the tomato slices, season with salt and pepper and cook for about 10 minutes on a moderate heat.

When the tomato slices are cooked replace the meat, together with any juices on the plate, sprinkle with oregano and cook for a few minutes. Serve the steaks covered with sauce.

Time: 20 minutes   *Serves 6*

Fruit Salad Cake

MACEDONIA IN TORTA

Ingredients	Metric/Imperial	American
banana	1	1
dessert apple	1	1
peach	1	1
strawberries	225 g/8 oz	1⅔ cups
pineapple slices	2	2
apricot jam	2 tablespoons	3 tablespoons
brandy	1½ tablespoons	2 tablespoons
white wine	2 tablespoons	3 tablespoons
dried (active) yeast	15 g/½ oz	½ ounce
butter	150 g/5 oz	½ cup + 2 tablespoons
plain (all-purpose) flour	200 g/7 oz	1¾ cups
eggs, separated	4	4
caster (fine granulated) sugar	150 g/5 oz	Scant ⅔ cup
lemon rind	1	1
oil	1 teaspoon	1 teaspoon

Prepare the fruit and cut into small pieces as for an ordinary fruit salad. Place in a large bowl, add the jam, brandy and wine, stir and leave to macerate.

Sprinkle the dried yeast over 2/3 tablespoons slightly warmed water and leave until frothy.

Melt the butter over a very low heat. Sift the flour into a bowl and stir in the melted butter, egg yolks, sugar, yeast mixture and grated lemon rind. Beat hard.

Beat the egg whites until they are stiff but not dry. Stir the fruit salad into the dough, then fold in the egg whites. Brush a 25 cm/10 in flan pan with oil and dust with flour. Pour in the cake mixture and bake in a moderately hot oven (200 C, 400 F, gas 6) for 40 minutes. Turn out on to a serving plate and serve warm or cold.

Time: 1 hour *Serves 6*

Fruit Salad Cake
1 Prepare the fruit by chopping into small pieces.
2 Add the jam, brandy and wine. Allow to stand to enable flavours to permeate the fruit.
3 Prepare the yeast batter. Stir in the fruit to the yeast mixture. Fold in the egg whites.

Menu

Vols-au-Vent with Tagliolini
VOL-AU-VENT RIPIENI DI TAGLIOLINI AL
POMODORO

Soup with Cheese Dumplings
GNOCCETTI DI FORMAGGIO AL BRODO RISTRETTO

Tournedos in Sherry Sauce
TOURNEDOS IN UMIDO

Strawberry Bavarois
BAVARESI ALLE FRAGOLE

Preparation

One day ahead
Prepare the soup and put it in the refrigerator.
Prepare the bavarois and put it in the
refrigerator still in the mould, covered with
plastic wrap.

Three hours ahead
Prepare the mushroom vols-au-vent; reheat 10
minutes before serving.

Two hours ahead
Prepare the sauce for the tournedos.

One hour ahead
Prepare and cook the dumplings. Keep warm
until ready to serve.

Half an hour ahead
Cook the tournedos and make the toast rounds
to serve them on.

Vols-au-Vent with Taglioni
1 Arrange the pastry cases on a greased baking sheet. Brush over with egg before cooking.
2 Add the tagliolini to the prepared tomato sauce for the filling.

Vols-au-Vent with Tagliolini

VOL-AU-VENT RIPIENI DI TAGLIOLINI AL POMODORO

Ingredients	Metric/Imperial	American
oil	2 tablespoons	3 tablespoons
butter	40 g/1½ oz	3 tablespoons
onion	1	1
plum tomatoes	450 g/1 lb	1 pound
salt and pepper		
basil leaves	6	6
medium-sized frozen vol-au-vent cases	12	12
egg yolk	1	1
tagliolini pasta	100 g/4 oz	¼ pound
Parmesan cheese, grated	25 g/1 oz	¼ cup
Mozzarella cheese	1	1

Preheat the oven to 230 C, 450 F, gas 8.

Heat the oil with two-thirds of the butter in a shallow pan. Add the finely chopped onion and cook over a low heat for a few minutes until transparent. Peel the tomatoes if using fresh, drain if canned, deseed and chop coarsely. Add to the pan, season with salt and pepper and leave on a medium heat for 20 minutes. Stir in the chopped basil at the end of the cooking time.

Meanwhile arrange the vol-au-vent cases, still frozen, on a buttered baking tray and brush the tops with beaten egg yolk. Put in the hot oven for 15 minutes until puffed up and golden.

Cook the tagliolini in plenty of boiling salted water until *al dente*. Drain well, add to the tomato sauce, sprinkle with Parmesan cheese and mix thoroughly.

Divide the tagliolini in tomato sauce among the baked vol-au-vent cases and arrange in a buttered ovenproof dish. Top each one with chopped Mozzarella cheese. Reheat for 10 minutes in a hot oven before serving.

Time: 40 minutes   *Serves 6*

Soup with Cheese Dumplings

Soup with Cheese Dumplings

GNOCCHETTI DI FORMAGGIO AL BRODO
RISTRETTO

Ingredients	Metric/Imperial	American
shin of beef	450 g/1 lb	1 pound
stewing veal	450 g/1 lb	1 pound
beef bone	1	1
calf's foot	1	1
chicken carcass	1	1
salt and pepper		
carrot	1	1
celery stalk	1	1
onion	1	1
chopped parsley	1 tablespoon	1 tablespoon
egg white	1	1
For the dumplings:		
butter	65 g/2½ oz	5 tablespoons
plain (all-purpose) flour	50 g/2 oz	½ cup
eggs	2	2
Parmesan cheese, grated	50 g/2 oz	½ cup
grated nutmeg	¼ teaspoon	¼ teaspoon

Put the meat, bone, calf's foot and chicken carcass in a large pan. Add 3 litres/5¼ pints/3 quarts of water, season with salt and pepper and bring slowly to the boil, removing the scum with a slotted spoon as it forms.

Meanwhile chop the carrot, celery and onion finely. Add them to the pan together with the chopped parsley, cover and simmer very gently for 3 hours.

Strain the soup and leave until cold. Then remove the fat from the surface and return the soup to the rinsed-out pan. Whisk the egg white until stiff and add it to the pan. Boil for about 30 minutes, then strain again.

To make the dumplings first melt the butter in a small pan and stir in the flour. Add 500 ml/18 fl oz/2¼ cups of the soup and stir vigorously. Cook, stirring constantly, until the mixture draws away from the sides; remove from the heat. Stir in the eggs, one at a time, the grated Parmesan cheese and the nutmeg.

Reheat the remaining soup in a separate pan. When it boils drop in teaspoonfuls of the dumpling mixture and cook for 10 minutes. Serve hot.

Time: 4 hours   *Serves 6*

Tournedos in Sherry Sauce

TOURNEDOS IN UMIDO

Ingredients	Metric/Imperial	American
carrot	$\frac{1}{2}$	$\frac{1}{2}$
celery stalk	1	1
small onion	$\frac{1}{2}$	$\frac{1}{2}$
oil	2 tablespoons	3 tablespoons
plum tomatoes	100 g/4 oz	$\frac{1}{4}$ pound
salt and pepper		
grated lemon rind	$\frac{1}{4}$ teaspoon	$\frac{1}{4}$ teaspoon
butter	40 g/1½ oz	3 tablespoons
tournedos fillets	6	6
thick slices of bread	6	6
sherry	125 ml/4 fl oz	$\frac{1}{2}$ cup
single (thin) cream	125 ml/4 fl oz	$\frac{1}{2}$ cup

Finely chop the carrot, celery and onion. Heat the oil in a small pan, add the vegetables and cook until golden. Peel the tomatoes if fresh and add to the pan. Season with salt and pepper, cover and cook over a low heat for about 20 minutes. Stir in the grated lemon rind and remove from the heat.

Melt the butter in a large heavy pan over medium heat, add the tournedos and cook for 3–4 minutes on each side. Remove, season with salt and pepper and keep warm.

Toast the bread slices and cut them to the size and shape of the tournedos.

Pour the sherry into the pan used to cook the meat and stir to mix in the meat juices; cook until reduced by half. Add the prepared tomato sauce, bring to the boil and add the cream. Cook for another 2 minutes only, stirring well.

To serve arrange the toast rounds on a serving dish with the tournedos on top and pour the sauce over.

Time: 45 minutes — *Serves 6*

Tournedos in Sherry Sauce

Strawberry Bavarois

BAVARESI ALLE FRAGOLE

Ingredients	Metric/Imperial	American
milk	400 ml/14 fl oz	1¾ cups
vanilla pod	½	½
egg yolks	6	6
sugar	150 g/5 oz	⅔ cup
gelatine	5 teaspoons	5 teaspoons
whipping cream	400 ml/14 fl oz	2 cups
strawberries	275 g/10 oz	2 cups
To decorate:		
wild strawberries	150 g/5 oz	1 cup
double (thick) cream	125 ml/4 fl oz	½ cup

Put the milk in a small pan with the vanilla pod and heat gently, then remove from the heat.

Beat the egg yolks and sugar in a bowl until soft and creamy. Remove the vanilla pod and stir the hot milk into the mixture. Sprinkle the gelatine into 50 ml/2 fl oz/¼ cup boiling water, stir until dissolved. Add to the custard mixture and cook on a very low heat, stirring continuously, until it thickens; then cool.

Whip the cream stiffly and fold it into the custard. Prepare the strawberries and push them through a sieve or purée them in a blender or food processor. Add the strawberry purée to the custard and mix well. Rinse a 20 cm/8 in mould out with cold water and fill with the strawberry mixture. Chill for 4–5 hours.

When ready to serve dip the mould briefly into boiling water and invert on to a serving plate. Decorate with wild strawberries and lightly whipped cream.

Time: 40 minutes + 4 hours: chilling　　　*Serves 6*

Strawberry Bavarois
1 Beat egg yolks and sugar until creamy. Stir in milk gradually.
2 Make up gelatine and add to the egg mixture.
3 Whip the cream stiffly and fold in carefully.

Menu

Melon Cocktail with Port
COCKTAIL DI MELONE AL PORTO

Rich Pigeon and Pasta Pie
TIMBALLO DI PENNE ALLA RICCA

Tuscany Veal
VITELLO ALLA TOSCANA

Chocolate Mousse
MOUSSE AL CIOCCOLATO

Preparation

One day ahead
Prepare the sauce for the pigeon pie and put it in the refrigerator. Make the pastry, wrap in foil and put it in the refrigerator.

Three hours ahead
Prepare the white sauce, cook the pasta and complete the pie ready for cooking.

Two hours ahead
Prepare the melons, retaining the shells, and put in the refrigerator. Prepare the roast and cook. Whip the cream for the chocolate mousse.

One hour ahead
Cook the pie. Prepare the mousse and refrigerate until ready to serve.

Half an hour ahead
Complete the melon cocktail. Carve the roast and keep it warm.

Melon Cocktail

Melon Cocktail with Port

COCKTAIL DI MELONE AL PORTO

Ingredients	Metric/Imperial	American
medium-sized melons	3	3
icing (confectioners') sugar	4 tablespoons	6 tablespoons
port	9 tablespoons	12 tablespoons
peaches	3	3
bananas	3	3
sorbet (page 268)		
mint sprigs	6	6

Cut the melons in half horizontally (or Vandyke as shown) and scoop out the seeds and any damaged flesh. Scoop out and cube the remaining flesh.

Put the empty shells in a bowl, sprinkle with the sugar and refrigerate for at least 2 hours. Also refrigerate the flesh.

When ready to serve pour a portion of the port into each melon shell and swirl it round well. Cut the peaches and bananas into chunks and pile into the shells mixed with the melon flesh. Add a scoop of sorbet and serve decorated with a sprig of mint.

Time: 20 minutes + 2 hours: chilling   *Serves 6*

Rich Pigeon and Pasta Pie

TIMBALLO DI PENNE ALLA RICCA

Ingredients	Metric/Imperial	American
For the pastry:		
plain(all-purpose) flour	300 g/11 oz	2¾ cups
salt and pepper		
butter	150 g/5 oz	½ cup + 2 tablespoons
whole egg	1	1
egg yolk	1	1
beaten egg to glaze		

Rich Pigeon and Pasta Pie
1 Divide the pastry into two pieces with one slightly larger for the lid. Line the pie dish with one piece. Arrange two-thirds of the pasta and pigeon mixture, distributing the pigeon evenly.
2 A tablespoon of sauce can be added before arranging the remaining pasta mixture on top.
3 Add the white sauce to the pie and sprinkle with the remaining cheese. Dampen the edges of the pastry with cold water. Roll out the lid and cover the pie.

dried mushrooms	25 g/1 oz	1 ounce
pigeons, plucked and drawn	2	2
butter	75 g/3 oz	6 tablespoons
onion	$\frac{1}{4}$	$\frac{1}{4}$
Parma ham	50 g/2 oz	2 ounces
Marsala wine	1½ tablespoons	2 tablespoons
stock	300 ml/½ pint	1¼ cups
plain (all-purpose) flour	25 g/1 oz	¼ cup
milk	225 ml/8 fl oz	1 cup
grated nutmeg	¼ teaspoon	¼ teaspoon
pasta quills	350 g/12 oz	¾ pound
cheese grated	4 tablespoons	6 tablespoons
oil	1 teaspoon	1 teaspoon

Put the dried mushrooms in a bowl of warm water to soak while making the pastry.

Sift the flour into a mixing bowl with a pinch of salt. Cut the butter into small pieces and add them to the bowl along with the egg and egg yolk. Rub the mixture between the fingertips until it forms into a ball. Wrap in foil and put it in the refrigerator to rest for at least 30 minutes.

Cut the pigeons into serving portions. Melt one-third of the butter in a heavy pan over moderate heat. Add the pigeon pieces, chopped onion and Parma ham, drained mushrooms and a pinch of salt and pepper. Stir well. When the portions are browned all over add the Marsala and cook until it has evaporated. Then add the stock, stir and leave over a low heat for about 40 minutes.

Meanwhile make a white sauce: melt half the remaining butter in a small saucepan, blend in the flour and season with a pinch of salt and the nutmeg. Gradually add the milk and bring to the boil, stirring constantly. When the sauce thickens remove it from the heat.

Preheat the oven to 200 C, 400 F, gas 6.

Cook the pasta in plenty of salted boiling water until slightly undercooked. Drain it well and mix with the pigeon sauce, remaining butter and half the grated cheese, preferably Parmesan.

Brush a 25 cm/10 in pie dish with oil.

Divide the pastry into two pieces, one slightly larger than the other, and roll it out. Use the smaller piece to line the base and sides of the pie dish. Put in two-thirds of the pigeon and pasta mixture, arranging the pigeon portions evenly. Cover with the remaining pasta, top with the white sauce and sprinkle with the remaining cheese.

Dampen the pastry rim, cover with the pastry lid and pinch the edges together well to seal. Decorate the top with pastry trimmings and brush with beaten egg. Mark the edges with a fork and pierce the top to allow steam to escape. Bake in the moderately hot oven for about 40 minutes or until golden brown.

Allow the pie to rest for a few minutes before cutting into wedges to serve.

Time: 2¼ hours　　　　　　　　　　　　　　*Serves 6*

Tuscany Veal

VITELLO ALLA TOSCANA

Ingredients	Metric/Imperial	American
fillet (tenderloin) of veal	1.2 kg/2¾ lb	2¾ pounds
plain (all-purpose) flour	25 g/1 oz	¼ cup
butter	50 g/2 oz	¼ cup
small onion	1	1
cooked ham	150 g/5 oz	5 ounces
red wine (Chianti)	50 ml/2 fl oz	¼ cup
salt and pepper		
stock	225 ml/8 fl oz	1 cup
garlic clove	1	1
lemon rind, grated	½	½ teaspoon
grated nutmeg	¼ teaspoon	¼ teaspoon

Tie the meat up with kitchen string, not too tightly, so that it will keep its shape during cooking. Roll it in flour. Melt the butter in a heavy pan over a medium heat and brown the meat all over. Finely chop the onion and ham and add to the pan. Lower the heat and cook for a few minutes.

Sprinkle in the wine and simmer until it evaporates. Season with salt and pepper, cover and cook for about 1½ hours, moistening from time to time with a little stock.

At the end of the cooking time, season the meat and cooking juices with crushed garlic, grated lemon rind and nutmeg. Remove the meat.

Carve the meat in thick slices and serve with the cooking juices poured over.

Time: 2 hours   *Serves 6*

Tuscany Veal
1 Tie the meat with string to keep the shape. Heat the butter in a pan and brown on all sides. Add the finely chopped onion and ham to the pan and cook for a few minutes.
2 Sprinkle in the wine and allow to evaporate. Cook for 1½ hours.
3 At the end of cooking, season the meat with lemon rind.
4 Sprinkle the meat with grated nutmeg to flavour the cooking juices.

Chocolate Mousse

Chocolate Mousse

MOUSSE AL CIOCCOLATO

Ingredients	Metric/Imperial	American
egg yolks	7	7
egg white	1	1
caster (fine granulated) sugar	100 g/4 oz	½ cup
plain (semi-sweet) chocolate	150 g/5 oz	5 ounces
milk	1 tablespoon	1 tablespoon
double (thick) cream	500 ml/18 fl oz	2¼ cups

Put the egg yolks, egg white and sugar in a double saucepan or in a bowl set over a pan of boiling water and beat with a whisk until the mixture becomes light in colour and thickens. Remove from the heat and continue beating until quite cold.

Break the chocolate up and melt it in the milk, also over boiling water. Stir until thick. Add the chocolate milk to the egg mixture and stir well. Leave until cold.

Whip the cream until stiff and add it to the chocolate mixture a little at a time. Pour the mousse into individual serving dishes and put in the refrigerator until ready to serve.

Note: Wine does not go well with this dessert – serve liqueur, whisky or Grappa.

Time: 1 hour　　　　　　　　　　　　　　*Serves 6*

Menu

Crab Cocktail
COCKTAIL DI GRANCHI

Soup with Green Dumplings
PASSATELLI VERDI

Casseroled Chicken with Peas
POLLASTRA IN CASSERUOLA ALLE PRIMIZIE

Apple Charlotte
CHARLOTTE DI MELE

Preparation

One day ahead
Prepare the soup and the apple charlotte.

Three hours ahead
Prepare the chicken casserole.

Two hours ahead
Prepare the crab cocktail and the custard sauce for the apple charlotte.

One hour ahead
Prepare the mix for the green dumplings.

Crab Cocktail

Crab Cocktail

COCKTAIL DI GRANCHI

Ingredients	Metric/Imperial	American
mushrooms	350 g/12 oz	¾ pound
lemon juice	1 tablespoon	1 tablespoon
French beans	350 g/12 oz	¾ pound
salt and pepper		
medium-sized tomatoes	2	2
canned crabmeat	350 g/12 oz	¾ pound
olive oil	1 tablespoon	1 tablespoon
lettuce leaves		
chopped chives	1 teaspoon	1 teaspoon

Clean the mushrooms, slice thinly and put in a large bowl. Sprinkle with lemon juice to prevent discoloration.

Top and tail the French beans and cook them in lightly salted boiling water until just tender; about 12 minutes. Drain immediately, leave to cool and then cut into 2.5 cm/1 in lengths. Add them to the bowl.

Peel and chop the tomatoes, taking care not to squash them, and add them to the bowl. Drain the liquid from the crab, chop the meat and add it to the bowl.

Sprinkle the mixture with a little olive oil, season with salt and pepper, mix well. Serve in individual goblets on a bed of lettuce leaves, topped with chopped chives or sprigs of parsley.

Time: 45 minutes   *Serves 6*

305

Soup with Green Dumplings

PASSATELLI VERDI

Ingredients	Metric/Imperial	American
shin of beef	450 g/1 lb	1 pound
stewing veal	450 g/1 lb	1 pound
beef marrow bone	1	1
calf's foot	1	1
chicken carcass	1	1
salt and pepper		
carrot	1	1
celery stalk	1	1
onion	1	1
chopped parsley	1 tablespoon	1 tablespoon
For the dumplings:		
spinach	350 g/12 oz	$\frac{3}{4}$ pound
eggs	3	3
Parmesan cheese, grated	75 g/3 oz	$\frac{3}{4}$ cup
plain (all-purpose) flour	1½ tablespoons	2 tablespoons

Soup with Green Dumplings
1 Whisk the egg whites and use to clear stock.
2 Chop the spinach finely and put in a bowl.
3 Add remaining dumpling ingredients and mix.

Put a large pan containing 3 litres/5 pints/3 quarts of cold water over a low heat. Add the beef, veal, marrow bone, calf's foot and chicken carcass; season with salt and pepper. Bring slowly to the boil, removing the scum with a slotted spoon as it forms.

Meanwhile chop the vegetables finely. Add them to the pan when the water boils along with the chopped parsley. Cover and simmer very gently for 3 hours.

Carefully pass the stock through a fine sieve. Leave it until cold and remove the fat from the surface. Return to the rinsed-out pan and put over a low heat. Whisk the egg white until stiff and add it to the stock to clear it. Simmer for a further 30 minutes and then sieve again, preferably through muslin.

To prepare the dumplings, wash the spinach thoroughly and cook it in the water remaining on the leaves for 5–10 minutes until tender. Drain thoroughly and squeeze out any remaining liquid.

Chop the spinach finely and put it in a bowl with the eggs, half of the grated Parmesan cheese, flour and a teaspoon of marrow scooped out of the marrow bone. Season with salt and pepper and mix well together either in a bowl or in a food processor.

Form the mixture into small dumplings and drop into the boiling soup. Cook until the dumplings rise to the surface.

Garnish the soup with grated Parmesan cheese and serve hot.

Time: 4 hours   *Serves 6*

Chicken Casserole with peas
1 Stuff the chicken and wrap in the remaining slices of Parma ham. Tie with string to form a parcel.
2 Melt the butter in a heavy pan and brown the chicken on all sides. Pour over the wine and allow to cook until it has evaporated.
3 Add the vegetables to the pan. Lower the heat and cook for about 45 minutes, adding stock from time to time to prevent the dish drying out. Add frozen peas.

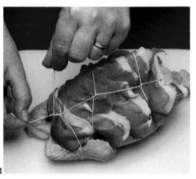

Chicken Casserole with Peas

POLLASTRA IN CASSERUOLA ALLE PRIMIZIE

Ingredients	Metric/Imperial	American
Parma ham	150 g/5 oz	5 ounces
garlic clove	1	1
sage leaves	2–3	2–3
salt and pepper		
oven-ready fresh chicken	1 (1.5 kg/3½ lb)	1 (3½ pound)
lemon	½	½
butter	50 g/2 oz	¼ cup
dry white wine	125 ml/4 fl oz	½ cup
fresh or frozen peas	600 g/1¼ lb	1¼ pounds
artichokes	4	4
asparagus	800 g/1¾ lb	1¾ pounds
onion	½	½
stock	225 ml/8 fl oz	1 cup
chopped parsley	1 tablespoon	1 tablespoon

Chop half the Parma ham. Chop the garlic clove and sage leaves finely. Mix together, season with salt and pepper and stuff into the chicken, followed by the half lemon. Wrap the chicken in the remaining slices of Parma ham and tie it up with string to form a neat parcel.

Melt the butter in a large pan over medium heat. Put in the stuffed chicken and brown it on all sides. Pour over the wine and leave it to evaporate.

Meanwhile prepare the vegetables. Shell the peas. Remove the hard outer leaves from the artichokes, cut the points of the remainder, and remove the stalks and chokes (the hairy part in the centre). Slice them thinly. Scrape the asparagus to remove any grit, cut away the white woody parts and wash well. Cut into 4 cm/1½ in lengths. Finely chop the onion.

Add the vegetables to the pan (do not add frozen peas), season to taste with salt and pepper and lower the heat. Cook for about 45 minutes more, adding stock from time to time if it dries out. If using frozen peas add 15 minutes before the end of the cooking time. When the chicken is tender take it out, cut away the string and remove and reserve the slices of Parma ham. Carve the chicken into serving portions.

Chop the Parma ham finely, together with any morsels of chicken left behind after carving, and add to the vegetables. Sprinkle with the chopped parsley. Return the chicken pieces to the pan to keep warm until required.

Time: 2 hours   *Serves 6*

Apple Charlotte

Apple Charlotte

CHARLOTTE DI MELE

Ingredients	Metric/Imperial	American
sultanas	50 g/2 oz	$\frac{1}{3}$ cup
walnut halves	75 g/3 oz	$\frac{1}{2}$ cup
small red apples	1.2 kg/2$\frac{3}{4}$ lb	2$\frac{3}{4}$ pounds
butter	65 g/2$\frac{1}{2}$ oz	5 tablespoons
granulated sugar	75 g/3 oz	6 tablespoons
cinnamon	1 teaspoon	1 teaspoon
apricot jam	100 g/4 oz	$\frac{1}{2}$ cup
rum	3 tablespoons	scant $\frac{1}{4}$ cup
milk	125 ml/4 fl oz	$\frac{1}{2}$ cup
sponge fingers	200 g/7 oz	7 ounces
For the sauce:		
egg yolk	1	1
caster (fine granulated) sugar	2 tablespoons	3 tablespoons
plain (all-purpose) flour	1 tablespoon	1 tablespoon
lemon rind, grated	$\frac{1}{2}$ teaspoon	$\frac{1}{2}$ teaspoon
milk	300 ml/$\frac{1}{2}$ pint	1$\frac{1}{4}$ cups

Put the sultanas in a bowl and cover with warm water to soften them. Crush the walnut halves, reserving a few for decoration.

Peel the apples, remove the cores and cut the flesh into segments. Put these in a saucepan with the butter and cook very gently into a pulp, stirring occasionally. Add the sugar, cinnamon, crushed walnuts and drained sultanas. Raise the heat and cook the mixture until it thickens. Stir in the jam and leave until cold.

Meanwhile line a plain mould or round cake pan with plastic wrap. Mix the rum and milk together and dip the biscuits in it. Line the mould with biscuits, fill it with the apple mixture and cover the top with more biscuits. Refrigerate until needed.

To make the sauce put the egg yolk and sugar in a small pan over very low heat and beat until frothy. Stir in the flour and grated lemon rind. Gradually add the milk and bring to the boil, stirring constantly. Remove from the heat and leave until cold, stirring occasionally.

To serve turn out the charlotte on a serving dish, pour over the sauce and decorate with the reserved walnut halves.

Time: 1 hour   *Serves 6*

Menu

Baked Stuffed Tomatoes
POMODORINI GRATINATI

Spaghettini with Herbs
SPAGHETTINI AGLI AROMI

*Cold Veal with Aubergine
(Eggplant)*
VITELLO FREDDO ALLE MELANZANE

Apricots with Chocolate Sauce
ALBICOCCHE AL CIOCCOLATO

Preparation

One day ahead
Cook the veal, grill the aubergine (eggplant) and leave in the marinade. Refrigerate until required.

Three hours ahead
Prepare and stuff the tomatoes ready for cooking later.

Two hours ahead
Prepare the sauce for the pasta and the apricots with their chocolate sauce.

One hour ahead
Complete the cold veal and heat the tomatoes.

Half an hour ahead
Cook the spaghettini, add the sauce and keep warm.

Baked Stuffed Tomatoes

Baked Stuffed Tomatoes

POMODORINI GRATINATI

Ingredients	Metric/Imperial	American
medium-sized red tomatoes	12	12
salt		
oil	1 teaspoon	1 teaspoon
butter	65 g/2½ oz	5 tablespoons
garlic clove	1	1
salted anchovies	4	4
fresh breadcrumbs	75 g/3 oz	1½ cups
freshly ground pepper		
black olives	12	12
chopped parsley	2 tablespoons	3 tablespoons

Wash the tomatoes and cut the top off each one with a very sharp knife. Gently scoop out the pulp with a teaspoon and put it in a bowl. Sprinkle the hollowed-out tomatoes with salt to draw out excess water. Leave for a few minutes, then drain well and put on to an oiled baking tray.

Melt the butter in a small pan over medium heat. Crush the garlic and add it to the pan. Wash the anchovies well, drain, remove the bone and chop the flesh. Remove the garlic from the pan and put in the anchovies. When they begin to disintegrate add the breadcrumbs and the pepper. Cook until brown, stirring continuously.

Stone the olives and chop the flesh finely. Add it to the pan together with the chopped parsley and reserved tomato pulp. Stir the mixture well and stuff the tomatoes with it. Cover them with their lids and bake in a hot oven (220 c, 425 f, gas 7) for about 15 minutes. Serve very hot.

Time: 45 minutes   *Serves 6*

Spaghettini with Herbs

SPAGHETTINI AGLI AROMI

Ingredients	Metric/Imperial	American
onion	1	1
garlic clove	1	1
plum tomatoes	450 g/1 lb	1 pound
oil	3 tablespoons	scant $\frac{1}{4}$ cup
dry white wine	50 ml/2 fl oz	$\frac{1}{4}$ cup
salt and pepper		
chopped pine nuts	2 tablespoons	3 tablespoons
majoram	$\frac{1}{4}$ teaspoon	$\frac{1}{4}$ teaspoon
chopped parsley	1 tablespoon	1 tablespoon
chopped basil	$\frac{1}{2}$ teaspoon	$\frac{1}{2}$ teaspoon
spaghettini	450 g/1 lb	1 pound

Finely chop the onion and crush the garlic. Peel the tomatoes if using fresh (put in boiling water for 1 minute to make it easy to remove the skins) and chop them roughly. Heat the oil in a heavy pan and cook the onion and garlic until soft but not brown. Pour in the wine and when this has evaporated a little add the tomatoes.

Simmer the sauce over a low heat for about 30 minutes, then season with salt and pepper and add the pine nuts, marjoram, parsley and basil.

Cook the spaghettini in plenty of boiling salted water until *al dente*. Drain well, mix with the sauce and serve at once.

Time: 45 minutes   *Serves 6*

Spaghettini with Herbs
1 Chop herbs and onion. Crush garlic.
2 Heat oil in a pan; cook onion and garlic.
3 When the tomato sauce is cooked add herbs, seasoning and pine nuts.

Cold Veal with Aubergine (Eggplant)

VITELLO FREDDO ALLE MELANZANE

Ingredients	Metric/Imperial	American
aubergines (eggplants)	4	4
salt and pepper		
carrot	1	1
celery stalk	1	1
onion	$\frac{1}{2}$	$\frac{1}{2}$
boned loin of veal	800 g/1$\frac{3}{4}$ lb	1$\frac{3}{4}$ pounds
oil	225 ml/8 fl oz	1 cup
chopped sage	$\frac{1}{2}$ teaspoon	$\frac{1}{2}$ teaspoon
chopped rosemary	$\frac{1}{2}$ teaspoon	$\frac{1}{2}$ teaspoon
wine vinegar	125 ml/4 fl oz	$\frac{1}{2}$ cup
garlic cloves	2	2
chopped basil leaves	$\frac{1}{2}$ teaspoon	$\frac{1}{2}$ teaspoon

Slice the aubergines thinly, sprinkle with salt and leave for 30 minutes to draw out excess water. Drain well and cook under a hot grill (broiler) without adding any fat or seasoning.

Chop the carrot, celery and onion. Put them in a large pan with the meat, a little salt and enough water to cover. Bring to the boil, then simmer gently for about 2 hours or until the meat is cooked.

Remove and drain the veal. Put 1 tablespoon of the oil in another pan with the sage and rosemary and brown the veal in it lightly. Pour over half the vinegar and leave until it evaporates. Remove the meat and leave to cool.

Chop the garlic finely. Put a layer of aubergine slices in a shallow dish and season with a little of the garlic, basil, remaining oil and vinegar and salt and pepper. Continue until all the aubergine slices are used up and pour over any remaining oil. Leave to marinate for 1 hour, or longer if convenient.

To serve carve the veal into slices and arrange them on a plate alternately with slices of aubergine. Strain the marinade over the dish.

Time: 2 hours + 1 hour: marinating   *Serves 6*

Cold Veal with Aubergine
1 Brown prepared aubergine under a hot grill.
2 Cover the meat with water and add vegetables.
3 Put the drained veal in a pan with oil. Brown on all sides with sage and rosemary added to the pan.
4 Layer the aubergine in a dish and season with garlic, basil, oil and vinegar. Use all the aubergines and allow to marinate.
5 Arrange alternate slices of veal and aubergine on a serving plate.

Apricots with Chocolate Sauce

Apricots with Chocolate Sauce

ALBICOCCHE AL CIOCCOLATO

Ingredients	Metric/Imperial	American
large ripe apricots	12	12
butter	25 g/1 oz	2 tablespoons
sugar	100 g/4 oz	$\frac{1}{2}$ cup
whipping (thick) cream	300 ml/$\frac{1}{2}$ pint	1$\frac{1}{4}$ cups
Amaretti biscuits	100 g/4 oz	$\frac{1}{4}$ pound
egg yolks	2	2
plain (all-purpose) flour	2 tablespoons	3 tablespoons
milk	300 ml/$\frac{1}{2}$ pint	1$\frac{1}{4}$ cups
plain (semi-sweet) chocolate	100 g/4 oz	$\frac{1}{4}$ pound

Wash the apricots, cut in half and remove the stones. Spread a large shallow baking dish with butter and sprinkle it with 1 tablespoon of the sugar. Put the apricots in it and bake in a moderate oven (180 C, 350 F, gas 4) until tender but not mushy.

Meanwhile whip the cream. Put the biscuits in a plastic bag; crush with a rolling pin and add them to the cream. Arrange the apricots in 6 individual serving dishes, top with the cream mixture and set aside.

Beat the remaining sugar and egg yolks in a bowl until light and fluffy. Gradually add the flour and milk. Put the bowl over a saucepan of boiling water and cook the mixture, stirring constantly, until it is creamy. Break up the chocolate and add it to the mixture; as soon as it has melted remove the bowl from the heat. Leave until cold, stirring occasionally.

To serve pour a portion of chocolate sauce over each dish of apricots.

Time: 1 hour + 1 hour: chilling   *Serves 6*

5

Menu

Savoury Tartlets

TARTELLETTE DELICATE

Cream of Mushroom Soup

CREMA DI CHIODINI

*Rolled Veal with Walnut
Stuffing*

ROTOLO DI VITELLO ALLE NOCI

*Cold Zabaione with Home-
made Biscuits*

ZABAIONE GELATO CON CIALDE

Preparation

One day ahead
Prepare the tartlets but not the filling. Make
the biscuits to serve with the zabaione.

Three hours ahead
Prepare the zabaione and put in the
refrigerator until well chilled.

Two hours ahead
Prepare the rolled veal and put it on the stove
to cook. Make the filling for the tartlets.

One hour ahead
Prepare the mushroom soup and the croûtons
to serve with it.

Half an hour ahead
Fill the tartlets and put in the oven to heat.

Savoury Tartlets

TARTELLETTE DELICATE

Ingredients	Metric/Imperial	American
frozen puff pastry, thawed	225 g/8 oz	½ pound
oil	2 teaspoons	2 teaspoons
butter	25 g/1 oz	2 tablespoons
salt		
grated nutmeg	¼ teaspoon	¼ teaspoon
plain (all-purpose) flour	1 tablespoon	1 tablespoon
milk	225 ml/8 fl oz	1 cup
eggs	2	2
Mozzarella cheese	225 g/8 oz	½ pound
cooked ham	100 g/4 oz	¼ pound

Preheat the oven to 200 c, 400 f, gas 6.

Roll the pastry out thinly and divide between 6 well-oiled individual 7.5 cm/3 in flan pans. Line each one with a small disc of foil and weigh down with a few dried beans. Put in the moderately hot oven for 10 minutes.

Meanwhile make the filling. Melt the butter in a small pan, add a pinch of salt and freshly grated nutmeg to taste. Add the flour and stir well. Pour in the milk and bring to the boil, stirring constantly. Remove from the heat and add the beaten eggs, cubed Mozzarella cheese and very finely chopped ham.

When ready to serve remove the foil and beans from the tartlets, fill to within 1 cm/½ in of the edge and put in a moderate oven (180 c, 350 f, gas 4) for 10 minutes.

Time: 45 minutes   *Serves 6*

1 Make a thick sauce. Pour in milk, stirring.
2 Add eggs, cubed cheese and finely chopped ham.
3 Fill the partly-cooked tartlet cases and bake.

Cream of Mushroom Soup

Cream of Mushroom Soup

CREMA DI CHIODINI

Ingredients	Metric/Imperial	American
button mushrooms	450 g/1 lb	1 pound
butter	65 g/2½ oz	5 tablespoons
oil	50 ml/2 fl oz	¼ cup
salt and pepper		
plain (all-purpose) flour	50 g/2 oz	½ cup
milk	450 ml/¾ pint	2 cups
stock	1 litre/1¾ pints	1 quart
single (thin) cream	225 ml/8 fl oz	1 cup
Parmesan cheese, grated	25 g/1 oz	¼ cup
chopped parsley	1 tablespoon	1 tablespoon
slices of bread	8	8

Wipe the mushrooms with a clean damp cloth and chop roughly. Melt one-third of the butter in a pan with a little of the oil and cook the mushrooms over a medium heat for 5 minutes.

Melt the remaining butter in a large pan, add a pinch of salt and stir in the flour. Pour in the milk, bring to the boil then cook, stirring constantly, until the sauce thickens. Season with a pinch of pepper.

Sieve or blend some of the mushrooms, then add these to the sauce along with the remainder. Gradually add the stock and bring to the boil. Simmer for 20 minutes, then add the cream, Parmesan cheese and parsley.

Remove the crusts from the bread and cut the bread into small cubes. Heat the remaining oil in a heavy pan over a high heat and fry the cubes until crunchy and golden. Drain on paper towels and keep hot.

Serve the soup hot and hand the croûtons separately.

Time: 1 hour   *Serves 6*

Rolled Veal with Walnut Stuffing

ROTOLO DI VITELLO ALLE NOCI

Ingredients	Metric/Imperial	American
slice of boneless leg of veal	800 g/1¾ lb	1¾ pounds
shelled walnuts	75 g/3 oz	½ cup
Fontina cheese	100 g/4 oz	¼ pound
Parma ham	100 g/4 oz	¼ pound
chopped parsley	1 tablespoon	1 tablespoon
butter	40 g/1½ oz	3 tablespoons
salt and pepper		
milk	450 ml/¾ pint	2 cups

Trim the meat of any excess fat and beat it well with a meat mallet to flatten and enlarge it. Finely chop the walnuts; remove the rind from the cheese and slice the cheese.

Arrange the slices of ham and cheese over the meat and top with walnuts and chopped parsley. Roll up and tie tightly with kitchen string to keep the filling in place during cooking.

Melt the butter in a flameproof casserole over a medium heat, add the rolled veal and brown it lightly on all sides. Season with salt and pepper, add the milk and lower the heat. Cover the casserole and cook for about 1½ hours, stirring occasionally, until most of the milk has evaporated and the cooking juices are creamy.

Remove the string, cut the veal into thick slices and serve covered with the cooking juices.

Time: 2 hours　　　　　　　　　　　　　　*Serves 6*

Rolled Veal with Walnut Stuffing

Cold Zabaione with Home-made Biscuits

ZABAIONE GELATO CON CIALDE

Ingredients	Metric/Imperial	American
For the zabaione:		
egg yolks	6	6
caster (fine granulated) sugar	75 g/3 oz	9 tablespoons
sweet white wine	125 ml/4 fl oz	$\frac{1}{2}$ cup
double (thick) cream	300 ml/$\frac{1}{2}$ pint	1$\frac{1}{4}$ cups
For the biscuits:		
oil	1 teaspoon	1 teaspoon
butter	125 g/4$\frac{1}{2}$ oz	generous $\frac{1}{2}$ cup
caster (fine granulated) sugar	125 g/4$\frac{1}{2}$ oz	$\frac{1}{2}$ cup + 1$\frac{1}{2}$ tablespoons
plain (all-purpose) flour	125 g/4$\frac{1}{2}$ oz	1 cup + 2 tablespoons
egg whites	4	4
vanilla sugar	1 tablespoon	1 tablespoon

First make the zabaione: Beat the egg yolks in a bowl with the sugar until pale and fluffy. Put the bowl over a pan of boiling water, add the wine and cook, stirring constantly, until the mixture thickens. Remove from the heat and leave until cold, stirring from time to time.

Whip the cream stiffly and stir it into the egg mixture. Turn into sundae glasses and put in the refrigerator for 2 hours to become really cold.

Preheat the oven to 220 c, 425 f, gas 7. Oil a baking sheet liberally.

To make the biscuits first allow the butter to come to room temperature. Beat it with a wooden spoon until creamy, then add the sugar, sifted flour and vanilla sugar. Beat the egg whites until standing in stiff peaks and fold gently into the mixture.

Put the biscuit mixture in a piping (pastry) bag fitted with a large nozzle and pipe it on to the baking tray in strips about 5 cm/2 in long, leaving plenty of space between them. Put in the hot oven for just a few minutes in order to harden the biscuits, then remove and leave to cool on the baking tray.

Serve the zabaione decorated with some of the biscuits and hand the remaining biscuits separately.

Time: 40 minutes + 2 hours: chilling   *Serves 6*

Cold Zabaione with Home Made biscuits
1 Beat batter until creamy, then add sugar and mix well before adding flour.
2 Fold the stiffly beaten egg whites into the mixture carefully.
3 Pipe strips onto a greased baking tray.

Menu

Fresh Pea Soup with Ham
ZUPPA DI PISELLI AL PROSCIUTTO AFFUMICATO

Poached Brill with Piquant Sauce
ROMBO LESSATO CON SALSA FANTASIA

Fillet of Beef en Croûte
FILETTO DI BUE DEL BUONGUSTAIO

Queen Cake
TORTA REGINA

Preparation

One day ahead
Prepare the Queen cake and the accompanying banana sauce. Store the cake at room temperature, the sauce in the refrigerator.

Three hours ahead
Prepare the fillet of beef ready for cooking.

Two hours ahead
Prepare the pea soup and croûtons, but do not put together until the last moment.

One hour ahead
Put the beef fillet in the oven and prepare the poached brill and sauce.

Half an hour ahead
Finish the pea soup and remove the banana sauce from the refrigerator.

Fresh Pea Soup with Ham

ZUPPA DI PISELLI AL PROSCIUTTO AFFUMICATO

Ingredients	Metric/Imperial	American
fresh peas	1.2 kg/2¾ lb	2¾ pounds
raw smoked ham	100 g/4 oz	¼ pound
onion	½	½
butter	100 g/4 oz	½ cup
salt and pepper		
chopped parsley	1 tablespoon	1 tablespoon
stock	1 litre/1¾ pints	1 quart
croûtons		
Parmesan cheese, grated	40 g/1½ oz	3 tablespoons

Shell the peas; finely chop the ham and onion. Melt 25 g/1 oz/2 tablespoons of the butter in a large pan, add the ham and onion and cook until the onion is golden. Add the peas and leave for a few minutes to absorb flavour.

Season with a pinch of salt and pepper, add the chopped parsley and 300 ml/½ pint/1¼ cups of the stock. Cover and cook over a low heat for about 30 minutes. Add the remaining stock and bring to the boil.

Meanwhile prepare the croûtons, using the remaining butter to fry them. Divide between 6 soup bowls and sprinkle with grated Parmesan cheese and the hot butter.

Immediately before serving pour the boiling soup over the croûtons.

Time: 50 minutes   *Serves 6*

Fresh Pea Soup with Ham

Poached Brill with Piquant Sauce
1 Add vinegar to fish, water and vegetables.
2 Remove the fish, cool and fillet into portions. Keep warm.

Poached Brill with Piquant Sauce

ROMBO LESSATO CON SALSA FANTASIA

Ingredients	Metric/Imperial	American
brill or halibut	1 (1.4 kg/3 lb)	1 (3 pound)
carrot	1	1
onion	1	1
celery stalk	1	1
bay leaf	1	1
wine vinegar	2 tablespoons	3 tablespoons
salt and pepper		
For the sauce:		
pickled green (sweet) peppers	350 g/12 oz	¾ pound
capers	1 tablespoon	1 tablespoon
anchovy fillets in oil	25 g/1 oz	1 ounce
garlic clove	1	1
chopped parsley	1 tablespoon	1 tablespoon
oil	1½ tablespoons	2 tablespoons

If the fish has not already been cleaned, slit open along the body, remove the insides. Wash under running cold water, scraping the outside to remove scales. Trim the fins. Place in an oval pan or fish kettle.

Chop the vegetables finely and add them to the pan together with the bay leaf, vinegar, a little salt and just enough cold water to cover. Bring to the boil, then simmer very gently for 15 minutes or until the fish is just tender. Remove the fish very carefully, so as not to break it, and cut it into portions. Arrange these on a heated serving dish.

While the fish is cooking prepare the sauce: chop the peppers, capers, anchovies and garlic finely. Mix thoroughly with the chopped parsley. Heat the oil in a small pan, add the chopped mixture and cook over a low heat for about 20 minutes. If the sauce becomes dry, moisten with a little water.

Cover the fish with the hot sauce and serve at once.

Time: 1¾ hours   *Serves 6*

3 Chop peppers, capers, anchovies and garlic.
4 Heat oil in a pan and cook chopped mixture.
5 Divide the hot sauce over the fish portions.

Fillet of Beef en Croûte

FILETTO DI BUE DEL BUONGUSTAIO

Ingredients	Metric/Imperial	American
butter	25 g/1 oz	2 tablespoons
beef fillet	1.2 kg/2¾ lb	2¾ pounds
salt and pepper		
asparagus	800 g/1¾ lb	1¾ pounds
frozen puff pastry, thawed	350 g/12 oz	¾ pound
Parma ham	100 g/4 oz	¼ pound
egg	1	1

Fillet of Beef en Croute
1 Roll out the pastry, arrange a layer of ham and asparagus on the pastry. Lay meat on top and cover with remaining asparagus and ham.
2 Wrap over the pastry and seal the edges.
3 Prick the pastry and decorate with scraps. Brush with beaten egg before cooking.

Melt the butter in a heavy pan, add the piece of beef and brown it lightly on all sides. Season with salt and pepper and leave to cook for about 15 minutes, allow to cool.

Meanwhile clean the asparagus well, removing the white woody parts. Tie it in bundles, stand upright in a tall pan with water to just below the tips and cover the tips with a dome of foil. Bring to the boil and cook for 10 minutes. Drain well.

Preheat the oven to 200 C, 400 F, gas 6.

Put the pastry on a floured work surface and roll out to a rectangle about 5 mm/¼ in thick. Place a layer of ham on the pastry, a layer of asparagus, then the meat; add another layer of asparagus and finish with ham. Brush the pastry with water and seal the ends well to ensure that the pastry parcel will not open.

Prick the pastry with a fork in several places and brush with beaten egg.

Cook the beef en croûte in the moderately hot oven for about 20 minutes or until the pastry is golden.

Time: 1½ hours *Serves 6*

Queen Cake

Queen Cake

TORTA REGINA

Ingredients	Metric/Imperial	American
For the sauce:		
egg yolks	2	2
caster (fine granulated) sugar	75 g / 3 oz	9 tablespoons
milk	225 ml / 8 fl oz	1 cup
vanilla sugar	25 g / 1 oz	2 tablespoons
overripe bananas	2	2
brandy	2 tablespoons	3 tablespoons
For the cake:		
granulated sugar	200 g / 7 oz	1 cup
butter	50 g / 2 oz	¼ cup
egg	1	1
cocoa powder, unsweetened	50 g / 2 oz	½ cup
vanilla sugar	25 g / 1 oz	2 tablespoons
milk	125 ml / 4 fl oz	½ cup
natural yogurt	150 g / 5 oz	½ cup
bicarbonate of soda (baking soda)	1 teaspoon	1 teaspoon
plain (all-purpose) flour	100 g / 4 oz	1 cup

First make the sauce: Beat the egg yolks in a bowl with the sugar until light and fluffy. Heat the milk and add it to the egg mixture with the vanilla sugar. Put the bowl over a pan of boiling water and cook, stirring constantly, until it begins to thicken. Remove from the heat. Mash the bananas, stir them into the sauce with the brandy and leave it to cool.

Preheat the oven to 200 c, 400 f, gas 6.

To make the cake, mix together in a large bowl the melted butter, sugar, egg, cocoa powder, vanilla sugar, milk, yogurt and the bicarbonate of soda. Sift the flour over the top a little at a time and mix well.

Grease and flour a 20 cm / 8 in cake pan and bake the cake in the moderately hot oven for 40 minutes. Allow to cool before serving accompanied with the banana sauce.

Time: 1 hour 20 minutes   *Serves 6*

Menu

Salmon in Pastry
PATE AL SALMONE

Duck with Orange and Rice
ANATRA ALL'ARANCIA CON RISO

Walnut Salad
INSALATA ALLE NOCI

Raspberry Meringue
MERINGATA AI LAMPONI

Preparation

One day ahead
Prepare the salmon in pastry, cover with foil and put in the refrigerator. Remove 4 hours before serving time.

Three hours ahead
Prepare the meringue and raspberry sauce and put in the refrigerator.

Two hours ahead
Wash and prepare the salad but do not mix with the dressing. Prepare the duck ready for cooking.

One hour ahead
Cook the duck in the orange sauce.

Half an hour ahead
Cook the rice and complete the duck dish.

Salmon in Pastry
1 Cool the salmon and remove the bones.
2 Layer the salmon, egg, seasoning and herbs.
3 Cover with the remaining pastry and decorate.

Salmon in Pastry

PATE AL SALMONE

Ingredients	Metric/Imperial	American
For the pastry:		
plain (all-purpose) flour	275 g/10 oz	2½ cups
salt		
butter	165 g/5½ oz	⅔ cup
egg	1	1
egg yolk	1	1
For the filling:		
fresh salmon	1.4 kg/3 lb	3 pounds
bay leaf	1	1
garlic clove	1	1
salt		
dry white wine	125 ml/4 fl oz	½ cup
hard-boiled (cooked) eggs	3	3
chopped thyme	½ teaspoon	½ teaspoon
olive oil	1 tablespoon	1 tablespoon
milk	1 tablespoon	1 tablespoon

First prepare the pastry. Sift the flour into a bowl with a pinch of salt. Chop the butter into small pieces and rub it into the flour with the fingertips until the mixture looks like breadcrumbs. Add the beaten egg and egg yolk with 1 tablespoon of cold water and mix until firm. Roll the dough into a ball, wrap in foil and refrigerate for at least 30 minutes.

Meanwhile put the salmon in a large pan with the bay leaf, crushed garlic clove, a pinch of salt, the wine and 225 ml/8 fl oz/1 cup water. Bring to the boil, then cook over a very low heat for 10 minutes. Take out the salmon, remove the skin, head and backbone and flake the flesh on to a plate.

Preheat the oven to 180 c, 350 f, gas 4.

Roll out two-thirds of the pastry and use it to line a small loaf pan, overlapping the edges. Put a layer of salmon on the pastry, then a layer of coarsely chopped egg; season with a pinch of thyme, salt and pepper and sprinkle with a little oil. Continue in this way until all the ingredients are finished.

Roll out the remaining pastry to make the lid. Fold in the overlapping pastry and dampen with water; press the lid on firmly. Decorate the top with pastry trimmings and brush the surface with the milk. Punch a small hole in the centre and insert a little roll of foil, to allow steam to escape during cooking.

Bake in the moderate oven for 1½ hours until golden brown. Allow to cool for 10 minutes and turn out on to a serving dish and cool before serving.

Time: 2 hours + 2 hours: chilling   *Serves 6*

Duck with Orange and Rice

Duck with Orange and Rice

ANATRA ALL'ARANCIA CON RISO

Ingredients	Metric/Imperial	American
medium-sized oven-ready duck	1	1
salt and pepper		
butter	1½ tablespoons	2 tablespoons
dry white wine	125 ml/4 fl oz	½ cup
oranges	4	4
lemon	½	½
long-grain rice	350 g/12 oz	1⅔ cups
sugar	1 tablespoon	1 tablespoon
brandy	2 tablespoons	3 tablespoons

Season the duck with salt and pepper. Melt all the butter except 1 teaspoon in a large flameproof casserole, add the duck and cook until lightly browned all over. Add the wine, juice of 2 oranges and ½ lemon and the stock. Put in a moderately hot oven (200 C, 400 F, gas 6) for about 1 hour.

Cook the rice according to type.

Meanwhile peel the remaining oranges and slice them thinly. Chop the rind finely and plunge into boiling water for 1 minute. Put the rind in a small pan over high heat with the sugar, brandy and remaining butter. Cook until the sugar caramelizes.

When the duck is cooked pour the sauce over it and add the orange slices. Return to the warmed oven to keep hot.

Put a portion of rice and duck on each plate, pour some of the sauce over and garnish with orange slices. Serve very hot.

Time: 1¼ hours   *Serves 6*

Walnut Salad

INSALATA ALLE NOCI

Ingredients	Metric/Imperial	American
red lettuce (radichio)	1	1
walnuts	150 g/5 oz	5 ounces
Fontina cheese	150 g/5 oz	5 ounces
mustard powder	2 teaspoons	2 teaspoons
oil	3 tablespoons	scant ¼ cup
salt and pepper		

Wash and dry the lettuce and slice it finely. Shell the walnuts and chop the kernels; remove the rind from the cheese and dice the cheese. Put all three in a salad bowl.

To make the dressing put the mustard, oil and salt and pepper in a screw-top jar and shake well. When ready to serve pour the dressing over the salad and mix thoroughly.

Time: 20 minutes   *Serves 6*

Walnut Salad

Raspberry Meringue

MERINGATA AI LAMPONI

Ingredients	Metric/Imperial	American
egg whites	3	3
icing (confectioners') sugar	200 g/7 oz	scant cup
double (thick) cream	300 ml/½ pint	1¼ cups
fresh raspberries	600 g/1¼ lb	4 cups

Put the egg whites in a mixing bowl and beat until stiff. Gently fold in 175 g/6 oz/¾ cup icing sugar, then beat again until smooth and satiny and standing in peaks.

Line two baking trays with rice paper. Pipe half the meringue mixture on to each tray so as to make a large disc. Cook in a moderate oven (160 C, 325 F, gas 3) until dry and light, but not golden.

Meanwhile whip the cream and sweeten it with 2–3 tablespoons of icing sugar. Add a few of the raspberries, folding them in gently to make sure they do not get squashed.

Place one meringue on a large dish. Pile on the Chantilly cream and top with the second meringue. Put in the refrigerator for 1 hour or in the freezer for 30 minutes.

Meanwhile purée the remaining raspberries. Pour the purée into a sauceboat and serve separately with the meringue.

Time: 1 hour + 1 hour: chilling   *Serves 6*

1 Pipe the meringue with a plain pipe starting in the centre to make a round disc.
2 Pile the cream in the centre of the cooked meringue and top with the second disc; chill.
3 Purée the raspberries to serve as a sauce.

Menu

Salmon Roll in Gelatine
ROTOLO DI SALMONE IN GELATINA

Soup with Semolina Dumplings
BRODO CON MORBIDELLE DI SEMOLINO

Veal in Green Sauce
VITELLO AL VERDI

Crêpes with Confectioners' Custard
CREPES ALLA CREMA PASTICCIERA

Preparation

One day ahead
Prepare the salmon roll, cover it with foil and put it in the refrigerator. Boil the rolled veal loin and prepare the meat stock for the dumplings.

Three hours ahead
Prepare the crêpes and the confectioners' custard ready for stuffing.

Two hours ahead
Prepare the mushrooms and the sauce for the veal.

One hour ahead
Complete the veal and prepare the mixture for the dumplings.

Half an hour ahead
Cook the dumplings in the stock. Complete the crêpes and keep them warm.

Salmon Roll in Gelatine

ROTOLO DI SALMONE IN GELATINA

Ingredients	Metric/Imperial	American
French beans	450 g/1 lb	1 pound
salt		
plain (all-purpose) flour	100 g/4 oz	1 cup
eggs	2	2
milk	175 ml/6 fl oz	$\frac{3}{4}$ cup
oil		
slices of smoked salmon	150 g/5 oz	5 ounces
gelatine	1 envelope	1 sachet
lemon	$\frac{1}{2}$	$\frac{1}{2}$

Top and tail the French beans and cook them in lightly salted boiling water for 12 minutes or until just tender. Drain and leave to cool.

Put the flour and ½ teaspoon salt in a small bowl and add the eggs. Beat until well mixed, then gradually add the milk, beating constantly to make a smooth batter.

Brush a small non-stick shallow pan with oil and place it over medium heat. Pour in 1 tablespoon of batter at a time and swirl it around to make a very thin pancake. Cook for about a minute, until pale brown underneath, then turn the pancake with a spatula and brown the other side. Slide it on to a plate and continue until all the batter is used up, brushing the pan with oil when necessary.

Lay a pancake on the work surface and put a slice of smoked salmon on top. Add another pancake, then a thin layer of French beans. Continue in this way, stacking 6 pancakes at a time until all the ingredients are used up. Roll each 6 pancakes up as tightly as possible into a cylinder. Refrigerate for about 1 hour.

Slice the rolls carefully with a sharp knife and lay the slices in a serving dish. Make up the gelatine by sprinkling it into 225 ml/8 fl oz/1 cup boiling water and stirring until dissolved. Allow to cool and pour a little over each slice of salmon roll. Stand in the refrigerator until set. Serve garnished with lemon slices and any remaining smoked salmon.

Time: 1¾ hour + 2 hours: chilling *Serves 6*

1

2

3

4

Soup with Semolina Dumplings

Soup with Semolina Dumplings

BRODO CON MORBIDELLE DI SEMOLINO

Ingredients	Metric/Imperial	American
shin of beef	350 g/12 oz	$\frac{3}{4}$ pound
veal bone	350 g/12 oz	$\frac{3}{4}$ pound
salt		
carrot	1	1
celery stalk	1	1
onion	1	1
bunch of parsley	1	1
butter	40 g/1$\frac{1}{2}$ oz	3 tablespoons
Parmesan cheese, grated	60 g/2$\frac{1}{2}$ oz	$\frac{2}{3}$ cup
eggs, separated	3	3
nutmeg	$\frac{1}{4}$ teaspoon	$\frac{1}{4}$ teaspoon
semolina	150 g/5 oz	1 scant cup

Put the beef and veal bone in a large pan with 3.5 litres/6 pints/3$\frac{1}{2}$ quarts of cold water and a pinch of salt. Bring slowly to the boil, removing any scum which forms with a slotted spoon.

Meanwhile roughly chop the carrot, celery, onion and parsley. Add all the vegetables to the pan with the meat, cover and simmer over a very low heat for 3 hours. Remove any scum which forms during cooking with a slotted spoon. Strain the stock and pour it back into the rinsed-out pan.

Put the softened butter into a small bowl and beat into it some of the Parmesan cheese, the egg yolks, a pinch of salt, the nutmeg and semolina. Beat the egg whites until stiff and fold them into the semolina mixture.

Bring the stock to the boil. Add the semolina mixture half a teaspoon at a time; little dumplings will form immediately. Allow to cook for 15 minutes and serve hot, garnished with the remaining Parmesan cheese.

Time: 3$\frac{1}{2}$ hours   *Serves 6*

Salmon Roll in Gelatine
1 Lay one pancake on a flat surface with a slice of smoked salmon on top.
2 Cover with a pancake and then beans.
3 Continue until there are six layers. Roll tightly into a cylinder and chill.
4 Cut the pancake rolls into slices.
5 Arrange on a plate and pour on the gelatine.

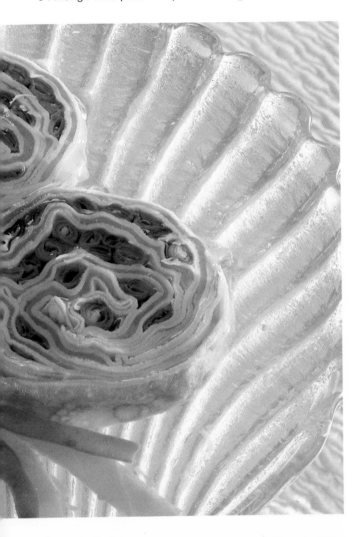

Veal in Green Sauce

VITELLO AL VERDI

Ingredients	Metric/Imperial	American
rolled veal loin	1.2 kg/2¼ lb	2¼ pounds
onion	1	1
celery stalk	1	1
carrot	1	1
salt and pepper		
egg	1	1
mushrooms	600 g/1¼ lb	1¼ pounds
oil	125 ml/4 fl oz	½ cup
lemon juice	50 ml/2 fl oz	¼ cup
garlic clove	1	1
large bunch of parsley	1	1

Put the veal in a casserole. Prepare and chop the onion, celery and carrot into small dice. Add to the casserole, season with salt and cover with cold water. Bring to the boil and simmer for 2 hours, covered, over a low heat. Remove the meat and allow to cool. Strain and reserve the cooking liquid.

Meanwhile hard-boil (cook) the egg for 8 minutes or until hard; cool it under cold running water. Clean the mushrooms, remove the stalks and slice the caps thinly. Mix the oil, lemon juice, crushed garlic clove and salt and pepper together in a shallow dish. Marinate the mushroom caps in the mixture for 1 hour.

Make a sauce by puréeing the mushroom stalks with the egg, chopped parsley and a little reserved cooking liquid in a blender or food processor.

Carve the meat and put the slices on a serving plate. Arrange the mushroom caps on top and cover with the sauce.

Time: 2½ hours   *Serves 6*

1 Marinate the mushrooms in oil and seasoning.
2 Blend the mushroom stalks with egg, parsley and a little cooking liquid.
3 Arrange carved meat with mushrooms and sauce.

1

2

3

Crêpes with Confectioners' Custard

Crêpes with Confectioners' Custard

CREPES ALLA CREMA PASTICCIERA

Ingredients	Metric/Imperial	American
lemon	1	1
plain (all-purpose) flour	200 g/7 oz	1¾ cups
caster (fine granulated) sugar	100 g/4 oz	½ cup
eggs	3	3
milk	1 litre/1¾ pints	1 quart
egg yolks	2	2
butter	75 g/3 oz	6 tablespoons
icing (confectioners') sugar		
cognac	50 ml/2 fl oz	¼ cup

Put a teaspoon of lemon rind in a bowl with 175 g/6 oz/ 1½ cups of flour, 40 g/1½ oz/3 tablespoons of sugar and the 3 whole eggs. Beat the mixture well with a whisk, then beat in half the milk to make a smooth batter.

Brush a small shallow pan or a hot plate with oil and use the batter to make a large number of small pancakes or crêpes.

Beat together the egg yolks and remaining sugar in a pan. When the mixture becomes light in colour add the remaining flour and a little lemon rind. Gradually add the remaining milk, stirring continuously. Put the pan on a low heat and bring to the boil, stirring. Remove from the heat and allow to cool.

Spread each crêpe with custard, then fold it in half and in half again to form a triangle shape.

Heat the butter in a large heavy pan and add a little icing (confectioners') sugar and the cognac. Put in the crêpes and cook them for a few minutes, just enough to get them hot. Dust them with more of the sugar and serve at once.

Time: 30 minutes   *Serves 6*

Menu

Saffron Dumplings
GNOCCHETTI ALLO ZAFFERANO

Bass with Sweet Peppers
BRANZINETTI ALL MUGNAIA SAPORITI

Fillet Steak Salad
FILETTO IN INSALATA

Diplomats Trifle
BUDINO FREDDO ALLA DIPLOMATICA

Preparation

One day ahead
Prepare the trifle, cover and put in the refrigerator. Prepare the sweet peppers for the bass and leave to marinate in a cool place.

Three hours ahead
Prepare the mushrooms for the steak salad, brush with lemon juice to prevent blackening and put in the refrigerator.

Two hours ahead
Prepare the dough for the dumplings and leave to rest. Cook the bass and keep hot. Turn out the trifle, decorate and return to the refrigerator.

One hour ahead
Complete and cook the dumplings. Prepare the steak salad.

Half an hour ahead
Prepare the saffron sauce for the dumplings. Add the prepared sweet peppers to the bass.

Saffron Dumplings

Saffron Dumplings

GNOCCHETTI ALLO ZAFFERANO

Ingredients	Metric/Imperial	American
plain (all-purpose) flour	350 g/12 oz	3 cups
fresh breadcrumbs	200 g/7 oz	3½ cups
eggs	2	2
egg yolk	1	1
cooked ham	100 g/4 oz	¼ pound
cheese, grated	75 g/3 oz	¾ cup
milk	175 ml/6 fl oz	¾ cup
grated nutmeg	¼ teaspoon	¼ teaspoon
salt and pepper		
saffron strands	½ teaspoon	½ teaspoon
butter	40 g/1½ oz	3 tablespoons
small onion	¼	¼
single (thin) cream	225/ml/8 fl oz	1 cup

Sift the flour on to a work surface and mix in the breadcrumbs. Break the eggs and egg yolk into the centre, add the chopped ham, grated cheese, milk, nutmeg and a pinch of salt. Mix well together and knead for about 10 minutes until the mixture forms a ball. Cover with a tea-towel and leave to rest in a warm place for about 1 hour.

Knead the dough for about 5 minutes, then cut it into finger-sized strips and squash them lightly with a fork to form the dumplings.

Soak the saffron strands in a little very hot water.

Cook the dumplings in plenty of salted boiling water for a few minutes then remove with a slotted spoon.

Melt the butter in a large pan. Chop the onion finely and add it to the pan together with the dumplings; cook, stirring with a wooden spoon, until golden. Add the saffron liquid to the cream and pour into the pan. Season generously with pepper, stir well and serve at once.

Time: 1 hour + 1 hour: resting   *Serves 6*

Bass with Sweet Peppers

BRANZINETTI ALLA MUGNAIA SAPORITI

Ingredients	Metric/Imperial	American
red (sweet) peppers	3	3
oil	2 tablespoons	3 tablespoons
garlic cloves	1	1
basil leaves	4	4
salt and pepper		
bass	6 (225 g/8 oz)	6 ($\frac{1}{2}$ pound)
flour	40 g/1$\frac{1}{2}$ oz	6 tablespoons
butter	100 g/4 oz	$\frac{1}{2}$ cup
chopped parsley	1 tablespoon	1 tablespoon
lemon	$\frac{1}{2}$	$\frac{1}{2}$

Put the red peppers under a hot grill (broiler) or in a flame to char the skins; plunge into cold water. Peel,

Bass with Sweet Peppers
1 Dip the fish in seasoned flour. Heat the oil in a pan and fry the fish with garlic and basil.
2 Put on a heated plate; sprinkle with parsley and lemon juice.
3 Arrange the peppers on top of the fish.

deseed and remove the stalks. Rinse and dry, then cut into slivers. Put the oil in a shallow container with the crushed garlic, chopped basil leaves and a pinch of salt and pepper. Add the peppers and leave to marinate for a few hours or overnight.

Prepare the bass ready for cooking, wash and dry on paper towels. Dip in seasoned flour. Melt the butter in a heavy pan, add the bass and cook, turning once, until golden brown and just tender. Arrange in a heated serving dish and sprinkle with parsley and lemon juice. Remove the garlic from the peppers and cover the fish with them. Pour over the cooking juices and serve at once.

Time: 50 minutes + 4 hours: marinating   *Serves 6*

Fillet Steak Salad

FILETTO IN INSALATA

Ingredients	Metric/Imperial	American
mushrooms	450 g/1 lb	1 pound
lemon juice	125 ml/4 fl oz	$\frac{1}{2}$ cup
truffle paste	2 teaspoons	2 teaspoons
oil	3 tablespoons	scant $\frac{1}{4}$ cup
salt and pepper		
beef tomato	1	1
fillet steak	450 g/1 lb	1 pound

Prepare the mushrooms by wiping them with a clean damp cloth; do not wash. Dip them in lemon juice and slice thinly (if they are to stand for any length of time put them in the lemon juice and refrigerate).

Mix the truffle paste with the oil and a little lemon juice, season and leave for the flavours to blend. Plunge the tomato briefly into boiling water, peel and dice.

Cut the fillet steak into thin slivers. Put in a bowl with the truffle mixture, the mushrooms; add the diced tomato, arrange and serve.

Time: 30 minutes   *Serves 6*

1 Mix truffle paste with oil and lemon juice.
2 Peel the tomatoes and dice.
3 Cut the beef into thin strips; mix with truffle.

Diplomats Trifle

BUDINO FREDDO ALLA DIPLOMATICA

Ingredients	Metric/Imperial	American
crystallized fruit	100 g/4 oz	$\frac{1}{4}$ pound
Kirsch	125 ml/4 fl oz	$\frac{1}{2}$ cup
gelatine	5 teaspoons	5 teaspoons
egg yolks	6	6
caster (fine granulated) sugar	150 g/5 oz	$\frac{2}{3}$ cup
milk	350 ml/12 fl oz	$1\frac{1}{2}$ cups
vanilla pod	1	1
double (thick) cream	350 ml/12 fl oz	$1\frac{1}{2}$ cups
sponge finger biscuits	200 g/7 oz	7 ounces

Slice the crystallized fruit finely and soak in the Kirsch. Sprinkle the gelatine on to 125 ml/4 fl oz/$\frac{1}{2}$ cup of boiling water and stir until dissolved.

Beat the egg yolks and sugar together for about 15 minutes until light and fluffy, then add the warmed milk and vanilla pod. stir in the prepared gelatine, put in a pan over very low heat and cook, stirring continuously, until thick. Remove from the heat, take out the vanilla pod and leave to cool.

Whip the cream and stir into the cooled custard. Remove the crystallized fruit from the Kirsch. Add a little water to the Kirsch and lightly dip the sponge fingers in it. (Reserve a little of the fruit for decoration.)

Rinse out a 20–23 cm/8–9 in soufflé dish or mould with cold water and pour in a layer of custard. Arrange some of the biscuits on top, followed by crystallized fruit. Continue in this way until all the ingredients are used up, finishing with custard. Cover and refrigerate.

When ready to serve immerse the mould in warm water for a few seconds and invert on to a plate. Decorate with reserved fruit.

Time: 50 minutes + 2 hours: chilling   *Serves 6*

Diplomats Trifle

Menu

Soup with Spinach Dumplings
BRODO CON GNOCHETTI VERDI

Sea Bream (Porgy) with Anchovy Butter
DENTICE AL BURRO D'ACCIUGA

Chicken Breasts Rossini
PETTI DI POLLO ALLA ROSSINI

Mascarpone Cheese Dessert
DOLCE DI PITTORE

Preparation

One day ahead
Prepare the soup and the anchovy butter for the bream and put in the refrigerator.

Three hours ahead
Prepare the dumplings.

Two hours ahead
Prepare the Mascarpone cheese dessert and put in the refrigerator.

One hour ahead
Put the fish in the oven. Prepare the sauce for the chicken breasts.

Half an hour ahead
Drop the dumplings in boiling water and leave to cook. Complete the chicken breasts. Slice the anchovy butter.

Soup with Spinach Dumplings

Soup with Spinach Dumplings

BRODO CON GNOCCETTI VERDI

Ingredients	Metric/Imperial	American
For the soup:		
shin of beef	450 g/1 lb	1 pound
stewing veal	450 g/1 lb	1 pound
beef or veal bone	1	1
salt and pepper		
carrot	1	1
onion	1	1
celery stalk	1	1
bunch of parsley	1	1
For the dumplings:		
butter	65 g/2½ oz	5 tablespoons
plain (all-purpose) flour	50 g/2 oz	¼ cup
cooked spinach	100 g/4 oz	¼ pound
Parmesan cheese, grated	40 g/1½ oz	3 tablespoons
salt		
grated nutmeg	¼ teaspoon	¼ teaspoon
eggs	2	2

Put the meat and the bone in a large pan, add 3 litres/5¼ pints/3 quarts of cold water, salt and peppercorns and bring to the boil, removing the surface scum every so often with a slotted spoon. Chop the carrot, onion, celery and parsley finely and add to the pan. Cover and cook for 3 hours over a low heat.

Strain the broth through a sieve, leave until cold and remove any surface fat.

To make the dumplings first melt the butter in a small pan and stir in the flour, then the drained and chopped spinach. Add 600 ml/1 pint/2½ cups of cold broth and cook until the mixture is coming away from the sides of the pan. Remove from the heat and stir in the grated Parmesan cheese, a pinch of salt, the nutmeg and the eggs, one at a time.

Bring the remaining broth to the boil in a large pan. Add the dumpling mixture in teaspoonfuls, cook for about 10 minutes then serve at once.

Time: 4 hours   *Serves 6*

Sea Bream (Porgy) with Anchovy Butter

DENTICE AL BURRO D'ACCIUGA

Ingredients	Metric/Imperial	American
salted anchovies	100 g/4 oz	$\frac{1}{4}$ pound
garlic clove	$\frac{1}{2}$	$\frac{1}{2}$
sprig of parsley	1	1
butter	100 g/4 oz	$\frac{1}{2}$ cup
sea bream (porgy)	1 (1.2 kg/2¾ lb)	1 (2¾ pound)
fresh breadcrumbs	50 g/2 oz	1 cup
salt and pepper		
oil	1 tablespoon	1 tablespoon

Rinse the anchovies under running water, remove the tails and backbones and chop the flesh finely.

Finely chop the garlic and parsley. Bring the butter to room temperature, mix with the anchovies, garlic and parsley and form into a cylinder about 2.5 cm/1 in across. Wrap in foil and put in the refrigerator.

Clean the fish, removing the insides and gills but keeping the head on. Put the fish in a baking pan, sprinkle with the breadcrumbs, salt and pepper to taste and brush with oil. Bake in a hot oven (220 C, 425 F, gas 7) for about 20 minutes.

Lay the fish carefully on a heated serving dish and garnish with slices of cold anchovy butter. Serve at once.

Time: 30 minutes   *Serves 6*

Sea Bream with Anchovy Butter

Chicken Breasts Rossini

PETTI DI POLLO ALLA ROSSINI

Ingredients	Metric/Imperial	American
onion	1	1
carrot	1	1
butter	75 g/3 oz	6 tablespoons
flour	1 teaspoon	1 teaspoon
stock	125 ml/4 fl oz	½ cup
dry white wine	50 ml/2 fl oz	¼ cup
sprig of parsley	1	1
salt and pepper		
boneless chicken breasts	6	6
Madeira wine	1½ tablespoons	2 tablespoons
slices of crusty bread	6	6
liver pâté	100 g/4 oz	¼ pound
small truffle (optional)	1	1

Finely dice the onion and carrot. Melt one-third of the butter in a small pan, add the onion and carrot and cook over a medium heat until golden. Stir in the flour, then gradually add the stock, white wine, chopped parsley and seasoning. Leave to cook over a low heat for about 25 minutes. Sieve the sauce and keep warm.

Melt the remaining butter in a large heavy pan and brown the chicken breasts lightly on both sides, cooking for at least 8–10 minutes. Season to taste, sprinkle with Madeira, remove and keep warm. Fry the bread in the hot butter and cooking juices.

Arrange the fried bread on a heated serving plate. Put a chicken breast on each piece and top with a small slice of pâté and slivers of truffle. Pour over the prepared sauce.

Time: 40 minutes *Serves 6*

Chicken Breasts Rossini
1 Add onion and carrot to butter; make sauce.
2 Sieve the sauce and keep warm.
3 Heat butter in a pan and fry chicken.

Mascarpone Cheese Dessert

DOLCE DI PITTORE

Ingredients	Metric/Imperial	American
eggs, separated	3	3
caster (fine granulated) sugar	50 g/2 oz	¼ cup
Mascarpone cheese	350 g/12 oz	¾ pound
sponge finger biscuits half covered in chocolate	150 g/5 oz	5 ounces
brandy	175 ml/6 fl oz	¾ cup
milk	50 ml/2 fl oz	¼ cup
cocoa powder	1 tablespoon	1 tablespoon
sugar	1 teaspoon	1 teaspoon
cornflour (cornstarch)	1 teaspoon	1 teaspoon
strong black coffee	50 ml/2 fl oz	¼ cup

Beat the egg yolks and sugar in a bowl until light and fluffy, then incorporate the Mascarpone cheese. Beat the egg whites until they form soft peaks and gently fold them into the cheese mixture.

Dip the sponge finger biscuits in the mixed brandy and milk and lay them in a deep serving dish. Pour over the Mascarpone cream.

In a small pan, mix the cocoa with the teaspoon of sugar and cornflour. Stir in the coffee, place over a low heat and cook, stirring constantly for a few minutes, until syrupy.

Using a spoon, decorate the top of the cream with artistic swirls of syrup. Put the dessert in the refrigerator for 2 hours before serving.

Time: 20 minutes + 2 hours: chilling   *Serves 6*

4 Fry bread slices until golden each side.
5 Top bread with chicken, arrange a slice of pâté on each portion and pour over the sauce.

Mascarpone Cheese Dessert

Menu

Individual Spinach Soufflés
PICCOLI SOUFFLE AGLI SPINACI E MOZZARELLA

Crab Soup
ZUPPA DI POLPA DI GRANCHIO

Stuffed Breast of Veal
PETTO DI VITELLO FARCITO BRASATO

Zarina's Sweet
DOLCE DELLA ZARINA

Preparation

One day ahead
Prepare and cook the stuffed breast of veal but do not carve. Prepare the dessert without decorating it. Allow both to cool, then cover and put in the refrigerator.

Three hours ahead
Prepare the soufflé mixture up to the stage before the egg white is added. Complete the dessert. Remove fat from veal cooking juices. Remove veal from refrigerator.

Two hours ahead
Prepare the crab soup and the accompanying toast but do not put the two together until ready to serve.

One hour ahead
Complete the soufflés and heat the oven ready to cook them. Reheat the veal.

Half an hour ahead
Carve the veal and keep hot. Cook the soufflés.

Individual Spinach Soufflés

PICCOLI SOUFFLE AGLI SPINACI E
MOZZARELLA

Ingredients	Metric/Imperial	American
fresh spinach	800 g/1¾ lb	1¾ pounds
butter	25 g/1 oz	2 tablespoons
plain (all purpose) flour	25 g/1 oz	¼ cup
salt		
milk		
grated nutmeg	¼ teaspoon	¼ teaspoon
oil	2 teaspoons	2 teaspoons
dried breadcrumbs	2 tablespoons	3 tablespoons
eggs, separated	4	4
Mozzarella cheese, diced	200 g/7 oz	7 ounces

Wash the spinach thoroughly in several changes of cold water. Remove any coarse stalks or ribs. Put in a large pan and cook over a low heat in the water clinging to the leaves until tender; about 10 minutes. Drain and allow to cool. Press out excess liquid and blend finely.

Melt the butter in a small pan over a low heat; stir in the flour and a pinch of salt. Gradually add the milk, stirring constantly, bring to the boil and simmer until the sauce is thick and smooth. Stir in the chopped spinach, season with nutmeg and leave to cool.

Preheat the oven to 220 C, 425 F, gas 7. Brush 6 ramekins or individual soufflé dishes with oil and sprinkle with the breadcrumbs.

Add the egg yolks to the spinach mixture. Beat the whites until they stand in stiff peaks. Stir the Mozzarella cheese into the spinach, then carefully fold in the beaten egg whites. Pour into the prepared dishes.

Put in the hot oven for 20 minutes until the soufflés are well risen and golden brown. Serve at once.

Time: 1½ hours   *Serves 6*

Individual Spinach Soufflés
1 Add cooked spinach to sauce with nutmeg.
2 Stir in egg yolks to spinach mixture.
3 Whisk egg whites until light and fluffy.
4 Fold into spinach and pour into dishes.

Crab Soup

leave to dry. Reserve a few sprigs for garnishing the soup and chop the rest finely with the garlic.

Heat the oil in a large high-sided pan over a moderate heat, add the prepared vegetables and cook for 5 minutes. Pour in the fish stock all at once, add salt if necessary and bring to the boil. Simmer for 20 minutes, then purée in a blender, food processor or vegetable mill.

Pour the soup back into the rinsed-out pan, add the drained crabmeat and simmer for a further 10 minutes. Meanwhile toast the slices of bread and cut them into small squares.

To serve divide the toast amongst 6 soup bowls and cover with soup. Garnish with chopped parsley and season with freshly ground black pepper.

Time: 40 minutes   *Serves 6*

Stuffed Breast of Veal

PETTO DI VITELLO FARCITO BRASATO

Ingredients	Metric/Imperial	American
dried mushrooms	25 g / 1 oz	1 ounce
large onion	1	1
butter	75 g / 3 oz	6 tablespoons
salt and pepper		
Ricotta cheese	225 g / 8 oz	$\frac{1}{2}$ pound
egg	1	1
cooked ham	100 g / 4 oz	$\frac{1}{4}$ pound
chopped parsley	1 tablespoon	1 tablespoon
boned breast of veal	800 g / 1$\frac{3}{4}$ lb	1$\frac{3}{4}$ pounds
carrot	1	1
celery stalk	1	1
ripe tomato	1	1
garlic clove	1	1
dry white wine	125 ml / 4 fl oz	$\frac{1}{2}$ cup
stock	125 ml / 4 fl oz	$\frac{1}{2}$ cup

Put the mushrooms to soak in a little warm water for 20 minutes.

Finely chop the onion. Melt one-third of the butter in a small pan over moderate heat, add the onion and cook for a few minutes until golden. Drain the mushrooms and add to the pan; season with salt and pepper and leave to cook over a low heat, adding a little water if the mixture starts to dry out.

Put the Ricotta cheese, egg and chopped ham into a bowl. Add the mushroom mixture, including any liquid, along with the chopped parsley and mix well together. Stuff into the veal and sew the pocket up with fine string, making sure there are no gaps.

Crab Soup

ZUPPA DI POLPA DI GRANCHIO

Ingredients	Metric/Imperial	American
large potato	1	1
ripe tomato	1	1
courgettes (zucchini)	2	2
garlic clove	1	1
bunch of parsley	1	1
oil	4 tablespoons	6 tablespoons
fish stock (page 152)	1.5 litres / 2$\frac{1}{2}$ pints	1$\frac{1}{2}$ quarts
salt and pepper		
canned crabmeat	200 g / 7 oz	7 ounces
slices of bread	6	6

First prepare the vegetables: finely dice the potato; peel and dice the tomato. Peel and finely chop the courgettes (zucchini). Wash the parsley, removing the stalks, and

Melt the remaining butter in a heavy pan or flameproof casserole, add the veal and brown it lightly on all sides. Meanwhile finely chop the carrot, celery, tomato, garlic clove and remaining onion. Add them to the pan, season with salt and pepper and pour over the wine. Cook over a low heat for about 1¼ hours, stirring in the stock halfway through.

To serve remove the string, carve the meat into slices, put on a heated serving dish and strain over the cooking juices.

Time: 2 hours   *Serves 6*

Stuffed Breast of Veal
1 Cook the chopped onion in some of the melted butter. Add the drained mushrooms and cook for a few minutes. Put the cheese, egg and ham in a bowl, tip in the mushroom mixture with any liquid and chopped parsley. Mix well.
2 Stuff the cheese mixture into boned pocket of the veal. Sew the edges up with fine string or secure with skewers.
3 Melt the remaining butter in a heavy pan and cook the meat until golden on both sides. Add the chopped vegetables with the seasonings and pour over the wine.

Zarina's Sweet

Zarina's Sweet

DOLCE DELLA ZARINA

Ingredients	Metric/Imperial	American
egg yolks	2	2
caster (fine granulated) sugar	75 g/3 oz	9 tablespoons
plain (all-purpose) flour	25 g/1 oz	¼ cup
milk	400 ml/14 fl oz	1¾ cups
cognac	3 tablespoons	scant ¼ cup
sponge fingers	225 g/8 oz	½ pound
mixed fresh fruit (strawberries, pears, bananas, kiwi)	1 kg/2 lb	2 pounds
double (thick) cream	200 ml/7 fl oz	scant cup
plain (semi-sweet) chocolate	100 g/4 oz	¼ pound

Put the egg yolks in a small pan with the sugar and beat together until light and creamy. Stir in the flour with 300 ml/½ pint/1¼ cups of the milk and bring to the boil over a low heat, stirring constantly.

Add the cognac to the remaining milk and dip the sponge fingers briefly in the mixture. Arrange them around the sides of a glass serving dish.

Prepare the fruit as for a fruit salad. Stir into the custard and pour the mixture into the dish. Fill any gaps with leftover biscuits.

Whip the cream stiffly and, using a piping (pastry) bag, decorate the top of the sweet. Finish with finely grated chocolate.

Time: 30 minutes   *Serves 6*

Menu

Salmon Turban with Prawn Sauce
TURBANTE DI SALMONE CON SALSA DI GAMBERI

Dumplings au Gratin
GNOCCHETTI ALLA PARIGINA GRATINATI

Fillet Steak and Asparagus in Pastry
FILETTO AGLI ASPARAGI IN CROSTA

Stuffed Pineapple
ANANAS RIPIENO

Preparation

One day ahead
Prepare or thaw the puff pastry for the fillet steak and put it in the refrigerator. Clean and cook the asparagus. Prepare the prawn sauce and put it in a sealed container in the refrigerator.

Three hours ahead
Prepare the dumplings, place in an ovenproof dish and cover with the cheese sauce ready for cooking.

Two hour ahead
Prepare the stuffed pineapple and put in the refrigerator, then prepare the salmon turban.

One hour ahead
Prepare and cook the fillet steak in pastry.

Half an hour ahead
Put the dumplings in the oven and reheat the prawn sauce.

Salmon Turban with Prawn Sauce

TURBANTE DI SALMONE CON SALSA DI GAMBERI

Ingredients	Metric/Imperial	American
canned salmon, drained	450 g/1 lb	1 pound
rolls	2	2
milk	125 ml/4 fl oz	½ cup
salt and pepper		
lemon	½	½
chopped marjoram	¼ teaspoon	¼ teaspoon
Parmesan cheese, grated	1½ tablespoons	2 tablespoons
grated nutmeg	¼ teaspoon	¼ teaspoon
eggs, separated	3	3
oil	2 teaspoons	2 teaspoons
For the prawn sauce:		
onion	½	½
chopped parsley	1 tablespoon	1 tablespoon
bay leaf	1	1
chopped thyme	1 teaspoon	1 teaspoon
white peppercorns	4	4
whole uncooked Dublin Bay prawns	450 g/1 lb	1 pound
butter	50 g/2 oz	¼ cup
brandy	50 ml/2 fl oz	¼ cup
dry white wine	125 ml/4 fl oz	½ cup
plain (all-purpose) flour	50 g/2 oz	½ cup
tomato paste	1 teaspoon	1 teaspoon
paprika	¼ teaspoon	¼ teaspoon
double (thick) cream	125 ml/4 fl oz	½ cup

Salmon Turban with Prawn Sauce
1 Drain and blend the salmon. Stir in softened bread.
2 Add seasoning, lemon juice and rind, herbs, cheese and nutmeg. Mix with egg yolks.
3 Fold in stiffly beaten egg whites and cook in a ring mould.
4 Shell the prawns, retaining a few for garnish.
5 Crush the shells and cook in half the melted butter until golden. Add the brandy and wine.
6 Reduce the liquid and rub through a fine sieve.
7 Make the sauce; add prawns and cream.

Drain the liquid from the salmon and remove any pieces of skin and bone. Put in a blender or food processor to obtain a thick mixture.

Pull out the soft centres from the rolls and soften them in the milk. Squeeze well and add to the salmon with seasoning, the juice and finely grated rind of the lemon, marjoram, Parmesan cheese and nutmeg. Mix well and stir in the egg yolks one at a time. Beat the egg whites until they form stiff peaks and fold them into the mixture. Preheat the oven to 200 c, 400 f, gas 6.

Brush an ovenproof ring mould liberally with oil. Fill it evenly with the salmon mixture. Bake in the moderately hot oven for 45 minutes or until well risen and golden brown.

Meanwhile prepare the prawn sauce. Finely chop the onion and put it in a saucepan with half the parsley, the bay leaf, thyme and peppercorns. Add 600 ml/1 pint/2½ cups of cold water and bring to the boil. Drop in the prawns, reduce the heat and cook for about 4 minutes. Drain, reserving the liquid.

Shell the prawns, reserving a few whole ones for garnishing. Chop most of the prawns but leave some whole. Crush or grind the shells and brown them in a saucepan with half the butter and the remaining parsley. Add the brandy and wine, cook until slightly reduced, then press through a fine sieve.

Dumplings au Gratin

GNOCCHETTI ALLA PARIGINA GRATINATI

Ingredients	Metric/Imperial	American
milk	500 ml/18 fl oz	2¼ cups
butter	100 g/4 oz	½ cup
salt		
grated nutmeg	¼ teaspoon	¼ teaspoon
plain (all-purpose) flour	275 g/10 oz	2½ cups
eggs	5	5
Parmesan cheese, grated	75 g/3 oz	¾ cup
oil	1 teaspoon	1 teaspoon
For the sauce:		
butter	40 g/1½ oz	3 tablespoons
plain (all-purpose) flour	25 g/1 oz	¼ cup
milk	500 ml/18 fl oz	2¼ cups
egg yolk	1	1
cheese, grated	65 g/2½ oz	5 tablespoons

First make the dumplings by heating the milk in a deep pan with the butter, a pinch of salt and the nutmeg. When it is boiling add the sifted flour and, stirring constantly, cook until the mixture leaves the sides of the pan. Leave until tepid, then beat in the eggs one at a time with the Parmesan cheese.

Bring a large pan of salted water to the boil. Drop in teaspoonfuls of the dumpling mixture and cook until they turn yellow. Remove the dumplings with a slotted spoon and keep warm in a well-oiled ovenproof dish.

Next make the sauce. Heat the butter in a deep pan over a low heat, stir in the flour and a pinch of salt. Gradually add the milk, stirring continuously, and bring to the boil. Cook and stir until creamy.

Remove the sauce from the heat, stir in the egg yolk and cheese; pour it over the dumplings. Put the dish under a hot grill (broiler) for a few minutes until the top is golden brown. Serve hot.

Melt the remaining butter, add the flour, the juice from the prawn shells, the tomato paste, a pinch of salt, the paprika and the reserved prawn liquid. Bring to the boil, stirring constantly. When the mixture is thick add the cream and prawns.

Allow the salmon turban to stand for a few minutes when it comes out of the oven then turn on to a serving plate and allow to cool. Fill with prawn sauce. Serve cold, garnished with reserved whole prawns.

Time: 2½ hours　　　　　　　　　　*Serves 6*

Time: 1 hour 20 minutes　　　　　　*Serves 6*

351

Menu

Ham Mousse
MOUSSE DI PROSCIUTTO

Pasta with Seafood Sauce
TAGLIOLINI MARE E MONTI

Chops with Asparagus
COSTOLETTE AGLI ASPARAGI

Chocolate Chestnut Roulade
ROTOLO DI CIOCCOLATO AI MARRONI

Preparation

One day ahead
Prepare the ham mousse and put it in the refrigerator. Prepare the chocolate roulade and put it in the freezer.

Three hours ahead
Prepare the dough for the pasta and leave to rest coated in flour. Remove the roulade from the freezer to the refrigerator.

Two hours ahead
Prepare the sauce for the pasta. Cook the asparagus to go with the chops.

One hour ahead
Turn out the ham mousse and garnish to taste. Cook the chops and keep warm.

Ham Mousse

Ham Mousse

MOUSSE DI PROSCIUTTO

Ingredients	Metric/Imperial	American
butter	25 g/1 oz	2 tablespoons
plain (all-purpose) flour	25 g/1 oz	$\frac{1}{4}$ cup
salt and pepper		
milk	150 ml/$\frac{1}{4}$ pint	$\frac{2}{3}$ cup
Parma ham	350 g/12 oz	$\frac{3}{4}$ pound
double (thick) cream	150 ml/$\frac{1}{4}$ pint	$\frac{2}{3}$ cup
thin bread slices	6	6
Garnish:		
watercress		
lettuce leaves		

Melt the butter in a small pan over medium heat. Stir in the flour, season with salt and pepper and gradually add the milk. Bring to the boil, stirring constantly with a wooden spoon, and cook until thick and smooth.

Remove all fat from the Parma ham and slice the lean into strips. Add it to the sauce and sieve or blend. Leave to cool.

Whip the cream until stiff and fold it into the cold ham mixture.

Brush a mould with oil or line it with foil. Pour in the mousse and refrigerate for at least 2 hours.

When ready to serve invert the mould on to a serving plate and garnish the mousse with watercress and lettuce leaves. Toast the bread, cut it into triangles and serve wrapped in a serviette to keep warm.

Time: 40 minutes + 2 hours: chilling   *Serves 6*

Pasta with Seafood Sauce

TAGLIOLINI MARE E MONTI

Ingredients	Metric/Imperial	American
For the pasta:		
plain (all-purpose) flour	450 g/1 lb	4 cups
eggs	4	4
salt		
oil	1 tablespoon	1 tablespoon
For the sauce:		
garlic clove	1	1
butter	40 g/1$\frac{1}{2}$ oz	3 tablespoons
mushrooms	350 g/12 oz	$\frac{3}{4}$ pound
squid or baby octopus	450 g/1 lb	1 pound
dry white wine	125 ml/4 fl oz	$\frac{1}{2}$ cup
mussels	1 kg//2 lb	2 pounds
ripe tomatoes	2	2
salt and pepper		
peeled cooked shrimps	450 g/1 lb	1 pound
chopped parsley	1 tablespoon	1 tablespoon

Sift the flour on to a large work surface and break the eggs into the centre with a generous pinch of salt and the oil. Work to form a smooth firm dough and roll out, not too thinly. Leave to rest and dry out for a while. Then roll the sheet up and cut into thin strips with a large sharp knife. Spread the strips out on a work surface or pastry board and sprinkle with a little flour to stop them sticking together.

To make the sauce first crush the garlic clove and melt the butter in a heavy pan over a low heat. Add the garlic and cook until soft but not browned. Clean the mushrooms, slice thinly and add to the pan.

Prepare the squid by cutting off the tentacles close to the head. Slit open the body bag and pull out the head, intestines and clear spine. Wash the bag and tentacles well under running water and chop finely. Add to the pan along with the wine, cover and cook very gently for about 40 minutes.

Meanwhile open the mussels by putting them in a pan over heat; discard any which do not open.

Peel and chop the tomatoes and add them to the mushroom mixture. Season with salt and pepper and cook for a further 15 minutes. Then add the shelled mussels, shrimps and chopped parsley. Stir together for a few minutes and keep warm.

Cook the pasta in plenty of salted boiling water until *al dente*. Drain well, pour over the seafood sauce and serve.

Time: 1$\frac{1}{2}$ hours + 30 minutes: resting time   *Serves 6*

Pasta with Seafood Sauce
1 Heat the butter in a heavy pan and add the garlic. When the garlic is brown add the mushrooms and then the squid.

2 Gradually stir in the tomatoes and seasoning.
3 After 15 minutes add seafood and parsley.

Chops with Asparagus

COSTOLETTE AGLI ASPARAGI

Ingredients	Metric/Imperial	American
asparagus	1 kg/2 lb	2 pounds
salt and pepper		
veal rib chops	6	6
plain (all-purpose) flour	20 g/$\frac{3}{4}$ oz	3 tablespoons
butter	65 g/$2\frac{1}{2}$ oz	5 tablespoons
dry white wine	50 ml/2 fl oz	$\frac{1}{4}$ cup
chopped parsley	1 tablespoon	1 tablespoon

Wash the asparagus well and remove the white woody parts with a knife. Tie in bunches and stand upright in a tall pan. Add enough cold salted water to come just below the tips, cover the tips with a foil dome and cook over a medium heat until the asparagus is just tender –

about 8–18 minutes from the time the water boils, depending on the thickness of the asparagus.

Drain the asparagus, reserving a little of the cooking liquid. Leave to cool and cut into 2.5 cm/1 in lengths.

Trim the veal chops, season with salt and pepper and dip in flour. Melt the butter in a heavy pan or casserole over a medium heat and add the veal, turning once to brown on each side. Pour over the wine, cover and cook for 10 minutes.

Take the veal out of the pan on to a plate. Put in the asparagus and the reserved liquid and cook for a few minutes to reheat the asparagus and reduce the liquid. Replace the veal, sprinkle with chopped parsley and keep warm until ready to serve, stirring occasionally.

Time: 45 minutes   *Serves 6*

Chops with Asparagus
1 Prepare the asparagus and tie in bundles.
2 Fry the chops in butter and add the wine.
3 Remove chops; reheat asparagus and return chops.

Chocolate Chestnut Roulade

ROTOLO DI CIOCCOLATO AI MARRONI

Ingredients	Metric/Imperial	American
eggs, separated	4	4
caster (fine granulated) sugar	50 g/2 oz	$\frac{1}{4}$ cup
plain (all-purpose) flour	2 tablespoons	3 tablespoons
cocoa powder	4 tablespoons	6 tablespoons
For the filling: whipping (thick) cream	400 ml/14 fl oz	$1\frac{3}{4}$ cups
chestnut purée	3 tablespoons	scant $\frac{1}{4}$ cup
cognac	1 tablespoon	1 tablespoon
marrons glacés (candied chestnuts)	10	10

Put the egg yolks and sugar in a bowl and whisk until light and frothy. Add the flour and cocoa powder and fold in for 2–3 minutes. Beat the egg whites with a whisk until they stand in stiff peaks and gently fold them into the mixture.

Brush a large piece of foil with oil and put it on a rectangular baking tray. Pour on the cake mixture and spread it out evenly to 1 cm/$\frac{1}{2}$ in thick. Bake in a hot oven (220 C, 425 F, gas 7) for 15 minutes or until cooked. Slide cake and foil off the baking sheet and leave to cool.

Whip the cream until stiff. Blend the chestnut purée with the cognac and stir it into the cream. Chop the marrons glacés finely and add them to the cream. Spread the cream over the cake, reserving a little. Roll the cake up lightly and spread with the reserved cream.

Present the cake whole on a serving plate and slice it at the table.

Time: $1\frac{1}{4}$ hours   *Serves 6*

Chocolate Chestnut Roulade

Menu

Cream of Leek Soup
CREMA DI PORRI DELICATA

Monkfish (Goosefish) Mould
with Hollandaise Sauce
SFORMATO DI PESCATRICE CON SALSA AGRA

Ragout of Pheasant
FAGIANO IN SALMI

Pears in Wine Sauce
PERE ALLA CREMA CON CIALDE FRIABILE

Preparation

One day ahead
Prepare the pears in wine sauce. Cook the prawns and artichokes for the fish mould. Prepare the pheasant for cooking and put in the marinade. Boil the potatoes for the leek soup. Put everything in separate covered containers and stand in the refrigerator.

Two hours ahead
Prepare the fish mould ready for cooking.

One and a half hours ahead
Prepare the leek soup and cook the pheasant.

One hour ahead
Cook the fish mould.

Half an hour ahead
Prepare the hollandaise sauce and remove the pear dessert from the refrigerator.

Cream of Leek Soup

CREMA DI PORRI DELICATA

Ingredients	Metric/Imperial	American
medium-sized potatoes	2	2
salt and pepper		
leeks	3	3
butter	50 g/2 oz	$\frac{1}{4}$ cup
milk	225 ml/8 fl oz	1 cup
stock	1 litre/1$\frac{3}{4}$ pints	1 quart
chopped parsley	1 tablespoon	1 tablespoon
egg yolk	1	1
single (thin) cream	225 ml/8 fl oz	1 cup
Parmesan cheese, grated	25 g/1 oz	$\frac{1}{4}$ cup
slices of bread to serve	6	6

Wash the potatoes and boil in salted water in their skins for about 30 minutes. Allow to cool slightly, then peel and mash.

Meanwhile prepare the leeks: remove the roots, tough outer layers and most of the green parts. Slice horizontally, wash thoroughly under running water and drain well. Melt half the butter in a large pan, add the leeks and cook over medium heat until golden. Add the milk and mashed potato and season to taste. Pour in the stock, stirring well with a wooden spoon. Reduce the heat and leave to simmer for about 30 minutes.

Put the parsley in a bowl with the egg yolk and cream; add 4 teaspoons of the grated Parmesan cheese. Mix carefully and stir into the soup. Simmer for 2–3 minutes, then remove from the heat.

Cut the slices of bread in quarters. Just before serving melt the remaining butter in a shallow pan and fry the bread until golden brown. Remove and sprinkle with the remaining Parmesan cheese.

Time: 1 hour   *Serves 6*

Monkfish Mould with Hollandaise Sauce

Monkfish (Goosefish) Mould with Hollandaise Sauce

SFORMATO DI PESCATRICE CON SALSA AGRA

Ingredients	Metric/Imperial	American
monkfish (goosefish)	1 kg/2 lb	2 pounds
bay leaves	2	2
garlic clove	1	1
salt and pepper		
black peppercorns	6	6
dry white wine	125 ml/4 fl oz	$\frac{1}{2}$ cup
bread roll	1	1
milk	1 tablespoon	1 tablespoon
grated nutmeg	$\frac{1}{4}$ teaspoon	$\frac{1}{4}$ teaspoon
Parmesan cheese, grated	$1\frac{1}{2}$ tablespoons	2 tablespoons
chopped parsley	1 tablespoon	1 tablespoon
eggs, separated	4	4
king prawns	225 g/8 oz	$\frac{1}{2}$ pound
artichokes	2	2
lemon juice	$1\frac{1}{2}$ tablespoons	2 tablespoons
oil	2 teaspoons	2 teaspoons
Hollandaise sauce see page 36		

Put the fish in a large pan with the bay leaves, crushed garlic clove, a pinch of salt, the peppercorns, wine and 225 ml/8 fl oz/1 cup of cold water. Cover and simmer over a medium heat for about 15 minutes. Soak the inside of the bread roll in a little milk.

Drain and skin the fish; remove the backbone. Put the flesh in a bowl and mash with a fork. Season with salt, pepper, the grated nutmeg, Parmesan cheese and parsley. Squeeze the bread roll and add it to the fish mixture along with 4 egg yolks. Beat well together.

Beat the egg whites until standing in stiff peaks and fold them into the fish mixture.

Boil the king prawns in salted water for 6 minutes; drain and shell. Preheat the oven to 200 C, 400 F, gas 6. Clean the artichokes and boil in water with lemon juice added, drain when the outer leaves come away easily. Remove outer leaves and the choke, cut into segments.

Oil a plain 20 cm/8 in soufflé dish or mould liberally. Spread half the fish mixture in the base and cover with the king prawns and artichoke leaves. Spread over the remaining fish mixture and cook in a moderately hot oven for 30–35 minutes.

Remove the mould from the oven, invert on to a serving dish and cut into slices. Pour over the sauce.

Time: $1\frac{1}{2}$ hours *Serves 6*

Pheasant Ragout

FAGIANO IN SALMI

Ingredients	Metric/Imperial	American
pheasant (cock or hen)	1	1
dry white wine	600 ml/1 pint	2½ cups
celery stalks	2	2
carrot	1	1
onion	1	1
salt		
bay leaves	2	2
thyme	½ teaspoon	½ teaspoon
marjoram	½ teaspoon	½ teaspoon
juniper berries	6	6
cloves	2	2
garlic cloves	2	2
plain (all-purpose) flour	2 tablespoons	3 tablespoons
butter	50 g/2 oz	¼ cup

When the pheasant is prepared for cooking make sure the liver is reserved. Wash and dry the bird and cut into serving pieces. Make a marinade using the wine; chopped celery, carrot and onion; salt and a muslin bag containing the herbs, spices and garlic cloves. Marinate the pheasant pieces for 12 hours.

Drain and dry the pheasant pieces and coat them in flour. Melt the butter in a large heavy pan over a medium heat and brown the pieces lightly on all sides. Pour in the entire marinade, cover and simmer gently for about 1 hour or until the pheasant pieces are tender.

Remove the pheasant pieces to a flameproof casserole. Discard the muslin bag and sieve or blend the pan contents together with the reserved raw liver. Put this sauce into the casserole and cook over a high heat to heat and thicken it slightly. If it becomes too thick stir in a little stock.

Serve hot straight from the casserole.

Time: 1½ hours + 12 hours: marinating   *Serves 6*

Pheasant Ragout
1 Joint the pheasant. Make a marinade with wine, vegetables, seasoning and herbs. Add the pheasant pieces and leave for 12 hours.
2 Drain the pheasant and dip in flour. Heat the butter in a pan and brown the joints on all sides.
3 Put the pheasant in a casserole. Sieve or blend the sauce with the liver and pour over pheasant.

Pears in Wine Sauce

PERE ALLA CREMA CON CIALDE FRIABILE

Ingredients	Metric/Imperial	American
milk	300 ml/½ pint	1¼ cups
pieces of lemon rind	3	3
egg yolks	4	4
caster (fine granulated) sugar	170 g/5½ oz	⅔ cup
plain (all-purpose) flour	40 g/1½ oz	6 tablespoons
salt		
cooking pears	6	6
white wine	225 ml/8 fl oz	1 cup
lemon juice	1 teaspoon	1 teaspoon
piece of cinnamon	1	1
plain (semi-sweet) chocolate	150 g/5 oz	5 ounces

Put the milk in a pan with 2 pieces of the lemon rind and heat gently.

Beat the egg yolks with 100 g/4 oz/½ cup of the sugar for 10 minutes. Stir in the flour, a pinch of salt and the hot milk. Put in a pan over a medium heat and cook, stirring constantly, until thick. Allow to boil for a few minutes, then remove from the heat.

Peel the pears without removing the stalks and trim the bases so they will stand upright. Put them in a pan just large enough for them, sprinkle with 225 ml/8 fl oz/ 1 cup of water, the wine, lemon juice, cinnamon and remaining sugar. Cover the pan, bring slowly to the boil and simmer until tender.

Stand the pears upright in a glass serving dish. Strain the cooking juices, stir into the prepared egg yolk mixture and pour over the pears. Finely grate the chocolate over the top straight away so that it melts slightly.

When cool cover with plastic wrap and chill until required.

Time: 45 minutes   *Serves 6*

Menu

King Prawn Flan
TORTA DI SCAMPI

Veal with Mustard
VITELLO ALLA SENAPE

Green Bean and Mushroom Nests
NIDI DI FAGIOLINI AI FUNGHI

Mascarpone Cheese Cups
COPPETTE DI MASCARPONE

Preparation

One day ahead
Prepare the mascarpone cheese cups, cover with plastic wrap and refrigerate until ready to serve.

Three hours ahead
Prepare and cook the king prawn pie.

Two hours ahead
Prepare and cook the veal with mustard. Cook the green beans and mushrooms.

One hour ahead
Make up the bean and mushroom nests ready to cook.

Half an hour ahead
Carve the veal and complete the sauce. Heat the nests and keep warm until ready to serve.

King Prawn Flan

TORTA DI SCAMPI

Ingredients	Metric/Imperial	American
frozen pastry, thawed	225 g/8 oz	½ pound
Dublin Bay prawns, cooked	600 g/1¼ lb	1¼ pounds
butter	40 g/1½ oz	3 tablespoons
garlic clove	1	1
brandy	1½ tablespoons	2 tablespoons
salt and pepper		
eggs	4	4
plain (all-purpose) flour	2 tablespoons	3 tablespoons
double (thick) cream	225 ml/8 fl oz	1 cup
chopped parsley	1 tablespoon	1 tablespoon

Remove the shells from the prawns. Melt the butter in a heavy pan, add the prawns and crushed garlic clove and fry for 2 minutes. Pour over the brandy, season with salt and pepper and remove from the heat.

Preheat the oven to 220 C, 425 F, gas 7.

Roll out the pastry and line the base and sides of a 20 cm/8 in flan dish. Beat the eggs in a bowl with the flour and a little salt and pepper until creamy. Add the cream, the prawns with their cooking juices and the chopped parsley. Pour into the pastry shell.

Bake in the hot oven for 15 minutes, then reduce the oven temperature to moderate (180 C, 350 F, gas 4) for 20 minutes or until the top is golden, the pastry crisp and the filling set. Serve warm or at room temperature.

Time: 1¼ hours   *Serves 6*

King Prawn Flan

1 Remove the shells from the prawns. Heat butter in a pan; add garlic, prawns and then brandy and seasoning.

2 Roll out the pastry and line the dish. Trim the edges with a sharp knife and mark the rim neatly.

3 Make up the egg mixture. Mix in the cream, the prawns with juices and parsley. Pour into the pastry case.

Veal with Mustard

VITELLO ALLA SENAPE

Ingredients	Metric/Imperial	American
leg of veal	1.2 kg/2¾ lb	2¾ pounds
garlic clove	1	1
chopped rosemary	½ teaspoon	½ teaspoon
butter	65 g/2½ oz	5 tablespoons
onion	1	1
mustard	4 tablespoons	6 tablespoons
salt and pepper		
milk	400 ml/14 fl oz	1¾ cup

Make small incisions all over the surface of the veal with a sharp knife. Chop the garlic finely, mix it with the rosemary and push a little of the mixture into the incisions.

Melt the butter in a flameproof casserole. Chop the onion finely, add to the pan and cook for 4 minutes until golden. Add the veal and half the mustard. Brown the veal on all sides, then season with salt and pepper and pour in the milk. Cook on a low heat for about 1½ hours, until the sauce has reduced a little and the veal is cooked.

Remove the veal, carve it and arrange the slices on a heated serving plate. Stir the remaining mustard into the sauce and pour over the meat. Serve hot.

Time: 1¾ hours   *Serves 6*

Veal with Mustard

Green Beans and Mushroom Nests
1 Soak the dried mushrooms. Slice the fresh thinly.
2 Arrange slices of cheese and ham on the bread.
3 Make the cooked beans into 'nests' on the ham.
4 Fill the centres with cooked mushroom mixture.

Green Bean and Mushroom Nests

NIDI DI FAGIOLINI AI FUNGHI

Ingredients	Metric/Imperial	American
dried mushrooms	25 g / 1 oz	1 ounce
fresh mushrooms	350 g / 12 oz	¾ pound
dwarf green beans	800 g / 1¾ lb	1¾ pounds
salt and pepper		
onion	½	½
garlic clove	1	1
butter	75 g / 3 oz	6 tablespoons
chopped parsley	1 tablespoon	1 tablespoon
slices of bread	6	6
slices of Cheddar cheese	6	6
slices of Parma ham	6	6

Soak the dried mushrooms in warm water. Clean and thinly slice the fresh mushrooms. Top and tail and remove any strings from the beans. Cook the beans in salted boiling water for about 12 minutes, until just tender. Drain immediately and set aside.

Finely chop the onion, crush the garlic and heat 40 g/ 1½ oz/3 tablespoons of the butter in a heavy pan. Cook the onions and garlic until soft but not brown. Drain the dried mushrooms and add them to the pan along with the fresh ones. Season with salt and pepper, lower the heat, cover and cook for another 20 minutes. Stir in the chopped parsley.

Put the slices of bread on a baking tray and top each one with a slice of cheese, then a slice of ham. Melt the remaining butter and toss the beans in it. Make a 'nest' of beans on top of each serving and fill the centres with the mushroom mixture. Bake in a moderately hot oven (200 c, 400 f, gas 6) for 10 minutes.

Time: 1 hour   *Serves 6*

Mascarpone Cheese Cups

COPPETTE DI MASCARPONE

Ingredients	Metric/Imperial	American
eggs, separated	3	3
caster (fine granulated) sugar	100 g/4 oz	½ cup
Mascarpone cheese	225 g/8 oz	½ pound
brandy	1½ tablespoons	2 tablespoons
strong black coffee	225 ml/8 fl oz	1 cup
milk	50 ml/2 fl oz	¼ cup
sponge fingers	200 g/7 oz	7 ounces
plain (semi-sweet) chocolate	50 g/2 oz	2 ounces

Beat the egg yolks with the sugar until light and frothy, soft and creamy. Beat the egg whites with a whisk until they stand in stiff peaks.

Add the Mascarpone cheese to the egg yolks, mix well and then add the brandy. Gently fold in the egg whites.

Put the coffee in another bowl with the milk. Dip the sponge fingers briefly in the mixture and use them to line 6 individual goblets. Pour the cheese mixture on top and decorate with grated chocolate.

Cover with plastic wrap and refrigerate until ready to serve.

Time: 25 minutes + 1 hour: chilling   *Serves 6*

Mascarpone Cheese Cups

Menu

Mushrooms on Toast
CROSTINI AI FUNGHI

Soufflé with Tagliatelline
SOUFFLE DI TAGLIATELLINE

Savoury Pork Chops
COSTOLETTE DI MAIALE SAPORITE

Grape Flan
SFOGLIATA ALL'UVA

Preparation

One day ahead
Prepare or thaw the pastry for the flan and bake it blind. Wash and drain the mushrooms for the toasts and store in an airtight container in the refrigerator.

Three hours ahead
Prepare the confectioners' custard and complete the grape flan.

Two hours ahead
Cook the pork chops and prepare the topping for the mushrooms on toast.

One hour ahead
Prepare the soufflé and complete the mushrooms on toast.

Half an hour ahead
Cook the soufflé and reheat the chops just before serving.

Mushrooms on Toast

Mushrooms on Toast

CROSTINI AI FUNGHI

Ingredients	Metric/Imperial	American
dried mushrooms	15 g/½ oz	½ ounce
fresh mushrooms	800 g/1¾ lb	1¾ pounds
butter	40 g/1½ oz	3 tablespoons
garlic clove	1	1
salt and pepper		
slices of bread	12	12
oil	2 tablespoons	3 tablespoons
plain (all-purpose) flour	1½ tablespoons	2 tablespoons
milk	125 ml/4 fl oz	½ cup
chopped parsley	1 tablespoon	1 tablespoon
Parmesan cheese, grated	40 g/1½ oz	3 tablespoons
lettuce	1	1

Put the dried mushrooms to soak in a little warm water.

Clean the fresh mushrooms and slice them thinly. Heat the butter in a heavy pan over a medium heat. Add the garlic clove and mushroom slices and cook until lightly browned. Drain the dried mushrooms and add them to the pan. Season with salt and pepper and leave to simmer for a few minutes.

Remove the crusts from the bread slices and brush each one with a little oil. Lay them on baking trays and put in a moderately hot oven (200 c, 400 f, gas 6) for a few minutes.

Sprinkle the flour into the pan of mushrooms and stir well. Pour in the milk and remove the garlic clove. Cook over a low heat, stirring occasionally to make sure the mixture does not stick. When it is cooked add the chopped parsley and grated Parmesan cheese.

Meanwhile wash the lettuce and dry the leaves thoroughly.

Spread the mushroom mixture over the toast, put two on each plate and garnish with lettuce leaves.

Time: 40 minutes　　　　　　　　　　　　　*Serves 6*

Soufflé Tagliatelline
1 Prepare the cheese, ham and the sauce. Allow sauce to cool. Add the ham and cheeses.
2 Gradually beat the egg yolks into sauce. Taste for seasoning.
3 Add the cooked tagliatelline to the sauce and mix well.

Soufflé Tagliatelline

SOUFFLE DI TAGLIATELLINE

Ingredients	Metric/Imperial	American
cooked ham	100 g/4 oz	¼ pound
Fontina cheese	100 g/4 oz	¼ pound
butter	50 g/2 oz	¼ cup
plain (all-purpose) flour	40 g/1½ oz	3 tablespoons
milk	500 ml/18 fl oz	2¼ cups
Parmesan cheese, grated	40 g/1½ oz	3 tablespoons
eggs, separated	3	3
fresh tagliatelline	450 g/1 lb	1 pound
salt and pepper		
grated nutmeg	¼ teaspoon	¼ teaspoon
dried breadcrumbs	1 tablespoon	1 tablespoon

Chop the ham finely. Remove the rind from the Fontina cheese and cut the cheese into little cubes.

Melt the butter in a small pan over a low heat. Stir in the flour and cook for a few minutes, making sure it does not brown. Gradually add the milk and bring to the boil, stirring continuously. Cook for a few more minutes until creamy and remove from the heat.

When the mixture is cool add the ham, Fontina and Parmesan cheeses and the egg yolks.

Preheat the oven to 200 c, 400 f, gas 6.

Cook the tagliatelline in plenty of boiling salted water until just tender, *al dente*. Drain it well and add it to the soufflé mixture.

Beat the egg whites until stiff but not dry and fold them into the mixture with the grated nutmeg.

Brush a 20 cm/8 in soufflé dish, or a high-sided ovenproof dish, with oil and coat with the breadcrumbs. Fill with the tagliatelline mixture. Put into the moderately hot oven for 30 minutes or until the soufflé is well risen and golden brown. Serve at once straight from the dish.

Time: 1 hour   *Serves 6*

4 Whisk the egg whites until they are stiff but not dry. Fold into the mixture carefully.
5 Brush the soufflé dish with oil and coat evenly with breadcrumbs. Fill with the mixture and cook.

Savoury Pork Chops

COSTOLETTE DI MAIALE SAPORITE

Ingredients	Metric/Imperial	American
pork or veal chops	6	6
salt and pepper		
plain (all-purpose) flour	1 tablespoon	1 tablespoon
yellow (sweet) peppers	4	4
oil	125 ml/4 fl oz	½ cup
garlic cloves	2	2
plum tomatoes	400 g/14 oz	14 ounces

Savoury Veal Chops
1 Heat the oil and cook the peppers.
2 In a separate pan heat more oil and cook the chops with crushed garlic until brown.
3 Arrange chops on a plate with peppers and sauce.

Flatten the pork or veal chops with a meat hammer. Season with salt and pepper and coat lightly with flour.

Char the skin of the peppers, either by putting them under the grill (broiler) or holding them over a flame. Remove the skins and deseed and chop the peppers coarsely. Heat some oil in a heavy pan, add the peppers, sprinkle with a little salt and fry gently for 10 minutes.

Heat more oil in a separate large pan over a medium heat. Add the crushed garlic cloves, sprinkle with salt and fry until golden brown. Remove and add the chops. Brown for a few minutes, then set aside on a plate.

Peel the tomatoes if using fresh, drain if canned and chop them roughly. Add to the pan and stir to incorporate the meat juices. Season to taste with salt and pepper. Simmer for 15 minutes, then add the chops and cook for a further 10 minutes.

Arrange the chops in an ovenproof serving dish, cover with the peppers and pour the sauce over. Reheat for 15 minutes in a moderate oven (180 c, 350 f, gas 4).

Time: 1 hour   *Serves 6*

Grape Flan

Grape Flan

SFOGLIATA ALL'UVA

Ingredients	Metric/Imperial	American
puff pastry	225 g/8 oz	½ pound
black and white grapes	225 g/8 oz	½ pound
egg yolks	2	2
caster (fine granulated) sugar	75 g/3 oz	9 tablespoons
plain (all-purpose) flour	40 g/1½ oz	3 tablespoons
lemon rind, grated	¼	¼
milk	500 ml/18 fl oz	2¼ cups
vanilla sugar to decorate		

Make or thaw the pastry. Halve and deseed the grapes. Brush a 23 cm/9 in flan tin with oil.

Preheat the oven to 220 c, 425 f, gas 7.

Roll the pastry out thinly and line the base and sides of the flat tin, trimming the edges neatly. Prick the base all over with a fork, line with foil, cover with baking beans and bake blind in the hot oven for 20 minutes or until the pastry is crisp and golden brown.

Meanwhile make the filling. Beat the egg yolks with the sugar and flour in a small saucepan. Add the grated lemon rind and milk. Bring to the boil, stirring constantly. Remove from the heat and leave to cool.

Remove the beans and foil from the pastry shell. Pour in the custard. Arrange the grapes on top and sprinkle with vanilla sugar.

Time: 40 minutes + 30 minutes: cooling   Serves 6

Menu

Chicken Consommé
RISTRETTO DI POLLO CON JULIENNE

Cold Salmon with Caviar
SALMONE AL CAVIALE

Beef Fillet with Asparagus Sauce
FILETTO DI MANZO ALLA CREMA D'ASPARAGI

Ginger Ice Cream with Strawberry Sauce
GELATO ALLO ZENZERO CON CREMA DI FRAGOLE

Preparation

One day ahead
Prepare the chicken consommé, ginger ice cream and strawberry sauce. Put all three into separate lidded containers; stand the consommé and sauce in the refrigerator and the ice cream in the freezer.

Three hours ahead
Cook the salmon.

Two hours ahead
Cook the beef.

One hour ahead
Prepare the caviar sauce for the salmon.

Half an hour ahead
Prepare the asparagus sauce for the beef.

Chicken Consommé

RISTRETTO DI POLLO CON JULIENNE

Ingredients	Metric/Imperial	American
oven-ready chicken with giblets	1 (2 kg/4 lb)	1 (4 pound)
carrot	1	1
leek	1	1
sprigs of parsley	2	2
sprig of thyme	1	1
bay leaf	1	1
salt	1 teaspoon	1 teaspoon
minced (ground) beef	350 g/12 oz	1½ cups
egg white	1	1
For the julienne:		
small carrot	1	1
celery stalk	1	1
small onion	1	1
leek	1	1
butter	25 g/1 oz	2 tablespoons

Cut the chicken into joints (see page 176). Put into a large pan with the giblets, add 2 litres/3½ pints/2 quarts of water and bring to the boil. Skim off the scum as it forms.

Clean and chop the carrot and leek. Add to the pan when the water comes to the boil, together with the herbs and salt. Reduce the heat, cover and simmer very gently for 1 hour, skimming the surface fat from time to time with a small strainer. Remove the chicken and use for another meal.

Mix the beef and lightly whisked egg white together. Remove the pan from the heat, rapidly whisk in the beef mixture, return to the heat and simmer for another 50 minutes. Pass through a fine strainer.

To prepare the julienne clean all the vegetables and cut into very fine strips. Melt the butter in a heavy pan, add the strips and cook over a low heat for a few minutes. Add a ladleful of the chicken broth and, cook until softened.

Add the julienne to the soup and serve hot. Some strips of chicken may be added.

Time: 3 hours　　　　　　　　　　　　*Serves 6*

Cold Salmon with Caviar

SALMONE AL CAVIALE

Ingredients	Metric/Imperial	American
salmon trout	1 (1.4 kg/3 lb)	1 (3 pound)
onion	½	½
sprigs of parsley	3	3
sprig of thyme	1	1
bay leaf	1	1
peppercorns	10	10
coarse salt	1 teaspoon	1 teaspoon
white wine vinegar	125 ml/4 fl oz	½ cup
dry white wine	50 ml/2 fl oz	¼ cup
lettuce leaves and lemon slices to garnish		
For the sauce:		
hard-boiled (cooked) egg yolks	3	3
mustard powder	¼ teaspoon	¼ teaspoon
salt		
olive oil	350 ml/12 fl oz	1½ cups
lemon juice	1 tablespoon	1 tablespoon
caviar	25 g/1 oz	¼ cup

Prepare the salmon by removing the insides through a slit in the stomach, wash well. Lay the salmon gently on the rack of a fish kettle. (If a fish kettle is not available use a large roasting pan. Cover with foil and cook in a moderately hot oven (180 c, 350 f, gas 4)). Cover with finely chopped onion, parsley and thyme sprigs, crumbled bay leaf, peppercorns and coarse salt. Pour in the vinegar, wine and 225 ml/8 fl oz/1 cup of water. Put on a medium heat and bring quickly to the boil, then reduce the heat and simmer for 15 minutes.

Remove the salmon from the heat immediately and leave to cool in the liquid. Drain well and remove the skin. Arrange the whole fish on a serving plate and garnish with lettuce leaves and lemon slices. Serve by removing portions from the centre bone. Alternatively, you can remove the fish fillets from the bone before arranging them on a serving plate.

To prepare the sauce put the egg yolks in a bowl and mash with a spoon. Sprinkle on the mustard and a pinch of salt, then gradually add the oil, stirring constantly. When the mixture is smooth and creamy add the lemon juice and caviar and pour into a sauce boat.

Note: Do not make the sauce too far ahead as it is delicate and will only keep for a few hours.

Time: 45 minutes + 1 hour: cooling　　　　*Serves 6*

Cold Salmon with Caviar (p. 375)

Beef Fillet with Asparagus Sauce
1 Chop herbs with garlic and mix with seasoning.
Stuff into slits in the beef.
2 Wrap ham around beef and tie with string.

Beef Fillet with Asparagus Sauce

FILETTO DI MANZO ALLA CREMA D'ASPARAGI

Ingredients	Metric/Imperial	American
fillet of beef	1 (1.4 kg/3 lb)	1 (3 pound)
large sprig of rosemary	1	1
sage leaves	8–10	8–10
garlic clove	1	1
salt and pepper		
Parma ham	100 g/4 oz	$\frac{1}{4}$ pound
butter	50 g/2 oz	$\frac{1}{4}$ cup
dry white wine	50 ml/2 fl oz	$\frac{1}{4}$ cup
asparagus	1 kg/2 lb	2 pounds
milk	450 ml/$\frac{3}{4}$ pint	2 cups
plain (all-purpose) flour	1 teaspoon	1 teaspoon

Make incisions all over the piece of beef. Remove the rosemary leaves from the woody stems and chop finely with the sage leaves and garlic. Mix with salt and plenty of pepper. Fill the incisions with the herb mixture.

Wrap the beef in the slices of Parma ham and secure with kitchen string. Melt 2–3 tablespoons of the butter in a large heavy pan, add the beef and cook over a medium heat, turning frequently, until lightly browned on all sides. Add the wine and leave until it has evaporated.

Meanwhile prepare the asparagus: trim off any woody ends and scrape off tough skin at the lower ends. Rinse under cold running water and cut into short lengths.

Add the asparagus, pour the milk over the beef and continue to cook over a low heat for 40 minutes. Then take out the beef, remove the string, put the pieces of ham back in the pan and keep the meat warm.

To make the sauce blend or sieve the asparagus, ham and cooking juices; mix the remaining butter with the flour. Put the asparagus mixture into a small pan over a low heat and gradually add the blended butter and flour, stirring constantly, until the sauce is thick and creamy.

Carve the beef medium thick, arrange on a heated serving plate and pour the asparagus sauce over.

Time: 1½ hours　　　　　　　　　　　　　　*Serves 6*

3 Melt butter in a pan and brown the meat on all sides. Add the wine and leave to evaporate.
4 Trim the asparagus and chop into short lengths. Add the asparagus to the beef.
5 Pour the milk over the beef and cook over a low heat for 40 minutes.

Ginger Ice Cream with Strawberry Sauce

GELATO ALLO ZENZERO CON CREMA DI FRAGOLE

Ingredients	Metric/Imperial	American
milk	500 ml/18 fl oz	2¼ cups
vanilla essence (extract)	¼ teaspoon	¼ teaspoon
egg yolks	6	6
caster (fine granulated) sugar	225 g/8 oz	1 cup
single (thin) cream	500 ml/18 fl oz	2¼ cups
ground ginger	1 tablespoon	1 tablespoon
small strawberries	350 g/12 oz	¾ pound
icing (confectioners') sugar	2 tablespoons	3 tablespoons
egg white	1	1

Ginger Ice Cream with Strawberry Sauce

Put the milk and vanilla in a small pan over very low heat.

Beat the egg yolks with a whisk in a bowl until they just begin to lighten in colour. Gradually add the warm milk and the cream, beating constantly. Put the bowl over a pan of simmering water and cook, stirring constantly, until the mixture coats the back of the spoon. Stir in the ginger and leave to cool, stirring occasionally to prevent a skin from forming.

Put the cold mixture into a shallow metal container and freeze for at least 1 hour. Remove and purée in a blender until creamy; replace in the freezer for another hour. If it is not creamy enough by then repeat the process.

Wash and dry the strawberries and sprinkle with icing sugar. Purée in a blender. Beat the egg white until stiff. Fold into the strawberry mixture and pour into a bowl or jug.

Serve the ice cream in individual dishes topped with strawberry sauce and any remaining sauce can be served separately.

Time: 2½ hours   *Serves 6*

Menu

Artichoke Pie
TORTA DELICATA

Fish Cutlets Italian Style
TRONCE DI PESCE ALL'ITALIANA

Steak with Olive Sauce
FILETTO ALLE OLIVE

Flambé Bananas
BANANA ALLA FLAMINA

Preparation

One day ahead
Prepare and cook the artichokes ready for the pie. Cover with plastic wrap and put in the refrigerator, removing them an hour before they are needed.

Three hours ahead
Complete and cook the artichoke pie. Prepare the filling for the flambé bananas.

Two hours ahead
Prepare and cook the fish cutlets ready for final browning.

One hour ahead
Prepare and cook the steak and olive sauce.

Half an hour ahead
Reheat the artichoke pie. Complete the flambé bananas but to not set alight until the moment of serving.

Artichoke Pie

Finely chop the onion and crush the garlic. Melt the butter in a heavy pan, add the onion and garlic and cook for a few minutes over a medium heat until golden. Drain and dry the artichoke segments and stems; add to the pan along with the wine. Cook over a low heat until the wine has evaporated. Season with salt and pepper, add a little water or stock, cover and cook over a moderate heat for 30 minutes.

Sprinkle on the chopped parsley. Put the artichoke segments on one side and purée the stems and cooking juices in a blender or food processor. Pour into a bowl and add the lightly beaten eggs, Parmesan cheese and cream. Beat well together.

Preheat the oven to 230 c, 440 f, gas 8.

Line a 25 cm/10 in round ovenproof dish with foil. Roll out the pastry to 3 mm/$\frac{1}{8}$ in thick and put it in the dish, trimming to fit neatly. Mark the edges with a fork. Arrange the ham on the pastry base, followed by the sliced Fontina cheese. Remove pieces of furry choke from the artichoke segments; place the segments in the pie. Finally pour over the blended artichoke mixture.

Put in the hot oven for 10–15 minutes or until the top is golden and the pastry cooked. Serve hot.

Time: 1$\frac{1}{2}$ hours   *Serves 6*

Young tender artichokes are essential for this dish. Alternatively canned or frozen may be used.

Artichoke Pie

TORTA DELICATA

Ingredients	Metric/Imperial	American
puff pastry, thawed	225 g/8 oz	$\frac{1}{2}$ pound
young artichokes	5	5
lemon	1	1
small onion	1	1
garlic clove	1	1
butter	50 g/2 oz	$\frac{1}{4}$ cup
dry white wine	125 ml/4 fl oz	$\frac{1}{2}$ cup
salt and pepper		
chopped parsley	1 tablespoon	1 tablespoon
eggs	3	3
Parmesan cheese, grated	2 tablespoons	3 tablespoons
single (thin) cream	125 ml/4 fl oz	$\frac{1}{2}$ cup
cooked ham	75 g/3 oz	3 ounces
Fontina cheese	75 g/3 oz	3 ounces

Remove the stems and outside leaves from the artichokes and cut the tips off the remaining leaves. Peel the stems and cut into small pieces; cut the heads into segments. Put in water and lemon juice to prevent discoloration.

Fish Cutlets Italian Style

TRANCE DI PESCE ALL'ITALIANA

Ingredients	Metric/Imperial	American
bream (porgy)	1 (1.8 kg/3$\frac{3}{4}$ lb)	1 (3$\frac{3}{4}$ pound)
bay leaf	1	1
garlic clove	1	1
salt and pepper		
dry white wine	175 ml/6 fl oz	$\frac{3}{4}$ cup
butter	75 g/3 oz	6 tablespoons
plain (all-purpose) flour	25 g/1 oz	$\frac{1}{4}$ cup
mushrooms	100 g/4 oz	$\frac{1}{4}$ pound
small bunch of parsley	1	1
grated nutmeg	$\frac{1}{4}$ teaspoon	$\frac{1}{4}$ teaspoon
single (thin) cream	1$\frac{1}{2}$ tablespoons	2 tablespoons
Parmesan cheese, grated	25 g/1 oz	$\frac{1}{4}$ cup
breadcrumbs	25 g/1 oz	$\frac{1}{4}$ cup

Prepare the fish by scraping off the scales, cutting off the head, fins and tail and cleaning out the inside. Cut the body into 6 serving pieces.

Make stock with the fish head and tail by putting them in a pan with the bay leaf, crushed garlic, a little salt and 600 ml/1 pint/2½ cups of water. Cover and simmer for about 30 minutes; strain and set aside.

Put the pieces of fish in a pan in a single layer, cover with the wine, 225 ml/8 fl oz/1 cup of water and season with salt and pepper. Put over a low heat, bring slowly to the boil and simmer for 15 minutes. When cooked drain the fish, reserving the cooking liquid. Remove the skin and bones and arrange the fish in a single layer in an overproof dish. Strain the reserved liquid.

Melt one-third of the butter in a small pan over medium heat, stir in the flour and strained fish liquid and bring the mixture to the boil, stirring constantly. Cook until it forms a smooth thick sauce, then remove from the heat.

Put the fish head stock in a small pan and heat until reduced to less than half. Clean the mushrooms and chop them finely with the parsley.

Return the sauce to the heat, add the mushroom and parsley mixture and cook gently for 10 minutes. Stir in the reduced fish stock until a good pouring sauce is obtained; add salt, pepper, nutmeg and cream. Stir well and pour over the fish.

Mix together the Parmesan cheese and breadcrumbs and sprinkle over the fish. Melt the remaining butter and pour over the top of the dish.

Put under a hot grill (broiler) for 10 minutes or until golden brown and serve hot.

Time: 1 hour 20 minutes   *Serves 6*

Fish Cutlets Italian Style

1 Clean mushrooms and chop finely with the parsley. Return the sauce to the heat and add the mushrooms and parsley. Cook on a low heat.
2 Stir in the reduced fish stock to make a pouring sauce. Add seasoning, nutmeg and cream. Stir well and pour over the fish.
3 Sprinkle with breadcrumbs and Parmesan cheese. Garnish with a few sliced mushrooms (optional).

Steak with Olive Sauce

FILETTO ALLE OLIVE

Ingredients	Metric/Imperial	American
garlic clove	1	1
salt and pepper		
fillet of beef	1.2 kg/2¼ lb	2¼ pounds
butter	75 g/3 oz	6 tablespoons
dry white wine	50 ml/2 fl oz	¼ cup
stock	225 ml/8 fl oz	1 cup
plain (all-purpose) flour	1 tablespoon	1 tablespoon
green olives	225 g/8 oz	1½ cups
chopped parsley	1½ tablespoons	2 tablespoons

Cut the garlic into small slivers and dust with salt and pepper. Make small slits all over the meat and push the garlic slivers inside.

Melt half the butter in a flameproof casserole over a medium heat. Add the meat and brown it lightly on all sides. Sprinkle on the wine and continue cooking until it has evaporated. Add the stock, cover and cook for 20 minutes. Remove the meat and keep hot.

Melt the remaining butter in a small pan, stir in the flour and cooking juices from the meat. Cook over a low heat for 10 minutes, stirring occasionally. Finely chop the stoned olives and add them to the sauce with the chopped parsley.

Serve the meat sliced and covered with the sauce.

Time: 1 hour   *Serves 6*

Flambé Bananas

BANANA ALLA FLAMINA

Ingredients	Metric/Imperial	American
shelled walnuts	100 g/4 oz	1 cup
icing (confectioners') sugar	3 tablespoons	4 tablespoons
brandy	225 ml/4 fl oz	½ cup
Ricotta cheese	350 g/12 oz	¾ pound
bananas	6	6
caster (fine granulated) sugar	100 g/4 oz	½ cup
plain (all-purpose) flour		
eggs, beaten	2	2
butter	65 g/2½ oz	5 tablespoons

Chop the walnuts finely, put in a bowl and mix to a paste with the icing sugar and 3–4 tablespoons of the brandy. Stir in the Ricotta cheese with a fork. (This can be done in a food processor)

Peel the bananas and slit lengthways, taking care not to cut right through. Stuff with the cheese mixture. Sprinkle with some of the caster sugar; dust with flour, dip in beaten egg then dust with flour again.

Melt the butter in a large heavy pan over a high heat. When it is very hot add the bananas and cook for a few minutes until golden. Arrange on a heat-resistant serving plate and sprinkle with the remaining caster sugar. When ready to serve pour over the remaining brandy, set it alight and take the dish, flaming, to the table.

Time: 20 minutes   *Serves 6*

Steak with Olive Sauce

Menu

Cream of Artichoke Soup
CREMA DI CARCIOFI

Bass Bellavista
BRANZINO IN BELLAVISTA

Entrecôtes in White Wine
LOMBATINI AL VINO BIANCO

Winter Cake
DOLCE DELIZIA D'INVERNO

Preparation

One day ahead
Prepare the cake but do not decorate.

Three hours ahead
Cook the bass and set in gelatine.

Two hours ahead
Complete the bass in gelatine and prepare the artichokes.

One hour ahead
Prepare the artichoke soup and decorate the cake. Make the cheese toasts to serve with the soup.

Half an hour ahead
Prepare the entrecôtes in white wine.

Cream of Artichoke Soup

Cream of Artichoke Soup

CREMA DI CARCIOFI

Ingredients	Metric/Imperial	American
large artichokes	6	6
lemon	$\frac{1}{2}$	$\frac{1}{2}$
butter	50 g/2 oz	$\frac{1}{4}$ cup
white sauce (page 25)	450 ml/$\frac{3}{4}$ pint	2 cups
stock	450 ml/$\frac{3}{4}$ pint	2 cups
slices of bread	4	4
Parmesan cheese, grated	2 tablespoons	3 tablespoons
single (thin) cream	225 ml/8 fl oz	1 cup
chopped parsley	1 tablespoon	1 tablespoon

Remove the large outer leaves and stalks from the artichokes; cut the sharp points off the remaining leaves. Put into boiling water and lemon juice and simmer for 15 minutes until part-cooked. Drain well, remove the chokes from the centres and cut the artichokes into slices. Melt half the butter over a low heat, add the slices and cook for 5 minutes or until tender. Purée in a liquidizer or food processor.

Prepare the white sauce. Add the artichoke purée and simmer for about 10 minutes. Pour in hot stock, a little at a time, and bring slowly to the boil.

Meanwhile melt the remaining butter, dip the slices of bread in it and sprinkle on both sides with grated Parmesan cheese. Bake in a moderately hot oven (200 C, 400 F, gas 6) for 10 minutes until golden and crisp.

To finish the soup stir in the cream and chopped parsley. Remove from the heat at once. Serve the soup hot with the cheese toasts, cut into small pieces, in a separate dish.

Time: 45 minutes   *Serves 6*

Bass Bellavista

BRANZINO IN BELLAVISTA

Ingredients	Metric/Imperial	American
For the court-bouillon:		
white wine vinegar	175 ml/6 fl oz	$\frac{3}{4}$ cup
onion, chopped	1	1
carrot, sliced	1	1
lemon slice	1	1
sprigs of parsley	4	4
bay leaf	$\frac{1}{4}$	$\frac{1}{4}$
peppercorns	4	4
coarse salt	1 teaspoon	1 teaspoon
bass	1 (1.4 kg/3 lb)	1 (3 pound)
mayonnaise (page 34)	225 ml/8 fl oz	1 cup
For the glaze:		
hake	150 g/5 oz	5 ounces
egg whites	2	2
leek	1	1
chopped parsley	1 tablespoon	1 tablespoon
gelatine	5 teaspoons	5 teaspoons
To garnish:		
green leek leaves	4	4
egg, hard-boiled (cooked)	1	1
lemon slices	3	3

1 Put the fish in a pan, cover with court-bouillon and simmer.

2 Remove skin from fish leaving the head and tail on the fish.

3 Lay the fish on the set gelatine and arrange the garnish.

First prepare the court-bouillon. Put 3 litres/5½ pints/3 quarts of cold water in a large pan with the vinegar, vegetables, lemon slice, herbs and seasoning. Bring to the boil, then simmer for 30 minutes. Strain and allow to cool.

Meanwhile scale, gut and wash the fish and make the mayonnaise.

Put the fish in a large oval pan or fish kettle and cover with at least 2 litres/3½ pints/2 quarts of cold court-bouillon for every 1 kilo/2 pounds of fish. Bring to the boil and simmer for 15 minutes. Cool in the cooking liquid, drain and lift carefully on to a plate.

Strain the cooking liquid through a piece of damp muslin. Sprinkle the gelatine on to 125 ml/4 fl oz/½ cup of boiling water and stir until dissolved.

Chop the raw hake and mix it with the whisked egg whites, the chopped leek and the finely chopped parsley. Add this mixture to 1 litre/1¾ pints/1 quart of fish stock and allow to bubble on a medium heat. Turn the heat to low, skim the liquid and cook for about 30 minutes, stirring occasionally; do not allow to boil. Strain it through the muslin and pour a thin layer on to a serving dish big enough to take the whole fish. Put the plate in the refrigerator; cool the remaining liquid without allowing it to set.

Carefully remove the skin from the fish, leaving the head and tail untouched. Lay it on the set gelatine and apply the garnish. Make petals with the white of the egg and arrange on the fish like flowers; mash the yolk to make their centres. Blanch the leek leaves briefly in boiling water and cut into leaf and stem shapes. Carefully pour on the remaining liquid gelatine in a thin layer to set the garnish in place. Cut the lemon slices in half and arrange them around the plate.

Serve the fish with the mayonnaise in a separate bowl.

Time: 2 hours   *Serves 6*

Entrecôtes in White Wine

LOMBATINI AL VINO BIANCO

Ingredients	Metric/Imperial	American
For the sauce:		
onion	1	1
sage leaves	4	4
sprig of rosemary	1	1
dry white wine	225 ml/8 fl oz	1 cup
butter	25 g/1 oz	2 tablespoons
plain (all-purpose) flour	25 g/1 oz	¼ cup
stock	125 ml/4 fl oz	½ cup
chopped parsley	1 tablespoon	1 tablespoon
beef bone marrow, cooked	150 g/5 oz	5 ounces
butter	50 g/2 oz	¼ cup
sirloin or entrecôte steaks	6	6
salt and pepper		

To make the sauce, finely chop the onion, sage and rosemary together. Put the wine in a small pan, add the onion and herb mixture, bring to the boil and simmer until reduced by about half.

Melt the butter in a separate pan, stir in the flour then gradually add the stock, stirring constantly; bring to the boil. Add the wine mixture and the chopped parsley, mix well and remove from the heat but keep hot.

Slice the bone marrow and steep in boiling water for about 10 minutes; drain and reserve.

To cook the steaks melt the butter in a large heavy pan over a high heat and fry them, turning several times, until done to taste. Season with salt and pepper. Arrange on a heated serving plate, top with a slice of bone marrow and pour over the hot sauce.

Time: 30 minutes   *Serves 6*

Entrecôtes in White Wine

1 Peel the chestnuts; also remove inner skin.
2 Add milk and cook chestnuts for 15 minutes.

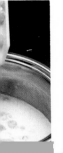

3 Purée chestnut mixture. **4** Mix with ingredients.
5 Pour in a third of purée; cover with biscuits.

Winter Cake

DOLCE DELIZIA D'INVERNO

Ingredients	Metric/Imperial	American
chestnuts	1 kg/2 lb	2 pounds
granulated sugar	100 g/4 oz	½ cup
vanilla pod	¼	¼
salt		
milk	225 ml/8 fl oz	1 cup
butter	100 g/4 oz	½ cup
drinking chocolate	50 g/2 oz	2 ounces
rum	125 ml/4 fl oz	½ cup
Amaretti biscuits	100 g/4 oz	¼ pound
toasted almonds	50 g/2 oz	½ cup
marrons glacés	9	9
double (thick) cream	125 ml/4 fl oz	½ cup

Remove the hard outer skins from the chestnuts and put the chestnuts in boiling water for 5 minutes. Drain and remove the inner skins.

Bring 600 ml/1 pint/2½ cups of water to the boil in a large heavy pan with the sugar, vanilla pod and a pinch of salt. Add the chestnuts and simmer for 45 minutes. Add the milk and cook for a further 15 minutes. Remove the vanilla pod.

Purée the chestnut mixture using a coarse sieve, blender or food processor and put back in the pan over a low heat. Cook, stirring continuously, until it thickens. Allow to cool, then add the softened butter, drinking chocolate and half the rum; beat well. Soak the Amaretti biscuits in the remaining rum.

Line an 18 cm/7 in round cake pan with damp muslin. Pour in one-third of the chestnut mixture and cover with half the biscuits. Repeat these layers and spread the remaining cake mixture on top.

Put the cake in the refrigerator for several hours, then turn out on to a plate. Remove the muslin and decorate with almonds, marrons glacés and whipped cream.

Time: 1½ hours + 3 hours: refrigeration   *Serves 6*

Menu

Asparagus with Watercress Sauce
ASPARAGI CON SALSA AL CRESCIONE

Mushroom Pie
PASTICCIO DI FUNGHI IN CROSTA

Stuffed Veal
CODINO DI VITELLO ALLE ZUCCHINE

Pistachio Boats
BARCHETTE AL PISTACCHIO

Preparation

One day ahead
Prepare the pastry for the pistachio boats and store at room temperature. Make the mushroom filling for the pie and store in a covered container in the refrigerator.

Three hours ahead
Prepare the stuffing for the veal, pack into the meat and sew it up.

Two hours ahead
Cook the veal and prepare the pistachio filling for the boats.

One hour ahead
Clean and prepare the asparagus ready for cooking. Complete and cook the mushroom pie

Half an hour ahead
Cook the asparagus and prepare the watercress sauce.

Asparagus with Watercress Sauce

ASPARAGI CON SALSA AL CRESCIONE

Ingredients	Metric/Imperial	American
asparagus	2 kg/4½ lb	4½ pounds
salt and white pepper		
bunches of watercress	2	2
butter	150 g/5 oz	½ cup + 2 tablespoons
egg yolks	3	3
lemon juice	2 tablespoons	3 tablespoons

Trim any woody ends off the asparagus and scrape off tough skin at the lower ends. Rinse under cold running water and tie into bundles. Stand in a pan and pour in salted water to reach two-thirds of the way up the asparagus; cover the tips with a foil dome. Bring to the boil and simmer for about 20 minutes.

Drain the asparagus, cut off the hard lower ends and put the tips on a heated serving dish; keep warm.

Wash, drain and finely chop the watercress. Dice the butter and put one piece in a double saucepan or a bowl set over simmering water. Add the egg yolks and lemon juice and beat with a wooden spoon until the butter had melted. Add the remaining pieces one at a time, beating continuously.

When the sauce resembles mayonnaise season with salt and pepper and stir in the watercress. (If it fails to thicken sufficiently beat in ½ tablespoon of cold water.) Keep warm over simmering water until ready to serve. *Note:* The asparagus stems can be used for making stock for soup.

Time: 50 minutes   *Serves 6*

Mushroom Pie

PASTICCIO DI FUNGHI IN CROSTA

Ingredients	Metric/Imperial	American
frozen puff pastry, thawed	350 g/12 oz	¾ pound
large flat mushrooms	1 kg/2 lb	2 pounds
shallots	2	2
butter	50 g/2 oz	¼ cup
salt and pepper		
plain (all-purpose) flour	1 tablespoon	1 tablespoon
single (thin) cream	1 tablespoon	1 tablespoon
chopped parsley	1 tablespoon	1 tablespoon
eggs, beaten	2	2
Fontina cheese	100 g/4 oz	¼ pound
cooked ham	100 g/4 oz	¼ pound

Divide the pastry in half and roll each piece out thinly.

Line a large rectangular pie pan with foil, then with pastry, covering the rim.

Clean and chop the mushrooms; finely chop the shallots. Melt the butter in a heavy pan, add the shallots and cook over a medium heat until golden. Add the mushrooms and season with salt and pepper. Cover the pan, reduce the heat and cook for a further 20–25 minutes.

Preheat the oven to 220 c, 425 f, gas 7.

Sprinkle the flour into the pan, add the cream and stir gently. Remove from the heat and add the chopped parsley and most of the beaten egg (reserve a little to glaze the top). Pour a little of the mixture into the pastry-lined pan and cover with a layer of sliced Fontina cheese, then a layer of ham. Repeat until all three ingredients are used up.

Dampen the pastry rim and put the remaining piece of pastry on top.

Press the edges well together and trim. Mark the edges with a fork and decorate the top of the pie with pastry trimmings. Pierce the top to allow steam to escape and brush with reserved beaten egg.

Bake the pie in the hot oven for about 30 minutes until golden brown. Serve at once.

Time: 1½ hours   *Serves 6*

Mushroom Pie

Stuffed Veal

CODINO DI VITELLO ALLE ZUCCHINE

Ingredients	Metric/Imperial	American
fillet of veal	1 (1 kg/2 lb)	1 (2 pound)
slices of crustless white bread	2	2
milk	50 ml/2 fl oz	$\frac{1}{4}$ cup
courgettes (zucchini)	450 g/1 lb	1 pound
onion	$\frac{1}{2}$	$\frac{1}{2}$
oil	2 tablespoons	3 tablespoons
salt and pepper		
eggs	3	3
Parmesan cheese, grated	25 g/1 oz	$\frac{1}{4}$ cup
chopped parsley	1 tablespoon	1 tablespoon
butter	50 g/2 oz	$\frac{1}{4}$ cup
sprig of rosemary	1	1
dry white wine	50 ml/2 fl oz	$\frac{1}{4}$ cup

Slit the veal partway through horizontally so as to form a bag. Put the bread to soak in the milk.

Top and tail the courgettes, peel, wash, dry and cut into slices. Chop the onion finely. Heat the oil in a heavy pan, add the onion and cook over a medium heat until golden. Add the courgettes, season lightly with salt and pepper, mix well and cook for 15 minutes.

Remove the pan from the heat and add the lightly beaten eggs, Parmesan cheese and parsley. Squeeze the bread and mix with the other ingredients.

Stuff the courgette mixture into the pocket in the veal and sew up with kitchen string so that no openings remain.

Melt the butter in a heavy pan with the rosemary leaves. Add the meat and cook on medium heat, turning frequently, until browned all over. Pour in the wine and leave until it evaporates. Season with salt and cook for 1–1$\frac{1}{4}$ hours until the meat is tender. Slice and serve hot.

Time: 2 hours   *Serves 6*

Stuffed Veal

1 Heat the oil and cook the onion and courgettes.
2 Remove from heat, add eggs, cheese and parsley.

Pistachio Boats
BARCHETTE AL PISTACCHIO

Ingredients	Metric/Imperial	American
For the pastry:		
Plain (all-purpose) flour	200 g/8 oz	2 cups
butter	100 g/4 oz	½ cup
sugar	75 g/3 oz	9 tablespoons
eggs yolk	1	1
Marsala wine	1 tablespoon	1 tablespoon
lemon rind, grated	1 teaspoon	1 teaspoon
For the filling:		
pistachio nuts	150 g/5 oz	5 ounces
egg yolks	4	4
caster (fine granulated) sugar	100 g/4 oz	½ cup
plain (all-purpose) flour	40 g/1½ oz	6 tablespoons
milk	500 ml/18 fl oz	2¼ cups
butter	25 g/1 oz	2 tablespoons
rum	2 tablespoons	3 tablespoons

First make the pastry: sift the flour into a mixing bowl; put the butter on top with the sugar, egg yolks, Marsala and lemon rind. Knead quickly to form a dough, wrap in foil and put in the refrigerator to rest for 30 minutes.

Preheat the oven to 180 c, 350 F, gas 4.

Roll the pastry out thinly on a floured work surface and use to line 12 individual oval tartlet pans. Prick all over with a fork and bake in the moderate oven for 15 minutes or until golden. Allow to cool before removing from the tartlet pans; fill with the pistachio cream the following day.

To make the pistachio cream first toast the nuts in a moderate oven. Rub in a clean tea-towel to remove the skins. Chop very finely or crush with a pestle in a mortar.

Beat the egg yolks with the sugar for about 10 minutes until pale then add the flour and prepared nuts. Warm the milk, add to the nut mixture and put in a small pan over medium heat. Cook, stirring constantly, until thick. Boil for a few minutes then stir in the butter and rum and leave to cool.

Time: 1¼ hours *Serves 6*

3 Add bread to make a stuffing. Insert into veal.
4 Heat butter, add rosemary and brown the meat.

English index

Italian index